the

NEFERTITI

the search fr
NEFERTITI

The True Story of a Remarkable Discovery

JOANN FLETCHER

HODDER

Copyright © 2004 by Joann Fletcher

First published in Great Britain in 2004
by Hodder and Stoughton
A division of Hodder Headline
This edition published in 2005

The right of Joann Fletcher to be identified as the Author of
the Work has been asserted by her in accordance with the
Copyright, Designs and Patents Act 1988.

A Hodder & Stoughton paperback

1

A CIP catalogue record for this title is available from the British Library

ISBN 0 340 83172 3

Typeset in Monotype Sabon by
Rowland Phototypesetting Ltd,
Bury St Edmunds, Suffolk
Printed and bound by
Mackays of Chatham Ltd, Chatham, Kent

Hodder Headline's policy is to use papers that are natural, renewable
and recyclable products and made from wood grown in sustainable forests.
The logging and manufacturing process are expected to conform to the
environmental regulations of the country of origin.

Hodder and Stoughton
A division of Hodder Headline
338 Euston Road
London NW1 3BH

For 'AJ'

ACKNOWLEDGEMENTS

Amongst the many wonderful friends, colleagues and relatives who have provided help, information and support over the years, I'd like to give particular thanks to the following individuals:

Dr David Allen; Andrea Bates; David Beaumont; Roger & Jenny Beaumont; Juliet Brightmore; Prof. Don Brothwell; Dr Stephen Buckley; Christine Carruthers; Julie & Adam Chalkley; Dr Bill Cooke; Dr Vanessa Corby; James Stevens Cox; Sian Edwards Davies; John Emery; Prof. Earl Ertman; Dr Martin Evison; Janice Eyres; Prof. Mahmoud Ezzamel; Vanessa Fell; Alan & Christine Fildes; Martin Foreman; Dr Diane France; Andy Gaskin; Marilyn Griffiths; Graham Hannah; Kerry Hood; Teresa Hull; David Ireland; Nyree Jagger; Nicola & Michael Jamieson; John & Joan Johnson; Dr John Kane; Mary Kershaw; Dr Sandra Knudsen; Jacqui Lewis; Jackie Ligo; Mark Lucas; Sarah Lucas; Dr Bridget McDermott; Barbara McDermott; Alistair Mackenzie; Sarah McLellan; the late Joan McMahon; Prof. John Maunder; Freda Morgan; David Moss; Gillian Mosely; Peta Nightingale; the late Alec Norris-Jones & Sheila Norris-Jones; the late Dennis Northmore; Prof. Terry O'Connor; Delia Pemberton; Michael & Jane Pickering; Jerry Preston; Tim Radford; Magdy el-Rashidy; Dr Howard Reid & family; Dr Alison Roberts; Annie Roddam; Carol Rowbotham; the late Julia Samson; Bob Saxton; Dr Damian Schofield; Ian Scorah & family; Ali Hassan Sheba & all the family – including Michael; Prof. Mohammed el-Shafie; Briar Silich; Sam and Neil Silk; Alastair Smith; Jack Smith; Penny Smith; Neil Staff; Dr John Taylor; Angela Thomas; the late Jean Thompson; Dr Gillian Vogelsang-Eastwood; Dr Kirit Vora; the late Carole Walker; Roxie Walker; Alison Walster, Rowena Webb and Bob Wilson.

A special heartfelt thanks must also go to my sister Kate, my parents Garry and Susan and of course to Django.

CONTENTS

FOREWORD
by Professor Earl Ertman

Almost every week new information is discovered on excavations in Egypt. New insight can be gained from this excavated material once a thorough analysis of its many types are conducted and evaluated, as can the study of objects that may have lain unrecognised in museum and private collections for years. This inevitably means that revisions are often required from what we believe we 'know' as new findings cause us to alter or modify our original interpretation.

There are many facets to most professions – Egyptology is no exception. New areas of study are being added as each specialisation becomes more refined. In years past, few, if any, individuals specialised in areas that, more recently, have added appreciably to an overall understanding of this ancient culture, from mummies and museums to sculpture and relief scenes.

One of the more unusual areas of specialised study is ancient body adornment, including hair, its arrangement, significance and symbolism as represented in art, together with all manner of surprising information that can be derived from a study of the hair itself.

In the forefront of this area of research is Dr Joann Fletcher, whose somewhat unusual and highly diverse career path has given her a first hand knowledge of ancient hair in particular has allowed her to find clues relating to everything from wig construction and the use of dyes to social status and health problems.

Her collaboration on various projects over the last few years has focussed her specialised expertise on previously unanswered questions. It has also helped provide more evidence in attempts to establish a more reliable means of dating through a classification of hairstyles and the types of wigs that were so popular amongst ancient Egypt's elite. Similar criteria can also be applied to art work in which the most noticeable element is often the style of hair or wig worn by the individual portrayed in an uninscribed fragment or incomplete sculpture, thereby providing evidence for not only dating but potential identification.

When I first heard Joann Fletcher give a lecture back in 1995 at an international Egyptology congress in Cambridge, England, I was taken by her humour and seemingly unorthodox manner which held the audience's interest whilst still proving her points. I am sure readers will find her writing both insightful and at times humorous, for her approach reflects her view of Egyptology and of the world as she sees it.

Her career continues to blossom, and in addition to her long-term research into ancient hair, she has already made a mark on the archaeological scene with her work on the pharaoh Amenhotep III as well as suggested identification of the mummy of the 'Younger Woman' in tomb KV.35 in the Valley of the Kings as that of the legendary Nefertiti.

And while a certain degree of controversy presently surrounds this identification, time and on-going research will undoubtedly confirm this to the satisfaction of the majority of Egyptologists and laymen alike.

Earl L. Ertman
Professor Emeritus,
University of Akron,
Ohio
USA

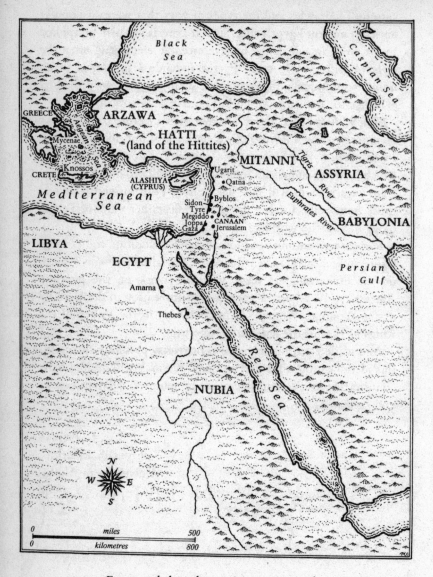

MAP 1. Egypt and the other major powers in the ancient
Near East during the Amarna Period

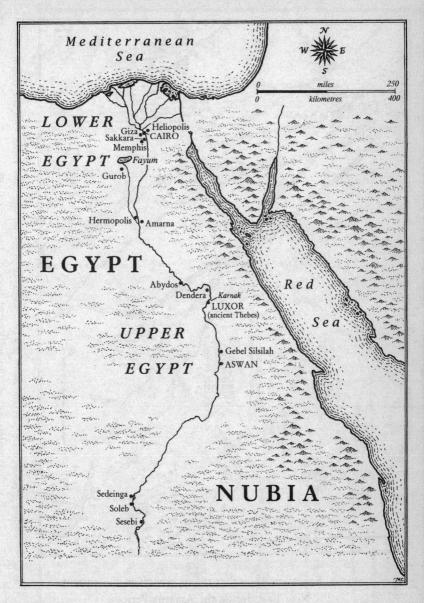

MAP 2. Egypt and Nubia

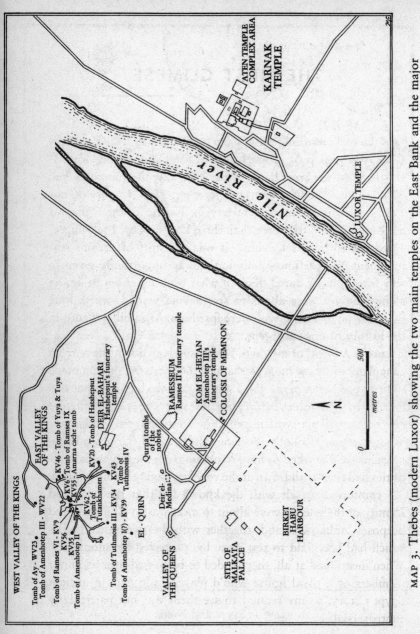

WEST VALLEY OF THE KINGS

Tomb of Ay - WV23 •
Tomb of Amenhotep III - WV22

EAST VALLEY OF THE KINGS

Tomb of Ramses VI - KV9
KV46 - Tomb of Yuya & Tuya
KV6 - Tomb of Ramses IX
KV56
KV55 - Amarna cache tomb
Tomb of Amenhotep II
KV35
KV62 -
Tomb of
Tutankhamen
KV20 - Tomb of Hatshepsut

DEIR EL-BAHARI
Hatshepsut's funerary temple

Tomb of Tuthmosis III - KV34   KV43
Tomb of Amenhotep I(?) - KV39   Tomb of
                                Tuthmosis IV

EL - QURN

Qurna tombs
of the
nobles

RAMESSEUM
Ramses II's funerary temple

KOM EL-HETAN
Amenhotep III's
funerary temple
COLOSSI OF MEMNON

Deir el-
Medina

VALLEY OF
THE QUEENS

SITE OF
MALKATA
PALACE

BIRKET
HABU
HARBOUR

Nile River

ATEN TEMPLE
COMPLEX AREA

KARNAK
TEMPLE

LUXOR TEMPLE

N

0   500
    metres

MAP 3. Thebes (modern Luxor) showing the two main temples on the East Bank and the major temples, tombs and settlement sites on the West Bank

1

THE FIRST GLIMPSE

As the early morning mist began to rise slowly from the silent waters, our boat crossed over to the Land of the Dead. It was here on the west bank of the Nile that the pharaohs had been buried some four thousand years ago, and we were on our way to the most famous cemetery in the world, the Valley of the Kings. With little more than three hours' sleep, I felt unprepared for what was to come. It was the stuff of dreams, the fulfilment of a lifetime's ambition and an opportunity given to very few. I hardly dared think of what we were about to do, let alone who we were about to see, having waited twelve long years for an audience with perhaps the most familiar figure in the history of ancient Egypt.

Lost in a world of my own, I made my way down the narrow gangplank to where the water lapped the shore. As the sun made its first appearance of the day, I stepped into the bus. I'd made this journey so many times before, but now it was very different, and nerves began to play with my mind. What if the tomb was empty? What if there was nothing there? And what if the official permissions we'd worked so hard to obtain from the Egyptian authorities had been withdrawn at the very last minute? It did happen.

I comforted myself with the knowledge that the perceived identity of the one we were about to meet was to all intents and purposes 'unknown', and, together with the two other bodies which had been laid to rest close by, protected by anonymity. When mentioned at all, they tended to be passed over as minor members of a royal house who'd played little part in ancient Egypt's story, so my request to see them was not particularly controversial.

As the ancient landscape whizzed past my window and the two colossal stone figures of Amenhotep III loomed up in front of us, I could almost hear the blood pumping through my head. I had to stay calm, I kept telling myself. I was about to meet Egypt's Head of Antiquities, Zahi Hawass, who was at this very moment flying in from Cairo to meet me inside the tomb. It was important at least to try to maintain an appearance of professionalism – not that I'd ever been much good at playing that game. The word 'nervous' doesn't even begin to describe it.

We passed lush green fields fringed with palm trees, farmers off to work and overburdened donkeys trotting along beneath great bales of sugarcane, all of them reassuringly familiar on this otherwise emotionally fraught morning. Even the bleary-eyed children getting ready for school still managed a smile or a wave at the funny-looking *hawajaya* (foreigner) with her big orange hair and little black glasses looking at them from the bus.

The hillside of Qurna stretched up before us, a fabulous back-drop of colourful houses built alongside the ancient tombs. Turning right, the bus sped on past the temple of Ramses II, Shelley's Ozymandias, and then to Deir el-Bahari, built by one of Egypt's great female pharaohs, the mighty Hatshepsut. Today, however, my mind was firmly fixed on one who came after her, and who wielded no less power.

In case I needed any reminding why the Valley of the Kings was a place familiar to everyone, we turned left at 'Castle Carter', home of the twentieth century's most famous archae-ologist. Howard Carter, the man who discovered the tomb of Tutankhamen in 1922, has always been something of a hero for me, a working-class lad made good who stuck two fingers up at the sneering establishment by making the greatest archaeological discovery of all time. Carter and Tutankhamen are very much part of this story, both of them closely linked to the three who now awaited us in the valley whose barren, limestone sides loomed on either side. As the bus rattled on and the summer temperature began to rise steadily towards its 40°C June average, I spared a thought for Carter and his trusty donkey.

Slowing down, the bus stopped at the first of numerous security checks, the legacy of the terrible events of 1997 when Islamic extremists had murdered foreigners and Egyptians alike in their attempt to destabilise Egypt's secular government. And in today's political climate another attack can never completely be ruled out. But thanks to a stack of official paperwork and security clearances, we were waved through the barrier where vehicles normally have to stop to offload their passengers, and drove right up to the entrance gates of the Valley itself. Carrying nothing more dangerous than a camera, torch and my trusty umbrella, I began the final walk up to the tomb.

I had first come here as a dumbstruck teenager, unable to take it all in as tomb after tomb revealed some of the most beautiful images I had ever seen. Their hidden chambers and sealed doorways only fired my long-held determination to become an Egyptologist, and by the time of my second visit I was an Egyptology student at last, able to start making sense of the complex blend of wall scenes, passageways, corridors and side chambers unique to each tomb. Many more visits followed, initially for postgraduate research, then accompanying groups of tourists, students and television researchers, and most recently as part of a team excavating KV.39, quite probably the first royal tomb to have been built here. Yet today was something else, a visit to a very different royal tomb. Unlikely to be repeated, it was surely my one and only chance to confirm what I had believed for so long.

Approaching the small group of officials and police who clustered around the tomb's entrance, I was greeted by the local antiquities inspector and his staff, smiling nervously and chain smoking as they awaited their new boss. Several local workmen with their tools and baskets were also waiting, beside a temporary sign announcing that the tomb was 'Closed for Restoration'. We had in fact been given permission to remove a wall and enter the tomb's remaining sealed chamber – the ultimate

archaeological cliché, perhaps, but an amazing prospect nevertheless.

As walkie-talkies beeped and crackled into life, a voice announced that Dr Hawass was on his way from Luxor airport
and would be here within the hour. With official permission to
proceed, I took a deep breath, stepped through the entrance and
began the descent into the depths of the rock-cut tomb.

As I made my way down the endless steps of the corridor
which penetrated deep into the cliff face, I could feel both temperature and humidity rising steadily. The ground levelled off
momentarily to pass through the first chamber and a modern
bridge took me safely over the deep well shaft, designed to trap
the floodwaters which periodically hurtle down the valley and
the tomb robbers whose ancient ropes have been found at its
bottom. I went on through the first pillared hall, down the final
flight of steps and out into the vast burial chamber, its walls
covered in row upon row of animated little black stick figures
acting out scenes from the Book of Amduat. This is the guide
book to the Afterlife, in which the dead are confidently assured
safe passage with the sun god on his eternal journey through
the Underworld.

Above me, the star-spangled ceiling of midnight blue and gold
was supported by six great square columns, each decorated with
three of ancient Egypt's greatest gods: Osiris, lord of the underworld and resurrection; the jackal-headed Anubis, god of mummification and the guardian of the Valley; and Hathor, goddess of
love, here appearing as the Lady of the West who takes the souls
of the dead into her protective care. All three of them held out
an ☥ ankh sign to bestow eternal life on their son, the dead king
Amenhotep II, whose twenty-six-year reign saw the building
of this impressive tomb in which he had been buried around
1401 BC.

At almost six feet tall, Amenhotep was a giant of a king
whose vast empire dominated the ancient world. In response to
a rebellion in Syria, this ultimate warrior pharaoh executed the

rebel leaders personally in gruesome fashion, strung their corpses from the prow of his ship, sailed home and hung what remained of them from the city walls of Thebes. His legendary belligerence is also reflected in claims that he could fire arrows from his chariot through copper targets three inches thick, using a bow that no one else had the strength to use. Typical pharaonic boastfulness, perhaps, but when this tomb was discovered in 1898 Amenhotep II's flower-bedecked mummy still lay within the quartzite sarcophagus that now stood before me, his favourite longbow beside him.

According to their report, the excavators of 1898 had found themselves almost knee-deep in debris left behind by ancient looters, including fragments of linen, furniture, statues, funerary figurines, model boats, large blue amulets, glass vessels, cosmetics objects, storage jars and papyrus rolls that had all been provided at the time of the original burial to sustain Amenhotep II's soul in the Afterlife. The most amazing discovery was the group of royal mummies hidden away in the two small side rooms leading off the burial chamber. These bodies had obviously been placed here after their own tombs in the Valley had been ransacked and their mummies ripped apart in the search for the precious amulets traditionally placed inside the wrappings, ironically to protect the bodies from harm.

As robberies increased during the eleventh century BC, priests, embalmers and tomb inspectors were all kept busy moving the mummies to places of safety where they could be tidied up and rewrapped prior to reburial. This restoration of the royal dead seems to have been carried out in a number of places. Ancient graffiti listing new supplies of linen wrappings and labels for 'corpse oil' have been discovered in several nearby tombs, and vast quantities of wrappings, embalming materials and implements were found during our own work at tomb KV.39.

The illustrious figures who received such attentive treatment before their reburial with Amenhotep II included his son and successor, Tuthmosis IV, and his grandson, Amenhotep III,

Egypt's very own 'Sun King'. There were also a whole series of later pharaohs alongside them, from Ramses II's son and successor, Merenptah, to Seti II, Siptah and Ramses IV, V and VI. All had been wrapped up neatly, carefully relabelled, placed in restored coffins and respectfully laid to rest in the first side chamber. However, since every one of them had been taken off to the Cairo Museum shortly after their discovery, this first chamber now stood empty. But the second chamber was another story altogether, and this was why I was here.

When the archaeologists of 1898 had first entered the tomb, they described how this second chamber contained the usual pile of fragmentary statuary and furniture, together with three further mummies. Because they bore no identifying inscriptions, were unwrapped and had simply been left on the floor without a coffin between them, they were assumed to be of little importance – probably some of the relatives of Amenhotep II, whose tomb this was. After making a quick sketch and taking a few photographs it was eventually decided to leave them much as they were found, anonymous and discarded.

Yet for me, the combination of their anonymity and the absence of any attempt to rewrap them in ancient times suggested something rather different, if not downright sinister. The three had clearly been singled out and kept separate from the other royal mummies in the tomb, even though there would have been enough space to house them all together in that single chamber. And one body in particular had clearly been the victim of malicious damage which could not be explained away as a side-effect of tomb robbery. Her face was bashed in and one arm had been ripped off just below the shoulder. Someone had clearly been trying to make a point. But who? And why? After years of painstaking research, I believed I was about to discover the answers to a whole series of mysteries.

With the head man, in his pristine white turban and flowing gallabaya, directing proceedings, the first workman began to chip slowly away at the plastered wall in front of us. After a few minutes the first brick was levered out of position, then the second and the third. But despite the best attempts of the large electric fans which whirred away in the background, the heat was increasing by the minute and soon the second workman had to take over from his mate. This was a far cry from the icy-cold sepulchres of legend; Egyptian tombs are *hot*! Even just standing still and watching, I was beginning to sweat.

As the second workman paused for breath, I found myself unable to wait any longer and asked if I could look through into the darkness. Glad of a chance for a minute's break, the men stepped aside and I raised my torch.

What I saw next will stay with me for the rest of my life. For there, looking right at me, were three people who had died over three thousand years ago. And yet I recognised each of them, so clear were their features as they continued to stare back, looking for all the world as if they had been expecting me. And all I could say was, 'Oh, my God. It's you!'

2

THE ORIGINS OF THE SEARCH

So how did I come to be in the Valley of the Kings on an early June morning looking into the faces of three people who had died over three thousand years ago? It's a long story.

It began thirty-seven years ago in Barnsley, an industrial town in Yorkshire. Anyone born in Yorkshire will generally tell you so within the first few minutes of meeting, and although I'm no exception, my flat vowels give the game away even sooner. I'm obviously not a product of the Home Counties, and I've never pretended to be. Yet for all its finer points, Barnsley isn't known as a hotbed of Egyptological research. So why did I want to become an Egyptologist and study mummies?

Much of it can be traced back to my wonderful aunt, born the year before Tutankhamen's tomb was discovered. Some of her earliest memories were of the spectacular finds that appeared in the press during the decade-long, painstaking clearance of the tomb by Howard Carter and his team, and she was one of thousands gripped by 'Tutmania'. Remaining fascinated with ancient Egypt for the rest of her life, she inspired much of my own passion for the subject following my introduction to it via my parents' history books. These included *Tutankhamen: Life and Death of a Pharaoh* by French *grande dame* of Egyptology Christiane Desroches-Noblecourt, its colour plates a source of great fascination to me even before I was able to read.

The discovery of the tomb by Carter and his patron, the Earl of Carnarvon, was a tale regularly told to me by my aunt, with plenty of colourful touches added from her childhood memories of pictures of golden thrones, lion-headed couches and gilded statues appearing from the depths of the tomb. In 1968 the BBC screened Tutankhamen's 'post-mortem', the first re-examination of the king's remains since Carter's day. My aunt's descriptions of the royal mummy beneath the famous gold mask had tremendous appeal, adding to my growing interest in bodies, burials and all things relating to the graveyard which developed throughout my childhood. One of my special treasures was an Airfix model of a human skeleton, which stood in my bedroom side by side with an Egyptian doll, resplendent in golden headdress and snake bracelets, which still sits on my desk today.

In 1972 the UK braced itself for Tutankhamen's treasures as they toured the world. As a six-year-old completely besotted with the boy-king, I watched television pictures of huge numbers of people queuing for hours in the London streets surrounding the British Museum. But I wasn't going to be one of them. Events closer to home took precedence, for my sister was born that year and my parents were kept busy at home.

I did, however, acquire a nice collection of Tutankhamen memorabilia – books, newspaper cuttings and posters which family and friends collected for me. I spent hours reading and rereading all my books, as well as everything the local library had to offer about ancient Egypt. One of my favourite books demonstrated how the ancient Egyptians removed the brain during mummification. When I told my parents about this over dinner one day, they told me that it was actually possible to study Egyptology as a subject. Apparently it was even a career for some people, and there was nothing to stop me becoming an Egyptologist. So there I was at the age of eight, my life and career all mapped out. Everything seemed pretty straightforward, the only catch being that I would have to work hard at school before I could finally go to university and study.

School was fine most of the time, except for the occasional run-in with one or two history teachers as a result of my growing obsession. Even though ancient Egypt was not part of the curriculum, I tried every way I could to bring my favourite subject into as many lessons as possible. At O-level I concentrated on the arts, including Latin, figuring this was as close as I would get for the time being. But as I soldiered on with Romulus, Remus and those most tortuous verbal constructions, the Romans really made me suffer – and I've still not forgiven them.

My final year at school, when I was fifteen, coincided with my aunt's retirement, and to mark the occasion she had planned a two-week trip to Egypt. As I was so determined to become an Egyptologist, my parents felt it would be the perfect opportunity to test the water. With considerable foresight, they let me accompany her. And despite the assassination of Egypt's President, Anwar Sadat, only days before we were due to leave, we kept to our plans.

The effect of that first visit was incalculable – mind-blowing is perhaps a more apt description. Completely mind-blowing. Flying into Cairo at night, we saw the Nile sparkling below us and I was nearly sick with excitement. On that first night the sight of the famous river right outside my window made so much of an impression that I hardly slept at all, and I was ready to leave several hours before our guide, Miss Azmar, arrived to take us to the Cairo Museum on our first scheduled tour. At last I was going to see King Tut's treasures and all the things I'd read about for so long.

The museum is an enormous building with a great domed roof. After passing through the gardens with their pool filled with papyrus and lotus, ancient Egypt's heraldic plants, we entered the huge foyer. Right in front of us, flanked by monumental statues, was the largest object in the place, a colossal statue of Tutankhamen's grandparents, Amenhotep III and his wife, Queen Tiy, their smiling faces distinctly recognisable from the books I knew so well. There were statues and artefacts in every direction, just like old friends in a crowd. I could hardly wait to see all these things up close, as our guide set off at a cracking pace. We followed her from room to room, craning our necks to glimpse the things she was pointing out. 'King Djoser, builder of the Step Pyramid at Sakkara . . . King

Mycerinus with the goddess Hathor from his pyramid at Giza
. . . the female pharaoh Hatshepsut with her false beard . . .'

With only a few minutes at each piece, soon we reached the
Amarna Room with 'the heretic pharaoh Akhenaten and his
beautiful wife Nefertiti', and some of the most extraordinary-
looking figures I'd ever seen. And then we were off again, puff,
pant, up the stairs. Although the Mummy Room had recently
been closed after Sadat had declared it disrespectful to Egypt's
ancient kings, we headed on to King Tut's treasure. We struggled
to keep up as we passed black and gold statues and animal-
headed couches, the reclining black jackal, flower bouquets from
his coffin, his clothing, sandals, wig box – wig box? – and
amazing jewellery, past the human-headed canopic jars for his
mummified entrails, and then, with a flourish, to the golden
death mask as a finale!

Desperate to do it all again, but more slowly, we were instead
herded back on to the bus and carted off to Giza to see the
pyramids. Now although an Egyptologist shouldn't really say
it, I can take or leave the pyramids. Of course they are very big
and very impressive and very old, but I just couldn't relate to
them, especially after such an intense morning in the museum.

Looking up in awe, my aunt described how my uncle and his
friends, when serving in North Africa during the Second World
War, had taken part in the challenge to hit a gold ball from the
top of the Great Pyramid in an attempt to clear the sides. Yet
none of them was able to do so on account of its sheer size.
This really brought home how big these things were, and like
every visitor before and since I wondered how on earth they
had been built. Then I started to think about who had built
them and, ultimately, why?

The Giza Plateau was perhaps the best place to try to understand what ancient Egypt was all about, and why thousands of
people would risk their lives to create something to commemor-
ate a single individual, just because they were told to. And this
is when I twigged that there must have been far more to it –

that these people were motivated by something other than wage packets and clocking-off time. Built to glorify the king, the pyramids also glorified the country and the people themselves, who truly believed that their efforts would guarantee them a place in the Afterlife. Eternity in paradise had obviously been a great motivator.

As we gazed up at the largest pyramid ever built, some four and a half thousand years ago, our guide rattled off statistics like a bookie on race day. 'The Great Pyramid', she announced with a flourish, 'was originally 481 feet high, its base is 756 feet long, the angle of incline is 51 degrees and it contains 2,300,000 limestone blocks, each weighing as much as 2.5 tons . . .' It was built as the final resting place of King Khufu, known later to the Greeks as Cheops. There have, however, always been those who for some reason need to believe that the pyramids were built for anything other than the purposes of burial, even though assorted mummified body parts have been found in many a pyramid burial chamber.

Although Khufu himself was no longer at home, the opportunity to venture inside the Great Pyramid was not to be missed. It was definitely a bit of a hike through the steep ascending passageway, especially in the hot, stale air, until suddenly the narrow passage opened out above us into the Grand Gallery, its soaring roof an awesome piece of architectural achievement. At the top, when we reached the red granite-lined chamber at the pyramid's heart, it was impossible not to think about the million tons of rock pressing down on the cantilevered roof above our heads. Yet I was also struck by just how plain and simple the room was. Although we were told this was the royal burial chamber, there were no wall scenes, no inscriptions, nothing except the monolithic stone sarcophagus which had once held Khufu's mortal remains. As whispers ricocheted round the walls of the atmospheric, almost eerie room it wasn't difficult to imagine the king's final burial rites by the light of a flickering torch. As the funerary priests withdrew for the last time, a series of stone portcullises would slowly have descended to seal the room for eternity, while the king's soul came and went at will, rising up through narrow shafts to join the stars in the night sky.

A sudden clap of hands signalled that it was time to leave, and back down in the daylight we ended our whistle-stop tour at the Great Sphinx. Made in the likeness of the pharaoh Khafra, Khufu's son, and eventually regarded as an image of the sun god, his friendly face had watched over the site for four and a half thousand years. Having gazed out at over one million, six hundred and sixty thousand sunrises, the Sphinx now stars each evening in the cheesy yet strangely wonderful 'Sound and Light' show against a backdrop of coloured lights.

Although Giza was still an impressive place, it was difficult to imagine its original appearance because so much of the ancient stonework was dragged off to build Cairo. Founded in AD 969, much of the early city was made of the limestone that had once given the pyramids their smooth-sided, gleaming surface. This reuse of ancient blocks also explains why rows of hieroglyphs can be spotted halfway up the city walls. The mosques and minarets which give Cairo its distinctive skyline were also on our itinerary, the unexpectedly glitzy interior of el-Rifai mosque with its carpets, glassware and fragrant woods providing an appropriately plush backdrop for the remains of Egypt's last king, Farouk. We also saw the burial place of the newly interred Shah of Iran, who had spent his last months in Egypt following the Iranian Revolution of 1979, whilst next door the altogether more austere interior of the Sultan Hassan mosque gave us views across to the massive citadel of the famous Saladin, who had battled with the Crusaders in the Middle Ages.

Yet the thing which struck me most about Old Cairo was the City of the Dead, the vast cemetery that houses the dead and living literally side by side. Cairo's population had long since outstripped the available housing, and we were told that the homeless had been living here since the fourteenth century.

Today the addition of TV aerials, shops and cafés has made the marble-lined tombs a viable form of dwelling. People also visited the tombs of loved ones with picnics on holy days, and although the religious authorities were trying to stamp out such 'un-Islamic' activities, the Egyptians have long been comfortable in the company of their dead.

Leaving Cairo's sprawling mass behind us, a day-trip out into unspoilt palm-fringed countryside brought us to Memphis, Egypt's first capital, established around 3100 BC. Known in ancient times as Ineb-hedj, 'White Walls', the city was sacred to the creator god Ptah who was believed to have simply thought the world into being. His vast temple here was known as the 'House of Ptah's Soul' or Hut-ka-Ptah, which the Greeks later pronounced Aiguptos, the origin of our word Egypt.

Although the ancient city had once spread for miles across the Nile's wide floodplain, some serious imagination was required to make anything of the few scattered ruins we were shown. In fact I realised I'd never seen an ancient house, whereas tombs and temples were all over the place. It was easy to see why people believed the ancient Egyptians were a morbid bunch obsessed with religion and death. We were told that in most cases the ancient housing simply lay underneath the modern settlements, although its absence also had a lot to do with the difference in building materials and location. Whilst ancient houses were made of mud-brick close to the river, tombs and temples were built of stone on the edge of the desert away from the limited amount of fertile land. It didn't take a genius to work out that one would last considerably longer than the other.

This was particularly clear at Memphis, where the city was long gone but the tombs of its ancient inhabitants survive up on the desert escarpment at nearby Sakkara, stretching out for some five miles to link up with the pyramids of Giza, Dahshur and Medum to form one vast graveyard. The most frequently visited part of Sakkara was the great Step Pyramid, the world's oldest monumental stone building, which had dominated the site for nearly five thousand years. It had even impressed the ancient Egyptians: across walls already 1500 years old appreciative graffiti had been scrawled by the scribe Hadnakht 'on a pleasure trip west of Memphis'.

The pyramid was the final resting place for King Djoser, whose stern, long-haired statue we'd seen a few days before in the Cairo Museum. The discovery of assorted body parts in one of the pyramid's granite-lined chambers had long ago confirmed the building's original function, its seven great steps forming a stairway on which Djoser's spirit could climb up to heaven and join the gods, who are even described in some of the funerary texts as hauling him up by the hand. The pyramid's revolutionary stepped design was created by the king's chief architect, Imhotep, and although his own tomb has never been found, searches for it in the 1960s led to the discovery of millions of mummified ibis, left as offerings for Imhotep's immortal soul in vast secret catacombs beneath the sands. Sacred to the god of wisdom, these stuffed birds were felt to be the appropriate thing to offer to Imhotep, someone so revered he'd eventually been deified. Sakkara's subterranean catacombs had also housed a complete menagerie of mummified animals, from embalmed bulls to sacred cows, baboons and falcons; there is even said to be a lion cemetery out there somewhere beneath sands which have never been excavated.

Only a few years before our visit, archaeologists had begun to find the tombs of officials who'd served Tutankhamen and his father, Akhenaten, close to those built a thousand years before, during the Pyramid Age, for men such as the vizier Mereruka, the doctor Ankhmahor and Ty 'the Rich'. The walls were covered in intricate scenes of daily life, depicting all manner of busy little figures going about their everyday business, farming the land, producing food, haggling in the market, dancing and even having a punch-up, while all around flourished flora and fauna bursting with life. Crocodiles lurked in the shallows, hedgehogs munched on tiny insects and startled birds flapped about in riverside marshlands. The emphasis was completely on the now, the real and the tangible, and every scene seemed to scream out the command 'Live!' in its attempts to revive the soul of the deceased, using reminders of what life was all about and how to go on living it, albeit in another dimension. Since the ancients believed that a person's likeness could be magically reanimated in the Afterlife, it was essential to show every feature as clearly as possible. So figures in wall scenes have a clear profile of nose and mouth to allow them to breathe, and their eye is shown whole as if seen from the front, allowing them to see. So strong was this belief that the features of statues and wall carvings were sometimes hacked out to render the figures senseless and therefore harmless to the living – a superstition which persists to this day.

After several days in and around Cairo and Sakkara, we did what most tourists do and flew south to Luxor, the site of ancient Thebes. Once the religious capital of the Egyptian Empire, visited by people from across the ancient world, it was now tourist heaven, filled with visitors from the modern world attracted by its combination of perfect climate and a reputation as the largest open-air museum in the world. It was here, amidst the colonial charms of the Winter Palace Hotel, that Carter and Carnarvon had discussed their excavation strategy sixty years before, the rarefied atmosphere still present amidst the potted palms and polished floors. With the Luxor Temple looming large outside my window, the whole place was a revelation and, whereas Cairo had been a wonderfully chaotic assault on the senses, Luxor's easy-going atmosphere affected the mind in far subtler ways.

Having been in the business of showing off their ruins for the last two thousand years, the locals had developed their ability to deal with tourists into a finely honed art. First stop Karnak Temple, where we were once again bombarded with facts and figures, kingdoms and dynasties while trying to keep up with our guide. Known in ancient times as 'The Most Select of Places',

Karnak has always been tremendously impressive. Approached by a sphinx-lined avenue which once led from the Nile to a great pylon gateway, its 245 acres were home to the great state god Amen, 'The Hidden One'. He was worshipped here for over two thousand years, his mysterious rites performed in the darkness of his inner sanctuary by priests whose authority reached way beyond the temple walls. Indeed, their influence was felt the length and breadth of Egypt, and as each successive pharaoh tried to outdo his – or her – predecessor in the wealth presented to their 'divine father', Amen's priests grew ever more powerful. They had ruled in splendour behind doors through which mere mortals could not pass, yet it was now possible for anyone who bought a ticket to wander through the temple's sacred precincts and pylons and gape open-mouthed at its sheer size.

Although to modern visitors Karnak was the same dusty beige colour as just about every other temple we'd seen, ancient descriptions painted a very different picture of surfaces covered in all manner of precious stones and dazzling walls reflected in floors of beaten silver. Choosing colours and materials for their dramatic as well as symbolic effect, the ancient Egyptians were masters in the art of interior design and knew exactly how to decorate the homes of their gods. They believed that beautiful surroundings encouraged the divine to take up residence, and, with their powers harnessed through ritual and redirected for the benefit of Egypt, it was a reciprocal arrangement which kept things ticking over nicely for millennia.

Designed to be seen from as far away as possible, each temple entrance was flanked by massive flagpoles whose shape ⌐ formed the hieroglyphic sign 'netcher', meaning 'god'. Fluttering pennants showed the world that the gods were at home, and as we stood in front of the first pylon gateway we could clearly see the massive grooves where the flagpoles once stood, made of the same Lebanese cedar as the immense double doors of the pylon entrance.

Stepping through into the sacred precincts and vast courtyard beyond, our guide pointed out a small alabaster sphinx with the face of Tutankhamen which crouched to the right of us, and up ahead on the left a huge statue of Ramses II, with one of his many wives standing at his feet on mere human scale. Then just beyond lay the most famous part of the temple, the Hypostyle Hall with its 134 massive stone columns representing the primeval swamp of creation. With rising flecks of dust caught in shafts of sunlight, it had all the air of a medieval cathedral. Yet, in spite of the symbolic grandeur, I also remembered it as the place where a great stone block was pushed from the top of one of the columns in an attempt to crush the person standing below in the film version of Agatha Christie's *Death on the Nile*. Special effects or not, it still makes you look up and think.

Towards the end of the forest of columns stood a pair of pink granite obelisks, the largest one of four set up by the female pharaoh Hatshepsut in honour of 'her father' Amen. Functioning as a kind of esoteric lightning conductor, the obelisks had once been covered in polished electrum to reflect the sun's life-giving rays around the temple, and as she said herself in true pharaonic fashion on the obelisk's inscription, 'Never was the like made since the beginning of time.'

The more intimate surroundings of the temple's inner precincts led to the 'holy of holies' which had once housed Amen's golden statue, close to which were statues of Tutankhamen and his wife Ankhesenamen. Since they were children of the god their faces were sculpted in his image and his name was included in theirs, Tutankhamen meaning 'The living image of Amen' and Ankhesenamen 'She lives in Amen'. Not far away sat their great-great-grandfather, the warrior pharaoh Amenhotep II. His statue had once incorporated two figures until the second had at some time obligingly disappeared, leaving the royal arm still stretched out as if inviting the curious to sit down.

Our tour ended by the Sacred Lake in which the ancient clergy had once come to bathe, beyond which was what appeared to be a building site. This turned out to be one of the pylon gateways which had been dismantled to remove the thousands of small blocks making up the internal filling. The blocks had originally come from buildings erected by the so-called heretic pharaoh Akhenaten, Tutankhamen's father, which had been demolished soon after his death and their stone reused by later pharaohs. Each block was carved with tantalising fragments of scenes and inscriptions from the original temple buildings, and archaeologists had spent years trying to fit them back together – rather like trying to do a massive jigsaw puzzle without knowing what the picture was. As their work progressed, amazing scenes had started to appear, showing Akhenaten and his wife Nefertiti worshipping the sun god Aten, and done in a style so different from anything else at Karnak that it was perhaps no surprise they'd ended up as the next generation's building rubble.

Just past the dismantled pylon and associated building site another huge gateway led to a second sphinx-lined avenue, this one running for just over a mile and connecting up with the smaller Temple of Luxor. Its use as a fort in Roman times had earned it the Arabic name el-Aksur, 'The Castles', from which the modern town derived its name. Once again dedicated to Amen, Luxor Temple had been built by Akhenaten's father Amenhotep III who proudly described it as 'wide, very great, and exceedingly beautiful'. With sandstone walls covered in gold, its pavements in silver, and surrounded by gardens, it was certainly a suitable place to celebrate the annual Opet festival when Amen's golden statue was brought from Karnak to recharge the powers of the king. In secret rites within the darkness of the innermost sanctuary pharaoh's soul would merge with that of the god, and then, brimming with divine power, he would re-emerge into the daylight to the acclamation of the crowds.

And there in Amenhotep's colonnade hall we were shown the assembled masses portrayed on the walls, singing, dancing and literally turning back-flips. One man stepped forward to play a trumpet fanfare while the priestesses provided a lively accompaniment on their sistrum rattles – all so different from the gloom-laden way Egyptian religion was usually perceived. These people were really having a good time.

The temple remained unfinished at Amenhotep III's death, and since his son Akhenaten was apparently preoccupied with his own projects these scenes were eventually completed by Tutankhamen. He had obviously wanted to be seen as the heir and successor of his illustrious grandfather, and by skipping a generation he was able to leave out all reference to his father Akhenaten. With their creator erased from history almost as soon as his reign had ended, Akhenaten's own buildings were systematically demolished and his statues broken up. Yet if his only crime was a somewhat eccentric desire to do his own thing, as everything I'd read seemed to suggest, complete obliteration seemed a bit steep. There'd surely been more to it than that – and we soon saw that there had been.

Beyond the colonnade in Amenhotep III's open-air sun courts, its perfectly proportioned lotus columns held evidence of some-one else trying to rewrite history. The name 'Amen' had been hammered out wherever it occurred, even from the king's own name, Amenhotep, which ironically meant 'Amen is satisfied'. Not with that, I wouldn't have thought. It was well known that the Egyptians considered an individual's name vital for the survival of the soul, so I was amazed to discover that the damage had been inflicted by none other than Akhenaten. Having failed to carry out the expected duties of son and heir by finishing his father's temple, he had then defaced what had already been achieved, even to the extent of erasing his own father's name. So much for the benign, misunderstood dreamer whose memory had been cruelly treated by his successors. Looking up at the evidence in front of me, it seemed he'd received exactly what he'd deserved.

As we passed through into the rear section of the temple, raised floors and lowered ceilings increased the feeling of sanc-tity. This part of the building had been turned into a church by the Romans when they converted to Christianity in AD 395, then Islam arrived with the Arab Conquest of AD 640 and the mosque of Abu el-Haggag was built at the front of the temple. In an astonishing piece of religious continuity, Luxor Temple has been a place of constant daily worship for the last three and a half thousand years.

Trying to comprehend such a vast timescale, I found it helped to write everything down, although at times I still found it all quite overwhelming. Just when I thought I had something figured out, something else would come along to contradict it. As well as all those dynasties and kingdoms, the names were endlessly confusing – was it Amenophis or Amenhotep, Tuthmosis or Tuthmose? Then there were all the gods and goddesses – was it Amen, Amun or Amon? And why did Isis wear Hathor's head-dress? And why did Ra and Horus look the same? In fact, why did so many things conflict with what the books had told me?

Up at six the following day, we crossed the Nile by ferry to the West Bank, the traditional land of the dead where the royal tombs and funerary temples were spread out in a kind of ancient theme park. In contrast to the temples at Karnak and Luxor built on the East Bank to house the gods, those on the West Bank, known poetically as 'Mansions of Millions of Years', were funerary temples, commemorating and sustaining the soul of each pharaoh. We were going to start with the greatest of them all, at Kom el-Hetan.

When the bus pulled up at the side of the road, all I could see were a pair of enormous stone statues sitting alone in the middle of a farmer's field. But at almost sixty feet high, they were a pretty impressive pair none the less. Two of Egypt's oldest tourist attractions, the so-called Colossi of Memnon were named by the Greeks after one of their own heroes, and their huge feet were covered in the Greek and Latin graffiti of visitors who'd gathered to hear Memnon 'sing' each dawn. This curious sound effect is thought to have been caused by the breeze whistling through the cracks in the northernmost statue. However, all performances were unintentionally cut short by repairs carried out by the Roman emperor Septimius Severus (193–211 AD).

Yet for all their later fame in the classical world, the two figures had nothing at all to do with Memnon, and after an earthquake in 27 BC were pretty much all that remained of the vast funerary temple of Amenhotep III. With his usual flair for interior decor, his greatest temple had once featured his favoured combination of golden walls and silver pavements together with hundreds of statues, carted away by later kings too lazy to carve their own. Many, including large numbers of the seven hundred and more black granite statues of the lioness goddess Sekhmet, were eventually taken abroad to various museums. One even ended up over the entrance of Sotheby's auction house in Bond Street, where the ferocious Egyptian goddess and bringer of plague today stares down on London's busy traffic.

The huge figure of the king and queen we'd seen in the Cairo Museum had also once stood here, and I now stood looking up at the two remaining figures of the king, his mother Mutemwia on his left and chief wife Tiy on his right, their long, wavy hair topped by diadems. Once they had flanked the temple entrance, whose original design featured the same type of sun-filled court-yard we'd seen at Luxor Temple. The odd column base sticking out of the grass was also inscribed with lists of the places Egypt had once laid claim to, with sites from as far afield as the Aegean revealing the increasingly cosmopolitan nature of the royal court during Amenhotep III's reign.

In the Theban Hills beyond, tombs riddled the landscape, their black rectangular entrances stark against the sun-bleached limestone. They had been built to face the eastern horizon so that the rising sun could rouse the dead from slumber. Yet their original mummified inhabitants were long gone, destroyed in the search for any wealth they might possess not only by locals, who then at least took over the vacant tombs to house their families and livestock, but by an endless stream of foreign explorers and collectors who had simply desecrated the graves for financial gain or personal acquisition.

We drove along parallel to the hills, where great mounds of loose chippings represented centuries of illicit digging, through a landscape that had been reshaped by ancient funerary beliefs. Then as the bus swung left I caught sight of the building up ahead, its multiple layers built into the base of limestone cliffs which curved round in a great sweep. A centre of religious life for over three thousand years, Deir el-Bahari was the place where the goddess Hathor as Lady of the West took dead souls into her care. By building her funerary temple here, the female pharaoh Hatshepsut had taken full advantage of this prime location with its fast track to the Afterlife. She had planned the temple, built directly opposite Karnak, as 'a garden for my father Amen', and when the site was excavated in the early twentieth century the archaeologists discovered tree roots from the original acacia and sycamore planted here. Sacred to Hathor, these trees formed a shady oasis to encourage her spirit to dwell in her special grove.

The original tree-lined causeway led up to a vast structure built on four levels, with lively interior wall scenes recording the key events in Hatshepsut's life. Her great stone obelisks at Karnak were shown being brought by barge from the quarries in the south, and trading expeditions sent down to the mysterious land of Punt obtained the tons of fragrant incense needed for Amen's rituals. There were even scenes of her divine conception and birth, clearly demonstrating that Amen was her true father and that she had ruled Egypt as his child.

Yet for all her efforts, later pharaohs refused to admit her into their Old Boys' Club, smashing up her temple statues and erasing her name from the records just as they'd done with Akhenaten. So it seemed doubly unfair that all reference to Hatshepsut's divine paternity had also been attacked by Akhenaten when he had ordered Amen's names and images erased.

Originally Amen, Hathor and Anubis were represented within

the temple to guard Hatshepsut's tomb. Located directly behind her temple over the cliffs in the Valley of the Kings, the royal tombs were hidden away, spiritually attached but physically separate from the highly visible funerary temples associated with them. After pyramids had eventually been rejected as useless from a security point of view, later Egyptian royals built their tombs in this remote site dominated by a huge pyramid-shaped mountain now known as 'the Qurn', an instant connection with their past without the drawbacks or indeed the cost. Beneath its peak, guarded by the great serpent goddess Meretseger, 'She Who Loves Silence', a whole network of secret tombs lay where the sun sank each evening, taking with it the souls of the dead and preparing them for a glorious, shining rebirth in the east each morning.

The Valley was first chosen as a royal cemetery around 1500 BC by the kings of the 18th dynasty, but the identity of the first pharaoh to be buried there was, we were told, a mystery. A village for the royal tomb builders had certainly been founded by King Amenhotep I and his formidable mother Ahmose-Nefertari, and they had presumably needed tomb builders to build a tomb for them, although where exactly was still not known. The earliest datable tomb in the Valley had certainly been completed by a woman when Hatshepsut ordered a large double burial chamber for herself and her earthly father Tuthmosis I. Via a complicated series of dynastic marriages, Hatshepsut was suc-ceeded by her stepson and nephew Tuthmosis III, an innovator in many fields, whose military exploits and stature earned him the modern title 'The Napoleon of ancient Egypt'. His tomb was the first in the Valley to feature painted wall scenes, and these were closely copied by his son, Amenhotep II, whom I remembered from his accommodating statue at Karnak; it was his tomb which was to be our first port of call.

As we went through the entrance, the passage immediately sank down into the rock, then passed across a deep well shaft and through a small chamber, and after that down another corridor, before emerging into a great burial chamber. Surrounded by hundreds of little black stick figures running around the walls, we were told this was the Underworld through which the sun god travelled each night – a scary place inhabited by two-headed creatures, snakes impaled on blades and the headless bodies of bound captives. In contrast to this Lowry-meets-Hieronymus Bosch version of the Afterlife was Amenhotep II himself, welcomed into the Beyond by friendly-looking figures of the gods. Hathor was the most prominent, easily recognisable in her great crown of cows' horns and blazing red sun disc, and she'd certainly done a good job protecting the king, for when the tomb was first discovered in 1898 his mummy still lay there.

As we looked down into his now empty sarcophagus, our guide pointed out a small chamber to the right where a further nine kings had been found. According to the guide book, the mummies had included Tuthmosis IV, Amenhotep III (him again), Seti II and Ramses IV, V and VI, all placed there for safety by the priests after their own tombs had been robbed. It is also said that they had all been removed to the Cairo Museum, where we had just missed our chance to see them following the closure of the Mummy Room.

Momentarily alone, I looked around at the other small chambers I could see. Two of them were wide open, but the nearest was still sealed up.

After taking a few more photographs I headed back up into what was now blazing daylight, catching up with my aunt and the rest of our group in a shady corner of a tomb doorway so enormous it was difficult to imagine how it could ever have been hidden. It couldn't have been more obvious if they'd rigged up a set of neon lights. Built for Ramses VI, whose mummified body had ended up in the side chamber of the tomb we'd just visited, it had been finished around 1136 BC. The tons of rock chippings removed during its construction had been dumped outside, completely concealing an earlier tomb only rediscovered three thousand years later by Howard Carter. The small area where we now stood was the very last part of the Valley he had cleared in his search for Tutankhamen's tomb, and soon after work began on 1 November 1922 he made the discovery of a lifetime. It affected far more people than he could ever have imagined, and was responsible for bringing countless thousands of people like us to Egypt to see the tomb for themselves.

After taking photographs by the famous tomb entrance, we went down the sixteen steps Carter had cleared to reach the sealed doorway at the bottom, where seal impressions of Tutankhamen told him he was on the edge of something potentially momentous. Passing through into the descending corridor beyond, we came to the second doorway, which Carter had reached on 26 November, his 'day of days'. It was here, in the company of Lord Carnarvon and his daughter, Lady Evelyn Herbert, and his friend Arthur Callendar, that Carter made a small opening in the plaster and held out a candle into the blackness beyond. 'At first I could see nothing,' he wrote, 'the hot air escaping from the chamber causing the candle flame to flicker, but presently, as my eyes grew accustomed to the light, details of the room within emerged slowly from the mist, strange animals, statues, and gold – everywhere the glint of gold.'

I tried to imagine how this empty room must have looked filled with all the wonderful treasures we'd seen in the Cairo Museum, originally stacked up in here with all the care and attention of a teenager's bedroom. Yet the chaotic state was the result of the attentions of ancient Egyptian tomb robbers who'd broken in on two separate occasions, and although they'd only taken a relatively small amount they'd still had time for a good rummage around. But while they were emptying boxes of linens, scooping out expensive perfumes and scattering the contents of jewel boxes across the floor, something seems to have disturbed them, and in their hurry to leave they dropped some of their stolen treasures. Carter found a set of gold rings still threaded on to a knotted handkerchief, and the robbers' fingerprints were still visible inside alabaster perfume jars.

In their attempts to tidy up the tomb, the authorities had then rushed about hastily repacking boxes and chests with whatever lay closest to hand, apparently in as much of a hurry as the robbers had been, in their attempts to keep the tomb's location secret. Yet this was only unknowingly achieved when Ramses VI's tomb was built close by, just in time to save Tut's tomb from the wholesale looting which accompanied the breakdown of royal authority soon after Ramses' death. Oblivious to such comings and goings above him, Tutankhamen slept on, safe within a golden cocoon of coffins and 'the only royal mummy who remained in the Valley of the Kings', or so it was said.

We had already seen two of his gold coffins in Cairo and now his mummy lay before us inside a third, its toes still covered with the perfumes used at his funeral, now blackened with age. Within a stone sarcophagus covered with a protective sheet of rather dusty glass, he lay in the centre of a burial chamber which, just like the much larger tomb of Amenhotep II, was adorned with amazing wall scenes. Although often dismissed as hastily painted, the figures were overwhelmingly beautiful, and whilst they might be the most powerful gods of the Afterlife they looked friendly enough to me. There was Hathor again, holding up her ☥ ankh to allow the king to breathe in the breath of life as jackal-headed Anubis gave him a reassuring pat on the shoulder. On the opposite wall the sky goddess Nut had come down from her usual heavenly perch to welcome him into the realm of the gods, and at the far end Osiris, dread lord of the Underworld, stretched out his arms to embrace his newly arrived son.

There was also the king's funeral cortège, the courtiers wearing white headbands – the ancient version of black armbands – followed by the royal mummy. As his upright mummy received the final rites to revive his soul, the figure in leopardskin robes performing these rites was Ay, Tutankhamen's elderly vizier, who succeeded him. In the familiar tale of the 'tragic boy-king' I'd always read and accepted as fact that Ay had also killed him, his sudden death and apparently hasty burial explaining why the tomb was so small and unfinished.

But hang on a minute! We'd just been into two other tombs which clearly contradicted all this. With only the burial chamber decorated, Amenhotep II's tomb too was described as 'unfinished' – and he'd ruled for twenty-seven years. And we'd also been into the enormous, fully decorated tomb of Ramses VI, who my guide book said had reigned from 1143 to 1136 BC – only seven years as opposed to Tutankhamen's ten. It just didn't seem to add up.

After a last look round the tomb of someone whom I, like many others, had long regarded as a familiar figure, I realised he was perhaps not quite as familiar as I'd thought. Fantastic as it had been finally to see all these things for myself, I concluded in my diary that evening that 'this has all been a very strange experience, after reading about the subject so many times'. It also began to dawn on me that, just because I'd read things in a book, it didn't make them true, and I'd have to try and find some things out for myself.

On our last day in Egypt my aunt and I went back to the museum in Cairo, this time taking things at our own pace. Little by little, my brain started to make its own connections between the objects and the places we'd just seen, as things gradually pulled together into some kind of focus. Revisiting Tutankhamen's treasures, we found some of the lesser-known pieces, such as the sandals with images of Egypt's enemies painted on the soles so he could trample upon them, their figures carved on the base of ceremonial staves so that he could grind them into the dust. There were also six chariots, and representations of the king firing arrows into everything from ostriches to Asiatics. Amongst a fearsome array of the weapons themselves were at least nineteen bows, arrows, scimitars, daggers, clubs and two large shields adorned with images of Tutankhamen attacking lions and trampling his enemies. These adult possessions were a far cry from the tragic, helpless little boy of legend, and I began to see a very different Tutankhamen in my mind. But if my cherished image of the 'boy-king' had been so misleading, what about others? This was a question which soon resurfaced when we reached the Amarna Room.

Like many other people I was familiar with the famous bust of Nefertiti in Berlin, and whilst there were several other similarly attractive images of the queen's face here in the museum, other portrayals of the fabled beauty revealed a big chin and scrawny neck. In some examples she looked so much like her husband Akhenaten that it was difficult to work out who was who. As the museum's own guide book said, 'their bodies seem deformed: long face, narrow neck, rounded breast, delicate, high waist, enormous buttocks, and bulging thighs'. Although one of the smaller statues of the king showed an average-looking king, four larger figures flanking the wall displayed elongated features and distorted body shapes which are routinely described as 'grotesque'. The guide book said these statues had been found in Akhenaten's short-lived temples at Karnak, built before he moved to a new capital, Amarna. Its remote location generally excluded Amarna from the standard itinerary, but I now very much wanted to see the place for myself. Even with the limited knowledge of a fifteen-year-old, I knew there were things that didn't add up and I wanted to know why. But for now the longed-for visit to Amarna would have to wait.

Back in England preparing for O-level exams, I found the careers advice I was offered unimaginative at best. 'Egyptologist' was certainly on no one's list, and although I took matters into my own hands and wrote to all sorts of museums and institutions, they either didn't reply or told me in their roundabout way to forget it, assuming this was yet another query from a teenager who'd 'grow out of it'. So I left school and went on to sixth form college, where I made my choice of A-level subjects on the basis of what seemed the most appropriate preparation for Egyptology: history, classical studies and geography, with general studies and archaeology thrown in for good measure.

My eventual aim was to study for an Egyptology degree close to the British Museum at University College London, whose world-famous Egyptology Department, the first in the country, had been set up in 1892 as a result of the efforts of Amelia Ann Blandford Edwards.

Something of a rarity in Victorian times, this independent single woman made her living as a writer. When bad weather on a sketching holiday in France sent her on to sunnier climes she ended up in Egypt, which changed her life and the entire future of Egyptology. Chartering a sailing boat in Cairo, the intrepid forty-one-year-old set out on a three-month river journey which she described in her classic work *A Thousand Miles up the Nile*, first published in 1877 and still in print.

Edwards's sense of adventure and evocative descriptions are refreshingly unspoilt by self-conscious academic niceties. In many ways a mistress of understatement, she describes through words and her own sketches the key sites from Cairo, Giza and Dendera down to Luxor, the Valley of the Kings and on to Philae, her text interspersed with unexpected and often unintentional humour. Sitting down to lunch with assorted travelling companions at Abu Simbel, she records the arrival of a hastily scribbled note from another member of their party: 'Pray come immediately – I have found the entrance to a tomb. Please send some sandwiches!' With a genuine respect for the people she met, she compares her own appearance with that of the Egyptians, declaring that 'one cannot but feel . . . that we cut a sorry figure with our hideous palm leaf hats, green veil and white umbrellas!'

Edwards also had very clear ideas on women's rights, and was indignant at the reluctance of male scholars to recognise the achievements of Hatshepsut; she herself praised the 'genius and energy of this extraordinary woman'. She was vice-president of the Society for Promoting Women's Suffrage, an event still forty years in the future, and so the notion of an omnipotent female pharaoh was no doubt an attractive one.

Yet it is Edwards's reaction to the ancient gods which is most surprising, and at the risk of offending her God-fearing Victorian readers she revealed that there were times when she felt she believed in them. She was also deeply upset by Christian vandalism of the monuments, and, seeing the damage still being done by both foreigners and locals, she realised that 'There is no-one to prevent it; there is no-one to discourage it. Every day, more inscriptions are mutilated – more tombs are rifled – more painting and sculptures are defaced.' The situation so affected her that, once back in England, she gave up all her other work and began a single-handled crusade to save Egypt's heritage by tapping into the widespread interest in finding historical verification for the Bible. To this end she set up the Egypt Exploration Fund, later Society, in 1882, and spent the rest of her life doing all she could to promote the study and preservation of Egypt's ancient monuments.

Her diplomatic skills were particularly required in defending the Society's archaeologist William Matthew Flinders Petrie. On his first visit to Egypt in 1880 to survey the pyramids of Giza, Petrie's careful excavation methods put him light years ahead of his treasure-hunting contemporaries and, recognising his potential, Edwards took him on. Yet Petrie's disagreements with the gentlemen of the Society's committee led to his dramatic resignation in 1886. So Edwards found him financial support from a wealthy Bolton businessman, inspired to visit Egypt after reading Edwards's book and one of her biggest fans. Although there were no strings attached to the funding, Edwards told Petrie that his financier was quite a religious man 'and if you could throw any light on the Bible . . . he would be gratified'.

Able to resume his work at numerous sites, Petrie had started to make tremendously important discoveries at Amarna when Edwards, aged only sixty-one, died from a combination of exhaustion and influenza. The Egyptian-inspired ankh and obelisk adorning her grave caused quite a scandal at the time. In her will she left £5000 worth of railway shares with instructions that these be used to establish Britain's first chair in Egyptology.

It gave Petrie a job for life as the Edwards Professor of Egyptian Archaeology and Philology, with an income of £140 a year.

It seems that Edwards chose University College as the home of her bequest rather than Oxford or Cambridge because it was the only university to admit men and women on equal terms regardless of religious belief. It had been founded in 1827 as an alternative to these other two universities, and, since it admitted students 'without distinction of colour, caste, creed or sex', became known as 'the godless and infidel establishment of Gower Street'. With the head and stuffed body of its founder, the philosopher Jeremy Bentham, still watching over the seat of learning he had created, it really was the perfect choice for me.

Ignoring much well-intentioned advice, I applied to study for a degree in ancient history and Egyptology at UCL. I knew they only took a very few students each year, but to my amazement they gave me a place. At just eighteen, I found the move south incredibly tough, with London the most unfriendly place in the world. Crippled as I was by a shyness misinterpreted as disinterest, from the personal standpoint my first year was truly hideous. Yet everything about the course was fantastic, despite the terrifying convolutions of hieroglyphic grammar. There were only three of us on the course that year, so classes were far less intimidating than they might have been. We also had access to an excellent library built around Edwards's own books, and the department as a whole was an amazing place. Some of the research fellows had actually studied with Petrie and his equally extraordinary colleague Margaret Murray, the first professional female Egyptologist in Britain.

Murray was born in Calcutta to a Northumbrian family and first came to UCL as a hieroglyphs student in 1894, only two years after Amelia Edwards's bequest had created the department. She later remembered that

there was still that splendid spirit which in 1827 had dared to start an English University on modern lines. It was revolutionary! Not only was there no religion but women were admitted! Everyone knew that women were anathema in a university, not only because of their inferior intellect but also on account of their innate wickedness they would be a terrible danger to the young men. I am not sure if the old universities believed the Almighty had created women for the sole use of the male sex, but they certainly acted as if they did!

Unsurprisingly, Murray was also an active supporter of women's suffrage, just like Edwards before her. Soon teaching hieroglyphs herself, Murray ended up running the department during Petrie's long absences making his name as an excavator. She also set up a proper curriculum which included ancient Egyptian history together with the basic principles of archaeology, mineralogy, anthropology and pathology, the latter with the help of a skeleton that she bought and christened George.

Murray also directed one of the earliest mummy examinations in 1906, made important discoveries while excavating in Egypt, Malta, Minorca and Syria, and published regularly on a wide range of subjects. Her lifelong interest in anthropology did cause problems, however, and she was told on more than one occasion that 'Anthropology is not a subject for women.' When established Egyptology journals refused to publish her articles about anything they considered 'indelicate' although they accepted the same type of material from male scholars, she was justifiably angry, since 'it showed that a man might write on such subjects and be praised for his knowledge and insight, but not a woman'.

Nevertheless she persevered and, pursuing her interest in folklore, began to study Egyptian customs. Particularly fascinated with those of women, she observed the various methods used to induce pregnancy, from swallowing scrapings taken from temple walls to visiting the mummies of the Cairo Museum. She was finally made Assistant Professor in 1924, and retired in 1935. After Petrie's death seven years later she kept his memory very much alive, and dedicated her best-selling book *The Splendour That Was Egypt* to him. She also used the new medium of television to pay him further tribute in a 1953 BBC programme marking the centenary of his birth. In a second BBC interview, describing her own career, she declared in the true spirit of the elderly, 'I'm a piece of archaeology myself, being ninety-six.' Having completed her output of 150 publications with her defiantly lively autobiography, *My First Hundred Years*, she died four months later. Despite a very long life dedicated to teaching, her tremendous contribution has tended to be obscured by the legendary Petrie. But whilst he was in many ways a genius who achieved incredible things, the 'Father of Egyptology' was only able to do much of this with the constant support of Murray, and of Edwards before her.

UCL's Petrie Museum had been formed around Edwards's personal collection of artefacts, since she had wanted to initiate 'the study of ancient Egypt by means of the objects found' rather than simply by the hieroglyphic language, as it was then taught. Much of her collection had come from Petrie's own excavations, and over the next forty years he continued to increase it through what he described as 'unconsidered trifles'. Of far more value to an Egyptologist than any amount of golden treasure, such relatively mundane objects as pots, beads, scarab-shaped seal stones and rings enabled him to establish a reliable means of dating Egyptian culture. Photographs from the late 1880s and 1890s also show him using a favourite seal ring as an innovative form of tie fastener.

Although he admitted that the rapidly expanding collection was almost getting beyond his control, it was finally displayed in 1915 in long galleries containing material from just about every period in Egyptian history. Alongside cases full of pottery and funerary figurines, beads, flints and scarabs, the museum housed objects that I found fascinating – the world's oldest dress, a set of tattoo needles, small bronze hair curlers, hair pins and combs, in fact all the things Egyptian men and women would have handled and used on a daily basis to create the well-groomed figures portrayed in their art.

Although Petrie seems to have discouraged anyone from touching the artefacts while he was in charge, for fear of them breaking, the department's second professor, Stephen Glanville, encouraged his students to handle what has been described in Egyptological terms as 'the greatest teaching collection in the world'. In museum classes we were presented with drawers full of items thousands of years old and taught to understand the basic features of each type of object, even being allowed to choose pieces we particularly liked for further study. I was already fascinated with dress and adornment, and there was a particularly attractive carving of a nobleman, with golden bangles around hands raised in prayer, gold necklaces tied on with tassels and a wonderful hairstyle carved with incredible precision. I'd made a decision to study hairstyles as part of my degree, and as I took notes on its date and find spot I discovered that my praying nobleman came from Amarna.

Most of the museum's Amarna objects had come either from Petrie's excavations or from those undertaken later by the Egypt Exploration Society. There were sculptures and carvings of Akhenaten, Nefertiti and their daughters; brightly coloured glazed tiles and inlays from the palaces in which they had lived; hundreds of scarab seals, amulets and rings; delicate glass and faience vessels; and pottery from as far afield as the Aegean. Everything painted a picture of a sophisticated and cosmopolitan city, and although I had not yet visited Amarna I was at least able to touch, feel and hold things once used by its ancient inhabitants.

During my time at UCL I met Julia Samson, who had first arrived in the department some fifty years earlier. In 1934, as Julia Lazarus, she had begun to study with Petrie's successor, Stephen Glanville. When she commented that there was a lot of work to be done in sorting through the thousands of objects, some still in the packing cases in which they'd arrived from Egypt, she was offered the job of registering everything from Amarna. In 1936 she was invited to join the Egypt Exploration

Society's excavations there. The excavation director, John Pendlebury, was keen to include the material Petrie had found but never had time to publish, so he asked Lazarus to write part of the excavation report, *The City of Akhenaten*, and bring the material together. Back in London, she continued to work on the material in the Petrie Museum until her plans to become a museum assistant were put on hold at the outbreak of the war in 1939.

After her marriage she finally returned to the museum in 1966 as Julia Samson, and published her catalogue *Amarna: City of Akhenaten and Nefertiti*, followed by a series of articles based on her meticulous examination of material she knew better than anyone else. This included the well-dressed nobleman figure who'd caught my eye, the hieroglyphs in the top corner spelling out part of the name of the sun god the Aten. When I checked Samson's descriptions of it, she explained that this was only part of a much larger limestone slab or stela, pieces of which had been recovered by both Petrie and Pendlebury and were now divided between the Petrie Museum and Cairo. She also described it as important for the information it revealed about the 'uncertain history' of Smenkhkara, a mysterious character confusingly described in the books I'd read as Akhenaten's son, son-in-law, brother or even lover! And because I'd never seen a picture of a man named Smenkhkara, he intrigued me even more.

My nobleman was carved on the reverse of the stela, its front inscribed with two pairs of cartouches – the ovals drawn around royal names. Although tradition dictated that each king had five names, only two were ever written in cartouches. So the two pairs of cartouches positioned here must contain the names of two kings, ruling together as equals. Since royal names are some of the first things a hieroglyph student learns, even I could read them. The first two named Neferkheperura-Waenra Akhenaten, better known as Akhenaten, whilst the second, less familiar, pair read 'Ankhkheperura Neferneferuaten', Akhenaten's co-regent, who was also described as his 'beloved'.

Samson had realised that Nefertiti was often described as being 'beloved of' her husband Akhenaten, and she also knew that Neferneferuaten was one of Nefertiti's names. And from her long studies of Amarna material she'd discovered the name Ankhkheperura written in a feminine form. Although the figures below the cartouches had been partly destroyed, the lower halves of the two individuals remained. And they clearly showed that the second figure was female. For Samson, this unassuming little stela was 'ultimate proof of Akhenaten's co-regency with a woman', whom she identified as Nefertiti, and who, after Akhenaten's death, had ruled as sole monarch with the throne name Smenkhkara. Indeed, Samson's catalogue of the Amarna collection was republished in 1978 with the provocative subtitle *Nefertiti as Pharaoh*.

Since her work completely contradicted most established views of the Amarna period, they were controversial to say the least. Yet they seemed to clarify so much of what had been confusing and difficult to explain. When I felt confident enough, I approached her after one of her lectures to talk about her work. She was incredibly kind, suggesting books and articles I should read, and even wrote to me with further information and a copy of one of her own publications.

And the more I read about this fascinating period, the more I was able to piece together just how exactly the accepted version of events had come about.

3

THE CREATION OF THE
AMARNA STORY

The most controversial part of ancient Egypt's long history is its most popular one, with a cast-list of famous names headed by Akhenaten, Nefertiti and Tutankhamen. People seem comfortable with the established characters of the Amarna Period, portrayed as the eccentric revolutionary, his beautiful queen and the tragic boy-king who played out their lives in palatial surroundings, beset with all the usual intrigue, murder, homosexuality and incest. After all, this *is* ancient Egypt.

With the limited amount of evidence available endlessly scrutinised and argued about, the few hard facts about the Amarna Period are inevitably set against a background of theory, supposition and possibility, and the means by which the 'established version of events' came about is a fascinating story in itself. Many of the mysteries and controversies associated with the Amarna Period and ancient Egypt in general began when the first European travellers visited the land of the Nile. Already familiar with the Egyptian statues and obelisks that the Romans had brought back to Italy in the early centuries AD, many pilgrims to the Holy Land took detours south to see the pyramids, which they believed to be 'the granaries of Joseph'.

The biblical version of Egypt as little more than the home of cruel pagans was then knocked off balance somewhat during the Renaissance, when translations of Greek and Roman texts revealed that the classical world had regarded Egypt as the source of all wisdom. The Egyptians were even believed to have been able to transform base metals into gold, the science of alchemy derived from the Arabic *al-keme*, which simply means 'of Egypt'. Even the Pope was impressed: for his Vatican apartments Alexander VI commissioned paintings of Egyptian gods alongside images of Moses; and the more adventurous of Europe's clergy were inspired to visit Egypt as part of the Grand Tour. One of the earliest tourists was a Yorkshireman, George Sandys, who saw the pyramids for himself in 1610 and was the first to realise that they were nothing to do with Joseph but were the tombs of Egypt's kings.

The first Europeans known to have ventured any further south were a couple of French Capuchin friars who toured Luxor and the Valley of the Kings in 1668. Their countryman Claude Sicard moved permanently to Cairo in 1712 until his death from plague fourteen years later. As a Jesuit, Sicard's travels around the country saving souls took him to remote places that no other European had ever seen. With considerable foresight the Regent Philippe of Orleans ordered him to investigate all the ancient monuments he saw and keep a written record.

On his first trip south, in 1714, Sicard sailed nearly 200 miles up the Nile and stopped off at the town of el-Ashmunein to see the large Christian basilica built on the ruins of a temple to Thoth, the Egyptian god of wisdom. The ancient Egyptians regarded picture writing as the 'words of Thoth', and this pictorial script was known by the later Greeks as 'hieroglyphs' or 'sacred carvings'. However their meaning was eventually lost and by Sicard's day the ancient language had been indecipherable for over thirteen hundred years.

As Sicard travelled on a few miles further west to the limestone cliffs of Tuna el-Gebel, he discovered a fourteen-foot-high inscription carved into the rock face. The lines of mysterious picture writing were topped by two strangely shaped, rather obese-looking human figures raising their arms to the sun, and beside the tablet-shaped stela were two groups of statues, their headless, distorted bodies reaching blindly forward to grasp at a smaller stela and hold out an altar. Before their mutilation, the curiously proportioned figures had once stared out across the Nile to the East Bank where the cliffs pull back in a vast arc, creating a wide desert plain. The plain itself was a windswept, barren place, uninhabited save for a few Beni Amran nomads, who had a reputation for shooting strangers on sight. It appears that Sicard wisely made no attempt to cross the Nile to convert them, and so the place was left free of curious foreigners until more French turned up right at the end of the eighteenth century, this time armed to the teeth.

These were the troops of Napoleon Bonaparte, who were not to be put off by the unsavoury reputation of a few villagers. But this was far more than a show of force. Bonaparte's military expedition included 164 of France's greatest scholars, there for the sole purpose of recording and documenting all they saw in a country that Bonaparte himself regarded as 'the cradle of the science and art of all humanity'. Under the protection of the troops his scholars catalogued, mapped and drew everything they saw in a country 'all but unknown to Europeans', and also made the most significant discovery in the history of Egyptology.

During the reinforcement of Egypt's coastal defences in the summer of 1799, a French officer of the Engineers uncovered a slab of rock while demolishing the wall of a fort at el-Rashid, also known as Rosetta. He noticed that it was inscribed in Greek, but there were also sections of the ancient Egyptian picture writing known as hieroglyphs, and, suspecting it might be something important, he took the intriguing slab of rock back to his general. The Greek part of the text revealed that this was a decree issued by ancient Egyptian priests as a means of announcing the great honours they would bestow on the pharaoh Ptolemy V in 196 BC in return for tax exemptions. And because they wanted the message to be understood by both Egyptians and Greeks, the priests put their words down in 'sacred writing (hieroglyphs), document writing (demotic) and Greek writing'. And so it was the Rosetta Stone, as it is now known, that finally provided the means of understanding the ancient culture through its own words.

As the French scholars headed south, recording and drawing

as they went, they became the first Europeans to set foot on the windswept plain first seen by Sicard, and here they made another discovery. The plain was covered in a huge expanse of ancient ruins, comprising brick-built walls, a large gateway and enclosure and a great wide roadway, all of which were now mapped out and drawn by surveyors and artists. The French team's map of the ruined city appeared as one of the three thousand illustrations in their thirty-six-volume blockbuster *The Description of Egypt*, which gave birth to the whole subject of Egyptology. Not only was it a priceless resource for scholars; it became something of a 'style Bible' for those swept up in the growing fashion for all things Egyptian and also initiated the craze for treasure hunting, even providing the maps!

In the meantime, the slow process of deciphering the hieroglyphs from the Rosetta Stone finally achieved success in 1822 when the brilliant young Frenchman Jean François Champollion (1790–1832) cracked the code. During his work, Champollion corresponded with the English classicist Sir William Gell, whose own fascination for hieroglyphs and all things Egyptian soon rubbed off on his protégé, John Gardner Wilkinson. When Wilkinson set out for Egypt in 1821, he was so enamoured of the place that he stayed for twelve years, continuing his studies of hieroglyphs and exploring as many of the ancient sites as he could.

In 1824 he too visited the mysterious ruin-strewn plain shown on the French map and discovered a whole series of rock-cut tombs in the surrounding cliffs to the north. 'These grottoes I had the good fortune first to notice on my way up the Nile in 1824,' he wrote, 'at which time they had not been visited by any modern traveller' – at least not since early tourists had left Greek graffiti in them some two thousand years earlier. Although the walls beneath were covered in figures and texts which mystified him, Wilkinson immediately realised their similarity to those on top of the great stela that Sicard had discovered a century before at Tuna el-Gebel: 'The sculptures are singular and nearly in plain style as those of Gebel Toona [sic], tho' not quite so much out of proportion. They are all of the same king as that Tablet [stela], who may possibly be some Persian, since the arms and drapes are not common in Egyptian sculptures.'

Finally deciding that the figures must be Egyptian, albeit rather strange ones, Wilkinson wrote to an acquaintance describing how 'the sun itself is represented with rays terminating in hands thus which is never seen in other parts of Egypt. In addition to this the name of the king (written in Hieroglyphics) has been purposefully effaced, tho I have managed to get a copy of it.' The damage seemed to have been done by those wanting to obliterate all trace of an apparently much-hated predecessor, and with the tombs lying open the scenes had been further vandalised by the early Christians. Politely referred to as 'hermits', these superstitious squatters had used the tombs as houses and churches, carving crosses and an apse into the ancient scenes and blinding the eyes of the ancient figures who looked down on them.

Wanting a second opinion on the tombs' mystifying scenes, Wilkinson went back to the site two years later with his friend James Burton, who seems to have been equally bemused. He also noticed that, unlike the scenes in tombs and temples he'd seen elsewhere in Egypt, 'No other deity but the sun is anywhere to be found, either sculptures, or, I believe, written.' He was also unimpressed with the scenes themselves, stating: 'I think the style of sculpture is very peculiar and very bad.' Nevertheless the pair made numerous drawings and, in the days before the camera, took wet paper squeezes by pushing against the carvings soggy blotting paper which dried to give a perfect, crisp image.

Their mutual friend Gell was equally perplexed by the images Wilkinson then sent him, and assumed that the figure of the king, and a second who was presumably his queen, must be 'two pregnant females'. Certainly there was little to choose between them, as both were portrayed with the same long neck, swelling breasts, broad child-bearing hips and massive thighs, not to mention saggy chins and elongated faces. A funny-looking couple, to be sure.

After discovering one of the site's alabaster quarries, Wilkinson and Burton believed the ruins on the plain to be the lost city of Alabastron, described by classical authors. However, Wilkinson subsequently gave the site its more familiar name of Tell el-Amarna by combining the names of the two local villages, el-Till and el-Amarieh.

When their friend Robert Hay visited the region in 1827, he made a pencil study of the great stela at Tuna el-Gebel which featured a self-portrait for scale, leaning in contemplation against the stela's base in the Turkish dress adopted by Europeans in an attempt to 'blend in' with the local people. Yet the Egyptians remained bemused by such foreigners and, believing the stela to be a doorway concealing hidden treasures in the cliffs, they asked Hay and his colleagues why they always shut the door as soon they saw them coming!

Over the next few years Hay made studies of many of the city's tombs, their walls filled with figures of the ill-proportioned king and queen standing beneath the sun accompanied by their small daughters, with their city, its people and palaces, temples and houses. These were all carefully drawn with the aid of a camera lucida, a device that assists a draughtsman by using a prism to concentrate the light from the object being drawn and project it on to a sheet of paper, enabling it to be traced accurately.

As news of Alabastron and its curious inhabitants, dubbed the 'Disc Worshippers', spread throughout the academic community, the great Champollion himself arrived in 1828. Still working towards a complete understanding of the ancient hieroglyphic language, he made notes of the inscriptions while his draughtsman, Nestor l'Hôte, began patiently recording every single hieroglyph. Although l'Hôte's eventual seventeen volumes remain unpublished, some of his papers were passed on to his family and fired the curiosity and imagination of his young relative Auguste Mariette (1821–81), the future founder of the Egyptian Antiquities Service.

In 1840 a couple of tourists visiting the famous northern tombs spotted a second huge stela ('Stela U'), similar to the one Sicard had found ('Stela A') but on the East Bank near the city and even bigger. Extending the full height of the cliff face, battered statues of the king and queen stood in deep recesses at each side, while the top featured more defaced images of these famous disc worshippers beneath the ever-present spider-like arms of their sun disc god. Soon another French team copying the northern tomb scenes found a third such stela, 'Stela S' (Fig. 1), again flanked by battered statues with the same curious proportions as those engraved on the stela top, a faceless king and queen with arms raised to the sun. Although the workmanship was described as 'beautifully fine', the profiles were 'hideous and the forms of the body outrageous' and quite unlike anything else seen hitherto in ancient Egyptian art. So who exactly were the mysterious Disc Worshippers of Alabastron?

The answer was finally provided in 1841 when Champollion's epic work *Egyptian Grammar* finally revealed the full meaning of hieroglyphs to the world. Sadly, it was a posthumous revelation, since the great man had been dead for nearly ten years, killed by a work-induced stroke at the age of forty-one. Today his remains lie beneath an Egyptian-style obelisk in Paris's famous Père Lachaise cemetery, which also houses Oscar Wilde and Jim Morrison.

Champollion's legacy allowed his successors to translate hieroglyphs for themselves, and when Karl Richard Lepsius arrived in Egypt in 1842 at the head of the Prussian Epigraphic Expedition their three-year progress up the Nile and back again provided a tidal wave of new information. With time to throw an impromptu birthday party on top of the Great Pyramid in honour of their sponsor, King Wilhelm IV of Prussia, Lepsius' team visited Amarna in 1843 and again in 1845, intensively copying absolutely everything. Although many of the names, like the

FIGURE 1. The scene on the top of Boundary Stela S showing Akhenaten, Nefertiti and their eldest daughters Meritaten and Meketaten worshipping the Aten, Nefertiti's imposing crown making her the tallest figure in the scene

faces, had been largely hacked away, what remained allowed them to identify the disc-worshipping duo as an Egyptian pharaoh and his wife. When their names were spoken aloud for the first time in over three thousand years, the king was finally revealed as Bech-en-aten, later corrected to Akhenaten, whilst his queen had been a woman named Nefertiti. But with no such names to be found in any of the ancient king lists or official records, what had they done to deserve such a fate?

As early as 1837 Wilkinson had made a few conclusions for himself, and in his *Manners and Customs of the Ancient Egyptians*, the first 'popular' – meaning readable – book on the subject, he astutely referred to a group of 'Stranger Kings' who 'introduced very heretical changes into the religion, they expelled the favourite god from the Pantheon, and introduced a Sun worship unknown in Egypt'. He also noted that 'their reign was not of very long duration; and having been expelled, their monuments, as well as every record of them, were purposefully defaced'.

Lepsius too had referred to several kings not found on the legitimate lists, and with the benefit of hieroglyphs he was able to make the connection between those who changed the religion and the disc worshippers. Lepsius declared that a king named Amenhotep IV had built a new royal capital at Amarna and had tried to abolish the entire religious system, replacing it with sun worship and erasing all other gods' names throughout the country. And because his own name contained the name of Amen he had changed it to Akhenaten, meaning 'Worshipper of the Aten', the great sun disc which dominated every scene.

Yet not everyone was convinced that this unusual king had been a man at all. When the French scholar Eugène Lefébure examined the images, he concluded that this was surely a woman in masquerade. Using the well-known female pharaoh Hatshepsut as a precedent, he supported his claim with the evidence of classical scholars who had mentioned that a woman had ruled after a king named Akhenkheres, whom Lefébure equated with Akhenaten. Although Lefébure has been described as an able man who made valuable contributions to Egyptology, he was also characterised as 'by nature a poet and a mystic' and his theories were largely ignored by subsequent scholars.

Ever more keen for new information on this revolutionary trans-sexual who was starting to take shape before them, the French returned to Amarna and worked there on and off between 1883 and 1902 under the direction of Gaston Maspero, the newly appointed Head of the French-run Egyptian Antiquities Service following the death of its founder, Mariette. During 1881, his first year in office, Maspero had to deal with two major discoveries. No fewer than five royal burial chambers were found inside the pyramids of Sakkara, covered in Pyramid Texts, the world's oldest body of religious writings. This was followed by the largest-ever find of royal mummies – over forty of them buried together in a single tomb in Luxor.

That same year, a villager at Amarna discovered the most exquisite carved stone plaque, obviously an *antika*, amongst the ruins. He sold it to a dealer and it was bought by a wealthy American collector for twenty-two piastres – quite a bargain at the equivalent of around 4p in today's UK currency. Having lain safe beneath the sand for the last three and a half thousand years, the plaque finally revealed the faces of the king and queen in pristine condition. It also showed what might yet lie undiscovered elsewhere around the site, so the locals began exploring the one place they knew no foreigner had so far ventured into – the remote and desolate Wadi Abu Hasah el-Bahri, the valley which cuts right through the eastern cliffs between the northern and southern tombs.

After scouring all the likely nooks and crannies along four miles of inhospitable, boulder-strewn dry river bed, they finally came across a great square doorway cut out of the rock in the valley floor. Summoning up their courage, they went inside. After going down some ninety feet into the darkness, they would have had to push their way through the remnants of a blocked doorway, coming out into a great square burial chamber strewn with all manner of debris. By the light of their flaming torches they made out the remains of a once lavishly appointed tomb whose floors were covered with fragments of granite sarcophagi, alabaster canopic equipment, and over two hundred smashed up funerary figurines. There were pieces of brightly glazed pottery, alabaster bowls and jars, seals from jars of vintage wine, bright blue amulets and colourful glass beads, and, no doubt to their great delight, jewellery of gold and precious stones. Yet most importantly of all, though certainly not regarded as such by the superstitious villagers, the tomb still contained mummified remains. They had found the tomb of Akhenaten himself.

Managing to keep the tomb's whereabouts secret, the villagers gradually sold off its contents piece by piece, from 'fragments of a royal mummy' to 'numerous trinkets in ivory, glass, alabaster, bronze and gold'. Although details of such illicit dealings are

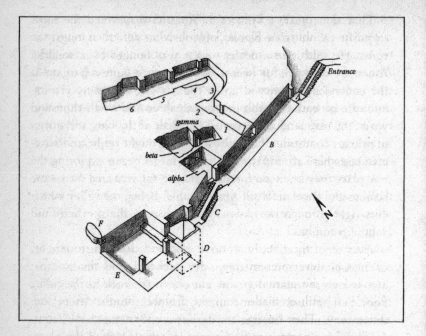

FIGURE 2. Plan of the Royal Tomb at Amarna, showing the
separate burial chambers used for members of the royal family
– Meketaten in chamber gamma, Kiya possibly in chamber
alpha and Akhenaten and possibly Tiy in pillared hall E. The
additional suite of rooms (1–6) thought to have been prepared
for Nefertiti were apparently never used

inevitably scarce, it is known that a local dealer sold some of
the jewellery to an Irish clergyman who happened to be passing
through the region in 1882. Looking for scarabs to add to his
antiquities collection, the Reverend W. J. Loftie bought a whole
range of 'trinkets', including gold foil scraped from a coffin, a
gold rosette from a linen funeral pall and a blue-glazed model
throwstick, together with parts of a jewelled collar, golden ear
studs and several rings, one of them a solid gold knuckle-duster
inscribed with the name 'Nefertiti'. Having purchased all he

could afford, in 1893 Loftie sold the pieces on via a London dealer to Edinburgh's Royal Scottish Museum, then returned to Amarna with more money to try to obtain what remained. Although, sadly, the gold foil 'winding sheets' inscribed with the name of Akhenaten's mother, Queen Tiy, were no longer around and had probably been melted down, he bought the two remaining large gold rings on behalf of fellow collectors, including the novelist H. Rider Haggard; both rings ended up in Liverpool's City Museum.

Apart from the French, who turned up in 1883 to do a few days' exploration amongst the low hills to the south, life went on much as it had always done in the nearby villages of el-Till, Hagg Qandil and el-Amarieh. Farmers worked their fields, fishermen cast their nets across the Nile and children ran about amongst the ever-present dogs and chickens. And the women attended to the eternal round of household tasks or dug for *sebakh*, a fertiliser made from the crumbly mudbricks of the ancient city. Then on one fateful day in 1887 a woman from el-Till, whose name is sadly unrecorded, made one of the most extraordinary discoveries in the history of Egyptology.

In her quest for compost she unwittingly wandered into the ruins of what could be described as an ancient office block. Just below the sand she found a box containing a pile of small clay tablets, each covered in tiny, wedge-shaped indentations. After digging around a little further she had uncovered several hundred more. To her they were just bits of useless old clay, so she sold them to a neighbour for the meagre sum of ten piastres. But the tablets were in fact some of ancient Egypt's most priceless records.

After the canny neighbour had made at least a hundredfold profit by selling them to a local dealer, they were picked up by the big-time middlemen who supplied foreign museums. Recognising the wedge-shaped indentations on the tablets as ancient cuneiform script, they approached one of their best customers, E. A. W. Budge, the British Museum's Keeper of Egyptian and Assyrian Antiquities, who was then touring the region. Offering to pay for his professional opinion, they handed him a few tablets to peruse. He instantly realised their significance: each lump of clay was an ancient communication between Egypt and her foreign neighbours. Although he must have been beside himself with excitement, Budge was a shrewd character and stayed deadpan, managing to take away eighty-two pieces to the British Museum for further study.

Now known as the Amarna Letters, the tablets contain correspondence between the kings and queens of Egypt and their opposite numbers abroad, using cuneiform as the international language of diplomacy. The earliest had been sent to Amenhotep III and Queen Tiy about 1360 BC and brought from their palace at Thebes to Amarna by their son Akhenaten. He and his family received the bulk of the letters, which continued to be sent throughout the Amarna Period to end in the reign of his son Tutankhamen about 1330 BC, when the court had returned to Thebes.

Whilst the great potentates of Babylon, Mitanni (Syria) and Arzawa (Anatolia) address the omnipotent pharaoh as 'Brother', the smaller vassal states kiss the ground before their lord 'the Sun'. Egypt was then the most powerful and wealthy country in the ancient world, although some of Akhenaten's later correspondence revealed that all was not well with Egypt's empire. Palestinian rulers repeatedly asked for military support as they came under attack from their neighbours, but it seemed that Akhenaten was either unable or unwilling to deal with their pleas.

As news of the letters' existence spread throughout the scholarly world, Budge's acquisition for the British Museum was soon duplicated by the museums of Paris, Berlin and Cairo. Villagers worked overtime, digging gleefully through the ruins to meet demand. The letters' discovery also prompted the first real excavation of the ruins, by the indefatigable Flinders Petrie who arrived there in 1891. After the usual arguments with the French-run Antiquities Service in Cairo, who would not allow him access to the tombs on which the French themselves were working, Petrie set up camp on the plain where the village dogs kept him awake at night with their incessant howling. He quickly realised that 'It is an overwhelming site to deal with. Imagine setting about exploring the ruins of Brighton, for that is the size of the town.'

With only a six-month excavation season in which to undertake the task, it was impossible to do anything more than get an idea of where the main features had been. So with Lepsius' fifty-year-old plans in hand, Petrie walked the site trying to locate the palaces, houses and temples of ancient Amarna. Almost immediately he found the outlines of the Great Official Palace. Built, like all ancient dwellings, from mudbricks, its surface was littered with chunks of smashed stonework and statues, fragments of bright-coloured glazes, glassware and tiles glittering in the sunlight amidst hollows in the sand which had once been lush garden pools.

After three days' digging he uncovered parts of a truly palatial pavement covering an area of some 2700 square feet. Surrounded by a great painted border, its centre was a *trompe l'oeil* blue lake filled with fish and lotus flowers. It was immediately reminiscent of the painted designs discovered only a few years earlier at the Theban palace of Amenhotep III and Tiy, where their son Akhenaten had grown up. Naturalistic scenes of ducks flying up from the reeds where small calves frolicked were bisected by a contrasting pathway of bound Nubian and Asiatic captives, designed to be regularly trampled underfoot by the king and queen in a subtle piece of political theatre. Petrie realised, however, that the same actions by the growing numbers of tourists arriving by sailing boat and steamer would have disastrous results, and decided to conserve his pavement with a protective shelter and raised gangway. To the painted plaster surface itself he painstakingly applied a solution of tapioca with his fingertip, a cost-effective way of providing a transparent coating once it had dried.

Even more beautiful were wall scenes decorating the royal family's private quarters in the less formal 'King's House'. One large fragment showed two young princesses playing at Nefertiti's feet, all of them sitting on plump red floor cushions in surroundings which hinted at the original sumptuous luxury.

One of the first to appreciate Petrie's new discoveries was a seventeen-year-old Norfolk artist, in Egypt for the first time working on behalf of his patron, Lord Amherst. Hearing of the new discoveries being made at Amarna, Amherst was keen to add to his growing collection of antiquities and encouraged his young artist to offer his services to Petrie and 'learn something of his methods'. The artist was none other than Howard Carter, who in January 1892 joined Petrie at Amarna, the city where Tutankhamen is believed to have been born.

Carter was completely in awe of Petrie, calling him an archaeological 'Sherlock Holmes'. Petrie in turn described Carter as 'a good-natured lad whose interest is entirely in painting and natural history: he only takes on this digging as being on the spot and convenient to Mr Amherst, and it is of no use to me to work him up as an excavator'. Yet he soon changed his mind and conceded that, with Carter's help, he could achieve much more. After building his own accommodation, the young man was sent to work in the place where Akhenaten and Nefertiti had worshipped the solar disc, the Great Temple, which covered an area some 2500 feet by 800 feet.

Although everything inside had been systematically smashed to pieces, Carter recovered the remains of seventeen superb limestone statues which had been mutilated and unceremoniously dumped over the temple's boundary walls in ancient times. Sharing a feminine-looking physique, these figures of Akhenaten and Nefertiti were depicted holding out offering trays and clad in the finest linen robes, embellished with jewellery inscribed with the name of the sun disc Aten and a whole range of interchangeable crowns, head-dresses and wigs. They also wore the same costume on smashed up sections of the temple's wall scenes, which showed them standing beneath the Aten's myriad arms, offering up endless bouquets, incense, perfumes and precious ornaments to the tinkly accompaniment of their small daughters' sistrum rattles.

Carter was beginning to enjoy himself, and wrote to a friend, 'As regards the work I like it very much indeed and find it very exciting. I did not find anything of any great value until yesterday. One of my men found another gold ring.' The piece in question was decorated with seated figures of Akhenaten and Nefertiti facing each other beneath the sun disc.

Working their way through some of the private houses in the central and southern parts of the city, Petrie and Carter also came across images of the royal family in people's homes, set up as objects of worship. One of the finest, found by Carter, showed Akhenaten on a lion-footed throne with Nefertiti on his lap, her long, graceful feet swinging below the fringed hem of her linen robe while their baby daughters Meritaten and Meketaten clamber over her lap.

In addition to such great works of art, Petrie made some of his most historically important discoveries by looking in places his contemporaries would never have considered. Working through the rubbish heaps, 'where the waste was thrown from the palace', he found piles of broken Mycenean and Cypriot pottery alongside native Egyptian vessels, whilst further rummaging turned up large quantities of discarded amulets, seal stones and rings of brightly glazed pottery naming members of the Amarna royal family. Having located the ancient 'industrial estates' and glass factories, Petrie also discovered buildings which he dubbed 'The Foreign Office' where the Amarna Letters had been found. He even managed to fit in a spot of survey work, mapping out the plain and surrounding hills which enabled him to discover no fewer than seven more of the fourteen great stelae set up to mark the limits of the city. Pacing up and down, compass in hand, Petrie calculated that they covered between twenty and twenty-six miles a day, and Carter almost had to run to keep up.

Then Petrie refers to his 'disabled foot', and as the summer temperatures began to rise both men succumbed to a combination of exhaustion, malnourishment and 'stomach pains'. Life on a Petrie dig was famous for its complete lack of just about anything, and as one of his students, T. E. Lawrence, better known as Lawrence of Arabia, later remembered, 'A Petrie dig is a thing with a flavour all its own: tinned kidneys mingle with mummy-corpses and amulets in the soup.'

Eventually Petrie grew disenchanted with working at a site he described as 'so ransacked that I have got very little and am almost ready to close work here'. Nevertheless, he and Carter still managed to fill 160 packing cases with Amarna finds. After being informed that Oxford University had decided to give him an honorary degree, most of Petrie's share was, unsurprisingly, presented to Oxford's Ashmolean Museum. The rest was given to University College London, to Petrie's sponsors and to Lord Amherst, with pieces eventually ending up in places as diverse as New York and Harrogate.

Regardless of his initial disappointments, Petrie's excavations had revealed the basic facts of the entire period. He had worked out that Akhenaten's reign had lasted around seventeen years, and had been able to date the city to the fourteenth century BC on the basis of the Greek pottery he had found. He even concluded, on the basis of the dates on fragments of food and wine jars, that the place had only been inhabited for a total of twenty years. From broken and discarded amulets and finger rings he also discovered the names of those who had lived at the site, and even established the exact order of succession – not an easy thing to do when each pharaoh traditionally had five official names and these were known to change from time to time. He concluded that the third Amenhotep had been succeeded by his son, Amenhotep IV, under 'the vigorous and determined tutelege of his imperious mother', Queen Tiy, who Petrie believed had been a Syrian from the land of Mitanni. After five years Amenhotep IV had changed his name to Akhenaten, confirming

Lepsius' finding that Amenhotep IV and Akhenaten were one and the same person.

During his next twelve years' rule as Akhenaten the king apparently took a co-regent named Smenkhkara, described as 'beloved of Akhenaten'. Petrie also believed that this Smenkhkare 'may well have married' the eldest princess, Meritaten, and, after becoming the next king, was followed in turn by Tutankhamen. When Petrie asserted that the king's wife, Nefertiti, was also a Mitannian princess he revealed the little-seen romantic side to his usually rather dour nature, especially when describing how Akhenaten was 'truly devoted to his one queen'.

In response to continuing doubts about the pharaoh's gender and French descriptions of the king's 'effeminate plumpness', Petrie said he believed that this was simply the result of 'good living and luxurious habits'. He asked: 'Is it credible that the most uxorious king of Egypt, who appears with his wife on every monument, who rides side by side with her in a chariot and kisses her in public, who dances her on his knee, who has a steadily increasing family – that this king was either a woman in masquerade or an eunuch?' Petrie's admiration for this icon of family values knew no bounds; with his apparently revolutionary views on art, religion and ethics, he stated, 'Akhenaten stands out as perhaps the most original thinker that ever lived in Egypt and one of the great idealists of the world.'

Meanwhile, the French-run Antiquities Service had finally found out about Akhenaten's tomb, sending Alessandro Barsanti – an engineer, conservator, technician or odd-job man, depending on who is telling the story – to move what was left of the contents to the Cairo Museum and then fit metal security doors to all the tombs. Although the date when the tomb was 'officially' discovered by the authorities is unclear, Barsanti finally took Petrie, Carter and their friend Henry Sayce to see it on 20 January 1892, their small group clambering over four miles of rocks and boulders as they made their way up the valley's dry river bed. Once inside, they witnessed the way in which the tomb's contents were being hoovered up with little supervision, although it seems that the mummy – or at least part of it – was still around, having been dragged outside into the daylight and picked clean by treasure hunters. Sayce remembered that immediately outside the tomb the French 'found the remains of a mummy which had been torn to shreds not long after its interment, and which I still believe to be the royal heretic', as Akhenaten was often described.

These remains seem to have become more and more 'fleshed out' each time the tale was told, and by the time Sayce wrote his *Memoirs*, the fragments had turned into 'the body of a man which had been burnt some time after mummification'. Yet this 'burnt' appearance was far more likely to have been due to the resins used in the mummification process. Although they were presumably packed up and sent to the Cairo Museum, no trace of either the mummified remains or the mummy's wrappings was ever seen again. Rumours that the villagers had taken a body away and burnt it persisted into recent times.

Whilst Petrie could only look on as vital clues were lost for ever, Carter took up his sketchbook and drew some of the extra-ordinary carvings which then still covered much of the tomb's wall space. With an eye for the unusual, exaggerated proportions of Amarna art, his efforts, published in *The Daily Graphic*, represented his first time in print. The most interesting scenes related to the early death of Meketaten, second daughter of Akhenaten and Nefertiti, who are shown 'lamenting over the body of this little child – weeping and casting dust in the air, like the bereaved in a modern Egyptian funeral. Here, too, were inscribed the thoughts, the feelings, the outgushings from the hearts of a people long ago.'

There was soon considerable bad feeling amongst the local people, who objected to the fact that the gates being fitted to the tombs would deprive them of a potential source of revenue. Many of the unique scenes in the southern tombs were destroyed before Barsanti's gates materialised, and, believing that piles

FIGURE 3. Wall scene in Chamber Gamma of Amarna's
Royal Tomb showing Akhenaten and Nefertiti followed by
Meritaten, Ankhesenpaaten and Neferneferuaten 'Junior'
mourning the death of the second daugher Meketaten, her
figure standing beneath a flower-strewn shrine on the far left

of gold lay behind their doorway-like exteriors, in 1906 local
Christians used gunpowder to blow up the most southerly of
the great boundary stelae (Stela P). Even the palace pavement
so carefully conserved by Petrie was hacked to bits by farmers
fed up with the endless hordes of tourists arriving by Thomas
Cook steamer and trampling down their fields to get to the sites.

Some of the more intrepid tourists also made the long trek up
to the Royal Tomb, which still contained numerous fragments of
granite and alabaster from the sarcophagi and funerary goods.
As one of them described on a visit in the 1890s, 'We found the
tomb; it had only been lately rediscovered, but had been rifled
and destroyed thousands of years ago . . . I saw where the coffin
had lain. It had been a handsome red granite sarcophagus. I
picked up many little fragments, each showing remains of the
polished surface and some with traces of carving. I also found
many pieces of alabaster showing remains of hieroglyphs . . .'
Fragments of the sarcophagi were also being offered for sale by
local dealers, as well as pieces hacked out of the crumbling wall
scenes which were repeatedly the subject of vandalism as more
and more of Amarna's history was lost for ever.

In the face of such damage the Egypt Exploration Society decided to make a complete record of all the tombs and boundary stelae at the site, and in 1901 arranged to send out a brilliant artist named Norman de Garis Davies. A former clergyman from Ashton-under-Lyne in Lancashire, Davies had got to know a local woman, Kate Bradbury, who was a close friend of Amelia Edwards and, like her, greatly enamoured of ancient Egypt. Bradbury's family wealth had helped support the Egypt Exploration Society and the fledgling Egyptology Department at UCL, and would also help finance Oxford University's Griffith Institute, named after Bradbury's future husband. Bradbury herself is yet another of Egyptology's unsung, behind-the-scenes heroines who also provided a great deal of practical help, from sorting books for the Edwards Library to treating the ancient textiles that Petrie was known to bring to her house in a suitcase.

Having been inspired by Bradbury, Davies studied Egyptology for himself and, arriving at el-Till in January 1902, immediately began work. Over the next six years he made facsimile copies of all the decorated tombs of the ancient city's officials, including the Aten priests Meryra and Panehesy as well as those who served the royal household, including the chamberlain, Tutu, Tiy's steward Huya, and a second Meryra, 'Steward of the Household of Nefertiti'.

Here Davies copied an unfinished wall sketch in which the king and queen rewarded their loyal servant Meryra. Although their names had recently been hacked out by vandals, Davies checked the old copies made by Lepsius and found that Akhenaten's name had been replaced in ancient times by that of 'Ankhkheperura Smenkhkara', the same name Petrie had first discovered, and evidence that an individual named Smenkhkara must have ruled after Akhenaten.

The second cartouche, which had once named Nefertiti, had also been recarved, and Davies made out 'Meritaten', the name of the couple's eldest daughter. On the basis of this information, it was assumed that Smenkhkara must have married the royal heiress. The suggestion by the French scholar Henri Gauthier that Ankhkheperura might simply be Nefertiti made little impact, just like the comments of his fellow countryman Lefébure before him.

Having established the basics of the highly distinctive Amarna art style, Davies concluded his six volumes of tomb scenes with the wish that 'the new excavations which have been begun with such promise by Professor Borchardt will throw additional light on this interesting subject'. They would certainly do that.

Between 1907 and the start of the First World War, the Berlin-based Deutsche Orient-Gesellschaft, the German Oriental Society, undertook large-scale excavations at the city funded by a wealthy Berlin merchant, James Simon. Directed by the small, pith-helmeted figure of Ludwig Borchardt, hundreds of local workers grafted away amidst clouds of dust in scenes worthy of a Cecil B. de Mille epic. Concentrating his efforts on the city's southern suburbs, Borchardt uncovered the spacious country villa and studios of Tuthmose, 'Overseer of Works and Sculptor', one of the very few ancient Egyptian artists whose name has survived. Here, in Tuthmose's once-thriving workshop, he made the greatest-ever find of Amarna art when he discovered a whole range of statues and figurines, in a variety of materials, of the ancient city's most illustrious inhabitants. They included superb heads of some of the royal princesses, but the most famous of all Tuthmose's masterpieces represented their mother, Nefertiti, whose painted limestone bust has become the very icon of ancient Egypt.

The life-size image represents the queen in her signature flat-topped blue crown, perfectly balanced on a long, slender neck. Although recent analysis has revealed that the bust originally had a longer, thinner neck and shoulders of rather uneven height, for some reason, perfect proportions were subsequently achieved by applying gypsum plaster to even up the imbalance. The haughty grandeur of her slightly smiling face is by no means diminished by the fact that one of the inlaid eyes is missing, the incredibly life-like effect owing much to the subtle use of mineral-based pigments and the queen's tasteful choice of cosmetics.

This fabled image of Nefertiti, described in endless detail, has certainly eclipsed her other less aesthetic portraiture in which it can be hard to tell her apart from Akhenaten. Even her name is routinely interpreted to fit this single image, repeatedly translated as 'Beautiful' rather than the more accurate 'Perfect'. And whilst the ancient texts do indeed describe Nefertiti as 'lovely faced', they also say the same about Akhenaten. But for all its stunning qualities, the famous bust leaves me completely cold. Lacking the warmth of the glorious golden death mask of Tutankhamen, her only rival in the attention stakes, this version of Nefertiti has always unsettled me – even scared me a little with its expression of thinly disguised disdain.

When Borchardt found the great icon on 6 December 1912, unceremoniously stuck upside down in a sand-drift, he worked out that she'd originally been placed on a wooden shelf in a cupboard, side by side with a similar limestone bust of her husband, Akhenaten. When the shelf fell prey to termites and eventually collapsed the heads flipped over as they fell, and whilst Akhenaten was smashed Nefertiti landed upside down on her flat-topped crown. She had suffered little more than a few scratches and damage to her ears, although her left eye, presumably made of glass and stone like the right, was absent, having possibly been knocked from its setting.

What happened next is something of a mystery, whose details again depend on who is telling the story. It appears that Nefertiti's bust was taken to Cairo along with the other spectacular finds of the season, and, in the division of the artefacts, the head was allocated to the excavations' financial sponsor, James Simon. He gave it to the Berlin Museum in 1920, and Nefertiti was finally unveiled to the public three years later.

Her appearance in Berlin caused an absolute furore across the world. Following the discovery of Tutankhamen's treasures the year before, the Egyptian Government had tightened up export laws for antiquities and demanded her immediate return. By the early 1930s this had almost happened, but then Adolf Hitler took power and declared that 'what the German people have, they keep'. During the Second World War, Nefertiti was forced into hiding until liberated by American troops in 1945 and put back on display in what was then the western sector of Berlin.

Apparently her 'Aryan' looks had made her particularly attractive to the Führer, and this description was also applied to some of the amazingly life-like plaster-cast masks which Borchardt had found in Tuthmose's workshop. In 1927 the Keeper of Egyptian Antiquities at the British Museum described one of them as being 'not that of an Egyptian nor a Semite. It is that of a Northerner; it is a Nordic type.' He described another as 'no Egyptian woman; there never was any Egyptian woman like her, or Syrian or other Semite either. She is a European ... I believe that we have here a contemporary facsimile portrait, taken from her own face, of some Minoan Cretan lady belonging to the royal harem.' And although 'Nordic characteristics' may be somewhat far-fetched, the 'Minoan' description was not such an unreasonable assumption, given Petrie's discoveries of imported Aegean pottery.

Some of this varied interpretation reflects the different nationalities of the scholars in question, and with the English, French, Germans, Italians and Americans all involved in two catastrophic twentieth-century wars in which millions lost their lives, Petrie's peace-loving philosopher pharaoh must have seemed a very attractive character indeed. Petrie initially compared Akhenaten to the 'plundering, self-glorifying, pompous cruelty of his conquering forefathers', and this already high opinion was later confirmed in the inter-war years, when Petrie sadly noted that 'the world is still far from ready for such a leader as Akhenaten; he would have no chance in Europe at present, where truth and beauty are strangers to men'.

Each generation built on Petrie's highly influential opinions. The American Egyptologist James Henry Breasted, for instance, regarded Akhenaten as a man before his time, 'a brave soul, undauntedly facing the momentum of immemorial tradition, and thereby stepping out from the long line of conventional and colourless Pharaohs, that he might disseminate ideas far beyond and above the capacity of his age to understand'. Having studied the hymns of praise to the Aten sun god, which have repeatedly been likened to Psalm 104 of the Bible, Breasted followed the convention of the day and translated them into the antiquated English of the King James Bible: 'Praise to thee! When thou risest in the horizon, O living Aten, lord of eternity. Obeisance to thy rising in heaven, to illuminate every land, with thy beauty ... when thou risest, eternity is given [the king]; when thou settest, thou giveth him everlastingness. Thou begettest him in the morning like thine own forms.' Indeed, Breasted's Akhenaten was something of a religious fundamentalist, and

Among the Hebrews, seven or eight hundred years later, we look for such men; but the modern world has yet adequately to value or even acquaint itself with this man who, in an age so remote and under conditions so adverse, became not only the world's first idealist and the world's first individual, but also the world's first monotheist, and the first prophet of internationalism – the most remarkable figure of the Ancient World before the Hebrews.

Sigmund Freud, in his less familiar capacity as an amateur Egyptologist raised the hypothesis 'If Moses was an Egyptian and if he communicated his own religion to the Jews, it must have been Akhenaten's, the Aten religion.' So now Akhenaten had inspired Moses and initiated Judaism too. And given the distinctly 'supporting' role of women in the Christian and Jewish traditions it was unsurprising that Nefertiti was nowhere to be seen in either interpretation, even though the Hymns to the Aten involve both Akhenaten and Nefertiti in a form of worship traditionally reserved for gods and kings alone.

Set against the backdrop of the First World War Akhenaten became something of a hero, certainly for the British Egyptologist and theatrical impresario Arthur Weigall. As the first to write a biography of the king, he considered him a complete pacifist with a 'conscientious objection to warfare', and 'not only a Christ, but a nineteenth-century Romantic, with a touch of Hamlet thrown in for good measure'.

The Amarna royals were certainly a ready-made soap opera and perfect fodder for dramatists. Married to the archaeologist Max Mallowan, the crime writer Agatha Christie penned a couple of novels with Egyptian themes, whilst her little-known drama *Akhenaten* is full of the most wonderful 1920s'-style dialogue. Nefertiti is told by her sister, 'Darling, I know I'm frightfully indiscreet in the things I say ... That's why Akhenaten and I would never have got on. I don't believe he's got any sense of humour. He's so frightfully religious, too . . .' You can just see their bobbed haircuts and long cigarette-holders.

Christie was no doubt inspired by her husband's colleague Leonard Woolley, who directed work at Amarna in 1921–2 after permission to excavate the site had passed to the British. With the Egypt Exploration Society concentrating their efforts on the central and northern parts of the city, their sixteen seasons of digging were directed by a succession of learned men including, from 1930, John Devitt Stringfellow Pendlebury. Curator at the palace of Knossos in Crete, Pendlebury divided his time between the two ancient sites, and with increasing amounts of Aegean material turning up he was the perfect person to appreciate the cross-cultural connections.

Focussing largely on the architectural and domestic side of life (one of their dig houses was even built up from the ruins of an ancient dwelling), the British team began to uncover all manner of houses built of mudbricks stamped with the names of Akhenaten and Nefertiti. Surrounded by high walls, the grand villas of the wealthy revealed a luxurious standard of living with beautifully decorated reception rooms, shrines to the royal family and bedrooms complete with en-suite facilities. It was all quite different from the back-to-back housing of the workers' village which had been home to those who had built the city and its tombs. Their dwellings contained few luxuries – just their looms, tools and numerous amulets that related to the traditional gods, with little sign of excessive devotion to the royal family. Pendlebury believed that their village 'was set as far as it could be from the residential quarters of the city because the workmen were a rowdy lot'; it was in fact surrounded by patrol roads and guard houses along the main road to the city.

Further security arrangements were revealed by the discovery of the police headquarters with its offices, armoury and stabling. Beside it was the 'House of Life', where official inscriptions were composed and copied out by scribes, and next door again lay Petrie's 'Foreign Office' where the Amarna Letters had been found almost half a century earlier. Although its walls had by then almost entirely disappeared as a result of locals searching in vain for more of the precious tablets, the discovery of small ovens caused Pendlebury to wonder whether there could have 'been any hot drink corresponding to the perpetual coffee of modern government offices in the Near East'.

Beneath the floors of some of the houses, the archaeologists even discovered proverbial 'buried treasure' when a large pot was found to contain silver rings, earrings, an amulet of a god from the land of the Hittites (modern Turkey) and twenty-three gold bars, some of which were sold to the Bank of England and melted down to provide an unusual form of funding for the following season's work.

Using aerial shots of the site provided by the Egyptian Air Force, the team worked out the relationship between the Great Official Palace and the less formal King's House, where the royal family seemed to have spent 'quality time' relaxing on a day-to-day basis. Random daubs of coloured paints around the bottoms of some of the walls, and the presence of paintbrushes still scattered across the floor, led Pendlebury to identify the rooms as 'the quarters of the six princesses with their night-nurseries and their playroom'. The excavators also found the ruins of a third 'North Palace' with its own zoo and aviaries, and gathered more information about the types of temples in the city, from the Great and Small Aten Temples to the summer-house-type 'viewing temples' with their flying duck paintings and garden pools.

Such flashy excess didn't seem to impress Woolley. After his own excavations, he noted that

much has been written about Akhenaten, his religious reforms, his monotheism, his idealism and his enthusiasm for truth, and I think a good deal more has been read into his words than the Egyptian language warrants. 'By their fruits ye shall know them', and the archaeologist who works at Akhenaten's capital, Tell el Amarna, gets a very different impression of the Heretic King. That through sheer neglect of his duties he let the Egyptian Empire go to pieces is a matter of common knowledge, but at Tell el Amarna we can see how the Empire's wealth was frittered away in fantastic extravagance.

He pointed out the shoddy, hasty workmanship of many of the buildings and highlighted a self-indulgent, superficial ostentation which 'is scarcely consistent with idealism and a passion for the truth, and in one further respect our discoveries seem to challenge the reputation in which the king has been held'.

What's more, the archaeologists had started to find disturbing evidence that the name and image of Nefertiti had everywhere been replaced with that of the eldest princess, Meritaten. 'This was a public affront if she [Nefertiti] were still alive,' wrote Woolley, 'and if she had died the devoted husband would not have taken the opportunity to obliterate her memorials; we are driven to assume that even the family affection of the royal household was superficial and that a quarrel so serious as to lose Nefertiti her position had ended the idyll which had hitherto been the standing theme of the court artist.' The cosy family scenario was suddenly shattered. As imaginations worked over-time, questions turned to what the famous beauty had been up to. She had obviously fallen from favour, been in some way disgraced and so much have been banished from court to the extreme north of the city, where large numbers of small inscribed objects bore her name but apparently not that of Akhenaten. The area in which she'd lived out her last tragic days was the same place where the Egypt Exploration Society had built their dig house, a romantic notion which gave one of the team members, Mary Chubb, the title for her highly entertaining book *Nefertiti Lived Here*.

So while the beautiful, vulnerable queen sought sanctuary in the outermost reaches of the city, her position and even her second name, Neferneferuaten, were apparently taken by the mysterious Smenkhkara, 'the young prince whom Akhenaten had co-opted on to the throne towards the end of his reign'. And evidence for the kind of relationship which had apparently existed between this 'young prince' and the king was soon found on a small, unfinished stela belonging to a military officer named Pase. Similar to the scenes of domestic bliss found elsewhere in the city, showing Akhenaten and Nefertiti with the children, this one depicted affection between two unnamed royals whom Egyptologists had always identified as Akhenaten and Nefertiti. Yet both wear kings' crowns, and the British Egyptologists Howard Carter and Percy Newberry decided that they must both be kings – which of course meant that they must both be men. Hatshepsut was very much regarded as the exception who proved the rule, and the scholars were apparently unable to accept that the female-looking figure sitting with Akhenaten might just be Nefertiti herself wearing a king's crown. As a result, the stela was taken as proof of an 'intimate relationship' between the two men. Described in 1928 as the same kind of relationship which had existed between the Roman Emperor Hadrian and the young Antinous, this was 'the love that dare not speak its name'.

So now Akhenaten was gay and Smenkhkara his effeminate-looking young lover, and the pair had banished the inconvenient

Nefertiti from court. In an attempt to find more 'evidence' for their argument, the same scholars cast around for any conveniently uninscribed figures of royal males they could find. A newly discovered sculptor's trial piece showing two versions of Akhenaten's profile was suddenly redesignated 'almost certainly Akhenaten and his putative co-regent Smenkhkara'. And there he was again, Smenkhkara strolling in the garden with his young wife Meritaten, both delicately rendered on a small painted limestone scene showing an unnamed royal couple who are almost certainly Akhenaten and Nefertiti. Yet as recently as 1984 the scene was described as 'Meritaten and the young man her husband, Akhenaten's successor, King Smenkhkara. This interpretation has generally been accepted by the experts.'

Back in the 1920s only one expert, Norman Davies, seems to have ventured alternative suggestions, based on his own extensive work in the tombs at Amarna and Thebes. Having studied an ink inscription referring to a third regnal year of a certain King 'Ankhkheperura Neferneferuaten', Davies wondered who this might be. After discussing the possibilities of a male candidate, he then asked 'if Neferneferuaten can be Queen Nefertiti herself, who, having come into the king's disfavor in the thirteenth year of his reign (a broken idyll, of which there were some signs in the recent excavations [at Amarna]), set herself up, [reigning] like another Hatshepsut as rival of her husband till his death four years later'. Yet little seems to have been made of his comments at that time.

As the British continued to excavate at Amarna, Pendlebury ventured up the Royal Valley in 1931 and 1935. Sifting through the debris left by Barsanti's men in and around Akhenaten's tomb, his team recovered fragments of coloured glass and blue-glazed vessels, beads, inlays and fragments of a human skull. Pendlebury also told his team about the 'stories – about as wonderful as they are unreliable – about people at the end of the last century seeing a golden coffin carried down from the high desert . . . But when the tomb was excavated – in the [eighteen] eighties – a man's body *was* seen there, a body that had been burned some years after it had been mummified.' Based on earlier sketchy descriptions of burnt-looking mummified remains found in the vicinity of the Royal Tomb, there seems to have been some kind of romantic belief that Akhenaten's mummy, or at least part of it, had survived until very recently. As for the reference to the 'golden coffin', it is just possible that this may have been a reference to the 'gold mummy wrappings' which the locals briefly offered for sale to the financially embarrassed Rev. Loftie before they were, presumably, melted down.

Whatever the truth, Pendlebury realised there was still much to be learned from a careful study of the Royal Valley, including three unfinished rock-cut tombs built into the adjacent valley as part of a new dynastic cemetery, Amarna's version of the Valley of the Kings. But he never got the chance to publish what he found here, and 1936 was his last season in Egypt. In England later that year, visiting his family in Wigan, he gave a lecture to the town's Education Society whose 'interest in archaeological work was roused to fever heat about eighteen months ago by the visit of Sir Leonard Woolley'. So when Pendlebury turned up too, they were delighted. Before a spellbound audience, the archaeologist revealed that Akhenaten had become king when already married to Nefertiti, whom Pendlebury believed was his sister – 'an attempt to keep the royal blood pure'. Both 'were what today we would call religious fanatics', and their devotion to a universal god 'the result of the internationalism which had been creeping into Egyptian life'. Even the new 'revolutionary' art style was described as a direct result of Cretan artists working in the city.

Contrary to Petrie's belief in an ethical king, Pendlebury had found 'no ethics at all'. Not only was there 'no sense of sin whatever, but no idea of afterlife. The ancient Egyptians very often considered their present life as prelude to the one to come, but there they got the idea wiped out completely. It was the King's tragedy that he took away the standards his people already had, and gave them nothing in their place.'

Returning to his beloved Crete, Pendlebury continued excavations until the beginning of the Second World War when he joined up. Seriously wounded in the invasion of Crete, he was captured by the Germans and, refusing to reveal information, was put before a firing squad in May 1941, aged only thirty-seven.

In the bleak aftermath of the war, Amarna itself was left alone while scholars spent the next thirty years trying to make some sort of sense of the massive amounts of material recovered. As so often happens in Egyptology, many objects were only examined years after their discovery, if at all, and there are still many hundreds of ancient Egyptian artefacts whose significance remains unrecognised as they await rediscovery in the basements and storerooms of museums across the world.

The Amarna material sent to the Petrie Museum joined what Petrie himself had found but never had time to unpack, let alone deal with, and here it was studied in detail by Julia Samson who published some of it in Pendlebury's posthumous excavation report. Following her description of the museum's small 'co-regency' stela naming Akhenaten and his co-regent 'Ankhkheperura', the report's editor, Herbert Fairman, noted that one of the two figures accompanying the names 'seems to be that of a naked woman, though differing somewhat from the normal Amarna portraiture of the female form. Are we to conclude that here Smenkhkara was depicted rather like the extraordinary Akhenaten of some of the Karnak statues?' Although assuming that Ankhkheperura-Smenkhkara was a man who just happened to look like a woman, Fairman had nevertheless hit the nail on the head without realising it. Some of these Karnak statues did indeed depict the distinctly female form of Akhenaten's co-ruler and had been set up at Karnak in the traditional capital, Thebes, where Akhenaten and Nefertiti had spent the first five years of the reign.

The first of twenty-five huge painted sandstone colossi were discovered by the French on the eastern side of the temple at

Karnak in 1925, their distorted body shapes so extreme that they are regularly described as grotesque and even hideous. Widely regarded as showing the king as he really must have been, with elongated head, drooping jaw and malformed body, they are among the most complete statues of the reign. Conveniently ignoring statuary in which the king is portrayed 'normally', these are the images of Akhenaten that people remember, especially the one which appears to be naked, the so-called 'Sexless Colossus'. Presumed to be of a man, its lack of male genitals has long been seen as 'proof' of many things: that the king was a hermaphrodite, or a eunuch, or suffered from the pituitary gland disorder acromegaly, or had any one of a whole range of diseases and 'syndromes'.

In 1907 Grafton Elliot Smith, then anatomy professor at Cairo School of Medicine, stated that he believed the king had suffered from Froehlich's syndrome, an endocrine disorder which would have given rise to feminine-like fat deposits around the breasts and lower body and rendered him impotent and sterile. It was a convenient explanation for Akhenaten's body shape, and the logical extension of the argument was that Nefertiti's six daughters must have been fathered by a mystery lover – candidates ranged from Amenhotep III to Smenkhkara. Although most Egyptologists eventually dismissed the idea of Froehlich's syndrome as a non-starter, some have recently suggested that the symptoms resemble those of Marfan's syndrome. This genetic disorder creates similar physical abnormalities, but because it doesn't affect the sufferer's reproductive capabilities Akhenaten could still have fathered children.

The controversial statues originally stood in the Aten temple complex which Akhenaten and Nefertiti had set up in the very heart of Egypt's traditional religious capital. The walls of these new temples were built from thousands of small sandstone *talatat* blocks adorned with repeat scenes of king, queen and sun god being universally adored by their people. Dismantled after Akhenaten's death, the small blocks were recycled in the buildings of later kings, albeit defaced and upside down to render their offensive images impotent. Finally rediscovered in the inter-war years during reconstruction work by the French, over thirty thousand of these blocks were recovered from the foundations of Karnak's famous Hypostyle Hall and the second and ninth pylon gateways. Then the same thing happened just across the river from Amarna when the Germans discovered around fifteen hundred more blocks, dismantled from their original position and ferried over the river for use by later kings in the foundations of their own temples. But as it was 1939 and war was imminent the Germans were forced to leave Egypt after reburying the blocks, which were immediately dug up by locals and sold abroad, mainly to private buyers in the USA.

With these blocks dispersed and those at Karnak simply stacked up haphazardly in rows, their scattered scenes lay undiscovered and unappreciated until an American businessman, Ray Winfield Smith, visited Karnak in 1965. Finding it unthinkable that such important evidence should simply be neglected, he initiated the Akhenaten Temple Project the following year, opening up a revolutionary new chapter in Amarna studies. It would involve photographing each block and reassembling the immense jigsaw puzzle with the help of a computer. The project's work was then continued by Egyptologist Donald Redford and, beginning excavations at East Karnak in 1975, he was able to identify and locate several parts of the Aten temple complex, including the massive Gempaaten – 'The Aten Is Found' – Temple, which incorporated the potent benben stone, an ancient cult fetish of the sun god worshipped by troupes of musicians and singers.

Much to everyone's surprise, the scenes revealed that the rituals had been led by Nefertiti alone as she worshipped the Aten on the temple's 30-feet-high columns. In fact the archaeologists soon realised that not only was Nefertiti shown alone in the Benben Temple, but on all the other talatat blocks she appeared nearly twice as often as Akhenaten. As they rightly point out, 'It is hard to avoid the conclusion that this high profile which Nefertiti enjoyed in the first five years of the reign is evidence of her political importance.'

In front of these extraordinary scenes had once stood the so-called grotesque statues, their true meaning finally interpreted by a British Egyptologist, J. R. Harris. Building on Fairman's original comment, Harris was able to demonstrate that the royal figures represented the primeval creator deities Shu and Tefnut: Akhenaten as Shu in his tall feather head-dress, Nefertiti as the goddess Tefnut in a close-fitting gown. So that's why some of the sculptures looked like a woman! No eunuchs, no hermaphrodites, but a woman. And, just like the male figures, she clutched the royal regalia of crook and flail in her crossed hands and wore the traditional false beard of kingship, as the female pharaoh Hatshepsut had done before her.

The royal couple were also portrayed as the creator deities Shu and Tefnut on a wide range of objects, from the huge colossi to the gold signet ring found by Howard Carter at Amarna, each showing Akhenaten and Nefertiti as the two essential halves of the creative whole. While Harris was gathering more and more evidence that Nefertiti had indeed once wielded kingly powers, Julia Samson was independently coming to similar conclusions. Throughout the 1970s and 1980s the two of them published convincing evidence that Nefertiti and Smenkhkara were one and the same.

Just as Amenhotep IV had simply become Akhenaten, Nefertiti had adopted the name Neferneferuaten. Apparently made her husband's co-regent in his twelfth year as king, she then added the name Ankhkheperura to become co-ruler Ankhkheperura-Neferneferuaten. Then finally, at Akhenaten's death, she took the throne herself as King Ankhkheperura Smenkhkara. This standard use of multiple names by Egypt's ancient kings, which had so misled Egyptologists, seems to have confused even the ancient Egyptians themselves. Often at a loss to know which was the correct name to write during times of political confusion – whether under Hatshepsut and her co-regent Tuthmosis III,

Cleopatra VII and an assortment of male relatives, or indeed in the case of Nefertiti and Akhenaten – they often left the cartouches blank, figuring that no name was often better than the wrong name.

Regardless of the occasional blank cartouche, however, Nefertiti's regal status is confirmed in a whole host of other ways. The crowns, clothes and false beard worn by Akhenaten were worn by Nefertiti too, who also carries the royal crook and flail. To her, as the dominant, often exclusive, figure at Karnak the Aten extends both the ankh φ sign and the $\upharpoonleft$ sceptre, signifying dominion. She rewards her officials with gold collars, just like a king, and is shown sitting alone on the royal throne decorated with heraldic plant designs; one example even shows Nefertiti on the royal throne while Akhenaten perches on a stool. With her throne dais adorned with a long line of bound captives, Nefertiti is shown in an exclusively kingly pose executing prisoners with her scimitar, a bow and arrow case attached to the chariot she drives as another symbol of her kingly privilege. And, although generally ignored in the stampede to reach the 'beautiful' version, an amazing statuette found in the sculptor's workshop at Amarna represents a slightly older Nefertiti, wearing the cap crown and standing alone as sole ruler.

Yet even this wealth of evidence was not enough, and the establishment remained largely unconvinced. Nefertiti's use of kingly regalia was explained away as 'the devaluation of royal symbols', the assumption being that a woman's touch would presumably devalue their worth. Although credited at least with being 'ingenious', it was stated that Harris and Samson's hypothesis 'has won few adherents' and it was dismissed as 'unacceptable'.

Nevertheless, what had been revealed in the city of Amarna and Karnak Temple was by no means the only testimony for Nefertiti's growing powers, and Samson's UCL colleague Geoffrey Martin was engaged in re-examining the Royal Tomb based on Pendlebury's notes from the 1930s and his own work

FIGURE 4. Detail of a wall scene on a limestone block
originally from Amarna showing Nefertiti in her tall blue
crown and stripped to the waist, about to execute a foreign
prisoner with the scimitar she holds in her raised right hand

there in 1980. Managing to shed a great deal more light on its
chaotic history, Martin commented that the tomb had been not
just plundered but systematically reduced to the smallest fragments by 'iconoclasts, intent on obliterating everything associated with Akhenaten'. Yet he still managed to find pieces of the
original sarcophagi, numerous pot sherds, fragments of stone
vessels, wine labels, jar seals, parts of hemp ropes and pieces of
textile.

His meticulous methods also allowed much of the original
burial to be recreated on paper. Some of the pieces of jewellery
recovered from the tomb in the 1880s were 'exact parallels' to
pieces found in the mysterious royal tomb KV.55 in the Valley
of the Kings, and although he could find no trace of the human
skull fragments that Pendlebury had found, or any trace of the

'burnt' mummified remains, there were nevertheless still clues to who might once have been buried there.

A plain rectangular brick found by Pendlebury was identified as one of those used during the mummification process to support the corpse, whilst some of the granite sarcophagus fragments were splashed with a black goo-like substance. Although the splashes were initially thought to be from the unguents used during burial ceremonies, their appearance across the broken edges of the stone suggested that they must have appeared *after* the sarcophagi had been broken up. So, working on the assumption that those smashing up the tomb had allowed their flaming torches to drip over the work in progress, Martin sent off samples for chemical analysis which revealed that the goo was bitumen. Although this was believed to indicate a modern origin, more recent analysis has shown that bitumen was actually used as early as *c*.1400 BC, intriguingly as a coffin varnish.

Working from hundreds of fragments of granite, it was discovered that Akhenaten had been buried in a granite sarcophagus carved with his names and those of the Aten, although it was Nefertiti who dominated the entire piece. She had replaced the four protective goddesses who usually appeared at the corners, and, like them, had been placed there to give the maximum protection to the dead pharaoh in the Afterlife. This was hardly an action to have been carried out by a disgraced and banished queen. Her role of safeguarding the eternal future of the pharaoh suggested instead that Nefertiti had wielded tremendous powers over this world and the next.

There were also fragments of at least two more sarcophagi, one for the second princess, Meketaten, and another, according to more recent studies, belonging to Queen Tiy, who also seems to have been buried in the Royal Tomb. Its labyrinthine structure certainly incorporated several other rooms used as burial chambers for members of the royal family who had died before their own tombs elsewhere in the Valley were finished.

The wall scenes showing Meketaten's funeral, copied so long

FIGURE 5. Detail one of the four figures of Nefertiti carved
on the corners of Akhenaten's granite sarcophagus restored
from fragments found in the Amarna Royal Tomb, her figure
with arms outstretched replacing the traditional protective
funerary goddesses

ago by Howard Carter, were recopied by Martin. Although most
of the scenes had been reasonably intact when Carter and then
the French had drawn them in 1894, acts of vandalism as recently
as 1974 now made the work a matter of urgency. In his expert
scrutiny of these images Martin identified two separate sets of
funeral scenes, one relating to the princess and another, almost
duplicate, set which he believed was made for the burial of a
shadowy royal woman whose existence only came to light in
1959 after her name was discovered on a cosmetics jar.

This was Kiya, the 'Greatly Loved Wife' of Akhenaten and
Amarna's 'other woman'. As more and more evidence came to
light, scholars began to realise that Nefertiti had had a rival,
someone whose unknown existence had seriously misled earlier

archaeologists. For it was Kiya and not Nefertiti whose names and images had been hacked out and replaced by those of Princess Meritaten. Martin suggested that it was Kiya whose funeral was portrayed in the second series of wall scenes, and that, because she appeared to have died in childbirth, the child may have been the royal prince, Tutankhamen.

As for the large unfinished suite of rooms just inside the Royal Tomb's entrance, these may well have been begun for Nefertiti, although she does not seem to have been buried there and may well have planned to be buried in one of the other substantial tombs in the Valley. One is particularly grand, its entrance corridor cut down through the limestone some forty feet deeper than the king's own tomb and suggesting that it too was designed for a king; perhaps it was even for Nefertiti herself, if she outlived her husband – which more and more evidence seemed to suggest.

A fragmentary funerary figurine naming Nefertiti as simply 'the royal wife' was once interpreted as meaning that she could not have succeeded Akhenaten and must have died before him while still a queen, to be buried somewhere in the vicinity of the Royal Valley where the fragment was found. Yet preparations for royal burials – including the manufacture of hundreds of such funerary figurines – generally began well within the individual's lifetime. In some cases funerary equipment was even stockpiled close to the tomb rather than having to be hastily thrown together during the seventy-day mummification period. Nor do such figurines prove where an individual was buried, since similar figures naming Queen Tiy have been found in the tomb of her husband Amenhotep III back in Thebes, even though she is now believed to have been interred in the Royal Tomb at Amarna where fragments of her sarcophagus were also found.

With so much of Amarna's history based on such small pieces of evidence, be they broken figurines, fragments of stonework or sherds of pottery, it is certainly true that the most unlikely-looking objects can often hold significant clues to Egypt's ancient past. This was certainly true of my own choice of specialist subject, ancient hair, which to many people can look quite unappealing. Yet if we give it the same attention as the ancient Egyptians themselves obviously did, it can start to reveal some fascinating clues.

4

HAIR, WIGS AND ANCIENT
HISTORY

With so many distinguished Egyptologists devoting entire careers to the Amarna Period, it was difficult to imagine how anything could be added to the subject which hadn't been considered a hundred times before. Yet, inspired by Julia Samson's belief that a study of the regalia and wigs worn by the Amarna royals could help us understand more about this extraordinary period in history, I was greatly encouraged in my own research.

A quick glance at my family history shows that those of us not employed in the funeral trade were generally involved with hairdressing. As far back as 1884 my maternal great-grandfather was apprenticed to a gentleman's hairdresser's in Barnsley, and my uncle's family ran a large hairdressing business in the Channel Islands. On the other side of the family my paternal great-grandfather ran a barber's shop and hairdresser's in a small village just outside Barnsley, and my aunt managed one of the largest salons in the area. It was even my own alternative choice of career should Egyptology not work out, since hair and how people treat it has always intrigued me.

While studying Egyptology at UCL I decided to combine my interests and in 1985, with the encouragement of my tutor, a former student of Margaret Murray, I began research into the fascinating world of ancient Egyptian hair. I had assumed that masses would already have been written on such a fascinating subject, but was surprised to discover that hair had never really received the detailed treatment it so obviously deserved. Largely ignored by most earlier Egyptologists, who seemed to regard it as very much a 'woman's subject', it was seen as a rather bizarre choice of study when compared to the more mainstream areas that had been pored over by generations of learned men.

Whilst immensely important, of course, the tendency to over-emphasise obscure linguistic conundrums and grammatical niceties can sometimes create something of an imbalance in Egyptology. Less than 1 per cent of the ancient population were able to read and write, so could it really be the best way to study the lives of the vast majority of the population? I suppose the answer depended to a large extent on who you considered the ancient Egyptians to have been. For many early scholars, ancient Egypt appears to have been populated by a literate male elite of kings, priests and scribes, with the silent majority dismissed as little more than illiterate peasants. But it was these same peasants whose efforts created the culture in the first place, and regardless of their inability to leave behind a convenient written record, they too clearly deserved to be the subject of serious study.

Fortunately, the Egyptian climate provided a democracy of its own by preserving the people themselves. Since time immemorial ordinary burials had taken place in little more than a hole in the sand, and the hot, dry surroundings had often preserved skin and hair as effectively as any expensively prepared mummy within an elaborate tomb. By studying such remains, I felt it should be possible to obtain a good idea of how Egyptians throughout society had treated their hair and what they had done to enhance their appearance and demonstrate their status; in short, to find out what had made these people tick.

They had certainly regarded hair as potent stuff, and whilst many of them had worn hair extensions, others had shaved their heads and worn wigs, combining a desire for ornate and impressive hairstyles with the practical considerations of com-fort. In such a hot climate a shaven or cropped head would have been the coolest option, but some sort of head cover would then be needed to guard against the sun. A wig provided a better solution than a scarf or turban since it allowed body heat to escape through its net-like base at the same time as protecting the head. Inevitably wigs developed as a means of showing off wealth, status or religious affiliations, with certain styles only worn by certain people. I wanted to discover whether it was possible to identify otherwise anonymous individuals on the basis of their hairstyle.

I began with the Petrie Museum's hair-related material, from the beautifully coiffured Amarna nobleman carved on the back of the co-regency stela to the wide variety of ancient hairdressing tools, together with the different types of hair Petrie had found in both towns and tombs. I also spent a great deal of time down the road in the British Museum, wandering through its galleries, making notes of the sculptures, reliefs and paintings, and studying the museum's reserve collection of mummified heads. I was also given permission to examine an amazing wig acquired in the nineteenth century which was composed entirely of human hair set in light brown curls over several hundred dark brown plaits. Found along with its wig box in a tomb at the village of Deir el-Medina, it had been studied only once before, in 1975, by a leading hair specialist based in the Channel Islands. Given my own family's hairdressing links on the islands, we began to compare notes, and so began a rather unusual correspondence on matters relating to ancient hair.

Even when I had produced the required undergraduate dissertation I had still only scratched the surface of this vast subject, and very much wanted to carry on. By comparing surviving wigs and mummy hair with the way they were portrayed in art, I felt it might be possible to set up some sort of chronology which didn't rely solely on written evidence. Doing the job properly would mean looking through more than three thousand years' worth of paintings, reliefs, sculptures, wigs and the mummies themselves, all of which were scattered across the world, in collections, in store rooms and in Egypt itself.

Although this research would obviously take years I remained blithely undaunted, no doubt fuelled in part by naive enthusiasm. It was just as Margaret Murray had once described it, as 'having added to the knowledge of your subject, of having filled a small and possibly not very important gap, but still a gap. This is one of the purest joys that life can give ... it at once becomes a habit, and like dram-drinking you can't stop, you must go on.'

Armed with a degree in ancient history and Egyptology, followed by a year studying German to help me to track down some of the more obscure hair-related references, I was raring to go and decided to apply to Manchester University as a postgraduate student. Grants were pretty thin on the ground even then, so my first year was to be self-funded, on the understanding that I could apply to the university for a grant if my research looked promising.

Manchester was the perfect choice situated in the north and so relatively close to my hometown. Much of its fine collection of Egyptology material came from Petrie's excavations following his split from the Egypt Exploration Society in 1886. After this date he had received alternative funding from Amelia Edwards's friend, a wealthy Bolton manufacturer named Jesse Haworth. Having financed Petrie's work for nine years, Haworth donated his share of the antiquities to Manchester's University Museum.

A perfect complement to Petrie's own collection at UCL, Manchester ended up with a most impressive array of objects relating to daily life. Many were discovered at Kahun, a well-planned town that housed pyramid builders more than five hundred years before the Amarna Period. Amongst their personal possessions Petrie found equipment belonging to builders, carpenters, potters and even the town magician, together with pots of green and black eye paint, powdered red haematite for reddening the lips, and wooden cosmetics boxes with sliding lids. The finished effect would have been admired in the polished bronze mirrors he found, their handles shaped like lotus flowers or the head of Hathor, goddess of beauty, perhaps reflecting the hopes of the ancient owner to absorb a little of the goddess's legendary good looks. There were also ivory hair pins, fine-toothed wooden combs, small bronze hair-curlers, part of an intricately made wig and even a supply of carefully prepared lengths of hair assumed to be dolls' hair – the building it was found in dubbed the 'Toy-maker's Shop'.

There was a similar division between UCL and Manchester of finds from Petrie's excavations at Gurob, the town in northern Egypt where he discovered burials of blond-haired people whom he believed were of Aegean origin. Gurob was also the site of Amenhotep III's country retreat, an old royal palace enlarged to house his vast entourage of wives, female relatives and children. It seems to have been a place where the royal family could escape the pressures of royal life, and its luxurious rooms were decorated and furnished with Egyptian and foreign designs similar to those seen further south in the official palace at Malkata.

In addition to fine blue-glazed Egyptian pottery, Aegean ware and Syrian-inspired vessels, the excavations also produced items of dress and adornment worn by the ancient inhabitants. There were detachable linen sleeves – a convenient way to keep clean those parts of a garment which get most dirty, especially when worn by children – as well as alabaster dishes and perfume pots, razors, combs, rings, necklaces, scarab seal amulets and an eye paint container naming Akhenaten's sister, Princess Henuttaneb. Even toys were found, such as a miniature horse and a pull-along boat on wheels complete with a ramming device and steering oar, which may have come from the royal nursery.

After Amenhotep III's death the palace had been inherited by Akhenaten and Nefertiti, and Queen Tiy seems to have spent much of her time at Gurob with her daughters. Beautifully dressed figurines of her female staff of servants and singers headed by Lady Teye were found in a tomb there by locals in the late nineteenth century, together with a magnificent head of the great dowager queen herself. Made from a combination of imported Cypriot yew wood and Egyptian acacia, the head, now housed in Berlin, is only about two inches high, yet her extraordinary face is so life-like that it conveys a powerful sense of the queen's determined personality.

Manchester also housed a fine selection of objects from

Amarna, discovered during the excavations of Petrie, Woolley and Pendlebury. Along with an exact copy of Nefertiti's famous 'beautiful' bust were fragments of the queen's statuary, pieces of carved stone reliefs and decorative inlays, feathers made of sandstone, glazed tiles set with small white daisies and green leaves, offering pots inscribed with the Aten's name, and part of a wand-like object inscribed 'Neferneferuaten Nefertiti, may she live forever and eternally'. This was part of a model throw-stick, based on the full-sized weapons used to catch wildfowl and often placed in kings' tombs for use in the Afterlife: one was found in Akhenaten's tomb and that of Nefertiti was discovered in the ruins of the city.

During my first year's research at Manchester I was finally able to visit Amarna when I was awarded a Nile Studentship by the Egypt Exploration Society, offered annually by Swan Hellenic to the Society's student members. I was the lucky recipient of a seventeen-day cruise, which the Society hoped 'would be an enjoyable and instructive experience' – possibly the understatement of the decade.

The six hundred-mile journey up the Nile began in Cairo. Revisiting the delights of the wonderful museum, I was able to make notes of everything that interested me, particularly the incredible collection of wigs worn by the priests of Amen around 1000 BC. They were huge things which looked like a cross between a bird's nest and an octopus, their impressive dimensions created by using bundles of date palm fibre as internal padding beneath the layers of carefully dressed hair.

The same room contained many of the fragmentary treasures which had been found in some of the royal tombs in the Valley of the Kings, including what was left of an anonymous wig hidden in a corner of one of the cabinets. Although the remains were much depleted, short hair, both brown and blond, was still attached to the well-made foundation cap, which had been constructed around a narrow centre parting. The short sections of detailed plaits displayed alongside could have added little to the wig's overall size, indicating that it must have been fairly short when worn; the plaits' differing lengths also suggested a layered effect of the sort seen in portrayals of the so-called Nubian wig. This was only a possibility, but it seemed the most likely explanation given the amounts of hair present.

Amongst the treasures of Queen Tiy's parents, Yuya and Tuya, were what remained of Yuya's 'ceremonial wig' – placed so high on a glass shelf that I could only make out a few plaited ends. I also revisited some of my favourite objects from the tomb of their great-grandson Tutankhamen – his wig box, eye paint containers, mirrors and clothing – and I also found the lock of hair which had belonged to his grandmother Tiy, thought to have been placed in his tomb as some sort of heirloom. A return visit to the rest of the family included the 'grotesque' statues of Akhenaten and Nefertiti and several quartzite heads of their daughters. There was also Akhenaten's heavily restored canopic box, which once held his mummified organs. Outside, in the museum gardens, was his granite sarcophagus. Restored from numerous small pieces, four figures of Nefertiti in a splendid wig of tile-like curls still protected each corner, her arms out-stretched in a permanent pose of protection.

As our boat set off on its stately progress down the Nile, we stopped at some of the more remote places that would be difficult to visit on a standard tour, enabling me to fill many of the gaps left from my first visit eight years before. Arriving at Sakkara, some of the smaller pyramids seemed far more interesting than their giant cousins of Giza: the rubble-heap pyramid of Unas, for instance, which you wouldn't really look at twice from the outside, contained a stunning burial chamber covered in the bright blue hieroglyphs of the so-called 'Pyramid Texts'. After a visit to the collapsed Pyramid of Medum with its blancmange-like outline we were shown the burial chamber of the mysterious bench-shaped tomb next door, its sarcophagus still wedged open by the wooden mallet of those who had robbed it more than four thousand years ago.

Docking at the dramatic cliffside location of Beni Hassan, we visited some of the rock-cut tombs of local governors who had controlled the region back around 2000 BC, their walls filled to bursting with scenes of all manner of daily activities. There was hunting in the desert and wrestling, dancing, weaving, farming and fishing, while Egyptians traded with a delegation of brightly dressed Palestinians who had brought supplies of the ever-popular black kohl eye paint in the saddle bags of their donkeys. But, best of all as far as I was concerned, the ancient barbers could be seen hard at work, shaving the heads of their customers, with their title written beside them in hieroglyphs featuring the razor symbol ⊐ as the tool of their trade.

Past the rock-cut shrine built high in the cliffs by the female pharaoh Hatsheput for the local lioness goddess Pakhet, 'She who Mauls', lay el-Ashmunein, which Sicard the Jesuit priest had first visited almost three hundred years ago. It had once been the sacred city of Thoth, god of wisdom, and a huge pair of quartzite statues of him set up by Amenhotep III were pretty much all that was left of the ancient temple. Yet, looking closely at the hieroglyphic inscriptions on their bases, it was clear that someone had been busy erasing all references to the state god Amen. For now we were in Akhenaten's territory, and the ancient city of Amarna lay just across the river. That evening we moored at the village of el-Till on the same stretch of river where the Amarna royal family would have arrived in the golden state barge. I was finally here, at the remote city where Tutankh-amen had been born, where the great Queen Tiy had spent her last years and where Akhenaten and Nefertiti had once lived and reigned.

As the early morning sun began to appear above the cliffs of Amarna, we trundled across the desert in a customised green trailer pulled by tractor, then the standard means of moving tourists across the large expanse of barren terrain to the North-ern Tombs of the city's officials. Although hacked about by Christian squatters who had done a little interior redesigning by putting in recesses and cutting out two of the columns supporting the roof, the walls in High Priest Meryra's great tomb were still covered in finely detailed carvings which in many cases still retained their original bright colours. Beside a huge bouquet of flowers made up of poppies, cornflowers and the ever-present lotus, Meryra, shaven headed in his priestly role, worshipped the rising sun in finely pleated linen embellished with four thick gold necklaces. On the opposite wall stood his wife Tenra in the finest linen pleats, her long, thick wig topped by one of the cone-shaped lumps of semi-solid perfume to show that she was expensively scented. And as husband and wife gave praise to the Aten and the king, Tenra expressed the wish that 'the king's great wife Neferneferuaten Nefertiti, living for ever and ever, may be by his side'.

Looking at the wall scenes beyond was rather like flicking through Meryra's photo album. At the high point of his career there he was, raised high on the shoulders of his colleagues to receive his promotion to High Priest, while Akhenaten and Nefertiti leaned out from their great Window of Appearances, well padded with a great squashy red bolster to cushion the royal elbows. Then, in a huge scene that dominated the entire wall, the royal couple were off, their robes streaming out behind them in the wind as they raced through the city each in their own chariot. Surrounded by their armed bodyguard, they arrived at the Great Temple where the staff had come out to greet them, lining up, raising their arms to the accompaniment of female clergy playing tambourines while a small girl waved a palm branch and danced. Some of the officials even held out bouquets. It all looked very like the typical public response when the British Queen goes walkabout today.

Standing in the midst of beautiful gardens with tall flagpoles at its entrance, the temple was shown in some detail, its columns flanked by the same statues of the king and queen which Howard Carter had found when excavating the temple site a century before. Inside were hundreds of open-air altars piled with offerings, and, as sacrificial cattle with elaborately decorated horns awaited their fate, Meryra accompanied the royal family into the temple. With Nefertiti's imposing feather crown making her easily the tallest figure in the scene, she and Akhenaten stood before an enormous offering table piled high with choice cuts of beef, geese, loaves of bread and bouquets. And as the nearby temple store rooms burst at the seams with provisions of every kind, Akhenaten and Nefertiti rewarded their High Priest for a job well done, telling the overseer of the Treasury to 'take the High Priest Meryra and put gold around all his neck and gold around his legs, because of his obedience to the royal will and for doing all he was told'. And there was Meryra, arms raised in triumph, almost punching the air for joy as servants swathed him in numerous gold collars and earrings to complement the costly perfumes he wore. Then, just before the couple took their leave in their chariots waiting close by, further offerings were made at another well-stocked altar, this time topped with burning incense from which clouds of smoke drifted up toward the sun disc uniquely adorned with a multi-coloured rainbow.

A little further on, the 'Royal Scribe and Fan Bearer on the King's Right Hand', Ahmose, stood at his tomb door. His figure was carved at either side of the entrance, coming forward with arms raised to worship the sun as if in greeting. He was dressed in fashionable linen robes, his ostrich feather fan of office slung across his back alongside the vicious-looking military axe that he would have wielded in his capacity as royal bodyguard. After long sections of hieroglyphic inscriptions describing the beauties of the Aten, much of the tomb was left unfinished. As a result its blank walls had been embellished with more than fifty snippets of ancient Greek graffiti – clearly this had been a popular spot with many early tourists. Yet on one wall the unfinished figures of Akhenaten and Nefertiti had been mapped out in red paint, now barely visible. This time sharing a chariot, Akhenaten held the reins as Nefertiti turned almost to touch his face with hers, while their eldest daughter, Meritaten, peered over the front of the chariot at the dancing plumes on the horses' heads. Accompanying the three was an escort of more than forty well-carved men, their varied dress and hairstyles identifying them as Egyptian, Nubian and Syrian. Although armed with clubs, spears, scimitars, axes, and bows and arrows, they were not in fact off to war but simply escorting the royal family on their daily visit to the temple.

The last tomb we visited on our Amarna tour was that of the priest Panehesy, whose name means 'the Southerner', carved with the king, queen and their three daughters offering the usual assortment of goodies to the sun disc. My guide book also drew attention to figures of the queen's sister Mutnodjmet, her hair dressed in a similar sidelock hairstyle to that worn by her nieces, the royal princesses, and accompanied by her two dwarf attendants.

To the right of the entrance were further figures of Akhenaten and Nefertiti, and there was no doubt that both were wearing the elaborate 'atef' crown of a king. Nefertiti was also described as 'the heiress, great of favour, mistress of all women, the wife of the king whom he loves', and the accompanying phrase 'she says all things and they are done' was surely evidence of her very real power.

As the royal couple drove out in their individual chariots to the temple, accompanied by what looked like half the army, Nefertiti, unlike her husband, used a whip to achieve greater speed. Once within the temple the royal pair stood at the high altar, side by side and so identical as to appear almost one figure as they performed their worship – despite the fact that a Coptic apse had been built later which interrupted the view of these ancient rituals.

At the foot of the cliffs, we were taken on to the North Palace, to which Nefertiti was once thought to have been banished. Now believed to have been equipped as a separate palace for her eldest daughter, Meritaten, it was an impressive spread of substantial mudbrick walls, white limestone column bases and small rectangular pools once flanked by beautiful gardens. As

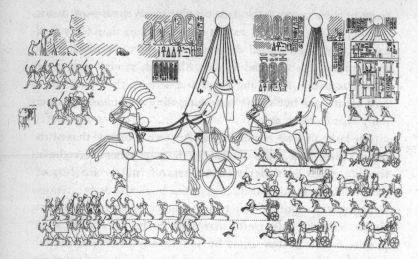

FIGURE 6. Part of a wall scene in the Amarna tomb of priest
Panehesy showing the royal couple surrounded by their
bodyguards driving out in chariots equipped with bowcases,
Nefertiti wielding her whip for greater speed

our small party made its way around we began to attract the attention of the local children, who do a nice line in woven baskets,
and before I knew it I was wandering about like some latter-day
offering-bearer with armfuls of the things.

Further gaps in my understanding continued to be filled in as
the cruise progressed south. In ancient times pilgrims flocked to
Abydos, cult centre of Osiris, Lord of the Underworld, to bring
him all manner of offerings, from the contents of pots which
still cover the site to locks of their hair. The god's cult fetish
itself was an elaborate wig mounted on a stand, and the wall
scenes in the superb temple built in his honour featured the long,
luxuriant sidelocks of royal children beside the multi-layered,
multi-coloured hairstyles of the goddesses Isis and Hathor. The
walls and ceiling of Hathor's temple at Dendera were a feast of
detail embellished by a carved ceiling relief of Egypt's oldest-

known zodiac (an exact copy replacing the original now in the Louvre in Paris). On the exterior walls were a huge figure of the legendary Cleopatra, and another of Hathor herself, 'Lady of the Beautiful Tresses and Breasts', named after her most prominent attributes.

At Luxor our boat tied up beside some of the huge floating 'gin palaces' which now ply the Nile. In the searing afternoon temperatures of early September, we wandered around the tombs in the Valley of the Kings at our leisure, each one giving a unique view on how the king would spend eternity in the company of favourite deities.

After the obligatory visit to Tut's tomb, our guide pointed out the ancient graffiti in the tomb of Ramses VI, one dated to 1120 BC revealing that the tomb had already been robbed and laid open a mere twenty years after it was completed. The king's mummy, salvaged and rewrapped by the priests, was eventually reburied in the tomb of Amenhotep II, our next port of call. And, just as on my earlier visit, the wall of that side chamber was still sealed up and gave absolutely nothing away.

Also in Luxor were the Tombs of the Nobles. High in the hills behind the village of Qurna lay the tomb of Sennefer, mayor of Thebes under Amenhotep II. Its uneven ceiling had been cleverly disguised as a vineyard and the tomb owner himself, sitting beneath large bunches of grapes, was resplendent in a range of black curly wigs and flashy gold jewellery which changed from scene to scene.

Sennefer's boss, the Vizier (Prime Minister) Rekhmire, had a much larger tomb, decorated with impressive scenes of tribute bearers arriving from every corner of the empire, all to emphasise his high-status role as the pharaoh's deputy. Syrians brought horses and fine wines, Nubians arrived with elephant tusks, gold and animal skins, and the Keftiu, the long-haired men of Crete, brought costly Aegean vessels to Egypt's pharaoh. Tribute bearers gave way to figures of the craftsmen working on the Temple of Amen across the river at Karnak, the region's largest employer. All were hard at work producing pottery, jewellery, sandals, metal vases, wooden furniture and mudbricks, or hanging off scaffolding to finish huge statues. On the opposite wall it was party time, and, at a banquet in full swing, a harpist sang the latest hit, 'Perfume the Hair of the Goddess of Truth', while the guests were attended by graceful servants with multi-plaited hair. In the nearby tomb of Userhet, a small group of men sat in the shade of a tree, patiently waiting their turn at the barber's; and rows of scribes in the tomb of Khaemhat bowed to receive perfume as a mark of honour from the king.

We ended in the tomb of Ramose, 'Master of All Wardrobes', whose job title was borne out by the stunning appearance of his family and friends. Figures of men and women in high relief, decked out in rippling wigs made up of individual zig-zag strands, appeared to be emerging from the walls as they watched us through black kohl-rimmed eyes startlingly defined against the white limestone background.

Ramose himself had at some stage been promoted, swapping wardrobe duties for the somewhat more stressful role of vizier to successive kings Amenhotep III and his son Akhenaten, still known as Amenhotep IV when the tomb was built. Although one scene depicted the newly crowned Amenhotep IV in the traditional style, the last scenes to be carved in the tomb within the first couple of years of the new reign suddenly changed. The beautiful people of Amenhotep III's court had somehow morphed into figures with the same curious proportions we'd seen at Amarna.

As the new king leaned forward from a Window of Appearances, framed by images of himself as a sphinx trampling his enemies, there beside him, making her first public appearance, was 'the King's Great Wife, his Beloved, Mistress of the Two Lands' (the two halves of Egypt) – Nefertiti herself. Wearing a short wig set in the face-framing layers of the Nubian style, and holding a drooping, queenly lily sceptre in her left hand, she looked the perfect image of the dutiful wife standing passively by.

FIGURE 7. Detail of a wall scene in the Theban tomb of
Vizier Ramose (TT.55) showing Nefertiti's first 'public
appearance'; wearing the Nubian wig and clutching the
queen's lily sceptre, she stands behind Akhenaten at the
Window of Appearances in their palace beside Karnak's Aten
Temple complex

The next stop was Luxor's Museum of Ancient Egyptian Art,
a building as small and pristine as the Cairo Museum is vast
and dusty. Among the larger objects displayed in the museum's
well-kept gardens was an image of the great warrior king Amenhotep II on a large red granite stela, firing arrows from his
chariot right through thick copper targets. And numerous representations of the smiling Amenhotep III inside were succeeded
by those of his son, including two more of the so-called grotesque
statues found at the Karnak Aten temples. These flanked a whole
wall of small sandstone blocks recovered from the Ninth Pylon

gateway at Karnak, reassembled in the museum to give a good idea of how the Aten temple walls might once have looked. The restored wall showed some of the key temple personnel at work: female musicians played lutes, flutes and tambourines while men in Syrian costume plucked the strings of a giant harp. There were also armies of busy little people in the temple's storehouses, warehouses, workshops and brewery; one man was even depicted sitting down to enjoy his meal of bread and onions at his lunch break.

Yet the focus of every scene was once again the royal couple. Akhenaten and Nefertiti stood as usual beneath the rays of the Aten, the king wearing a variety of crowns and head covers and Nefertiti the same Nubian wig she'd worn in the tomb of Ramose. According to the museum's guide book, 'Nefertiti and her daughters seem to have set a trend for wearing the Nubian wig . . . a coiffure first worn by Nubian mercenaries and clearly associated with the military.' The wig in question was adorned with the protective cobra at her brow and sometimes bound with a golden diadem, while matching golden Aten cartouches jangled at her wrists as she raised up endless offerings to the sun.

Before leaving Egypt I was also given a rare glimpse of Amarna art at Aswan, carved on one of the granite rocks which lay beneath part of the modern town. Although the waste pipe of the house above dripped a steady flow of water on to the scene, which could only be seen in the late afternoon light, it was still a vital piece of evidence for the reign. Carved around year 9 of Akhenaten, it showed the royal sculptor Bek worshipping a figure of Akhenaten, whose heavily defaced outline could still be made out beneath the Aten's rays. Here Bek actually described himself as 'the apprentice whom his majesty instructed', something he repeated on his pot-bellied statue now in Berlin. This suggests that he may well have been responsible for carving the so-called grotesque colossi of Akhenaten and Nefertiti which once stood at Karnak.

Back home after an amazing seventeen days on the Nile, a letter from Manchester University told me that I'd been awarded a three-year studentship to do my research. I was ecstatic – this would give me enough time to do the bulk of the work. Soon I began in earnest, starting with the University Museum's collection of mummified remains, a fantastic resource for anyone wanting to study the way in which the Egyptians had treated their dead.

The museum's first acquisition way back in 1825 was a mummy, the superbly preserved body of Asru, a shaven-headed priestess of Amen who had worked in Karnak Temple around 600 BC. Although Asru had been unwrapped by curious owners before they handed her over, the mummy of her colleague Perenbast, found by Petrie in a tomb at Qurna, remained tightly wrapped and strewn with lotus flowers, much as she would have been when placed in her tomb on the day of her burial. Other museum occupants included an Amen priest named Khary from around 1200 BC and a woman named Ta-aath from about 1000 BC. After Ta-aath's mummy had been unwrapped, photographed, then rewrapped, her owners donated her to the museum because she apparently brought them bad luck – typical of the way mummies were often given to museums by people who were uneasy at the thought of an ancient Egyptian watching them from the corner of the drawing room.

In 1907 the museum had also acquired the entire contents of an intact tomb, some four thousand years old, that Petrie had discovered at the cemetery of Rifeh, near Asyut. The mummies in question were two minor noblemen, half-brothers named Khnumnakht and Nekhtankh. When the indefatigable Margaret Murray arrived in Manchester in 1908 to catalogue the collection and give lectures, she also initiated one of the first scientific unwrappings of an Egyptian mummy as she worked on the brothers' remains. Although the earliest such event had taken place in Leeds in 1824, the Manchester unwrapping still represented a milestone; as Murray said, 'every vestige of ancient

remains must be carefully studied and recorded without senti-
mentality and without fear of the outcry of the ignorant.'

And so, on a typically wet Mancunian afternoon in May,
Murray, dressed for the occasion in a carefully pressed white
apron, gathered her small team of anatomist, chemist and two
textile experts in the university's chemist auditorium before an
invited audience of five hundred local worthies and interested
parties. Under the headline 'Unrolling a mummy: novel ceremony in Manchester', the local press reported the event as being

of great interest to Egyptologists. It was the unrolling of the 4,500
year old mummy of Ghnum-nakht [Khnumnakht] of the XII [sic]
Dynasty and his brother, a high priest of the time. The operation
was conducted under the superintendence of Miss Margaret Murray,
F.S.A. Scot., of University College, London, who has been delivering
a course of lectures on Ancient Egypt at Manchester University . . .
Miss Murray, having given an explanatory address the unfolding
was commenced. The operation, which was naturally conducted with
the greatest care, occupied considerable time.

In fact it took ninety minutes. The report concluded that 'those
who wished to have a piece of the mummy wrappings as a
memento were invited to leave their names and addresses', and
a small section of bandage mounted on a glass slide would be
sent to them in the post.

In addition to complete mummies, the museum's store rooms
housed a whole range of assorted mummified heads, hands, feet
and entrails – and, to my great delight, numerous hair samples
dating back over five thousand years from sites all over Egypt.
With so many different types of hair, the first requirement was
to work out the precise nature of each sample. Although hair
fragments tend to be labelled 'wigs', close examination often
reveals that this is not the case. I needed to work out whether
each sample consisted of the natural scalp hair, even if now
separated from the body, or had once been part of a wig or hair
extensions. Then there was always the possibility that the hair

was a votive or funerary offering, a practice found throughout ancient Egyptian history – although some archaeologists, at a loss to describe this custom, often ignore it and leave it out of their excavation reports.

Yet the ancient Egyptians are known to have placed locks of hair amongst mummy wrappings. Funerary texts refer to the 'Braided tress of Isis, which Anubis has affixed by means of the craft of the embalmer', and in earlier Pyramid Texts the mummy of the king is told to 'loosen your bonds, for they are not bonds, they are the tresses of the goddess Nephthys'. Locks of hair had also been found amongst the wrappings of both Tutankhamen and Ramses V, and since both of them were shaven or crop-headed this was clearly not a piece of their own hair which fell away during the wrapping. Perhaps it was hair's ability to regenerate when cut that made it a suitably potent substance to be placed in such close proximity to the mummy.

I looked at all the hair held in storage, and a simple visual examination using nothing more technical than a magnifying glass established basic facts about the hair's condition, colour, length and any evidence of styling techniques. Then, using a high-powered electron microscope put at my disposal by generous colleagues elsewhere in the university, I was able to find out all sorts of things about the ancient Egyptians via their hair.

Hair really does have tremendous potential, and can give information about diet, diseases, levels of environmental pollution and even the use of drugs and poisons, which remain in the hair shaft long after they have left the rest of the body. And often all that is needed for such analysis is a single hair.

As regards ancient styling techniques, close examination of the ends of the hair showed that very sharp blades had been used for cutting and trimming as early as 3000 BC. And although hair colour can fade over time or be changed by environmental conditions or even by the materials used during mummification, the multi-coloured hairstyles shown in art were not merely figments of the artist's imagination, because the Egyptians had been dab hands with hair dye. The most common was henna, which is still familiar today and which gave the hair an attractive orange-red tone.

One of the most intriguing results came from a body that Petrie discovered at Gurob, wearing 'a copious wig of black hair, reaching down to the waist, but beneath this on the scalp was yellow or light brown hair'. Taking this as evidence of an Aegean settler, he concluded that 'the person was light-haired during life, and wore a wig of black, hiding the foreign token'. Yet when I had the 'black wig' analysed, it turned out to be part of a dark blue woollen head cover; and, far from trying to play down the hair colour, it had actually been accentuated with a yellow vegetable colourant.

One of the oldest samples in storage was a portion of loose auburn hair, believed to date to around 3000 BC, which had been found at Abydos. Although the hair was in quite good condition, it was covered in the tiny white egg cases of the head louse, commonly known as nits, and a careful search recovered three adult lice each only a few millimetres long. To me this was hidden treasure of the most exciting kind, and, whilst not exactly the standard type of archaeological discovery, it did demonstrate another reason why the Egyptians had shaven off their own hair and worn wigs.

As early as 450 BC the Greek traveller Herodotus had noticed that 'Egyptian priests shave their bodies all over every other day to guard against the presence of lice, or anything else equally unpleasant, while they are about their religious duties'. Yet the desire to get rid of them was far more than religious or aesthetic, and as I pursued a growing fascination with these tiny creatures I discovered that lice can transmit diseases such as typhus, and have been responsible for more human deaths than any other insect except the mosquito.

As well as shaving off their hair, the ancient Egyptians devised a whole range of potions to prevent 'that which moves about on the head', one recipe recommending 'fruit of the castor-oil plant, ox fat and moringa oil: combine to a paste and apply every day'. Traces of lice and their eggs between the teeth of ancient combs resembling modern nit combs revealed another means of delousing, whilst wigs which were taken off on a regular basis would take the creatures away from their only food source, the scalp's blood supply. Lice were no respecters of class, preferring clean, well-groomed heads, since feeding was hindered if the head was dirty. Indeed, I've even found them hiding out in the hair of several princesses, queens and even one or two of the pharaohs themselves.

The lice were photographed using an electron microscope, and the resultant images were much in demand, and have even graced the British Museum's new mummy galleries. News of the unusual discoveries reached the local press and was soon picked up by the nationals, always in search of a quirky angle and daft headline; the *Daily Mirror* announced, 'Nits! The Curse of the Pharaohs', 'The Nit-Picking Pharaohs' appeared in *New Scientist*, and the *Guardian* went with 'The Oldest Nit in the World'. Interviews on local radio led to appearances on the World Service and Radio 4's *Midweek* programme, whilst the publicity even led to French-based chemical and cosmetics company Sanofi, the makers of Derbac louse shampoo, providing sponsorship for this unusual offshoot of my research.

Over the next few years I examined ancient hair, wigs and mummies in collections across the UK, in Europe, the USA and of course Egypt, and soon started to arrive at some interesting conclusions. Contrary to the general belief that ancient Egyptian wigs were made from wool or horse-hair, the material used was invariably human hair. And although no precise details were available to explain where the hair came from, it seems most likely to have been their own, or to have been traded for, since hair appears to have been a valuable commodity ranked alongside gold and incense in ancient accounts lists found at Kahun.

After removing any tangles or lice eggs with fine-toothed combs, the hair would have been styled into an assortment of braids, plaits or curls, depending on the fashion required. The individual sections were then attached directly to the natural hair as hair extensions, or could be used to create an actual wig by fastening them on to a mesh-type foundation. Again usually made from fine lengths of plaited or woven human hair, as in the case of a fabulous wig I was allowed to examine in the Berlin Museum, the base would have been made on a head-shaped wooden mount just like today's polystyrene equivalents. The whole lot was secured with a setting lotion made from warmed beeswax and resin which hardened when cool and kept the style in place, not only during the owner's lifetime but for a long time afterwards. It also coincidentally preserved hair which might otherwise have rotted away after burial in damp conditions.

Such sophisticated construction techniques and the skills of the ancient hairdressers produced wigs of similar quality to modern examples. Since some people had wondered whether these ancient wigs could have been responsible for some of the known cases of skull deformation among the ancient population, we decided to test this and after weighing a few were able to show that their lightweight construction would have made them as easy to wear as their modern counterparts.

With the office of 'Royal Wigmaker and Hairdresser' appearing by around 2500 BC I wanted to find the actual evidence for early wigmaking, and tracked down what was usually described as 'the world's oldest surviving false hair'. It had been dated to around 3000 BC and was discovered at Abydos by Petrie, who described it as a 'plait of hair and piece of false fringe found in the tomb of king Zer [Djer], probably belonging to his queen'. He also noted that 'the fringe of locks is exquisitely made, entirely on a band of hair, showing a long acquaintance with hair work at that age. It is now in the Pitt-Rivers Museum at Oxford.' Although Djer had ruled in about 3000 BC, the site of his tomb had been identified by later generations as that of the god Osiris, and ancient pilgrims travelled there to leave hair as a votive offering.

When I saw this piece for myself, the fringe and plait turned out to be just one item from three boxes full of hair made up into woven lengths, using construction techniques familiar from other examples dated to around 1500 BC and later. But soon I had tracked down the same type of samples from the same site in several other collections, and 'the world's oldest surviving false hair' was no longer quite so old, nor was it unique. Yet it did provide further evidence that Osiris, as god of resurrection, was closely associated with hair as well as with crops, since both were magical substances which continued to grow even after being cut.

Following the original discovery, however, it was assumed that even if the hair had been associated with Djer it probably belonged to his queen. This interpretation reflected an attitude which was not only alive and well a century ago in Petrie's day, but remains so in certain quarters today. There is still a tendency to assign anything vaguely decorative to a woman even if it is found in a man's burial, in the same way that weapons in a female burial are frequently assumed to have belonged to a man.

Yet even the briefest glance at ancient Egyptian art reveals elaborate hairstyles, not to mention generous quantities of make-up, perfume and jewellery, worn by both men and women of all ages right across society. Both sexes wore intricately styled hair of varying length, with hair both real and false playing an important part in love and seduction. This was most obvious in representations of women leading up to the Amarna Period, who were shown with all the attributes of the goddess Hathor, known for good reason as 'she of the beautiful hair and beautiful breasts'.

The art is also supported by the literature of the time, with the highly improper suggestion 'Put on your wig and let us lie together' featured in the oft-told 'Tale of Two Brothers'. A love poem of similar date also uses hair to suggest the intense feelings of a love-struck woman, who declares that 'My heart is once again invaded by your love when only half my hair is braided

. . . I'll trouble myself no longer over my hairdressing and put on a wig to be ready,' whilst in another love poem a similarly afflicted male tells how the object of his desire 'casts the noose on me with her hair', although whether the hair is actually her own he doesn't say.

As in many cultures, long hair was linked to male virility and strength and the magic powers of regeneration, and, whilst men frequently wore their hair long and flowing, women are also found with short, cropped or even shaven hair. Whether consciously or not, the modern world is still very much influenced by Christian attitudes dating back to the first century AD when St Paul dictated that men's hair should be shorter than that of women. This relatively modern attitude can cause all sorts of problems and misunderstandings when used to interpret ancient Egyptian material, giving rise to the tendency to assume that bodies with short or shaven hair are male and that those with long or intricately styled hair are female, this is simply not the case.

To take one example, a limestone figure in Birmingham City Museum was for years swooned over as an icon of feminine beauty, hailed as the 'Mona Lisa of Ancient Egypt' and 'The Birmingham Isis'. Yet this gorgeous individual is in fact a well-to-do man from around 1300 BC, wearing the typically elaborate 'double-style' wig fashionable at the time. The wonderful wig in the British Museum is set in exactly this style, yet again has often been described as 'a noblewoman's wig', as have others set in the same fashion. Amongst the enormous wigs I'd looked at in the Cairo Museum, one had been found in a wig box sealed with the name of a high priest. Yet it was still described as belonging to his wife, even though her wig was quite clearly the much smaller, more stylish creation of curls typical of the short feminine fashions popular around 1000 BC.

Women's wigs were generally less elaborate than those worn by men. The best-preserved example dates from the reign of Amenhotep III, around 1380 BC, and was found in the tall wooden wig box of a lady named Meryt. In the well-stocked tomb she shared with her husband Kha at the tomb builders' village of Deir el-Medina, the couple were even provided with his and hers cosmetics chests. Their numerous possessions are today displayed in Turin's Egyptology Museum, where I was able to examine Meryt's wig. It was made up of numerous wavy braids of dark brown hair attached to a narrow plait forming the central parting, just like the fragmentary wig in the Cairo Museum. Yet in contrast to this short style, Meryt's voluminous wig would have reached down to shoulder level, just like the beautiful long wigs worn by the women in the tomb of Ramose.

Whilst I was doing all this research, I was asked to contribute to the *Clothing of the Pharaohs* exhibition at Leiden's Rijksmuseum in the Netherlands. Since the textile historian organising the exhibition needed information about wigs, hairstyles and cosmetics, she invited me to write a couple of chapters for the accompanying book. She also told me about her work at Amarna in the 1980s when she studied the textiles found around the city, everything from ancient underwear to the textiles found in the Royal Tomb. We soon realised we had rather a lot in common – despite her Dutch married name, our families came from the same small village just outside Barnsley! This was a good omen for the work ahead, and we have remained friends.

To my great delight she also invited me to contribute to the Tutankhamen Textile and Clothing Project organised by the Textile Research Centre at Leiden University. Amongst the thousands of objects conserved and catalogued during the ten years it took Howard Carter to clear the tomb, the largest group of objects were the textiles. These included clothing which not only belonged to Tutankhamen but in some cases carried the names of Akhenaten and his mysterious co-regent Ankhkheperura, whom some Egyptologists believe to have been Nefertiti herself.

The majority of the garments were originally placed neatly inside storage chests and boxes, but the ancient thieves had pulled out many of them in their search for gold, and the officials sent in to tidy up had simply stuffed them back inside the nearest boxes. But, regardless of three thousand-year-old creases, Carter realised that the royal clothing was unique and would need very careful study. However, since immediate attention was focussed on the gold and works of art, the textiles lay largely neglected for seventy years until the Leiden researchers realised their importance.

With almost all the garments badly faded and some little more than a black, crumbly mass, exact replicas were made as a record of the fragile originals to save them from further damage. One of the discoveries made on examining these pieces was that Tutankhamen had a 31-inch chest, a 29-inch waist and 43-inch hips – possibly the origin of the pear-shaped body that seemed so exaggerated in portrayals of the Amarna royal family.

The replica garments provided a real understanding of how originals had been made, and I had great fun trying some of them on. This form of hands-on archaeology also solved some of the mysteries of how these garments had been worn. A number of the 'head-dresses' described by Carter turned out to be elaborate armbands which formed the wings of the falcon god, whilst other garments emblazoned with slogans such as 'Protector of the Country' and 'Vanquisher of All the Enemies of Egypt' were obviously designed to enhance royal status.

Amongst the sumptuous robes, gold-encrusted tunics and a large supply of neatly folded underwear were several pairs of royal socks. They were made with a gap between the big toe and the rest to accommodate the thongs of the forty-seven pairs of flip-flop sandals found in the tomb. The look was completed by golden collars, earrings, bracelets and one of a range of royal crowns, and it was my role to provide details of the finishing touches, from the sweet perfumed oils and thick black kohl eyeliner to the wig worn on the king's shaven head.

Working from Carter's original notes and photographs, I knew that the royal wig box had been found empty, tipped on its side with the lid pulled off. A portion of artificially curled, light brown human hair had been discovered in a small alabaster chest, its fragmentary state suggesting that the robbers had taken the original wig out of its box and ripped it apart to get at the jewelled decorations. The officials who restored the burial had then presumably collected up the hair fragments and dumped them in the chest in the same way that they'd restored an earlier burial of a queen, sweeping up the remains of her wig and hastily shoving them into a box of preserved meat! Even after such treatment, however, it was possible to work out the original style of the king's wig. The dimensions of the wig box meant that it could have been no more than fifteen inches in length, whilst the curled fragments suggested the relatively short curled style found in the art of the time.

But the ancient Egyptians hadn't all worn wigs: many men and women throughout society used hair extensions as a less costly alternative. One man buried in a simple sand-hollow around 1650 BC had lengthened his hair by attaching a single braid with thread. At the other end of the social spectrum, the wavy brown hair of a queen of slightly later date had been filled out around the crown and temples with numerous tapered braids to produce the top-heavy effect so fashionable at the time. She had also been buried with a duplicate set of braids as part of her funerary equipment – though none too carefully prepared, to judge from the sprinkling of lice eggs I found on them.

On a more practical level, such braids were also used to disguise baldness. For instance, an unnamed soldier from a mass grave of around 2000 BC at Deir el-Bahari had supplemented his own thinning locks with short, curly hair extensions. Since his burial was carried out hastily following battle, this hairstyle was unlikely to have been created by the morticians to prepare him for the Afterlife and must therefore have been worn during his life, perhaps to give his head that little bit of extra protection in the days before helmets, or simply for reasons of vanity. A similar technique had been adopted by the hairdressers of Egypt's elderly queens, whose mummies had been studied by

Manchester's anatomy professor, Grafton Elliot Smith, when he held the same post at Cairo University's School of Medicine between 1900 and 1909.

Most of the mummies he examined came from a great cache of royal bodies at Deir el-Bahari, discovered by locals in 1871 and ten years later by the authorities. Many had already been unwrapped by Gaston Maspero, head of the French-run Antiquities Service, in the original Cairo Museum located in an old palace at Giza. Then, when the current Cairo Museum was opened in 1902, some forty-five thousand artefacts were transferred, including the mummies. Maspero wanted Smith to re-examine them, as well as to unwrap and examine those discovered more recently in the second royal cache found in 1898 in the tomb of Amenhotep II (KV.35).

Smith's long-term studies of the royal mummies began with Akhenaten's grandfather Tuthmosis IV, when the king's mummy was 'unrolled' at 2pm on 26 March 1903 in the new museum before an invited audience, including Lord Cromer, the British Consul-General and the most powerful man in Egypt, Howard Carter 'and several ladies'. Later, when carrying out further examinations in more detail and presumably without the intimidating audience, Smith decided to X-ray the king's mummy to try to determine its age. Since Cairo's only X-ray machine was located in a private nursing home, Smith, assisted by Howard Carter, 'took the rigid Pharaoh in a cab to the nursing-home. It was the first [royal] mummy ever submitted to X-ray photography.'

Impressed by Smith's findings, and no doubt also by his initiative, Maspero invited him to make a thorough examination of all fifty of the royal mummies found in the two great caches at Deir el-Bahari and the tomb of Amenhotep II (KV.35), as well as the 160 priests and priestesses from a third cache discovered in 1891. Between 1903 and 1905 Smith practised on the clergy before tackling the pharaohs and queens. Then, between 1906 and 1909 Smith and his assistant, Dr Maynard Pain, occasionally helped out by Howard Carter, examined, described and photographed the remaining royal mummies.

After moving to Manchester to become anatomy professor, and apparently unaffected by 'the sudden transition from the sunshine and oriental glamour of Egypt to the smoky ungenial skies of Manchester' Smith continued to write up his notes, which finally appeared as 'The Royal Mummies, Catalogue Général des Antiquités Égyptiennes de la Musée du Caire, Nos. 61051–61100'. Published in 1912, it is still the standard reference work on the subject, and until its republication eighty-eight years later in paperback, this huge, rare volume was only to be found on the shelves of specialist libraries. Concentrating my attentions on the hair and wigs it described and portrayed, I worked my way through it chronologically.

Beginning with the mummy of the murdered pharaoh Seqenre, his hair still matted with blood from the wounds which had killed him, Smith went on to describe the mummy of his elderly mother Queen Tetisheri, her own sparse hair interplaited with false braids. Then came a whole succession of queens and princesses of the early 18th dynasty, many of whom had inherited the family trait of buck teeth. Seqenre's wife, Queen Inhapi, had plaited hair set with resinous setting lotion and dressed 'in a peculiar manner, which in itself is sufficient to indicate the beginning of the New Empire [Kingdom] as the date of this mummy'. The hair of the elderly princess Hentempet was streaked with grey, and she had been buried in a wig of long plaits with a second wig of artificially curled locks thoughtfully placed on her chest ready for a quick change in the Afterlife. Sadly, she no longer had access to it – using the old photographs, I had tracked it down, adrift and unlabelled, beside the priests' wigs in the Cairo Museum.

The first queen of the 18th dynasty, Ahmose-Nefertari, 'had very little hair on her head and the vertex was quite bald. Elaborate pains had been taken to hide her deficiency. Twenty strings, composed of twisted human hair, were placed across the top of her head; and to these were attached numerous tight plaits ... which hung down as far as the clavicle. Other plaits were tied to her own scanty locks.' The queen had been nursed by the much younger Lady Rai, 'the least unlovely' of all the mummies that Smith described, whose abundant masses of natural hair had been finely plaited and arranged in two sections which hung down over each shoulder, the upper parts twice as thick as the rest in order to create the fashionable top-heavy style of the day.

Then came a succession of 18th dynasty pharaohs beginning with King Ahmose, still garlanded with delphiniums and with his dark brown ringlets coated with thick resinous paste. Although his son and successor Amenhotep I has never been unwrapped, the mummy believed to be his successor, Tuthmosis I, had a completely shaven head whilst his son and successor in turn, Tuthmosis II, had a bald scalp surrounded by a wreath of dark, wavy hair. Smith suspected it had been artificially curled, and judging by the photographs it certainly looked as though his hairdresser had been creative with the curling tongs to make up for the pharaoh's own trichological limitations. The lack of hair continued with his son Tuthmosis III, 'the Napoleon of ancient Egypt', who seems to have had none at all – perfect for those long foreign campaigns.

Then Smith encountered a problem, because Tuthmosis III's son, Amenhotep II, was not amongst his relatives in Cairo but still lay in his tomb in the Valley of the Kings where he'd been found by Victor Loret, French head of the Antiquities Service, back in 1898. So, having a day to spare in 1907, Smith says he 'made a hasty examination' of the king's mummy with help from Arthur Weigall, then working as the antiquities inspector for the Luxor region. At around six feet tall Amenhotep II had been the tallest of the pharaohs, with greying brown wavy hair around a large bald patch. His arms were crossed over his chest, as with most of the pharaohs, and both hands were still clenched as if to grasp long-vanished sceptres. During his examination

Smith noticed the distinct impressions of jewellery and regalia in the resin coating the skin.

He then referred to three more mummies which in 1907 were still in the tomb with the king, inside one of the side chambers – apparently the same sealed-up room that had so intrigued me on my visits there. So who were they?

The first Smith simply called the 'Elder Woman', 'a small, middle-aged woman with long brown, wavy, lustrous hair, parted in the centre and falling down on both sides of the head on to the shoulders. Its ends are converted into numerous apparently natural curls'; as the photographs revealed, her amazing hair framed a truly regal face. Although much of her torso had been smashed in by ancient robbers searching for jewellery, her arms remained in place, 'the right arm placed vertically-extended [sic] at the side and the palm of the hand is placed flat upon the right thigh. The left hand was tightly clenched, but with the thumb fully extended: it is placed in front of the manubrium sterni, the forearm being sharply flexed upon the brachium.' Or, to put it plainly, she had her left arm bent up with the hand still clasped around a long-vanished sceptre in the well-known pose of a queen.

Smith described the second mummy as that of a boy around eleven years of age, his hair 'shaved from the greater part of [the] scalp: but on the right side of the head . . . the hair has not been cut and forms a great, long, wavy, lustrous mass . . . which from the nature of its waviness was probably plaited at some time'. This was the typical hairstyle of a royal child. Since this mummy had been found in the tomb of Amenhotep II, Smith followed Loret's initial suggestion that he was 'probably the Royal prince Ouabkhousenou' (his name also translated as Webensenu) whose wooden funerary figurines had been found amongst the tomb debris. He also stated that the mummy 'presented an extraordinary likeness to a beautiful statue of the god Khonsu, discovered at Karnak . . . Not only does the god wear a Horus-lock like that of this prince, but the statue is characterised also by his exceptional brachycephalism', which is defined as 'having a head nearly as broad from side to side as from front to back'.

In fact the statue Smith mentioned actually represented Akhenaten's son Tutankhamen, portrayed as Khonsu, son of Amen, to signify the young king's return to the traditional religion. I compared Smith's photographs of the boy's mummy, showing his wide-set eyes and pleasant, slightly smiling expression, with the Tutankhamen Khonsu statue, and they did indeed look quite similar. And, like Tutankhamen, the boy clearly had pierced ears, which from my own interest in body piercing I knew had only been adopted by royal males after Amenhotep II's reign.

It was on examination of the third mummy that Smith was most surprised. Loret had stated that this was the body of a man, 'whereas it requires no great knowledge of anatomy to decide that the excellently preserved naked body is a young woman's. Every later writer had followed Loret in his description of this mummy as a man. The only reason I can assign for such a curious and obvious mistake is the absence of hair on the head. All the hair had been clipped very short or shaved.' Smith also mentioned two small perforations in the remaining ear, the left one – although, turning to the photographs of the mummy, a front and side view, I couldn't make them out myself. Yet, looking closely at her profile, the complete lack of hair accentuating her long, graceful neck, I was suddenly struck with how familiar she seemed. She looked just like the famous head of Nefertiti in Berlin, the one we had a copy of in Manchester.

From the front, it was clear that the mummy's face had suffered terribly, presumably during the robbers' search for jewellery, and as with her companions, the Elder Woman and the boy, her chest had been smashed in. But a routine search for valuables could not explain why her face had been so savagely attacked, and the only reason I could think of for inflicting this kind of damage was a malicious one. Had someone wanted to destroy her features, and in doing so deprive her of the ability to breathe in the Afterlife? And not only that – the photographs and sketch that Smith had made showed that her right arm had been torn off. He said that in his notes, 'hurriedly made during my short visit to the tomb . . . I find no further reference to this arm: but these remarks occur . . . "along with these three mummies there is the well-preserved right forearm of a woman, which had been flexed at the elbow" and "the hand was clasped".' Clasped, of course, to hold a sceptre just like the Elder Woman buried with her. But in this case it was the right arm, which as far as I knew was only ever bent up when the deceased had been king.

With my brain working overtime, and trying desperately not to get completely carried away with the implications of all this, in my search for further clues I went on to read what else Smith had said. While trying to discover how old she was he admitted that 'the exact age cannot be determined', adding that 'in the remote Biban el Molouk [Arabic for Valley of the Kings], it is hardly feasible to examine the body with X-rays'.

Gazing out of the window, staring abstractedly towards the very house in which Smith had written up his notes on these mummies over eighty years before, I felt decidedly strange. I sat there thinking for some time, and was still there when a colleague called round later that evening. I decided to show her Smith's pictures of the 'Younger Woman' and see what she thought. I remember half-joking about it all in case she told me not to be so stupid. But she didn't laugh at all.

As we talked through some of the possible repercussions of such an identification, however unlikely, we became more and more fascinated with the idea that this might just be the great woman herself. Putting her former career as a graphic artist to good use, my friend began the first of a number of sketches, outlines and scale drawings of the mummy's profile in order to compare it in detail with the famous bust which it so closely resembled. Whilst in no way conclusive, and done as much for our own private interest as anything else, this work at least provided me with a starting point and I began to think of how I might get to see this intriguing individual for myself.

Since all three bodies were listed in Smith's royal mummies catalogue under their Cairo Museum accession numbers, I assumed they must now be stored somewhere in the museum. I also assumed that they must have been examined when all the royal mummies were X-rayed in the 1970s by a combined team from the universities of Alexandria and Michigan, who had begun to re-examine the mummies in 1967 to try to determine their state of health, the types of diseases they had suffered from, the mummification techniques used, their ages at death and, where unknown, their possible identities.

Although I couldn't find any reference to the shaven-headed woman in their *X-Ray Atlas of the Royal Mummies*, they had certainly X-rayed the boy. Although still calling him 'Prince Ouabkhousenou', they believed he might be as old as twelve or thirteen as opposed to Smith's estimate of eleven. Pointing out the difficulties of using statistics based on Western bodies in trying to interpret the ages of Egyptians, either ancient or modern, they noted that a Nubian or Egyptian child thought to be eleven years of age by American standards might actually be as old as thirteen.

Yet their findings regarding the Elder Woman made my eyes pop right out of my head. After X-raying the mummies they had worked out a set of measurements which allowed them to map out the contours of each face. Using a statistical approach called cluster analysis they compared all the royal females, and discovered that Tuya's mummy was 'more similar to that of the unknown mummy "The Elder Lady" than any other queen in the royal collection'. This finding suggested that the Elder Woman might be Tuya's daughter, Queen Tiy, a conclusion they later confirmed by comparing the hair of the Elder Woman with the lock of Tiy's hair found in Tutankhamen's tomb that I'd seen in Cairo Museum.

During the summer, when all this began to link together in my head, the newspapers had been full of rather more high-profile Egyptian discoveries being made at Highclere Castle in Hampshire, family seat of the earls of Carnarvon. As I knew from my childhood fascination with the whole story, the fifth earl, George Edward Stanhope Molyneaux Herbert, had first gone out to Egypt on medical advice while recovering from a serious car crash. Spending his winters in the luxury of the Winter Palace Hotel overlooking the Nile in Luxor, he had unsurprisingly succumbed to the lure of archaeology and in 1907 hired Howard Carter as his professional archaeologist. The two men spent the next sixteen years making a series of finds which culminated in the spectacular discovery of Tutankhamen's tomb in 1922.

Then, following the earl's tragic death from pneumonia in 1923, amidst spurious rumours of a curse, his family removed all traces of Egypt from their home. The late earl's fabulous collection of ancient artefacts was packed away by Carter and sold to the Metropolitan Museum in New York, except for 'a few unimportant antiquities' which were left in storage at Highclere. In the late 1980s these had literally started coming out of the woodwork, after the family butler found one hoard stashed away behind wall panelling, another stuffed in a drawer in the housekeeper's room and a third hidden away in the gun cabinet. Although certain quarters of the press were almost suggesting that golden treasures had been stuffed down the back of the drawing room sofa, the artefacts recovered were relatively modest. They were, nevertheless, fascinating.

Some of the pieces had come from the huge tomb of Tutankhamen's grandfather Amenhotep III during Carter's excavations in 1915. They included several funerary figurines with the king's characteristic large almond-shaped eyes and smiling lips, and part of a funerary figurine belonging to his great royal wife, Queen Tiy – quite possibly Smith's Elder Woman. There was also a superb archer's wrist-guard of red leather, which the king may well have worn when hunting lion and wild bulls, one of his favourite pastimes. Together with a whole range of canopic equipment, figurines, jewellery, caskets and pottery, these items formed the centrepiece of a conference to be held in June 1990 at Highclere Castle, in the library where Carnarvon and Carter had planned their excavations.

As soon as I heard about the forthcoming conference I put my name down, and in due course became one of the 150 delegates. The distinguished list of speakers included John Harris, who, together with Julia Samson, had done so much to prove Nefertiti's kingly status, and a member of the American team which had X-rayed the royal mummies and identified Queen Tiy. The presence of so many senior Egyptologists made this a tremendous event, and in the informal atmosphere of evening socialising I felt brave enough to ask a few questions. Following a lecture on the royal mummies by the expert from the American team, I got talking to him about some of the details of the work they had carried out.

Aware that the Elder Woman's bent left arm signified her queenly status, the team had started by trying to ascertain which queen was 'missing' amongst the royal mummies and wondered if she might be Hatshepsut or Tiy. When they discovered her close facial similarity to the mummy of Tuya, known to have been Tiy's mother, they presented their findings to the Egyptian authorities and asked to examine a sample of hair inscribed with Tiy's name which came from Tutankhamen's tomb and is now in the Cairo Museum. Using the scientific techniques of ion etching and scanning electron microprobe analysis, they compared it to a sample of the Elder Woman's hair. Their results were said to have demonstrated 'a near perfect superimposition'. This strongly supported their argument that 'the hair samples from both King Tutankhamen's tomb and the mummy from Amenhotep II's tomb are indeed those of the same person – Queen Tiy of the Eighteenth Dynasty, wife of Amenhotep III and mother of the heretic pharaoh Amenhotep IV or Akhenaten'.

But when I tracked down their findings in a science journal, there was another surprise in store. When they had begun to look for the mummy of the Elder Woman in order to X-ray her along with all the other royal mummies in the Cairo Museum in the 1970s, she seemed to have vanished. Eventually she was traced to the side chamber of the tomb where she'd been all the time. After X-rays of her skull had been taken she had been left there, walled up with the boy and, presumably, the shaven-headed woman. And to keep all three mummies safe the chamber had been sealed up again.

I couldn't believe it. Why had they been left there? I could only conclude that, with many authorities unconvinced by the team's findings, the three mummies were still to all intents and purposes anonymous. And without an identity, no one wanted to know.

Matters weren't helped by the fact that Victor Loret's original excavation plans had disappeared, leaving precious little to work from other than his article published in 1899 in an obscure French journal – one of the few our university library didn't have. Fortunately, however, his comments about the mummies he found in the tomb had been quoted in a recent book on the history of the Valley of the Kings, and they made fascinating reading.

By flickering candlelight in the darkness of the tomb, Loret had described each of the three bodies in turn. He had begun with the Elder Woman, Tiy, whose abundant hair spread out over the floor on either side of her head, and then moved on to the boy, who appeared to be totally bald apart from a magnificent tress on the right side of his head, which Loret referred to as the hairstyle of royal princes. Finally he came to the third body, which, much to Smith's later consternation, he had described as a man, whose 'head was shaved but a wig lay on the ground not far from him'.

A wig – the shaven-headed woman had been buried with a wig! But what sort was it? And where was it now?

Although these three mummies had been left in the tomb, all the other finds had gone straight off to the Cairo Museum where they were listed in one of the huge catalogues. On the shelves of the university library I eventually found the relevant details: a 'wig of wavy hair of dark brown colour, mounted on a net of lengths of plaited hair' and 'One long plait and four other fragments of hair perhaps once part of the aforementioned wig'. Although this description didn't give much away, the fact that Loret had assumed that the body was male argued against the wig being made up of long hair, which he would automatically have associated with a woman. Checking through my photographs of wigs from the museum, the fragmentary example which I believed had once formed the Nubian style seemed closest to the description. A letter from the museum's curators later confirmed that this was indeed the wig found in the tomb's side chamber beside the shaven-headed mummy. As the hairstyle most closely associated with the royal women of Amarna, another large piece was added to the puzzle.

Realising that I'd need more than a few ancient wig fragments to prove anything, I began the long search for corroborating evidence with the help of a few trusted colleagues. Each was able to add pieces to my jigsaw through their expert knowledge of Amarna art, pharaonic costume, palaeopathology and chemical analysis.

I also knew I had to find a way of getting into the sealed up chamber to see the three mummies for myself, and it wouldn't be easy.

5

A CAREER WITH THE DEAD

When I eventually finished my thesis, to emerge as a 'self-employed Egyptologist', cynics gave me six months. Admittedly there aren't many of us about, but I was determined to stay as far beyond the traditional career route as possible. Surely I could do the subject I loved and still be myself?

As luck would have it, three days later I received a phone call inviting me to join a small team examining the collection of ancient Egyptian mummies at Cairo University's Faculty of Medicine. It was not the sort of offer that comes along every day, let alone with such impeccable timing, and at first I thought someone must be playing a joke. But it was genuine enough, and on 16 January 1997 I arrived in Cairo, knowing only that I would be working on some extraordinary ancient Egyptians.

The Medical School was at Qasr el-Einy, the great Mameluke palace built in AD 1467 by Ahmed Ibn el-Einy, whose tomb, topped by a mosque, was part of the site. The palace was used as the official residence of the Turkish viceroys of Egypt until the French invasion of 1798; Napoleon held his Council of War there the night before the Battle of the Pyramids, and it was later turned into a military hospital. In 1890 it became the Medical School, occupying new premises built on the site by the British administration.

The first Professor of Anatomy had been Grafton Elliot Smith, who, given his well-known interest in ancient Egyptian bodies, was soon sent human remains from sites all over Egypt. Usually the very last things archaeologists were concerned with during their search for 'artefacts', mummies and body parts arrived at the school in ever-increasing numbers to form the core of the

Qasr el-Einy collection. Having taken delivery of '64 huge cases of prehistoric remains from Upper Egypt to be unpacked and arranged Museum shape', Smith was delighted with the contents, which he described as 'really most extraordinary, not to say marvellous. In some bodies the whole of the soft parts are retained in a desiccated state, and I have a large number of excellent brains (about 7,000 years old!), hair, beards, even eyes, nerves, muscles, genital organs and various viscera.'

By 1903 a wealthy American businessman named Theodore Davis had begun to fund large-scale excavations in the Valley of the Kings and, during a series of major tomb discoveries, Smith studied the mummies found inside. They included those of Queen Tiy's parents, Yuya and Tuya, and remains which he would identify as Akhenaten. Over the next two years Smith studied a growing collection of mummies in minute detail, providing a real understanding of ancient mummification techniques, their variations and their evolution through time – all excellent preparation for his matchless work on the royal mummies in the Cairo Museum (described in Chapter 4.)

After Smith's acceptance of a chair at Manchester his work in Egypt was continued by Douglas Derry, who had begun working there as his assistant back in 1905. After a stint at UCL's Anatomy Department, Derry returned to Cairo's Medical School in 1919 and was soon caught up in the Tutankhamen saga.

Having invited Derry and his assistant, Saleh Bey Hamdi, down to the Valley of the Kings in 1925 to examine the pharaoh's mummy, Carter noted in his diary that 'this scientific examination should be carried out as quietly and reverently as possible'. The diary also reveals that the work had to be put back several weeks when it was discovered that the mummy was going to be extremely difficult to remove from its protective nest of three coffins. After 'some two bucketfuls' of perfumed unguents had been poured over the innermost gold coffin during the king's burial rites the pitch-like substance had set rock-hard, and the mummy and its famous gold death mask were now stuck firmly to the base of the innermost coffin. Even leaving it in the hot sun for a few hours failed to melt the unguents and free the mummy. So, still in its heavy coffin, it was taken to the tomb of Seti II, which was being used as a laboratory by Carter's colleague Alfred Lucas, the Manchester chemist who was conserving the treasures. Carter had already removed the mummy's shrouds, jewellery and regalia, the flowers in the funerary wreaths suggesting that the king had been buried between mid-March and late April. Then, with Egyptian officials, Maspero's successor Pierre Lacau, Carter and Lucas all standing round the coffin, and a camera rigged up on a frame to take shots from above, Derry and Saleh Bey Hamdi finally began their examination of Tutankhamen's mummy on 11 November 1925.

As Carter stood by with his magnifying glass, Derry rolled up his shirt-sleeves and began to remove the wrappings. They crumbled at a touch, and became increasingly powdery and 'soot-like' the closer they were to the body. Yet the team was still able to determine the way in which the body had been wrapped in sixteen layers of linen; care had obviously been taken, since each finger and toe had been wrapped separately and fitted with an individual gold cover.

The internal organs had been removed through an embalming incision which ran in a horizontal direction from the navel across to the left hip rather than conforming to the standard position in which the incision is made vertically down the left side of the abdomen. Tutankhamen's body cavity had then been filled with resin-soaked linen which had set rock-hard, and his skin was brittle as a result of the lavish use of unguents. These also carried traces of the natron salts which had been used to dry out the body.

The king had been buried wearing golden sandals and an anklet above his right foot, and as the men worked their way up his body they began to find more and more jewellery and regalia. By the time they reached his folded arms, loaded with bracelets from elbow to wrist, they had recovered fifty-two items, including belts, amulets and large gold signet rings. By the fifth day they were up to his neck, which was swathed in more than thirty necklaces, amulets, pectorals and collars. In total, there were ninety-seven different groups of objects!

Once they had finally freed the head from the mask using heated knives, the protective linen padding was removed and Tutankhamen's eyes were revealed to the light of day for the first time in 3252 years. They were partly open and fringed by 'very long' lashes. As Carter and the king finally came face to face, the archaeologist wrote in his diary that 'sufficient of the head of the King was exposed today to show us that Tut-Ankh-Amen was of a type exceedingly refined and cultured. The face has beautiful and well formed features. The head shows strong structural resemblance by Akh-en-aten ... a resemblance in character which makes one inclined to seek a blood relationship.'

They discovered that Tutankhamen's brain had been removed via the nose as part of the mummification process. His nostrils had been plugged with resin-soaked linen, and his lips likewise sealed with resin. His ears had clearly been pierced, and his shaven head was encircled by a gold brow-band. His skull was covered with a fine linen cap covered in a beadwork design, with cartouches naming the Aten and four protective cobras, their sinuous bodies unconsciously mirroring the suture lines on the skull.

After the body had been studied, measured and photographed, Derry and Saleh Bey were 'able to definitely declare the age of the young king to be about eighteen years of age'. Since he was known to have reigned for just under ten years, that meant he must have come to the throne around the age of eight. Requesting Derry to contribute his findings to the second volume of *The Tomb of Tutankhamen*, which would be published in 1927, Carter told him 'the only thing I ask is that the text be of a kind comprehensible to the layman and the man in the street'. In his diary, Carter stated that the king's remains 'will be reverently re-wrapped and returned to the sarcophagus', as indeed they were in 1926, laid on a tray of sand inside the outermost gold coffin whilst everything else was sent to the Cairo Museum.

This, however, was not the only mummy found in the tomb. Later that year Carter had reached the piles of chests and boxes crammed into the small room adjoining the burial chamber, which had originally been guarded by a great reclining black jackal figure swathed in one of Akhenaten's old tunics. After finding a lock of Queen Tiy's hair inside a miniature coffin bearing her name, he came across a plain wooden box containing two more miniature coffins, which, like Russian dolls, contained two even smaller coffins within. Amazingly, each contained a tiny mummy.

Unwrapping the smaller of the two, Carter believed they were 'without doubt' the children of Tutankhamen and his wife Ankhesenamen, granddaughters of Nefertiti and Akhenaten, and 'had one of those babies lived there might never have been a Ramses'. Wanting to know if they had been born prematurely either as a result of foul play or because of 'an abnormality on the part of the little Queen Ankhesenamen', he sent them both to Cairo. Here they were eventually examined in 1932 by Derry, who discovered that the smaller of the two was a five-month-old foetus still retaining part of its umbilical cord. This prematurely born girl had clearly been mummified and was in an excellent state of preservation, but there was no sign of any of the internal organs having been removed. When the second body was unwrapped by Derry it proved to be, similar to the first, the seven months' foetus of a prematurely born girl. This time the internal organs had been removed through a tiny incision in her side.

Then, to discover how the brain had been treated during the mummification process, Derry states that he 'opened the head', one of the more extreme techniques employed over the next twenty years on material sent to him from excavations throughout Egypt. This included the remains of the 21st dynasty pharaohs buried at Tanis, the bodies of high officials found in their Giza tombs, mummified remains from the burial chamber of King

Djoser beneath Sakkara's Step Pyramid, and some of the mummies of royal women and nobility discovered at Deir el-Bahari on Luxor's West Bank.

Each was examined by Derry and his assistant Ahmed Batrawi, who eventually took over from Derry as anatomy professor in 1949 and continued to add a great deal to the understanding of mummification. And still the collection continued to grow, with the arrival of the remains of two pharaohs of the Pyramid Age, Djedkare and Sneferu, and, indeed, most of the ancient human remains discovered in Egypt since the First World War. Now known as the Derry-Batrawi Collection, this unique assemblage of ancient remains became the focus of research and conservation carried out by the Bioanthropology Foundation. It was this collection, with its great quantities of hair and wigs, that I was asked to examine in 1997.

Two days after my arrival in Cairo the Muslim month of Ramadan began, and with the students on holiday the faculty was fairly quiet. However, our work was punctuated each day by the loud call to prayer from the mosque next door – the same sound which had caused Smith to refer somewhat disrespectfully to Qasr el-Einy as 'The Palace of the Howling Dervish'.

The daily journey home often included a visit to the Cairo Museum, where I had finally managed to see some of the royal mummies for myself when eleven of those considered to be amongst the better-looking ones had been put back on display in 1994. Tuthmosis IV had made a particularly good impression with his relatively long, shoulder-length hair dressed with dark-colored resinous material, and I'd also spotted a couple of lice egg cases in the hair behind his clearly pierced ears – he was the first pharaoh to adopt this foreign fashion. He also had lovely long eyelashes and Smith, dismissing the pharaoh as 'effeminate', had also commented on his long fingernails. The majority of the other royal mummies were off-limits to the general public, but we were allowed to see them whilst we were working so nearby. As well as the warrior pharaohs Amenhotep II and Tuthmosis III and the great queen Ahmose-Nefertari, I finally got to meet Amenhotep III himself.

I have to admit that Amenhotep III has always been something of a hero of mine and I was then preparing to write a biography of him. Although he'd been dead for more than three thousand years I was overwhelmed to meet him face to face. His body had, however, suffered serious damage at the hands of the ancient plunderers. Presumably having been adorned with even more lavish quantities of gold than he had worn in life, the body may well then have been wrapped in gold foil 'winding sheets' of the type inscribed with Tiy's name and said to have been found at Amarna. These would certainly have been pillaged when his tomb was ransacked. After being salvaged and rewrapped in 1057 BC, according to the ink inscription on his restored linen wrappings, the king was reburied in one of the side chambers of KV.35. He was unwrapped again in 1905 by Smith, who found that the use of large quantities of resin had produced an almost statue-like mummy. Since the king's embalmers had clearly had the ability to create some of Egypt's most life-like mummies, especially those of his in-laws Yuya and Tuya, Amenhotep III's very different appearance was surely no accident. Because in life he'd declared himself a living god after ritually merging with the Aten sun disc, I wondered if his statue-like mummy was the result of being covered in huge amounts of shiny golden resins intended to symbolise his solar powers.

Whatever the motivation, Smith had long ago realised that this new form of mummification had begun at the start of the Amarna Period when things were being done differently. But whether or not the bodies of Amenhotep III's successors underwent a similar process 'is now impossible to say, because nothing but skeletons of some of them have come down to us'. And in the very next glass case lay the skeleton from tomb KV.55 which many Egyptologists believed to be that of his successor, Akhenaten himself. Tucked up beneath a linen covering dotted with dark splashes of resins, only his skull was visible, although missing nasal bones did suggest that the brain had been removed, and the discovery of canopic jars together with the body meant that the entrails had been taken out. In the original excavation report the remains are described as far more complete – the mummy of a 'smallish' person whose perfect teeth apparently crumbled to dust when touched. So too had most of the fine-textured linen wrappings, and when the cloth nearest the skin was removed 'it came off in a black mass, exposing the ribs'. The body had also been covered with sheets of gold, so perhaps, bearing in mind the use of golden resins for Amenhotep III and the gold sheets inscribed with Tiy's name, this body too had been imbued with the golden qualities of the Aten sun disc. If only we knew for sure who it was.

Looking at all those fascinating mummies in one room was an incredible privilege, as was being allowed to examine others on a daily basis at the Medical School, where it was my job to study their hair. All found in the 1920s and 1930s in the Deir el-Bahari region during excavations by Egyptologists from New York's Metropolitan Museum, the artefacts had been divided between the Cairo and New York museums, whilst the remains of the people themselves – including their hair – were generally sent north to Derry at Qasr el-Einy. After he'd examined them they became part of the Derry-Batrawi Collection, stored away for more than seventy years and effectively 'lost' until the Bioanthropology Foundation began their research and conservation programme.

My first subject was QA.39, a simple accession number which referred to Ashayet, one-time queen of Egypt and Great Royal Wife of King Montuhotep II. Having reunited Egypt around 2000 BC, he had been venerated down the centuries as a great warrior, and although his own body was destroyed in ancient times the remains of his chief queen had survived largely intact. Following the discovery of her tomb in 1921, her mummy was found inside a great limestone sarcophagus carved with scenes of daily life. Although the wrappings had already been ripped open by ancient robbers, photographs taken at the time reveal that the mummy itself was in an excellent state of preservation, with Ashayet endearingly described as 'a plump little person with bobbed hair done up in innumerable little plaits'. Derry himself reported that the body was in almost perfect condition when he examined it shortly after discovery, but this was certainly no longer the case – time had not been kind. Like the body from KV.55, Ashayet was now skeletal except for her left hand, her feet and part of her scalp and hair. After our conservator had cleaned her remains and the palaeopathologists had examined her bones, confirming that she had died in her early twenties, I began my work.

Her dark brown, quite fine mid-length hair had been carefully styled, and from the remaining plaits it was possible to obtain a good idea of how it would have looked when compared to the image on her sarcophagus. Each plait ended in a small open-centre curl secured with a drop of resinous fixing lotion, and although she hadn't used any false extensions her natural colour seemed to have been brightened with a henna-type preparation. A few lice eggs also remained in her hair.

Having branched out into the world of the ancient manicurist, I also examined her one remaining hand. It was delicate, and both the nails and the palm were stained orange-red, perhaps from the application of henna which is still used for decorative purposes of this kind in modern Egypt and the Middle East. The lack of wear and tear on the nails' surface bore evidence of a woman who clearly didn't do her own housework, and the likelihood of a privileged lifestyle was reinforced by their well-manicured appearance. Then I noticed that the thumbnail appeared to show traces of human teeth marks, and all of a sudden the Great Royal Wife became a human being, nervously nibbling her thumbnail during the grand state occasions in which she played a central role. Her feet were equally small and delicate, and, even allowing for some shrinkage during the mummification process, would only have been around a UK size 3.

After examining the queen I turned my attention to an entire family of bodies which the Metropolitan team had found at Deir el-Bahari, this time high in the hills overlooking the great female pharaoh Hatshepsut's splendid funerary temple. Inside an intact rock-cut tomb they had found a woman called Hatnefer and her husband Ramose, with some further women and children. But this was no ordinary family. Hatnefer and Ramose were the parents of the great state official Senmut, right-hand man, and some said lover, of Hatshepsut, and the man responsible for building both her funerary temple and tombs for himself and his family close by.

Intriguingly, the grandest coffin in Senmut's parents' tomb was made for his mother. Inside her gilded wooden coffin, beneath the golden mask, her mummy with its hundreds of hair extensions had been unwrapped and looked at *in situ* by those who had discovered it before being sent to Derry, who conducted his usual rigorous examination. Sixty years later, we decided to reconstruct Hatnefer's original hairstyle using the excavator's descriptions and original black and white photographs as our guide.

Presented with several bags full of hair, I began to sort through the curls and braids, discovering pieces of her original linen mummy wrappings and even one of her teeth. Her own short curls were heavily streaked with grey, and literally hundreds of thin, tapering plaits of dark brown human hair had been attached to create the top-heavy style found in art of the time. The plaits had originally been gathered into two sections at either side of the head, falling on to her chest in two rounded masses which the excavators believed had been wound around 'flat spiralled disks on the upper breast'. Yet when we X-rayed this part of the hair we found that no such discs had been used; instead, the ends had been kept in place by large quantities of resin fixative.

This distinctive style was associated with Hathor, the ancient Egyptian goddess of beauty also known as Lady of the Locks and Mistress of the Braid, and frequently shown wearing this exact coiffure. Given her additional status as Goddess of the West, believed to take the souls of the dead into her care within the Deir el-Bahari cliffs, the hairstyle also had funerary connotations. Hatnefer's extraordinary hairdo certainly seemed to be a post-mortem version of the style, since so many plaits attached to such fine sections of natural hair just couldn't have been worn in everyday life.

She would undoubtedly have presented an imposing figure, and, carefully prepared for burial in her finest jewellery, her fingernails stained a vibrant reddish shade, she appeared to have died between the ages of fifty-five and sixty-five. Although Derry thought her husband Ramose was of a similar age, our palaeopathologists felt he had been a much younger man, somewhere between twenty-five and thirty-five – the average life expectancy in ancient Egypt. But, much as I'd like to have imagined Hatnefer taking up with a toy boy, it seemed that she had simply lived longer than he had. Benefiting from her son Senmut's rise to power, as shown by her wealthy burial, she had been mummified in a superior way to that of her husband and other members of the family. This suggested that they had been exhumed and then laid to rest with the aged Hatnefer when she finally died.

Close to Hatnefer's tomb, the American archaeologists also found burials of people the family may well have known in life – contemporaries who had served at the court of Hatshepsut herself, including my own particular favourite, a man named Harmose. His coffin inscription revealed that he had worked as a singer, and alongside his body was his red lute, a chest containing his mummified entrails, a linen tunic and a pot of some sort of unguent. Although only his scalp seemed to have survived, Harmose's thick curly hair was neatly trimmed and fixed in place with a mixture which under the microscope appeared as a cracked coating – perhaps the contents of the jar buried with him. His unusually light brown to blond hair colour may also have been enhanced with some sort of yellow dye, perhaps a way to stress his connections with Hathor, the multi-faceted goddess who, as patron of musicians and daughter of the sun god, was herself known as the Golden One.

In addition to all these individuals I was even allowed to look at the remains of the two tiny foetuses from the tomb of Tutankhamen, which Carter had considered were the king's children by his wife Ankhesenamen. Although he'd wanted to know why they had been born prematurely (perhaps as a result of the family's in-breeding?), Derry had been unable to discover the reason. Then they had been 'lost' until 1978, when a team from Liverpool University located the older foetus. This they found to be 'damaged, particularly the skull which appears as though it has been squashed, in addition to Derry's post-mortem examination'. Nevertheless, their X-rays revealed that the baby girl had suffered from spina bifida, scoliosis and a shoulder deformity, and had she survived would have been quite severely disabled. With the second foetus rediscovered in 1992, I was able to look at what were believed to be the last in a long line of ancient royals, the flesh-and-blood relatives of Amenhotep III and Tiy, Akhenaten and Nefertiti, Tutankhamen and Ankhesenamen. I found the remains of the two tiny bodies lying in their separate boxes incredibly moving. Not having a scientific background, I've never been able to treat human remains with the correct amount of detachment, simply as artefacts or objects of study. Each one is an individual, prepared for burial by people who cared for them, and when you know their name or something about them it becomes doubly difficult.

My time at Qasr el-Einy gave me a real insight into what might be discovered, just by looking at their hair and nails, about people who had lived thousands of years ago. It had been possible to establish details of the lifestyles, habits, health and occupation of queens, priestesses, musicians and workers, most of them known by the names they had been given millennia ago.

I also did my first bit of television there for a Discovery series, appearing on the appropriately named *Post-Mortem* episode holding forth about Hatnefer's wonderful hairstyle. I hardly set the world alight with my screen presence, but I almost enjoyed it and found that, once I got the hang of it, it wasn't as difficult as I'd first thought.

Back home, I continued to write articles about mummification, ancient hair, cosmetics and tattoos, acting as a consultant and contributing chapters to one or two worthy tomes. I also wrote my first book, a small volume for the British Museum Press looking at the ways the ancient Egyptians had used perfume, not only as fragrance but also in medicine, magic and of course in mummification, where the ritual use of perfumes conveniently hid any hint of decay.

As a spin-off from my work at Qasr el-Einy I went out to Hierakonpolis in southern Egypt, the most important city in the country prior to the unification of north and south around 3100 BC. Excavations there had revealed a sizeable settlement, with large-scale pottery production and Egypt's earliest brewery. It was also the site of the country's first painted tomb and earliest-known temple, a large timber-framed structure dedicated to the falcon god Horus. Here, back in 1894, archaeologists had discovered a whole range of ritual artefacts including the famous Narmer Palette and a superb gold falcon head with eyes of black obsidian, both now in the Cairo Museum. Close by stood Egypt's oldest standing brick building, the enigmatic mudbrick enclosure thought to have been built by King Khasekhemwy around 2686 BC.

The site's continuing importance in later times was reflected by a series of rock-cut tombs built for New Kingdom dignitaries (c.1500–1100 BC). Yet in time-honoured fashion, the majority of the ancient population had been buried in holes in the sand where the hot, dry conditions had preserved much of their skin, hair and nails. So I was asked to examine material found in previous seasons and help recover that still being found during excavations at a workers' cemetery dating back to 3400 BC.

Here, amongst some of ancient Egypt's oldest mummified remains, was all kinds of hair. Most of it, like the vast majority of other ancient hair, was dark brown, although there were also a few red and even blond examples. The styles ranged from very short crops to mid-length waves and long ringlets for both sexes. The most amazing hairdo had belonged to a middle-aged woman, and we were able to reconstruct it from scattered fragments of her skull and hair recovered from her heavily plundered grave.

Clearly the result of many hours' work undertaken by someone other than the lady in question, her natural hair of slightly more than shoulder length had been transformed into an imposing crest-like coiffure using numerous hair extensions. Supplying the earliest evidence for the use of false hair anywhere in Egypt, the find became even more significant when we discovered that the woman's greying brown hair had been dyed, either just before her death or as a post-mortem treatment. The dye had coloured the brown parts auburn while turning the white hairs a bright orange, a characteristic of henna which I knew from personal experience.

The Egyptians in the nearby village told us that henna shrubs still grew at the site, and, kindly pointing out where the best leaves were to be found, allowed me to help myself. They also demonstrated the heavy circular stones they used to grind the leaves to a fine powder which they mixed with water to colour their own hair, skin and nails. Inspired, I carried out my own comparative tests using a range of modern hair samples of varying amounts of greyness supplied by members of our team. The results replicated the effects seen in the ancient samples.

The incredible kindness of the local people made my month at the site a tremendous experience, and when I swapped stories with the women using a combination of very basic Arabic and some rather inventive hand gestures, they usually asked about my pierced nose and reddish orange hair. One day while telling me about the types of jewellery and cosmetics they used, they insisted on making up my eyes by applying kohl in the traditional way – spitting on a short metal rod, dipping it in a small bottle of black powder and then pulling it horizontally between my closed eyelids. Then, with their characteristic generosity, they gave me the rod and bottle as a gift; I have kept them ever since.

Like many visitors, I have experienced much of this kind of hospitality in Egypt, and even have an adopted family in Qurna. I had first met them back in 1991 during one of my research visits when, as often happens, our taxi driver invited me to take tea with his family. The car left the road and headed up a hill honeycombed with ancient tombs, where we pulled up in front of a mudbrick house built right into the side of the Theban hills close to the tomb of Nakht, temple astronomer in the reign of Amenhotep III. What an incredible place to live!

Close by was the house where an excavator and collector named Yanni d'Athanasi had lived in the 1820s and 1830s, his furniture made from ancient coffins like that of his friend and neighbour, the Egyptologist John Gardner Wilkinson. Wilkinson's unusual tomb home contained all manner of fixtures and fittings, including a working library, and even had a garden at the front. As something of a commune of Egyptologists and artists developed in the nineteenth century, their numerous guests included the future British prime minister Benjamin Disraeli who turned up in 1831 on his Grand Tour. Apparently there were social evenings every Thursday, and one guest commented that 'never was the habitation of death witness to gayer scenes . . . and the odour of the mummies had long ago been dispelled'.

Many of the Qurnawi people had themselves lived in or beside the ancient tombs for a century or more, and the family I was visiting were no exception. Sitting with the children on the wooden bench by their front door we could look out at one of the best views in Egypt, the hill falling away before me and then flattening out before the ruins of the Ramesseum, the funerary temple of Ramses II, Shelley's Ozymandias. A little way beyond to the right, amidst the vivid green of the fields, stood the Colossi of Memnon, and even further round were the sands which covered the palace of Malkata. Sipping my sweet tea, I stared out into the distance where a pale haze hung over the river, hiding the temples of Karnak and Luxor on its banks.

This turned out to be the first of many visits. The family had six sons and five daughters, and although the boys spoke pretty good English, not to mention having a working knowledge of French, German, Italian and even some words of Japanese, picked up through working amongst Luxor's endless stream of tourists, the mother and daughters spoke only Arabic. This gave me the incentive to try to learn the language, through a combination of evening classes, tapes and the family's extremely patient, good-humoured coaching. As my visits to Egypt increased I spent more and more time with them, sitting talking, watching old black-and-white Arabic films, helping to make dinner, visiting the extended family in surrounding houses and, when the men were out, turning on the radio to practise our dancing. It's difficult to do justice to all that they've done for me over the years, but for some reason they have always treated me as one of their own, and I am proud to be able to call myself their daughter.

Their house was actually little different from the ancient houses of mudbrick: the walls were painted similarly bright colours, there were wooden benches and mats on the floor for sitting or sleeping, meals were eaten around a low table, and the chickens and donkey were never far away. There was no running water, so that having a shower involved locking yourself in with the chickens and dousing yourself in water which had been heated on the primus stove. Through a gap in one corner of the roof I could see the feet of the tourists walking past, although fortunately for them they never saw me.

Accompanying my parents and sister on their first visit to

Egypt, I gave a lecture about my work for the Egypt Exploration Society at the British Council in Cairo, which was reviewed in the *Cairo Times* under the headline 'Itchy the head that wears the crown' and accompanied by a wonderful cartoon of Akhenaten and Nefertiti checking their daughters for head lice. After my first book, *Oils and Perfumes of Ancient Egypt*, had been published I was approached to write a more general book on ancient Egyptian art and religion and then a third book, this time for children. Having established myself as a freelancer, I was also able to move back from Manchester to my beloved Yorkshire where, with the understanding of an ever-supportive bank manager, I bought the house of my gothic dreams beside a medieval graveyard overlooking the sea. I'd only been in the house a couple of weeks when I noticed what looked like a large, smooth stone protruding from the side of the hill by the gate. When I moved the surrounding soil a little I was certain I could see suture lines, the tell-tale marks of a skull. And after clearing away a little more soil, I discovered that it was human!

Human remains aren't something you find every day, and, although I appreciated this rather unorthodox house-warming gift, I decided to phone the police and report it. They turned up with bright yellow incident tape, but I assured them that there had been no foul play and that, from what I could see, the body was several hundred years old. Although my job description as an 'Egyptologist specialising in human remains' initially raised a few eyebrows, it was a great way to meet the local archaeologists who were told about the discovery and came along to decide what should be done. Given the body's precarious position they applied for Home Office permission to excavate, and the skeleton of a young woman estimated to be around five hundred years old now resides in storage in the local museum.

Briefly mentioning the unexpected discovery at a lecture I gave in London, I was contacted by the science editor of one of the daily broadsheets and asked if I'd like to contribute on anything of an archaeological natural that I found appealing. So I did, with updates on work in the Valley of the Kings, Tutankhamen's clothing, new research work into mummification and the body of what was supposed to be an ancient Egyptian princess but turned out to be someone quite different.

I also discovered that there was life beyond ancient Egypt when I was invited to look at some of the extraordinary mummies that had been produced in South America. Here was the world's longest continuous mummy-making culture, only brought to an end by the arrival of the Spanish in the sixteenth century. The Conquistadors had been amazed by mummies so life-like that they were regarded as living beings; indeed, the royal mummies were fed, clothed, consulted and carried aloft at state occasions.

In late 1998 I spent a month in the far south of Peru, studying mummies of the Chiribaya who eventually became part of the mighty Inca Empire. Situated between the windswept desert and the Pacific Ocean, the region is stunningly beautiful, and one of the most archaeologically rich sites in the world. It is home to literally thousands of mummies swathed in superb textiles, and, given the prevalence of grave robbing, the Bioanthropology Foundation had stepped in to help conserve and study these ancient human remains.

I carried out my examinations at their combined storage and study centre, surrounded by hundreds of neatly shelved crates and boxes of heads, torsos and entire bodies. Like most ancient South American cultures, the Chiribaya buried their dead with their knees drawn up, wrapped in many layers of decorated textiles to form a bundle. A few were even provided with gold death masks, although the great majority wore a variety of hats, caps, headbands and hairstyles. The extensive practice of skull deformation to mark out elite members of society also meant that, when their pointed hats were removed, the head beneath was often the same shape.

Such elongated heads were often enhanced with a fabulous range of hairstyles, although, as was also the case in Egypt, it was generally the men who sported the most elaborate styles. In many cases their hair was long – the Spanish conquerors had dragged away the last Inca king by his long hair – and braided into a multitude of thin plaits all over the head, a feature found in the textile designs of the Chiribaya and many other South American cultures and apparently connected to the serpent-like hair of the priestly shamans. Separate sections of hair left unplaited around the nape of the neck were then woven in the same way as textiles, forming a V-shaped braid down the back and neatly finished off with various coloured wools, which quite possibly contained information about the wearer. So intricate were some of these styles that they had to be the work of specialists. Women too sometimes grew their hair quite long, and enhanced their appearance with a form of red colourant on the cheeks. Both sexes also used more permanent forms of skin adornment, with beautiful tattoos of birds, frogs and spirals repeating the images featured in the textiles they wore.

Lacking any form of written script, the ancient South Americans used complex motifs on their textiles and forms of personal adornment in order to record information. The Spanish observed that the men wore distinguishing insignia on their heads, and the coded messages conveyed by people's dress were so important that it was a capital offence to wear attire inappropriate to one's social position. Studying their hair, headgear, cosmetics and tattoos was as close as one could get to being able to read about these people in their own words.

The dry climate had preserved just about everything, as had the frozen conditions in the high Andes, where the Inca regularly left their most beautiful young people, often drugged and accompanied by superb textiles and gifts of silver and gold, to freeze to death as gifts for the gods. Up to a hundred of their naturally mummified bodies had been discovered and DNA analysis had uncovered a family link between the mummies and the villagers who still lived at the foot of the mountains. I found it amazing that, whilst I had no idea what members of my own family looked like a mere century ago, these people could actually look into the faces of relatives from some thirty generations back.

My fascination with the mummified dead soon completely took over from my original narrower interest in hair and nails. The more I looked, the more there was to find out. My horizons expanded by my first trip to South America, I embarked on a series of extraordinary jobs working on mummies right across the world.

It all began when I was approached by a television company which was making a programme about the spread of mummification. The producer, who had a PhD in anthropology from Cambridge, was writing a book on mummification and wanted the Egyptian angle. As the programme came together we ended up filming in Egypt and tracing funerary practices across North Africa as far west as Morocco. We then went out into the Atlantic, to the Canary Islands. This wasn't the first place I'd have looked myself until I found out that the islands' ancient Guanche population, with their links to nearby North Africa, had not only built pyramids but mummified their dead.

We were able to confirm this when we were allowed to re-examine an anonymous Guanche mummy in Cambridge, first examined in 1968 by palaeopathologist Don Brothwell, now a professor at York University. He had discovered that the torso had been packed with filling inserted Egyptian-style through an incision in the abdomen. So we asked Don, one of the world's leading experts in ancient bodies, to return and help us re-investigate the mummy using state-of-the art computerised tomography (CT) equipment at Cambridge's Addenbrooke's Hospital. This process revealed massive facial injuries, which were presumably the cause of death. And to our surprise, carbon dating revealed that the mummy was only 650 years old, making it one of the very last links to an immemorial tradition only lost when the Spanish imposed their own beliefs on the native population, just as they had done in South America.

Don and I continued to keep in touch, and when the programme aired I also got an email from archaeological chemist Stephen Buckley. Completing a PhD on the materials used in Egyptian mummification, he wanted to know about the kinds of materials the Guanche had used to preserve their dead. And as we too began to correspond, the three of us eventually began to look at mummification practices throughout the ancient world.

My trips to Egypt continued, and as I began my book about Amenhotep III I also did some filming for a Channel 4 three-part series looking at the lives of the pharaohs and their people. At Giza's Human Remains Centre Dr Azza Sarry el-Din, one of Egypt's leading authorities on human remains, showed us what was left of those who had actually built the pyramids. The discovery of their town and cemetery in the early 1980s revealed that they had been not slaves, whatever Hollywood liked to think, but a core workforce whose numbers were regularly swelled by farmers, temporarily redeployed in massive job creation schemes during the three months every year when their fields were submerged by the Nile flood.

Lifting out bone after bone from the boxes on the shelves around her, the softly spoken Dr Azza began to bring the ancient workforce to life. The compressed vertebrae of those who had actually done the heavy labour, side-by-side with the more normal vertebrae of those of who had simply stood about as overseers, offered graphic evidence of the incredible effort which had gone into building these huge monuments. As more bones appeared on the table, a properly set, well-healed fracture on an ancient forearm showed that medical facilities had been on hand for the workforce. Although theirs was by no means a life of beer and skittles, they were at least provided with a degree of care. The most moving remains were those of a female dwarf who had died in childbirth, the matchstick-like bones of her baby showing that it had been of normal dimensions – with tragic results.

One of the programmes in the series looked at the Amarna royal family. Since much of the filming was done at Amarna I was able to spend time around the city, in its palaces and temples and up at one of the great boundary stelae, with its incredible views back across the plain and its criss-crossed roads where the city had once stood. Visiting the tombs of the officials, on this occasion I saw for the first time the Southern Tombs, including the largest of all, the extraordinary tomb of Ay and Ty with its forest of columns. Although Ay held several titles – Fan Bearer on the King's Right Hand, Master of the Royal Horses, Royal Scribe, and God's Father – none of these was really amongst the top jobs, and it has been suggested that the massive size of his tomb must have been due to some other connection to the royal family.

Although Ay is thought by many to have been Queen Tiy's brother, the only definite link with the royals can be found in the titles of his wife Ty, named as 'Great Nurse Who Nourished the Goddess', meaning Nefertiti. So this woman on the wall in front of me, with her superbly carved, long, rippling wig and finely pleated robes, had been instrumental in Nefertiti's childhood. This was my closest link so far with the elusive queen.

Ay's tomb inscriptions made fascinating reading, and after a bit more self-glorification ('My name has penetrated the palace because of my usefulness to the king') he said, 'I see the king's beauty when he appears in his palace.' This reference to the king's beauty, not the queen's, offers a clear contradiction of the modern world's long-standing belief in some sort of 'Beauty and the Beast' scenario in which Akhenaten's supposedly grotesque physical appearance is simplistically contrasted with the beauty of Nefertiti. Demonstrating his support for the Aten cult with a very long version of the Hymn to the Aten, Ay then paid extravagant honours to the royal couple, asking to be allowed to 'kiss the pure ground' before their feet. Then he prayed that the Aten bless the king and 'the Great Royal Wife, his beloved, abounding in her perfection, she who sends the Aten to rest with a sweet voice, and her perfect hands bearing two sistrums, the Mistress of the Two Lands, Neferneferuaten Nefertiti, living for ever and ever. May she be by the side of Akhenaten for ever and ever', inscriptions which revealed more about Nefertiti than any I'd seen before.

As in one of the Northern Tombs, Nefertiti wore the elaborate 'atef' crown of a king, appearing at the Window of Appearances side by side with Akhenaten whilst their youngest daughter touched Nefertiti's face in the way young children do when they want their mother's undivided attention. To the great cheers of the crowd, Nefertiti and Akhenaten rewarded Ay and Ty, making them 'people of gold' as they threw down the 'gold of honour' in the form of eighteen chunky gold necklaces. The two faithful courtiers were also showered with a hail of cups, goblets, jewelled collars, bead necklaces, signet rings, ornamental headbands and items of clothing. Some of the garments looked like tie-on sleeves or maybe even leggings of the sort the Leiden research team in the Netherlands had found amongst Tutankhamen's wardrobe – and perfect for those chilly nights in the desert. And among the lavish gifts piling up at their feet a pair of riding gloves, the preserve of royalty, were so unusual that Ay immediately put them on, and was seen holding out his hands for his colleagues to gather round and admire.

The tomb even featured scenes of palace life, with menservants sweeping the floors and preparing food whilst women were depicted eating, singing, and playing harps and lutes next door to what appeared to be a music room. Best of all, they were shown doing each other's hair; the unusual long curly style, coupled with some of their layered robes, suggested that some of these women were Syrians, presumably some of the foreign women who lived at the royal court. Packed with detail, this really was a fabulous tomb.

Then, for a complete change of mood, we spent a day out at

the remote and lonely burial place of Akhenaten and members of his family. As we made our way slowly up the boulder-strewn valley the wind suddenly picked up from nowhere, pelting the sides of the jeep with sand, and I had a distinct feeling of unease. Waiting for the generator to spark into life and bring some light to the tomb, my first impressions were of a very eerie place indeed.

Beyond a huge doorway, a superbly cut entrance corridor led right down into the depths, where my pocket flashlight made little impression as I stepped cautiously forward and headed slowly down towards the burial chamber. But even when the electric lights did finally come on, the atmosphere hardly seemed to change. Standing beside the plinth where the king's mummy had once lain, surrounded by what was left of the crumbling wall surface, it was difficult not to feel incredibly sad. Moving on into the suite of rooms containing funeral scenes of the dead princess Meketaten, mourned by a distraught Akhenaten and Nefertiti and three of her sisters, I felt deeply moved.

A few months later I was given the opportunity for more research into the ancient dead, this time nothing to do with Egypt. Following a tour around Peru, I hopped on to a small plane and flew south to Tacna where a car took me across the border into Chile, home to the world's oldest mummies. During the next few weeks I saw for myself some of the bodies that had been mummified an astonishing eight millennia ago – some three thousand years before the Egyptians had begun to mummify their dead.

Discovered on the coastal edge of the Atacama Desert, they had been created by small fishing communities of the Chinchorro culture. After the dead were defleshed, the bodies were dried and then reassembled; their hair was reattached as a wig, and their faces covered in a painted clay mask. Some showed signs of repainting, and since there were also signs of damage to the feet area the mummies may have stood upright and been treated as objects of veneration before their final burial in family groups.

Because the earliest mummies were those of children and foetuses, it was possible that Chinchorro women had been the first practitioners of mummification as a means of keeping their dead offspring with them. Certainly a condition known as auditory exostosis visible in male skulls indicated that the men had spent most of their time diving for food at sea, so the women who processed and prepared the daily catch of seals as well as fish may well have used the anatomical knowledge they gained from preparing sea mammals to prepare their own dead – an intriguing and highly persuasive theory.

In 2001 I was invited on what turned out to be the funniest trip to Egypt I've ever had. Ex-Python Terry Jones was going to front a history programme, and I was asked to take him on a tour through ancient and modern Egypt. The finished show also featured my Egyptian family, who soon became local celebrities themselves. Not surprisingly, the whole thing became quite surreal at times.

Within a few months I was back in Egypt with very different companions – two ex-FBI detectives. They had been sent out by the Discovery Channel to investigate whether there was any evidence to support the theory that Tutankhamen could have been murdered, and they needed an Egyptologist to provide some background information as they tried to build up criminal profiles of people who might have done the deed. Once again, television allowed me to visit places, see things and have experiences that would not otherwise have come my way. We spent a whole day filming in Tutankhamen's tomb, this time down in the actual burial chamber which is usually off-limits. Studying at point-blank range the king's gold coffin containing his body, and looking inside the small side room where the foetuses had been found, enabled me to study in detail parts of the tomb I'd never seen.

On another trip, this time filming at Karnak Temple, we were allowed to go right to the top of the first pylon from which there were extensive views across the temple and beyond. It had been off-limits for years since a tourist had fallen to his death, and the way up consisted of a very narrow, very long, pitch-black passage festooned with hundreds of drowsy bats sheltering from the daylight. But it proved to be well worth the hike when I looked right over the river to the West Bank, and then back the other way to where Akhenaten and Nefertiti had built their extraordinary Aten temples in Karnak's eastern quarter. I was even allowed into the long, low store rooms where the remains of these temples had ended up – the thousands and thousands of individual blocks carved with the Aten, the king and Nefertiti, whose figure cropped up time and time again.

Back home I had also begun to work with Stephen Buckley, now at York University, who was continuing his analytical research into mummification. Although it had long been assumed that everything about this complicated process was now fully understood, his work had started to show this was simply not so, and he had the scientific evidence to prove it.

At the end of 2001 we were both invited to Rome to look at two bodies which had just been discovered near the heart of the city. After uncovering a vaulted stone tomb close to the Appian Way, Italian archaeologists had found two stone sarcophagi containing the bodies of a woman and her son. Although this in itself was not particularly out of the ordinary, the fact that the son appeared to have been mummified certainly was. The burials dated from the first century AD and had obviously been influenced by Egyptian funerary traditions, for the woman had been buried in a carefully styled wig covered with a fine gold hair net. The hair had survived in amazing condition, and both bodies were swathed in floral garlands so huge that they were virtually covered. While I examined the wig and hair net, Stephen studied the bodies and gave advice on storage and conservation.

A couple of months later we received a call from the TV producer who had been writing a book on mummification: it had led him to a fascinating new discovery when a reader from Australia had written to say how much she'd enjoyed the book, although she could find no mention of the mummies in Yemen. He'd never heard of them, and when he phoned me I wasn't much help, as I hadn't either. In fact no one seemed to know anything about Yemeni mummies, and since this appeared to be an entire mummy-making culture unknown to the outside world we felt we needed to find out more. With the support of the Yemeni Government, Sanaa University and National Geographic I was asked to put a team together, and so, as the Anglo-Yemeni Mummy Research Project, Don, Stephen and I flew out to quite an adventure.

Previously the only Yemenis I had known about were Sheffield boxer Prince Nasim and the legendary Queen of Sheba. As Yemen's most famous figure she appears in the Bible, the Quran, the Ethiopian Orthodox Kebra Nagast and the Jewish scriptures. She also looms large in the country's colourful history as Queen Bilqis, who lived some time in the tenth century BC. I was now amazed to learn that a third famous Yemeni was also a woman – one who had ruled the country for an astonishing seventy-one years until her death aged ninety-two in AD 1138. This was Queen Arwa, patron of the arts and a great builder of aqueducts, schools and mosques, who had been buried in the mosque she had built in her capital, Jibla. Although her tomb had been vandalised in 1995 by fundamentalists unhappy with the historical reality of a woman in power, even so long ago, the vast majority of Yemenis still hold Arwa in great affection and the name remains a popular one.

Shortly after our arrival we met several hundred Yemenis all at once when we were invited to give a set of impromptu lectures to the university's archaeology students. Breaking the ice by apologising for not speaking better Arabic, I described what we'd be doing and what we wanted to find out from the mummies housed in their department's museum. Placed on their sides in the foetal position, the mummies' heads popped out of the top of the carefully stitched animal hides they were wrapped in. Some had also been dressed in leather clothing, and one of the mummies still bore a small label telling us he had been a priest. He had been buried with his ceremonial implements, and X-rays revealed that he was also wearing a rather fetching silver toe ring. Don took one of the mummies to the local hospital for CT-scanning, and we were also allowed to take samples for analysis back in the lab at York.

Then, with government permission, we travelled around this stunningly beautiful country to visit many of the major mummy sites and excavate some of the burial caves and ledges where the mummies had originally been placed. These were invariably hundreds of feet up in the most inaccessible cliffs, so we were fortunate to have with us two professional climbers trained in archaeological rescue. Their expertise proved invaluable, as did that of our minder, the grandson of Yemen's last Imam, whose influence kept us much safer than we would otherwise have been. Relations between the government and some of the more traditional communities have long been volatile, and there were a few sticky moments involving tribal feuding, a jail-break and a couple of murders in one remote site. Unsurprisingly, I suppose, when all the males over the age of about twelve carry the traditional curved knife and often a Kalashnikov as well, whilst in public the vast majority of women are veiled from head to toe and are seen but not heard.

As a Western woman with bright red hair I stood out even more than I usually do, but the Yemenis are tremendous people and made us all feel very welcome. When I was invited into their homes I experienced the same warmth and genuine friendliness I found amongst Egyptians, and during our stay we found evidence for trade links with ancient Egypt. The Yemenis mummified their dead as early as 1200 BC using preservative materials which seem also to have been in great demand by the Egyptians across the Red Sea, where they were additionally used for funerary and temple rituals and to make perfumes.

Although a return visit to Sanaa has been temporarily postponed by the world political situation, the murder of several foreign scientists and a belief that extremists still hide out in some of Yemen's remoter regions, our research on their mummies has continued in the rather more secure environment of York University. And as Don, Stephen and I began to compare their mummification practices with those of Egypt and beyond, we were also given the chance to examine an Egyptian mummy stored closer to home in Hull Museum.

An anonymous, undated individual of unknown sex and origin whom no one seemed to know very much about, it had obviously suffered when much of Hull was flattened by bombs during the Second World War. The museum itself had been destroyed, along with any details about the mummy's origins, but the mummy itself had survived, although its relocation in a riverside warehouse had done little for its long-term well-being. When new museum premises finally became available, the mummy was in such poor condition that its place was taken by one on loan from the British Museum whilst it remained in storage. Something had to be done, and a specialist conservator was brought in.

As regards its provenance and possible identity, the museum staff gave me some very useful leads. Old newspaper cuttings revealed that the mummy had originally come to Hull from Whitby, and in 1903 the small museum there had written to the British Museum for advice on a new acquisition which they described as 'the mummy of an Egyptian princess'. But when the museum was forced to sell off parts of its collection in 1935 the mummy was sent down the coast to Hull, where it took centre stage amongst Egyptian antiquities obtained from Petrie's excavations, which had been partly funded by Hull Museum. In the wake of the discovery of Tutankhamen's tomb, Hull's curator capitalised on the phenomenal interest in all things Egyptian by asking the Hull branch of the British Medical Association to X-ray his newly acquired mummy. Photographs of this unusual event were published in the local press.

Although the X-rays themselves had been lost in the wartime

bombing, I was able to obtain a copy of the photograph that had appeared in the newspapers. When the image was blown up, the shape of the pelvis suggested that the body could indeed be female, something which could be verified using the 3-d images provided by CT scanning. Although the mummy's fragile condition meant that we couldn't transport it to a hospital in the usual manner, Lister Healthcare very generously provided us with a portable CT scanner and three of their highly skilled staff, which meant we could examine the mummy with the minimum disturbance.

After slowly manoeuvring our mummy into position inside the scanner, we gathered round the screen to view the images as they appeared. There were the wide pelvis, gracile bone structure and delicate brow ridge that were all regarded as feminine traits. But what was that? Our supposed 'princess' had a penis! So much for his 'female characteristics', and a real lesson in treating 'typical' features with caution!

But who was he? Although all inscriptions from the coffin had been lost during the mummy's years of storage in damp conditions, the coffin's shape and style suggested a date between about 500 and 300 BC. The old press photograph showed traces of its original inscription around the leg area, and this was enlarged and enhanced and sent to coffin expert Dr John Taylor at the British Museum. Although the text was damaged in the area that stated the mummy's name, it turned out that he was the son of a priest and priestess of the fertility god Min who worked in the god's cult temple at Akhmim, just north of Luxor. And their unnamed son – our mummy – had followed in his parents' footsteps, working as a priest of Min and responsible for dressing and adorning the god's cult statue. And all of a sudden this anonymous, linen-wrapped mummy became a living, breathing individual, a graceful man who had once wafted round Akhmim Temple carrying his coloured scarves and perfume bottles, now at last able to reclaim his remains from the clutches of the fictitious Egyptian princess.

As more of ancient Egypt began to appear in my home county, I was also invited to Harrogate to look at the local museum's collection of Egyptian antiquities. The curators, with the help of enthusiastic volunteers, had begun to catalogue the hundreds of objects they had in storage. My role was to confirm the collection's authenticity and, as their consultant Egyptologist, give advice on their forthcoming exhibition, *Land of the Pharaohs*. Very little was known about the objects' background, most having originally been bought at auction by the Kent family for display in their home, a sturdy old farmhouse with stone-flagged floors, tallow candles and a large stone fireplace – typical of a traditional farm interior in every way except for the Egyptian mummy case and the thousands of ancient artefacts displayed in the upstairs rooms.

When the last direct member of the Kent family left these antiquities to Harrogate corporation, almost everything except the mummy case was placed into storage, along with artefacts donated by a local goldsmith, James Ogden. In the early 1920s Ogden had begun to correspond with two leading archaeologists – Leonard Woolley, just back from his excavations at Amarna, and Howard Carter, who had recently discovered Tutankhamen's tomb. Looking for specialists, Carter invited Ogden to work on samples of gold from the tomb, and while he examined part of Tutankhamen's treasures in his Yorkshire workshop Carter kept him informed of what was happening in the Valley of the Kings, including plans to examine the pharaoh's mummy. Ogden, a keen collector of ancient jewellery, gave much of his collection to Harrogate in 1930.

Despite such an illustrious pedigree, the combined Kent and Ogden collections had remained in storage due to lack of space. As they had started to come to light during the staff's cataloguing process, crate after crate had begun to reveal the most wonderful artefacts which hadn't seen the light of day for years. There was even a mask of the jackal god Anubis, most likely last worn by a priest during the highly secretive mummification rituals and unique. The collection also contained objects naming some of Egypt's greatest pharaohs – Tuthmosis III, Hatshepsut and the great Amenhotep III. One of Amenhotep's large scarab seals named his Great Royal Wife Tiy and revealed that the king had shot 102 wild lions 'with his own arrows', and there was a superb limestone relief fragment of the king celebrating one of his jubilees. Yet nothing prepared me for the biggest discoveries of all, a whole range of carved reliefs and statue fragments inscribed with the names of Amarna royalty.

Lifting up a piece of mottled red and black granite, I tilted it around under the light until the name 'Neferneferuaten Nefertiti' almost jumped out and grabbed me! Never in my wildest dreams had I ever imagined I'd find Nefertiti in the depths of a store room in North Yorkshire, but there she was. A second fragment in glowing white alabaster again carried her name, whilst a larger piece of limestone preserved her name alongside Akhenaten's, whose sandal-clad foot appeared in the corner. Another small chunk of alabaster depicted two gracefully rendered hands offering small pots of incense to the Aten's rays, whilst a section of red quartzite revealed the well-manicured fingernails of a royal right hand supporting the base of a wide offering tray, perhaps from one of the many statues of the royal couple which had once filled the central open-air court of the Great Aten Temple. There was even an image of one of their young daughters vigorously shaking her sistrum rattle for the Aten, who was named on piece after piece of limestone, alabaster, sandstone, quartzite and granite – all fragments of the vast temples and palaces which had once dominated the royal city of Amarna.

Needing to find out more we consulted the Kents' handwritten catalogue, and there on page 54, in neat, careful handwriting, we found them: complete entries for no fewer than twelve items 'from Tell-el-Amarna, Egypt, XVIII dynasty, Flinders Petrie Excavations'. This was clear proof that these completely unknown pieces relating to ancient Egypt's most popular yet controversial period had indeed come from the first excavations at the site, carried out by Petrie and Carter themselves. There was even an old black-and-white photograph of all the Kent Amarna pieces proudly displayed together.

I immediately emailed the news to my friend and colleague Earl Ertman in Ohio. He is one of the world's leading authorities on Amarna art, and I'd first met him in 1995 at the International Congress of Egyptologists, where I was presenting a paper on the wig fragment found in Tutankhamen's tomb and he a paper entitled 'Tut-Tut: Newly Identified Images of the Boy-king'. Since he was a fellow Egyptologist unafraid to admit to having a sense of humour we got on like a house on fire and kept in touch, working on joint projects including the use of jewellery during the Amarna Period.

As a seasoned archaeologist who had excavated in the Valley of the Kings for many years, Earl had even worked in the contro-versial tomb KV.55, burial site of Queen Tiy and, some believed, Akhenaten. Here he had discovered something missed by earlier archaeologists: a small piece of limestone on which had been drawn a plan of the tomb. As we discussed the Amarna material, I told Earl more and more about my attempts to gain access to the side chamber in the Valley of the Kings and see the three mummies for myself. He gave me great encouragement, pointing out that I was properly qualified, had excavation experience in Egypt and Yemen, was part of York University's Mummy Team, and was consultant Egyptologist to several museums. I was therefore 'respectable' – at least in terms of ticking all the right official boxes.

Soon afterwards, in 2002, I was invited to work in the Valley of the Kings itself, in the highest and apparently oldest royal tomb in the valley, the mysterious KV.39. Its spectacular location close to the Peak of Meretseger, the great serpent goddess known as She Who Loves Silence, had first been discovered in 1899 by Victor Loret, the year after he discovered the tomb of Amen-hotep II with the three mummies in the side chamber. Although it had been cleared by two local men looking for loot, Arthur

Weigall was intrigued by KV.39 and, despite finding it 'entirely ruinous' on his visit in 1908, believed its position corresponded perfectly with that given for the tomb of Amenhotep I in the reports of the ancient tomb inspectors. But Carter, who had fallen out with Weigall, believed he had found Amenhotep I's tomb at the other end of the region. Matters were not helped by the fact that these early royal tombs were never decorated, and so, with no name conveniently provided on the walls, the question could only be resolved by sifting through the immense piles of debris.

This was something I was very much looking forward to contributing to. I had first been approached to join the team working at the tomb some ten years earlier, to examine increasing numbers of hair fragments which were being found during the clearance of the tomb's passages and chambers. But I was then still trying to complete my PhD thesis, and there was no way I could find the money for a season's self-funded work in Egypt. So this was my second chance to look at the material, as one of a specialist team that included a surveyor, a geologist, a botanist and my old friend Stephen Buckley, who had been out there on several previous seasons in his capacity as an archaeological chemist.

Just as Stephen had told me, I found there was far more than hair to examine. Among the artefacts were mummified remains, linen wrappings and coffin fragments, not to mention fragments of gold and a pharaoh's large gold ring he'd analysed and conserved. It was also his opinion that there was more still inside the tomb, whose main burial chamber had a natural geological fault in the form of a perfect cross – so X really did mark the spot, whatever it said in Indiana Jones films. And, perhaps unsurprisingly since the tomb was so close to the home of the great serpent goddess high on the mountain peak above us, there were snakes living there. One of the workmen had been bitten during a previous season and needed immediate hospital treatment, and although I like snakes I took care nevertheless.

Climbing up to the tomb high in the Theban hills, I looked back the way I'd come to enjoy the splendid views down into the Valley of the Kings. Then, peering over the edge of the cliff not far from the tomb entrance, I could see right down to Deir el-Bahari thousands of feet below, and beyond to just about everything on the West Bank and the Nile itself. Midway between the land of the living and the Land of the Dead – what a fabulous place to be buried!

Donning a hard hat in case of rock falls, I made my way cautiously down the steep bank of loose chippings leading to the tomb entrance where the team's expert geologist was waiting to take me on a guided tour of the huge, labyrinthine structure. Soon we were slithering down the long, long passageways cut deep into the rock to reach the tomb's multiple burial chambers. Much of the tomb was still choked with tons of stone chippings and all kinds of intriguing debris, repeatedly churned up by a combination of tomb robbery, early excavations and catastrophic flash floods, when the tomb fills with water and everything is thrown around as in a giant cement mixer.

After looking at the new finds being made by the team, including yet more mummy wrappings, a piece of gold coffin and a coin of Ptolemy III, minted 1200 years after the tomb was built and evidence, perhaps, of early tourists visiting the area, I turned my attention to the things which had been found during previous seasons. All were stored in the official store rooms next door to Carter's house on the road which leads to the Valley of the Kings, in an area known as Elwat el-Diban or 'Mound of Flies'. Despite its lively insect population, the store room had a fairly level table and benches and we did have the use of a microscope. Alongside our chemist and botanist I began to go through the finds, beginning with the hair. There were seven separate fragments of different hair types recovered from the various parts of the tomb, and despite the chaotic state of the tomb's interior it was my job to try to work out exactly what each fragment had originally been.

The first clump of dark brown hair had been found with numerous coffin fragments and linen wrappings at the tomb entrance, presumably where the tomb's original occupants had been dragged outside into the light to be stripped of any valuables. The rest of the samples came from inside the tomb. Both auburn and dark blond hair were recovered from the south passage leading down to the lower burial chamber, and since the auburn piece was still attached to a fragment of skull this was obviously the individual's own hair. Yet the difference in colour and texture between the two samples suggested that they were not from the same person. All these remaining samples seemed to have been styled in some way, mainly plaited in a fashion which had been especially popular between about 1700 and 1500 BC.

Part of one wig had been found at the entrance to the Lower Burial Chamber, whilst intricately worked portions of at least two further wigs came from the main Burial Chamber itself. Although people had often been buried with a single wig or, very occasionally, with two, the only burials I knew to have contained more were the caches of royal mummies found over the hill at Deir el-Bahari in 1881, and the mass burial of clergy close by that had been discovered in 1891. So from a few scruffy-looking bits of hair we could certainly say we were looking at a high-status, possibly royal tomb, which may also have been employed as the final resting place for one or more royal women from the beginning of the New Kingdom, about 1600–1500 BC.

Previous long-term work at the tomb had shown that here were the remains of at least nine bodies, and although the majority were skeletal as a result of the regular water damage from flash floods, the few which had remained out of the water had miraculously retained their skin, hair and the substances used to embalm them. And because these materials changed over time, they gave some idea of when the bodies had been placed in the tomb.

The mummified remains had all been found in the main burial

chamber, and included a well-preserved child's hand as well as a female skull which still retained the skin on the lower half of the face and neck area together with parts of the original linen wrappings. The eye sockets were filled with thick resinous packing material similar to that which Smith had described on royal mummies including that of Amenhotep I's father. The upper teeth also appeared to project well beyond the lower incisors on both this skull and a second found nearby, a feature known as maxillary prognathism or, more familiarly, as buck teeth. Smith had said that 'the prominence of the upper teeth . . . may possibly be a family trait' which he had found in some of the leading members of the early 18th dynasty royal house, including Ahmose-Nefertari, Amenhotep I's formidable mother and co-regent, as well as his father, King Ahmose.

The same high status was reflected in the quality of the embalming materials studied by Stephen. In cases where the bodies themselves had long ago been ripped to pieces the thick resin coating used to mummify them had kept the original shape of parts of the arms, legs, vertebrae and entrails. The resins also gave the remains the appearance of having been burnt, even when this wasn't the case.

Stephen and I also wanted to look at the textiles and mummy wrappings – just as Carter had noted in his clearance of Tutankhamen's tomb, textiles made up the largest category of finds from KV.39. It was no exaggeration to say that the tomb had been almost knee-deep in mummy wrappings. There were also more than a hundred fragments of wooden coffins, and it was obvious that the tomb had been reused for many more than the original mummies buried there. Talking it through with my colleague at Leiden's Textile Research Centre, who had plenty of experience with this material, it was clear that there were pieces of wrapping here similar to those used to wrap 21st dynasty priests of the eleventh century BC – the men who had also been responsible for rewrapping many of the royal mummies down in the Valley. So what was going on?

Everything we'd seen so far supported the idea that KV.39 had originally been built as a royal tomb for Amenhotep I and some of his female relatives, but had then been used again several centuries later as one of the temporary storage places for some of the royal mummies brought up from the Valley after their original tombs had been robbed. After restoration, the re-wrapped royals were reburied elsewhere, either in the Valley in the tomb of Amenhotep II, KV.35, or over the hill at Deir el-Bahari in the caches of both royal and priestly mummies. With our tomb located midway between these two places, it would have been the perfect place for the priests and officials to bring the salvaged bodies and fit them out for reburial – when, presumably, more precise clues may have been left behind. It was time to open up more boxes.

On the basis of similar examples found at various sites including Tutankhamen's tomb and in houses at Amarna, we suggested that the curious lengths of twisted linen found in the main burial chamber were ancient lamp wicks – vital in the tomb's construction, during the arrangement of the burial equipment and, indeed, during its robbery. Evidence for some of the high-status burial equipment originally placed in the main burial chamber included well-carved wooden fittings familiar from the storage chests discovered in Tutankhamen's tomb. There was also a large wooden lion's foot, once part of a chair, a bed or even a lion-headed funerary bier of the kind known from other burials in the valley such as those of Yuya and Tuya, their daughter Tiy in KV.55, or Tut again. Although the gold had long ago been scraped off just about everything, large pieces of gold leaf had been discovered, along with a piece of gilded coffin decorated with coloured stripes, and other fragments still with one or two superbly carved hieroglyphs painted yellow on a black background. There were also inlaid eyes of ivory and obsidian, and a whole range of coloured beads and semi-precious stones including blue- and green-glazed faience, a large agate drop, carnelian and lapis lazuli, one or two carved with a series of parallel ridges exactly like those used on royal coffins and jewellery.

All these precious items had been discovered around the tomb entrance where the bodies would have been dragged up into the daylight to be stripped of their wealth, something which may also have been the case with the most spectacular find of all, a large gold ring inscribed with the name 'Menkheperre'. Whilst this is the throne name of Tuthmosis III, and may well have come from his mummy during its rewrapping in KV.39 prior to reburial just over the hill in the nearby royal cache at Deir el-Bahari, Menkheperre was also the name of a 21st dynasty high priest whose family were also buried in the Deir el-Bahari tomb together with the spectacular collection of priestly wigs in the Cairo Museum.

The only inscriptions were found on limestone fragments listing priestly titles, and a series of small sandstone dockets with faint traces of royal cartouches. Three appeared to name Amenhotep I, another was inscribed 'Tuthmosis I' and two more 'Amenhotep II'. Were these labels made by the priests to keep track of whose tomb the mummies had come from or were going to? Who knows.

Yet the most exciting piece of inscribed material turned up when I re-examined a rather unattractive-looking lump of mud found in 1993 at the tomb entrance. Turning it slowly around in the light, I slowly began to make out the original seal impression and wondered if this had once been part of the sealed-up entrance to the tomb. I began to see the head of an ibex or gazelle-like creature standing on its hind legs, its front legs resting in branches of foliage. The image of the gazelle, closely associated with the goddess Hathor, was used on the crowns and diadems of royal women who didn't enjoy the exalted status of Great Royal Wife. Indeed, Amenhotep I's own mother, Queen Ahmose-Nefertari, had worn a gazelle crown when still a young woman.

Yet when I came to check out this very specific rearing gazelle and tree motif, I could only find a few examples, all of them dating to the reign of Amenhotep III and the Amarna Period. Two were seal impressions discovered amongst the ruins of Malkata Palace whilst two more had been found during the excavations of Petrie and Pendlebury at Amarna. Having found both seal impressions and the actual mould used to mass produce the image as a cylinder seal, Petrie believed the gazelle motif did not appear to be Egyptian and was 'probably due to foreign influence', with later Egyptologists suggesting a Syrian origin.

The more I looked at it, the more I wondered. Was it even remotely possible that KV.39 had perhaps been the place where some of the royal mummies of the Amarna Period had been rewrapped and restored prior to their reburial down in the Valley of the Kings?

6

TOMB KV.35 AND ITS MUMMIES

Fired up by what I'd been able to discover by looking at excavated material for myself, I was more determined than ever to go back to the Valley and see the three anonymous mummies with my own eyes. But until that time came it was a matter of reading all I could about the tomb, from its discovery by Victor Loret in 1898 to the dramas of the next few years when the mummies played a leading role in the political manoeuvrings of the British and French authorities. Taken out of the tomb, then put back in again, they were also silent witnesses in a detective drama starring Howard Carter and the local Qurnawis. This eventful period was followed by almost a century of comparative peace punctuated by a brief visit from American and Egyptian scientists in the 1970s and the occasional check to monitor their condition, before our arrival in 2002.

To try to work out just what had happened, and why the three mummies had eventually been left where they were, I planned to assemble all the evidence I could, from journal articles, books and old photographs to the diaries of these involved and the first-hand account of one of the handful of people who had seen the three bodies in recent times. But first I had to understand who had found the tomb and how they had done so.

After the retirement of the great Gaston Maspero as Director General of the French-run Egyptian Antiquities Service in 1886, he was succeeded by several men whom Petrie regarded as unsuited to the job. The first of them was a French civil engineer, Jacques de Morgan, whom Petrie described as 'the son of Jack Morgan, a Welsh mining engineer . . . he knew nothing whatever about Egypt but, as a capable business man, made the most

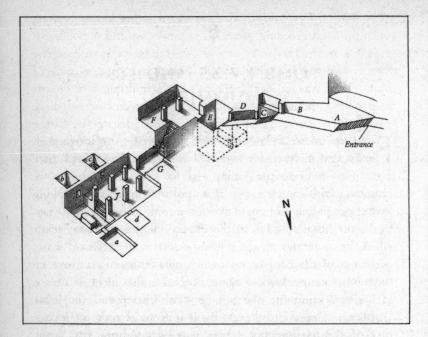

FIGURE 8. Plan of Amenhotep II's tomb KV.35 in the Valley of
the Kings, with Amenhotep II's mummy found in his
sarcophagus in the main burial chamber (J), the side chamber
Jb containing a cache of Royal Mummies now in Cairo
Museum, the three anonymous mummies sealed in side
chamber Jc and the mummy on the boat found in the first
pillared hall (F)

reputable head that the French could find', a comment which
reveals something of Anglo-French relations in Egypt at that
time. In 1897 de Morgan left Egypt and the Parisian Egyptologist
Victor Clément Georges Philippe Loret was appointed in his
place. Petrie continued to do his bit for Franco-British relations
by reporting that 'de Morgan was but a small devil, but Loret
is twenty devils'.

Despite the photograph accompanying Loret's entry in *Who*

Was Who in Egyptology, which shows a rather kindly looking old gent with receding white hair, pince-nez and a polka-dot cravat, Loret had arrived on his first visit to Egypt as an energetic twenty-two-year old with a shock of black hair, and, in terms of appearance, was far more believable as the multiple devil he was said to be. Although his subsequent stint as Director lasted a mere two years he managed to make a series of great discoveries during his systematic excavations there, adding to the list of those then known an astonishing eleven new tombs – including KV.39, where I had my own first experience of working in the Valley.

Having begun work in the Valley of the Kings in 1883 copying inscriptions in the tombs so far discovered, Loret had familiarised himself with the landscape and no doubt would have identified some of the most likely places to dig. Like all good archaeologists he also kept his eyes and ears open. He seems to have been aware that the Abd el-Rassul family of Qurna were claiming to know the whereabouts of another royal tomb after their great success discovering the first cache of royal mummies at Deir el-Bahari in 1871, a full ten years before the authorities came along and 'discovered' it.

Loret's achievements must also have owed much to his knowledgeable Egyptian head workman or, *reis*, literally 'the boss', Ahmed Girigar. After setting Girigar and his men to work in February 1898 at the southernmost end of the Valley, under the watchful eye of the local Qurna inspector, Loret left for Aswan. Here he received a telegram from the inspector to inform him of a new discovery, and nine days later was back in the Valley to inspect the newly revealed tomb of Tuthmosis III, the first royal tomb in the valley to have been decorated.

With the pungent odour of cedarwood filling the air, Loret and his men discovered that the tomb had been well and truly robbed in antiquity, its contents, including the fragment cedarwood furniture, stripped of their gold and smashed to bits. Yet the king's mummy had been salvaged by the ancient inspectors, and eventually reburied over the hill in the cache at Deir el-Bahari.

Because the route between the two places passes right by KV.39, a tomb filled with mummy wrappings and embalming material as well as the gold ring bearing one of Tuthmosis' names, it seems quite possible that his mummy could have been refitted there before reburial.

While Loret himself set to work on the careful clearance of Tuthmosis III's tomb, he sent workmen back down the Valley to explore another area at the base of the western cliffs. After digging a whole series of small test pits over the next few weeks they came to a large pile of loose boulders, and on 8 March they uncovered the beginnings of a rock-cut doorway. When pieces of broken pottery were found in the debris around the tomb entrance, together with a funerary statuette of Amenhotep II, it looked as though this was another plundered tomb. Yet they persevered, and by 7pm on the following day, enough of the doorway had been cleared to allow Girigar and then Loret to enter the black depths of the tomb.

Making their way as best they could down the steep entrance passageway, picking their way over piles of ancient debris as their candle flames leaped and spluttered in the stale and increasingly warm air, they eventually came to a stop at the edge of a deep well shaft. In no mood to turn back, Loret decided to work through the night and, calling for a ladder, edged his way forward into the black void.

After reaching the other side and emerging into the blackness of the room beyond, the two men, joined by a couple of local inspectors, found themselves in a pillared chamber, surrounded by the broken remains of cedarwood furniture, alabaster vessels, a large coiled wooden serpent and three large model funerary boats in bright colours. Stepping forward between the two columns to examine one of the boats more closely, Loret held up his candle and

spectacle effroyable [a terrifying sight], a corpse lay there upon the boat, all black, hideous, its grimacing face turning towards me and looking at me, its long brown hair in sparse curls around its head. I did not dream for an instant that this was simply an unwrapped mummy. The legs, the arms seemed to be bound. A hole exposed the sternum, there was an opening in the skull. Was this a victim of a human sacrifice? Was this a thief murdered by his companions, in a bloody division of the loot, or perhaps he was killed by soldiers or police interrupting the pillaging of the tomb?

Having just found an unexpected corpse late at night in the depths of an ancient tomb, Loret could be forgiven for letting his imagination run away from him. In fact the body was an unwrapped mummy, most likely that of Amenhotep II's son, Prince Webensenu, whose small wooden funerary figurines, along with fragments of canopic equipment, Loret would soon find further inside the tomb. After the mummy had been dragged up into this small chamber in ancient times to be unwrapped and stripped of its valuables it had been left where it was found by Loret, lying full length in one of the king's funerary boats, with the remains of its resin-soaked wrappings hanging down over the prow.

The Frenchman composed himself after his fright and continued forward down a set of stone-cut steps towards a doorway which 'opened into blackness. We advanced, the light grew brighter, and with stupefaction we saw an immense hall, entirely decorated, supported by two rows of three pillars on which were painted life-sized groups of a king in the presence of a god. It was really him! It was Amenhotep II.' Having checked the king's two name cartouches, Loret declared, 'There was no more doubt. It was the son of Tuthmosis III,' whose tomb he had found only weeks before.

The floor was covered in the debris left by the ancient looters – a thick layer of broken objects, beautifully summed up by Loret's terse description of 'un pêle-mêle unimaginable'. Over there was a large black wooden statue of the lioness goddess Sekhmet, and here a painted wooden head of her more benign bovine counterpart, Hathor, together with Anubis and several other gods. Scattered funerary figurines of alabaster and wood again named Amenhotep II and his son Webensenu, whilst portions of the king's canopic jars of alabaster still contained some of the mummified royal entrails. Loret also described shreds of the warrior pharaoh's red leather armour, blue-glazed throwsticks, part of a funerary text inscribed on a papyrus roll, pieces of pottery and large quantities of coloured glassware, which at the time of the king's burial had been all the rage. In fact more than two thousand items lay strewn before Loret in the same chaotic state in which they had been left some three thousand years before.

Delicately criss-crossing the floor, trying not to crush the debris beneath his feet, Loret eventually reached the furthest part of the great hall. Parallel with the last set of stone pillars he came to a flight of wide steps which led him down into the most low-lying part of the tomb, the crypt, and the king's quartzite sarcophagus. As he stood nervously before it, he could see

the sarcophagus, open, but was it empty? I couldn't dare to hope for the contrary, because no-one found pharaohs in the necropolis of the Valley of the Kings, all the royal mummies having been removed in antiquity to a safe place. I reached the sarcophagus with difficulty, being careful not to break anything underfoot. I could partially read the two names of Amenhotep II. I leant over the edge, bringing the candle a little nearer. Victory! A dark coffin lay in the bottom, at its head a bunch of flowers and at its feet a wreath of foliage . . .

It was a momentous occasion. Although the tomb had clearly been robbed of all its saleable treasures in ancient times, the tomb owner himself, Amenhotep II, remained where he had been buried. Yet as Loret could see, the king was not in the same state in which he had been interred. A single coffin of cheap *cartonnage* – ancient papier mâché – now stood in for the original nest of golden coffins.

Withdrawing from the pharaoh's presence, Loret turned his attentions to the four small side chambers which led off from the main hall, two on the left and two on the right. To the left of the sarcophagus was a chamber containing numerous large jars emptied out by the robbers, and a supply of carefully wrapped provisions including a shoulder of beef, dried meats and boxes of preserved ducks, pigeons, quails and olives – a sumptuous feast for Amenhotep's Afterlife. In the next chamber, to the left of the entrance, he found piles of broken bright blue pottery vases and vessels and ⚱ ankh-shaped amulets, which he had seen the gods holding up to Amenhotep's face on the columns all around. Also there were the black wooden figure of a lithe panther and a mummified human toe.

Then Loret entered the first of the two rooms on the right, the one closest to the entrance. The right side of the chamber was strewn with resin-covered wooden funerary statuettes which had been emptied out of their original small coffins and appeared to have been swept to one side. But on the left side of the room was *un spectacle inouï*, something unheard of:

Three corpses lay side by side at the back, in the left corner, their feet towards the door . . . We approached the three bodies. The first seemed to be that of a woman. A thick veil covered her forehead and left eye. A broken arm had been placed at the side, nails in the air. Torn cloth, ripped apart, scarcely covered her body. Abundant black hair, in waves, spread over the limestone floor, at each side of her head. The face, admirably preserved, had a noble and majestic gravity.

Black-and-white photographs taken on Loret's orders confirmed the woman's incredible appearance. Yet I could see no sign of the broken arm and, cross-checking Smith's Elder Lady Woman, as he called her, I confirmed that both her arms were present.

Leaning forward with his candle, Loret started to examine the middle of the three bodies. He described this second mummy as that of a child of about fifteen years. He was naked with the hands joined to the abdomen. At first, the head appeared totally bald, but, on closer examination, one saw that the head had been shaved, except to the right, on the right side of the temple, from which grew a magnificent tress of black hair. This was the coiffure of the royal princes, and I thought immediately of the royal prince Webensennu, this so far unknown son of Amenhotep II, whose funerary statue I had noticed in the great hall, and later I would find fragments of his canopic jars. The face of the young prince was laughing and mischievous; not at all did it evoke the idea of death.

The third body, the one nearest to the left-hand wall,

seemed to be that of a man. His head was shaved, but a wig lay on the ground not far from him. The face of this person displayed something horrible yet amusing at the same time. The mouth, running obliquely from one side nearly to the middle of the cheek, bit on a pad of linen whose two ends hung from the corner of the lips. The eyes, half-closed, expressed a strange amusement. This was perhaps unfortunate, as he could have died choking on a gag: he looked like a playful little cat snatching at a piece of cloth. Death, which had respected the severe beauty of the woman and the rebellious charm of the boy, seems to have amused itself with the man and had turned in derision.

It was an oddly moving description and, although the body had proved to be clearly female, I tried to put myself in Loret's position. Working in the darkness by candlelight, and clearly confused by the shaven head, he was not the first nor indeed would be the last to mistake the gender of the individual I believed might just be Nefertiti.

With only the fourth side chamber left to inspect, Loret must by then have been exhausted. Having hauled himself up to see over the top of the perilously balanced limestone blocks still sealing the entrance he held his candle aloft, although the room was so large that its flame made little impact. Then, slowly, as his eyes adjusted to the murky darkness,

I distinguished nevertheless nine coffins laid out on the ground, six at the back, occupying all the space, three in the front, leaving to the right a bit of empty space. There was only room, in the length of the chamber, for two coffins, in the width for six, so that the mummies touched at their shoulders, feet and head. Five coffins had lids. Four were without. It was not, at that moment, possible to think of entering the room and looking at the coffins more closely. I said to myself that they were probably members of the royal family.

He meant the family of Amenhotep II, an assumption based purely on the fact that they, like the three next door, had been found in this king's tomb.

Having satisfied himself of the contents, Loret and the three Egyptians accompanying him left the tomb, the whole experience having been something of an emotional roller coaster. 'Such were the impressions from my first visit to the tomb of Amenhotep II, impressions of an intensity I would never forget, dominated above all by the horror of seeing the corpse stretched out on the boat, and the joy of having contemplated, in its ancient position, the unhoped for coffin of the king.'

It was only when the tomb of Tuthmosis III had been cleared that Loret could return and begin to remove, one by one, the many hundreds of items in Amenhotep II's tomb, using a grid system to make a careful record of the exact position of each item. And only once these had all been packed up for eventual removal to the Cairo Museum could he finally look again at the mummies.

The body on the boat which had at first so scared him required delicate handling, since its bitumen-like coating had stuck tightly on to the boat, giving him the same problem Carter would experience a quarter of a century later when trying to move the resin-covered mummy of Tutankhamen. In the end Loret decided to move the whole thing together rather than risk damaging the mummy. Then he turned his attention to the three anonymous mummies, and at this point in my reading my heart beat a little faster.

Judging by the drawings made at the time, Loret's artist, Félix Guilmant, had sketched the three lying in their original position on the floor of the tomb. After commenting that the three together had given him far less trouble than the sticky lad on the boat, Loret described constructing for each mummy a made-to-measure wooden board, covered in linen and stuffed with cotton. Then 'the mummies, rigid as wood, were carefully lifted up and the boards slid beneath them', and each one was placed inside a long wooden packing case.

I couldn't understand this, and read it through again. I thought the mummies were still in the side chamber, so why had Loret packed them up? I read on, still looking for answers, but Loret had now shifted his focus to the king, whose body still wore a floral garland around its neck and a small bouquet of mimosa on its chest, which covered the name written on the wrappings.

There remained only the nine mummies in the final side chamber. Surrounded by broken figurines and discarded mummy garlands were the grey, dust-shrouded coffins. Approaching the nearest one Loret blew along the surface to try to read the names, which revealed themselves as those of Ramses IV, a king known to have died 253 years *after* Amenhotep II. 'Was I in the midst of royal coffins?' he wrote. 'I blew away the dust of the second coffin, a cartouche showed itself, illegible for an instant, painted in matt black on a shiny black background. I went over to the other coffins. Everywhere cartouches!' And as Loret moved around, blowing away the dust of millennia before him, he discovered a whole series of ancient pharaohs' names – in fact most of those who had been missing from the earlier cache at Deir el-Bahari.

The coffins were carefully lifted out into the now empty burial chamber, their lids removed and each mummy closely studied. Despite the fact that the coffins didn't necessarily belong to their current owner, those who had rewrapped the bodies had written the relevant names on the replacement wrappings. As Loret copied these out by candlelight he found the identities of Amenhotep II's son and successor, Tuthmosis IV, and his son and successor in turn, the great Amenhotep III. Then came Merenptah – although Loret at first read this as 'Akhenaten', who he described as 'the most quaint of all the pharaohs of Egypt'. He was followed by Seti II, Siptah, three of the kings named Ramses (numbers IV, V and VI), and finally an unknown woman with superbly curled hair, who some have since wondered might be the later female pharaoh Tawosret.

The shroud inscriptions also provided details of when these royal mummies had been restored. For instance, the inscription across the chest of Amenhotep III read, 'Year 12, fourth month of winter, day six. On this day renewing of the burial of Nebmaatra [Amenhotep III] by the High Priest of Amen-Ra, Pinudjem.' And since Pinudjem held office during the reign of King Smendes, this shroud could be dated to 1057 BC and the mummies would presumably have been placed in the tomb some time around that date.

All the mummies were then measured, recorded and photographed in the bright white light generated by magnesium flares, Loret's photographs of the three anonymous bodies next door showing them within their packing cases. He also declared his intention to have them all X-rayed once they arrived in Cairo. At the end of three weeks' work the tomb lay empty and, as the last packing case was nailed shut, all the material was made ready for the long sail north to Cairo. It included the three mummies from the side chamber who, like all the others, had been manoeuvred back up through the tomb's long corridors and finally out into the sunlight. Having been carried back down the Valley in a kind of rewind of the funeral service, they were taken along the four-mile track to the Nile, carried up the gangplank and placed inside the Antiquities Service's waiting boat.

So, according to Loret, the three anonymous mummies *had* left the tomb after all. But apparently politics had then intervened. The French-run Antiquities Service came under the control of the British-run Ministry of Public Works, headed by Sir William Garstin. With the rise of Egyptian nationalism, there was a growing feeling that foreigners were robbing Egypt's royal dead, so Loret was ordered to return all the mummies to the tomb. The only comment he made about this in his report was a rather pointed exclamation mark before he changed the subject. Most of the material I read, including Loret's own account, suggested that he replaced the mummies right away before the boat had even left its moorings. Certainly *The Times* had concluded its report – headlined 'Important Discovery at Thebes' – by saying that Garstin and the Ministry 'requested M. Loret to remove only the smaller objects and leave the mummies and the bodies in their present place'.

Elsewhere in the newspaper's account it was stated that the three mummies in the side chamber, a man, a woman and a boy, had not in fact been mummified but had simply dried out in the atmosphere of the tomb. Despite the fact that large chunks were missing from their torsos and one of them had had its face bashed in, they were said to be 'in a most complete state of preservation, with the features perfect', and the writer asserted that 'the hair upon each is luxuriant' – except of course for the Younger Woman, who had no hair at all! Finally, the newspaper report declared the three 'evidently met with violent deaths', and the unnamed correspondent hoped their discovery 'may throw some light on the vexed question of human sacrifices which now divides Egyptologists'.

Although Loret continued as head of Antiquities Service for a further year, finding yet more tombs in the valley, the British wanted to streamline the Antiquities Service. So they replaced him with the more cooperative Gaston Maspero, brought out of retirement in France to resume his old position. Maspero was given a staff of five Chief Inspectors, each taking a district of

Egypt. The twenty-five-year-old Howard Carter was appointed first Chief Inspector of Upper Egypt, an area that included Luxor and its Valley of the Kings.

Long fascinated by Carter and his incomparable knowledge of the region, I decided to consult his handwritten notebooks in Oxford to see if he had any information about just what had happened to the mummies from Amenhotep II's tomb. And Carter certainly had plenty to say.

Reading his words, wearing the regulation cotton gloves as I turned the precious pages, I became completely absorbed. Beginning with a long account of 'The Valley and the Royal Tombs', he described 'The Valley of the Tombs of the Kings – the very name is full of Romance, and of all Egypt's wonders, there is none that makes a more instant appeal to the imagination.' As I read on, all about 'the ultimate fate of the Theban necropolis and the destiny of the Royal Mummies', he said that the Royal Valley had been reasonably secure under the great pharaohs of the New Kingdom until a succession of 'worthless successors' and 'arrogant weaklings' saw a decline in security which 'gave rise to an orgy of temple and tomb robbing', for which he largely blamed the priests.

Twenty-five pages later he finally got on to the events of 1898 – the discovery of Amenhotep II's tomb and its cache of royal mummies. He wrote of the three bodies in the side chamber, and, contrary to Loret's belief that the shaven-headed body was that of a man, described them as 'two nameless women and a boy . . . found lying naked on the floor of one of the side Treasuries'. In Carter's version of events the mummies were indeed loaded on to Loret's boat, although it soon appeared that they had rather more of an adventure than was revealed by the official sources: 'Very rightly the Egyptian government, at the representation of Sir William Garstin, then under-secretary of state for the public works department, decided against their removal. M. Loret, however, did not think this prudent. He disregarded these orders, carefully packed the mummies, embarked them upon his *dahabêyah* (sail boat) and took them to the museum at Ghizah [Giza]', site of the first Cairo Museum.

There it was in Carter's hand: the three mummies had apparently set sail with their fellow royal mummies and reached Cairo. As a result, 'an administrative question arose and [Loret] received orders to replace them in the tomb. This he did, but left them still in their packing cases. Here they remained for two years. Under the directorship of M. Maspero, I replaced the mummy of Amenophis in his sarcophagus, with the flowers and foliage upon him as they were originally discovered', and the king's body was raised on trestles to allow him to be clearly seen by visitors.

Carter also returned the mummy on the boat to the antechamber, surrounding it with chicken wire to stop inquisitive visitors getting too close, whilst 'the three naked mummies I put back in the side treasury where they were found'. However, an early postcard photograph discovered in the late 1970s in a pile of old photographs in a Luxor shop shows that Carter replaced the three in a different order. After swapping the two female bodies around, he also placed the tops of their padded boards on a short trestle, making the three appear to be rising up and looking straight at the chamber's entrance.

However, when it came to the other nine mummies, who had also been returned to their side chamber next door, Maspero had a change of heart. According to Carter, 'the original plan was changed. It was decided to transport them on special government steamer [back] to the Ghiza Museum, near Cairo', and there they arrived for the second time in 1900. Maspero had persuaded the government officials that the nine named royals had been placed in the tomb only 'by accident' in ancient times, although he agreed that Amenhotep II should certainly stay in his own tomb. So too, he felt, should the body on the boat and the three anonymous bodies, all considered to have been buried with the king as 'victims of human sacrifice', a somewhat far-fetched notion which would nevertheless do wonders for tourist numbers. With the five mummies back home inside the tomb, Carter was ordered to make it 'accessible to the public, who were naturally eager to see this new discovery. The tomb', he wrote, 'I made secure with a steel gate and I placed a special guard over it' – although, as events would prove, even this would not be enough.

In his very personal account of what happened next, Carter confided that

as the reader will have noticed, I have been hurling boomerangs at those ancient Egyptian priest kings for their unskilful government. One of those missiles swerved, returned, and hit me – very, very hard. What happened was this. To stimulate popular sympathy towards Amenophis II, I purposefully gave us much publicity as possible to the fact that this mummy had been robbed in ancient times, and there was nothing of value left upon it. Perhaps that is where I made my mistake. For in spite of the fact, a modern tomb robber, possibly in connivance with the guard, forced upon the steel gate of the tomb and subjected Amenophis to another rifling.

The tomb guards told Carter that during the evening of 24 November 1901 a band of masked robbers threatened to shoot them, some of their number standing guard over them while the remainder broke into the tomb and robbed it. When Carter arrived, he found that the mummy on the boat had been forcibly removed from the boat, the broken body parts strewn about the floor and the boat itself stolen.

I breathed a sigh of relief with Carter that at least the three mummies in the side chamber had not been touched – their visibly unwrapped state clearly hid no valuables. But sadly there was more to come. The king's body had been pulled from his sarcophagus, and his wrappings cut through with a sharp blade. From his years of experience Carter realised that this was the work of 'an expert hand', and decided he would put all his energies into catching the culprits. First he needed evidence, and he 'therefore focussed my energies upon a thorough examination of the tomb itself'. As Carter turned detective, he examined broken locks and took casts of the footprints in the dust around the mummy. He already suspected the infamous Abd el-Rassul family, and when the tracks from the tomb led straight up to their front door he had three of the family arrested. When they were later released without charge, a fuming Carter turned his attentions to the one item he knew had been stolen, and

for eighteen months I made every possible search throughout Egypt for the boat. I employed secret police, port and frontier officials were supplied with photographs and were advised to prevent, if possible, the boat being exported by dealers or collectors. I am, however, happy to say that eventually I did find the boat; – but where? In a glass case in the Cairo Museum. It was purchased from an antiquity dealer out of state funds by an authority in the museum, but he never advised me of the fact. Subsequently it was revealed that Mohamed Abd-é-Rasool [had sold it] to a dealer al-Ghiza, near Cairo [sic].

Following the robbery, the tomb was treated as a crime scene and sealed until Maspero arrived with Carter to inspect the king's body in January 1902. Also in the party was Emma Andrews, variously described as the sister or cousin of a wealthy American businessman, Theodore Davis of Rhode Island, who had funded excavations in the Valley between 1903 and 1912. Accompanying her relative on his travels between 1889 and 1911, Andrews not only 'kept house for him on his boat at Luxor' but wrote a journal which provides valuable information on events at the time. After this visit to the royal tomb, she described how Amenhotep II's 'coffin and cartonnage had been lifted from the sarcophagus, laid on the floor, and the wrappings ripped from the feet to the head – and in a state of utter ruin . . .' After briefly examining the king's mummy, the two men replaced it in its sarcophagus with the wrappings arranged to reveal its face and chest. As part of plans to make the Valley more tourist-friendly, Maspero and Carter also brought electric lighting to five of the most popular tombs, including that of Amenhotep II.

As Andrews described on her next visit, the electric lights were a great advantage, resulting in 'no more stumbling about amongst yawning pits and rough staircases, with flickering candles dripping wax all over one' – and presumably, also, over the things being looked at. She went on to state that the king's 'rifled mummy has been restored to his sarcophagus, and decently wrapped with the torn mummy cloths – and Carter has arranged the thing most artistically. A shrouded electric light is at the head of the sarcophagus, throwing the fine face into splendid relief – and when all the other lights were extinguished the effect was solemn and impressive.'

A contemporary painting shows a crowd of European and American tourists, the men in flat caps or homburgs, the long-skirted ladies in large-brimmed hats and buttoned-up jackets, gazing intently down at the king's mummy from the top of the stairs. And no doubt they also paid the same close attention to the three 'sacrificial victims' in the side chamber – a regular freak show who even appeared on postcards. Yet tourists' attentions were soon diverted by events a short distance away across the Valley.

Following Loret's spectacular discovery of the tomb with its hidden collection of royal mummies Maspero gave Davis permission to organise a dig in the Valley, his money funding a set of equally astonishing discoveries over the next few years. With Carter supervising the workmen, in 1903 they discovered the tomb of Tuthmosis IV, the king's mummy having already been found by Loret in the tomb of Amenhotep II (KV.35). Then they excavated the long-known tomb of the female pharaoh Hatshepsut, although her remains had long since vanished. As Carter ominously declared, 'A king she would be, and a king's fate she shared.'

Carter's chequered career took him away from the Valley for a while, and Davis's excavations then involved Arthur Weigall. They literally struck gold with the discovery of the tomb of Queen Tiy's parents Yuya and Tuya (KV.46), stuffed full of wonderful things. Next came the young Englishman Edward Ayrton, who in 1907 discovered on Davis's behalf the controversial tomb known as KV.55. But with so many people involved in the tomb's excavation and clearance it had become very difficult to work out just what was found in there, and this has become the subject which Egyptologists love to argue about more than anything else.

After Ayrton found the doorway, fragments of alabaster and gold foil scattered beyond the partly blocked entrance showed that it had been robbed in ancient times. Firmly wedged in the small entrance corridor were also portions of a gilded shrine, and as Ayrton, Davis and Weigall looked more closely they could see that the shrine was decorated with the figure of a queen and a second figure who had been carefully erased, both of them standing beneath the rays of the Aten sun disc. When he saw the accompanying inscription which confirmed that the shrine had been made for the king's mother, Queen Tiy, Davis was ecstatic. 'By Jove! Queen Tyi [sic], and no mistake!' He later stated that 'It is quite impossible to describe the surprise and joy of finding the tomb of a great queen and her household gods, which for these 3,000 years had never been discovered.'

Queen Tiy herself was then very much in the public eye following the discovery of two superb likenesses, a small steatite stone head found in Sinai in 1904, and a second of wood discovered the following year in the Fayum oasis region. Both perfectly captured the determined pout of this amazing woman, who had surely taught Nefertiti everything she knew. Yet the burial chamber itself was a complete mess, strewn with rubble and debris. Water had seeped down through a great long crack in the ceiling during the flash floods which thunder through the Valley every few years, and the damp had caused the gilded shrine panels to decay. As the outside breeze blew gently round the tomb for the first time in thousands of years, tiny fragments of gold leaf began to swirl up through the air like a well-shaken toy snowstorm, sticking to the hair of those present. Davis's steady stream of visitors included one wit who sneezed and apparently 'found seven and six in his handkerchief'.

Having treated the shrine with paraffin wax in an attempt to keep the gold in place, Davis employed an artist to draw the figures of Queen Tiy and her carefully erased son Akhenaten, together with other material from the tomb. This artist, Harold Jones, is always described as a Welshman, but he was actually born in my home town, Barnsley, where his father was head of the local art school. After winning a scholarship to London's Royal College of Art Harold Jones had gone out to Egypt in 1903 as an archaeological artist. Following a stint at Hierakonpolis he began working for Davis in the Valley of the Kings, writing home: 'I expect I shall be here a week living at the tombs of the Kings.' In fact he remained there for the rest of his short life until his death from TB in 1911, working as Davis's official artist in place of Howard Carter, who was now employed by Lord Carnarvon.

Caught up in the general excitement of the tomb discovery, Jones told his family, 'I stayed till 10 o'clock having a fine time looking over the things [Davis] had found – gold diadem, canopic jars with beautiful portraits of Queen Thiy [sic] etc.' Amongst the numerous small items hidden in the debris were bits of jewellery, beads and amulets, only later recognised as exact parallels to those that had been found in the Royal Tomb at Amarna and suggesting a close connection. Yet much of the evidence was lost as a result of Davis allowing his endless stream of visitors to take small items as 'souvenirs', so when Jones asked if he too might take a handful of debris he was told, 'Certainly, take two!'

In the midst of the wreckage was a magnificent gilded coffin covered in a feathered design of carnelian and blue glass, 'so decorated that it looked as if a great mother bird had wrapped her wings around it from head to foot'. Although its golden face had been savagely ripped off, the blue inlay of part of the right eye remains, together with a blue and gold false beard; the arms were crossed at the chest. A protective uraeus snake was fixed over the brow, atop an amazingly constructed wig whose fringed layers were skilfully carved into individual ringlets to form the Nubian wig, the same style worn by the head-shaped stoppers of the four alabaster canopic jars which had once held the mummy's internal organs.

In the dampness of the tomb the lion-footed funerary bed beneath the coffin had collapsed, crashing to the ground, which knocked its lid aside to reveal the mummy within. Weigall could see bones 'protruding from the remains of the linen bandages and from the sheets of flexible gold-foil in which, as we afterwards found, the whole body was wrapped'. When the body was lifted from the coffin it soon began to fall to pieces.

Although the identity of this individual has been highly controversial ever since its discovery, whoever it was had been buried wearing a significant amount of jewellery. The damaged head was found partly covered with a golden vulture collar, dislodged from the chest when the bier collapsed and initially mistaken for a crown. Around the neck hung a broad collar made up of 'gold pendants and inlaid plaques connected by rows of minute beads, and ending in large lotus flowers of gold'. The left arm was bent with the hand on the breast, and the upper arm revealed 'three broad bracelets of very thin gold of fragile nature; the right arm was laid straight down by the side, the hand resting on the thigh, and remains of three similar bracelets round the wrist; no rings or other jewellery were found with the mummy'.

First examined *in situ*, the body was laid out in the pose associated with women, the right arm down by the side and the left laid across the chest. Needing a medical opinion, Davis was in luck and found two surgeons touring the Valley, an unnamed obstetrician and a certain Dr Pollock, who both declared the pelvis to be 'evidently that of a woman'.

Eventually all the small amulets, ritual implements, vessels of glass and stone, and canopic jars were packed up and taken to

Davis's boat on the Nile. After passing round the objects to show to distinguished guests, the party set sail for Cairo. Only the body, by now 'nothing but a mass of black dust and bones', remained behind.

After he had 'soaked the bones in paraffin wax so as to preserve them', Weigall placed them in a sealed basket and sent them, presumably by rail, to Elliot Smith in Cairo for examination. Unpacking what remained of the 'considerably damaged' body once it had arrived at the Medical School, Smith was clearly confused and immediately wrote to Weigall: 'Are you sure that the bones you sent me are those which were found in the tomb? Instead of the bones of an old woman, you have sent me those of a young man. Surely there must be some mistake.' But there seems to have been no mistake.

After examining them, Smith declared that the skull 'exhibits in an unmistakable manner the distortion characteristic of a condition of hydrocephalus [water on the brain]' whilst the bones 'formed the greater part of the skeleton of a young man, who, judged by the ordinary European standards of ossification, must have attained an age of about twenty-five or twenty-six years at the time of his death . . . without excluding the possibility that he might have been several years older'. Davis was stunned. Although he still went on to publish the find in 1910 as 'The Tomb of Queen Tiyi', based partly on the fact that Tiy's golden funerary shrine had been found in the tomb, he nevertheless accepted Smith's view that the body was that of a man and declared that 'the surgeons were deceived by the abnormal pelvis and the conditions of the examination'.

But Smith hadn't finished yet. After further examinations which revealed that the body might even be as old as thirty, he announced that the body was that of Akhenaten himself. 'The mummy . . . was found in its original wrappings, upon which were gold bands bearing the name of Akhenaten. It is hardly credible that the embalmers of the Pharaoh's mummy could have put some other body in place of it. Thus we have the most positive evidence that these bones are the remains of Akhenaten.'

Certainly there was no mention of Tiy anywhere on the coffin or the mummy, and although the cartouches had been carefully removed, the remaining titles and epithets on the coffin and gold bands were indeed those of Akhenaten, as were those on the ritual implements placed in the tomb. The coffin and canopic jars certainly displayed the Nubian wig hairstyle associated with royal women, and are now generally thought to have been made for Akhenaten's secondary wife Kiya, the 'other woman'; but it seems they were later adapted for a royal male, presumably Akhenaten, who had originally been buried in the Royal Tomb at Amarna. Then, after the Amarna Period when the court came back to Thebes, the bodies of both Akhenaten and his mother Tiy were brought back for burial in the Valley of the Kings during the reign of Tutankhamen, whose seals had been found on KV.55's blocked doorway.

It seems that the ancient tomb builders, when working in the area some two hundred years later, must have stumbled across KV.55 and presumably alerted the authorities responsible for security in the valley. These were none other than the priests of Amen, whose inspectors and police force regularly did the rounds, keeping a record of each tomb and checking for signs of robbery. If any was detected, as we know from surviving records, the matter would be investigated and the perpetrators brought to justice on the end of a very sharp spike. On hearing that one of the ancient tombs had been uncovered, the authorities must have consulted their records from which they would surely have identified whose burial place this was – something which they could indeed confirm by reading the inscriptions on the coffins and shrine. It was the name of the despised 'Great Criminal' himself!

Since he was lying beside his mother, Queen Tiy, whose husband, Amenhotep III, was still held in great esteem, the ancient authorities would have decided to remove and rebury her body. And if the Elder Woman is Tiy, then this reburial site was close to her husband and other rescued royals in the nearby tomb of Amenhotep II (KV.35). But, as a leading Egyptologist has pointed out, when they tried to remove her large gilded shrine in one piece, rather than patiently dismantling it, it got stuck in the entrance corridor and they simply left it where it was.

But her son, whose catastrophic policies had done so much damage to their livelihoods as well as to the country in general, must have been regarded as a different matter entirely. Akhenaten's image was excised from his mother's shrine, together with his name, and all trace of the original inscriptions was removed from the canopic jars and the gilded coffin. Having been rendered anonymous and impotent in the Afterlife, the coffin's gold face mask was then ripped off and it appears that a stone may have been used to partly crush the head within, presumably before the tomb was sealed up once and for all – or at least for 3032 years until it was again uncovered by workmen and the can of worms was opened up once more.

Although Smith and Weigall were both convinced that the body found in tomb KV.55 was that of Akhenaten, the coffin was soon seized upon in the ongoing hunt for evidence of Akhenaten's effeminate 'son-in-law' Smenkhkara, who was now popping up all over the place on conveniently uninscribed artwork and artefacts. If the coffin could be that of the young man, what about the body found inside it?

So Smith's successor, Douglas Derry, was asked to re-examine the bones. When he had done so he stated that they 'may be those of a man of not more than 23 years of age'. Rearranging the broken skull fragments and gluing them back together, Derry also found evidence for 'the very reverse of the shape produced by hydrocephalus', and stated that 'in width it exceeded any skull ever measured by the writer in Egypt'.

Derry had recently autopsied the mummy of Tutankhamen for Howard Carter, and, struck by the strong similarity between their two skulls, concluded that 'Smenkhkara', the individual from KV.55, and Tutankhamen had been brothers. More recent tests revealed that Tut and this body from KV.55 even shared the same blood group, confirming their close family relationship. This, of course, would also exist between father and son – Akhenaten and Tutankhamen. When the body was X-rayed in the late 1980s it was described as a male of 'rather fragile constitution' who was a close relative of Tutankhamen. But the teeth were now aged to the mid-thirties, whilst the 'long bones' in the limbs suggested an age 'in excess of' thirty-five.

So, as one leading Egyptologist said, 'Unless the anatomists change their minds yet again, it seems the impasse has at last been broken – in which case Akhenaten is found.' Inevitably, they did change their minds, and in January 2000 I was present when the body was re-examined yet again, this time by a human remains expert who declared it to be 'a man between the ages of twenty and twenty-five years'. From female to male, from old to young to old and back again, the burial remains 'Egyptology's most controversial archaeological find', with no fewer than thirty-one interpretations between 1907 and 2001, and many more since!

The main problem was that tomb KV.55 had contained material relating to more than one royal burial, and Egyptologists had argued among themselves that the body and the coffin could have belonged to no fewer than seven people. The usual suspects are Tiy, Akhenaten, Smenkhkara, Kiya, Meketaten, Meritaten and even Nefertiti – quite a list, which could well be narrowed down with help from the anonymous three walled up in the side chamber of nearby tomb KV.35.

The fact that the bones from KV.55 have been interpreted in so many different ways by so many different people has proved incredibly frustrating. It is all connected with the way in which ancient remains are aged, particularly with the age at which certain bones fuse or 'ossify', since each expert suggests something different. As Elliot Smith explained, 'The ages assigned by different anatomists as the times when the epiphyses [the ends of long bones] join and become consolidated present a considerable

The image by which Nefertiti is best known – the celebrated lifesize bust discovered in the ruins of sculptor Tuthmose's workshop at Amarna and widely regarded as an icon of beauty.

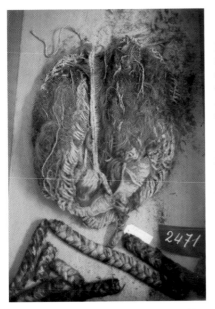

Fragments of the wig Victor Loret found in 1898 beside the body of the Younger Woman in side chamber Jc in the tomb of Amenhotep II (KV.35) in the Valley of the Kings.

(*below left*) Profile of the shaven-headed mummy of the Younger Woman initially described by Loret as male until subsequent examinations by anatomist Grafton Elliot Smith and others proved that it was female.

Side view of the bust of Nefertiti revealing a distinct profile with elongated neck and the wide brow-band beneath a tight-fitting crown most easily kept in place over a shaven head.

The three mummies lying on the floor of the tomb's side chamber as found, sketched by artist Félix Guilmant for Loret's excavation report published in the *Bulletin de l'Institut d'Égyptien* of 1899.

The mummies in February 2003. The position of the two female bodies had been switched around over a century before, when they were displayed to the public on padded boards made from Loret's original packing cases.

Small quartzite head of Amenhotep III, who is named on the reverse as 'King of Upper and Lower Egypt, the Ruler of Joy', wearing a short round wig and solar headdress identifying him as the son of the goddess Hathor.

Wooden head of Queen Tiy from the palace site at Gurob, her round headdress once covered with small blue beads set over an original headdress of silver. Although only 5cm high, the head still conveys a sense of forceful personality.

Funerary statuette of Prince Tuthmosis, eldest son of Amenhotep III and Tiy, his mummified body lying on a bier with his hair dressed in a sidelock and chest covered with a ba bird amulet representing his soul.

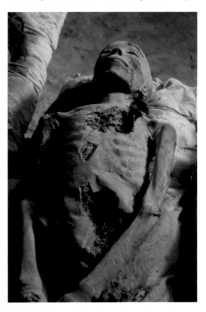

Mummy of the boy from the side chamber, his hair dressed in a sidelock and his chest hacked open with an axe-type blade. There is a similar wound to the left of his abdomen, possibly made to retrieve the gold plate placed over the embalming incision.

Unfinished quartzite head of a 'youthful' Nefertiti discovered amongst the ruins of sculptor Tuthmose's Amarna workshop, clearly showing her double-pierced ears and brow band.

Head of the younger of the two women in the tomb's side chamber, the impression of a tight-fitting brow band and double ear piercing clearly visible, together with the severe damage to the mouth area.

Wooden statuette of an unnamed, feminine-looking king of the Amarna Period wearing a pharaoh's blue khepresh crown, broad collar, gold bracelets and the right arm raised to hold the royal power symbols of crook and flail.

Yellow limestone statuette of Akhenaten wearing the striped nemes headcloth and holding both crook and flail in his right hand. The remains of a woman's supportive left arm behind him is that of his mother Tiy or his chief wife Nefertiti.

Two of the so-called 'grotesque' limestone colossi from the Karnak Aten Temple complex, originally all thought to portray Akhenaten but most likely representing both he (left) and Nefertiti (right, dubbed the 'Sexless Colossus') as the twin creator deities Shu and Tefnut.

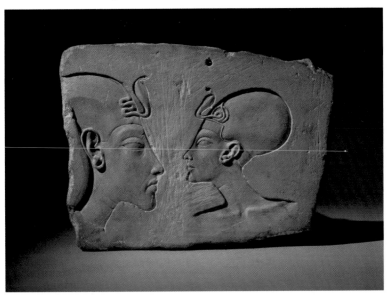

The Wilbour Plaque, a sculptor's trial carving on limestone of twin royal heads identified as Akhenaten (left, wearing the khat headdress) and Nefertiti (right, in her cap crown), bought at Amarna in 1881 for 22 piastres, a few pennies.

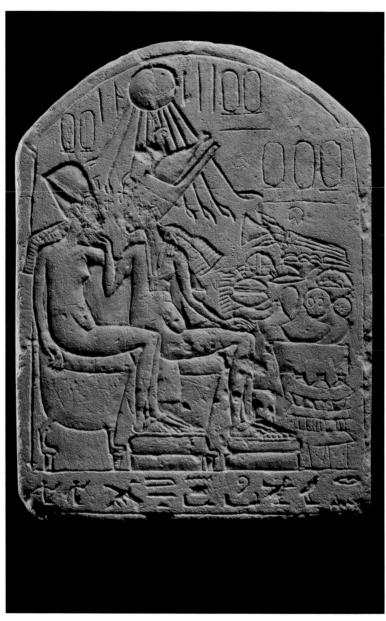

Unfinished limestone stela of Pase from Amarna. The two unnamed
figures in an intimate pose were once used as evidence for a
relationship between Akhenaten and the mysterious prince
Smenkhkare, but are in fact simply Akhenaten (right) and Nefertiti
(left) wearing kingly crowns.

range of variation . . . this condition may indicate an age of not more than 30 years, or than 25 or even 20 years, according to different authorities.' Such a wide fluctuation becomes even more problematic when dealing with bodies from ancient Egypt, where the average life expectancy was somewhere between thirty and thirty-five.

Smith also stated that he worked out the ages of ancient bodies using 'the ordinary European standards of ossification', which is not perhaps the most appropriate means of studying bones several thousand years old and from an entirely different part of the world. Indeed, as the American scientists explained during the second major study of the royal mummies in the 1970s, 'a comparison of our results . . . reveals that the pharaohs' ages at death as determined by the biologists are generally younger than what the written sources suggested. Part of this disparity may be attributed to a somewhat slower maturation in antiquity – as it is among modern Nubians, who reach puberty two to three years later than modern Americans.' But then along came another expert who looked at Tutankhamen's remains and contradicted all this, saying that 'it is recognized that among Eastern peoples maturation tends to take place earlier'.

In a recent work, published in 2001, which talks about the methods used to age bones it was stated that ageing children is

relatively easy and, at least when carried out using tooth eruption, a reliable chronological age can be arrived at. Once the epiphyses have fused, however, things change markedly for the worse, and for adults many bone specialists will talk about determining biological, as opposed to chronological age. This is because the ageing of adult skeletons depends upon the changes which take place in the morphology of the skeleton with advancing age and there is no *a priori* reason why these changes should proceed at the same pace in all individuals.

This was also repeated in a discussion at the Archaeological Science conference in Oxford in 2003, when a leading expert on ancient remains admitted that, whilst bones can certainly be aged as they are growing, it was 'not possible to be able to differentiate the ages of adults'.

Little wonder, then, that the widely varying ages given for the royal mummies are treated with caution. The situation has been well summed up by one leading Egyptologist:

whilst it is tempting to assume that the estimated ages of death of the royal mummies can be used as a starting point for establishing chronology, it appears that we must accept that not only the estimates given by Maspero and Smith, but also those based on recent scientific examination are not accurate enough to be used absolutely for this purpose, and that no historical or chronological arguments based solely on evidence of age at death of a mummy can be considered valid. It remains to be resolved as to how far such evidence should be allowed at all. Certainly, if it goes against what can be deduced from other sources, priority should be given to the latter.

This certainly seems to be true of the body from KV.55. Yet, clinging stubbornly to the belief that Smenkhkara was more than simply Nefertiti's throne name, many authorities *still* think that the body from KV.55 must be the tangible remains of the effeminate young royal 'himself', even though it has been pointed out that the name 'Smenkhkara' occurs nowhere at all in tomb KV.55.

Having looked at these most controversial of bones, Elliot Smith was then invited to examine the mummies that remained in the tomb of Amenhotep II. When at last he found a day to spare he 'made a hasty examination' of the king and the three anonymous mummies in the side chamber, assisted by Weigall, and reporting his findings in the royal mummies catalogue which had so inspired me in the first place. Estimating the Younger Woman's age at 'around 25', he admitted that the exact age couldn't be determined, adding that it wasn't practical to X-ray a body in such a remote location.

I was sure Amenhotep II was now in Cairo Museum, and began to wonder when exactly he had been moved from his tomb. In a subsequent publication Smith reported that he was still in his tomb in 1924, and again in an article published in 1934 it was stated that the king 'still lies in state beneath the glow of an electric lamp'. In fact this was no longer the case. With increasing sensitivity still surrounding the way in which Egypt's ancient dead were displayed, or at least how dead royals were displayed, the Government decided to take them all off display and place them in a huge mausoleum. Needing more details, I returned to Carter's diaries and once again found the information I was looking for. Apparently the mausoleum in question had been built for the great Egyptian statesman Saad Zaghlul Pasha, who died in 1927. The Government then decided that other notable Egyptians should be buried alongside him, but his widow refused permission. Unable to leave such an expensive monument so empty, the Government decided to turn the place into a Pantheon of Ancient Egypt, filling it with all the royal mummies, both from the Cairo Museum and from the tomb of Amenhotep II. But whilst the illustrious mummy of Amenhotep II was taken north by train to Cairo in 1931, apparently on the top bunk of a first-class sleeping car, the three mummies in the side chamber, presumably considered 'unworthy' of such a privileged burial, were left where they were, walled up for their own safety behind a sealed doorway.

Even that wasn't the end of the saga. Although Amenhotep II and all the rest of the royal mummies were transferred to the mausoleum in great secrecy in 1932, plans changed again a few years later. When Saad Zaghlul Pasha was finally interred in his purpose-built mausoleum in January 1937 the royal mummies, now superfluous to requirements, were returned to the Cairo Museum. And there has been 'Since then a marked silence.'

This was certainly true for the anonymous three walled up in the side chamber. Their peace was only briefly interrupted in 1975 when a sample of hair from the Elder Woman was taken to compare with the one labelled with the name of Queen Tiy found in Tutankhamen' tomb. Also during this inspection X-rays were taken of the Elder Woman's skull, from which the structure of her facial bones – her 'craniofacial morphology' – was declared to be closest to that of the mummy of Tuya, mother of Queen Tiy.

Tuya's mummy had been found with that of her husband Yuya in their small joint tomb (KV.46) in the Valley of the Kings. Their son-in-law Amenhotep III had honoured them with a grand burial, filling the tomb with fabulous gold coffins and death masks, a gilded chariot, inlaid furniture, well-stuffed cushions, a jewel casket and wig box, perfume jars and sandals. When it was discovered largely intact in 1905, with bouquets of flowers still as they were left in the entrance passage, the Valley's inspector, Arthur Weigall, told his wife, 'I really nearly fainted . . . The room looked just as a drawing room would look in a London house shut up while the people were away for the summer.'

Since their son-in-law's reign had marked a high point in the art of embalming, the mummies of Yuya and Tuya are without doubt the most technically perfect examples to have survived from ancient Egypt. Yuya in particular is regarded as the best-preserved Egyptian mummy, 'his eyes peacefully closed and his mouth a little open'. Both he and his wife also have bright yellow hair, originally taken as evidence for their supposed foreign origins; equally, perhaps, it may have been the effect of embalming fluids on their otherwise white hair, or evidence of a pale henna rinse.

Yuya and Tuya were taken off to the Cairo Museum, where the Americans X-rayed them both and announced that they were satisfied that the Elder Woman was their daughter, the great Queen Tiy. They also X-rayed the prince in the tomb, assuming he must be a son of Amenhotep II. But for some reason the mysterious shaven-headed Younger Woman was left alone, her secrets intact.

Although the identification of Tiy was accepted at first, some felt the evidence was not conclusive. And since no one else had actually seen the three mummies – just the head shots which appeared in Smith's royal mummies catalogue back in 1912, and

X-rays of the heads of the Elder Woman and Boy taken in the 1970s – many still felt all three were probably the relatives of Amenhotep II. After all, they had been found in his tomb and according to Smith had been mummified by the same techniques as those used on the body of the king himself.

One of the few alternative suggestions was made by Egyptologist Elizabeth Thomas in 1966. Discussing the shaven-headed state of the Younger Woman, she noted that 'such treatment of the head is noted elsewhere only for Tutankhamen, the other women having abundant hair as a rule and even supplementing it with a wig if necessary'. This was one of the factors which made her doubt that the Younger Woman could be either the mother or wife of Amenhotep II, and when describing the equally shaven-headed Tutankhamen she went further, asking: 'Does this feature suggest relationship in time with the lady?'

Although few seem to have picked up on this, Thomas's comment gave me real encouragement in challenging the accepted notion that the three were all related to Amenhotep II just because they had been found in his tomb. Some of the kings buried there had clearly died several centuries later, and as I read through Smith's examination reports I wasn't convinced that the mummification techniques used on the three were necessarily the same as those which had been used to prepare the body of Amenhotep II.

Nor did this explain the three's anonymity, the obvious lack of rewrapping when compared to the other mummies in the tomb, and the fact that they'd been placed in their own side chamber directly on to the floor and with such little care. And, of course, in the case of the Younger Woman, Loret had found the remains of that short wig; there was terrible damage to the face and the right arm had been ripped off. Smith clearly stated that this right arm was once bent up, which would be the pose of a king, and with its fingers still clutched around something, quite possibly a sceptre. It all suggested a woman who may once have wielded kingly powers.

7

THE RISE OF THE
FEMALE PHARAOHS

It is traditionally believed that it was virtually impossible for a woman to rule Egypt as king. Although no one can ignore the twenty-year dominance of the pharaoh Hatshepsut, she is generally explained away as an aberration, a fluke, the exception that proves the rule. And since Cleopatra was the last of the Ptolemies, the Greek dynasty that had ruled Egypt until her death in 30 BC, she was not technically Egyptian and is also conveniently dismissed. As for any other women known to have held power, they have generally been so 'little researched' – a euphemism meaning 'usually ignored' – that they hardly merit a mention in the standard scholarly tomes. Indeed, who beyond the narrow confines of Egyptology has heard of Merneith, Khentkawes, Neithikret, Sobekneferu and Tawosret? Egypt's great male pharaohs are well known, their modern epithets reflecting their achievements, be they Amenhotep the Magnificent, Ramses the Great, even Akhenaten the Heretic. But where are Hatshepsut the Mighty, Neithikret the Brave and Sobeknofru the Strong?

Despite the best attempts in certain quarters to sweep these women under the academic carpet, it is apparent that at least six ruled Egypt as absolute monarch – Neithikret in the 6th dynasty of the Pyramid Age, Sobeknofru in the 12th dynasty, Hatshepsut in the 18th, Tawosret in the 19th, Cleopatra in the dynasty of Ptolemaic pharaohs, and now, it seems, Nefertiti herself. The evidence shows that they ruled in their own right as female pharaohs, even if they are almost always subtly demoted by the use of the modern term 'queen', which usually signifies nothing more than marriage to a male king.

Nevertheless, the Egyptian scribe Manetho, whose work, written around 285 BC, forms the basis of ancient Egypt's chronology, states quite clearly that 'it was decided that women might hold the kingly office' as early as 3000 BC. He even places one of these female rulers at the end of the Amarna Period. So how much clearer does the evidence have to be?

Certainly female rulers should have been perfectly acceptable in a culture that believed the whole universe was a balance of male and female, a duality which was essential for the continuity of life and gave balance and order to all things. And the very symbol of cosmic order was a female deity, Maat, whose presence prevented the forces of chaos overwhelming the order that only she could maintain.

Maat laid down the rules by which each king must govern and judged him – or her – accordingly. Kings often incorporated the name of the goddess into their own, such as Hatshepsut's second name, Maatkara, and that of Amenhotep III, Nebmaatra. The latter's son Akhenaten took his loyalty to the goddess even further. He had himself portrayed in her company and routinely declared himself to be 'living by Maat', regardless of his supposed monotheistic credentials. In art and artefacts kings frequently had themselves shown holding up figurines of the goddess to her fellow gods, demonstrating to these deities that the king in question was ruling Egypt according to her guidelines in an endless cycle of divine intervention.

And even in death Maat would be there waiting, ensuring that each person had lived a good life before allowing him or her into Eternity. Within her ethereal Hall of the Two Truths where she presided with Osiris, Lord of the Underworld, the hearts of the dead would be weighed against her symbol, the feather of truth, which she always wore in her hair. Those whose hearts were light would be transformed into a gleaming spirit and allowed to pass into a blessed eternity. But for those with hearts heavier than Maat's feather, weighed down with sin, a second, much more terrible death was waiting as their hearts were tossed to the terrifying goddess Ammut, the Devourer of the Dead, and their souls were damned for ever.

Interacting through a complex cycle of myth and legend, which was often contradictory, Egyptian gods were both male and female or even combined male and female characteristics in one androgynous-looking body. This was clearly the case with the god Hapi, whose pendulous breasts and great paunch symbolised the life-giving waters of the Nile, his entire body a cornucopia brimming with plenty. Figures of Hapi were often included on the sides of the royal throne, but Amenhotep III took this a stage further by appearing in ceremonial attire as the god himself following a series of bumper harvests. Despite earlier misguided references to the king as little more than a fat old man with a dubious taste for cross-dressing, recent research has revealed that he simply wanted to be seen as the embodiment of the harvest, a plump and potent god bringing wealth to his people.

Yet the main focus of the king's divinity was the sun, and in his thirtieth year as king Amenhotep III became the self-styled Dazzling Aten, ritually merging with the sun disc to become god on earth. And in the same way that Hapi had male and female characteristics, so too did the Aten. In the hymns to the Aten, which first appear in Amenhotep III's reign, the sun disc is addressed as 'Creator of all, who makes them live . . . benificient mother of gods and men' and 'the mother and father of all creation'. For some reason rarely discussed, the role of king incorporated both masculine and feminine elements, and, together with predictable comparisons with male deities, the heroic warrior-pharaoh is also described as the embodiment of various goddesses.

With the line between the genders often blurred in ancient Egypt, 'male' and 'female' were not simply equated with 'active' and 'passive' – something clearly seen in the active roles allocated to female deities. The best example is the story of Isis and Osiris, in which Isis takes the active, dominant role in a legend that begins with the creation of the universe and ends with the resurrection of the dead.

Known as the 'oldest of the old', Isis ruled jointly with her brother-husband Osiris during a golden age on earth. But their jealous younger brother Seth, having ripped himself from the womb, desired power for himself and decided to murder his brother. Although Egyptian texts are always reticent when describing such a terrible event, later classical versions are more forthcoming. Tricking his brother into trying out a coffin, Seth sealed the lid and threw it into the Nile.

As Osiris drowned, death and conflict entered the world. Although Isis managed to retrieve the body Seth snatched it back and hacked it to pieces, scattering body parts across Egypt; this conveniently explains why so many places could claim to be his burial site, since they all had a bit of him. Seth then threw Osiris' penis back into the river, where unfortunately it was eaten by a fish. Yet Isis was resolute and, having tracked down all the other pieces of her dead husband, reassembled his body to create the first mummy. This transformation is reflected in Osiris' numerous titles – He Who Is within the Embalming Tent, He Who Is Put in the Linen, and He Who Is Everlasting in Perfect Condition, the prototype for the ideal mummy.

But Isis hadn't finished yet. After whittling up a false phallus she used her tremendous magical powers to bring Osiris back from the dead for one last passionate fling: 'Creating breath with her wings, rejoicing and joining with him, she raised his inertia and received his seed', a graphic description of the way in which life could literally spill forth from the dead.

Having conceived their son Horus, she raised him to avenge his father and succeed him as king on earth. The resurrected Osiris, the first to have experienced death, entered the land of the dead as the salvation of all who died; in this role he was aided by the omnipresent goddess Maat. Isis and her sister Nephthys gave maximum protection to all who died, comforting them and even leading them physically into the Afterlife; the dead were reassured that 'Isis has your arm and Nephthys has your hand, so go between them.'

With such an impressive track record, Isis came to be regarded as the most powerful of all the gods. By Roman times she had become the Egyptian deity par excellence and was known across three continents, even reaching northern Britain. In fact she was at one point neck-and-neck with Jesus Christ, who only just beat her in the race to become Rome's 'official' deity, and her temple at Philae in Egypt remained a bastion of the ancient religion until AD 550. Described as 'more powerful than a thousand soldiers', Isis was a typical example of the fact that a large proportion of the most formidable, if not downright fearsome, deities were female.

This is particularly true of the daughter of the sun god. Best known as the gentle goddess Hathor, the Golden One, all big hair and breasts, her flip side was Sekhmet, whose name means Powerful Female. Able to turn the sun's life-giving warmth into searing, murderous heat, Sekhmet was the gods' secret weapon, the beautiful goddess who could instantly transform into a terrifying lioness. As the sun god's agent of mass destruction, ancient tales tell how Sekhmet was unleashed against all who betrayed her father, including humans. The gleeful goddess hunted them down, wading through their blood, and revelling in the slaughter. Unable to call her off, the gods had to wait until she was sated and fell asleep; while she was out cold their priests mixed red ochre with seven thousand jars of beer, which they poured out over the land. When Sekhmet awoke, thinking it was blood she immediately began to lap it up. Soon she was so drunk that she forgot what she was supposed to do, returning home to her father's heavenly palace to sleep off her hangover. Spared their intended fate, the survivors became her devotees and ever after drank great quantities of beer to honour their Lady of Drunkenness, Hathor-Sekhmet.

She was also known as the Lady of Red Linen, on account of the blood-soaked clothing of her slaughtered foes, and since she was also the Bringer of Pestilence Sekhmet's priesthood, the ones who could appease her, logically functioned as Egypt's doctors. If she was sufficiently placated, Sekhmet's powers could be redirected for the benefit of king and country, with kings protected at all times by an impressive array of female deities often personified by their queens in appropriate regalia.

With several of the great warrior-pharaohs described as 'Sekhmet to those who defy him', the goddess's presence was a tremendous asset on the battlefield, riding alongside the king to whom she extended her protection. Ritual texts invoked her to aim her fiery powers at the bodies of the enemy. The Syrian warrior goddesses Anat and Astarte also protected the king in combat by acting as an impenetrable shield. Astarte was often depicted, as on the stela of one of her female devotees, in mid-charge astride her horse and brandishing her weapons in the air. The sister goddesses Isis and Nephthys were also sent to watch the king's back, whilst Hathor literally wrapped herself around the royal loins, so that the pharaoh could claim that 'My kilt that I wear is Hathor.' Similar protection came from Egypt's heraldic deities, Nekhbet and Wadjet, the Two Ladies represented by the vulture and cobra respectively. Also known as the Two Mighty Ones, they protected the king as far back as the Pyramid Age, their figures appearing on the front of the royal crown from where the cobra goddess was even able to spit fire into the eyes of the enemy.

Another great protector of the king was Neith, a goddess closely associated with warfare who came to be symbolised by a shield with crossed arrows. A very androgynous figure, Neith was referred to as 'the male who acts the female, the female who acts the male', although she also shared many of the characteristics of Egypt's mother goddesses, being both nurturing and destructive. Yet Neith was far more than that. As primordial creator deity who had emerged from the waters of chaos at the beginning of time, she had called the universe into being through her thunderous laughter. With powers so great that she could even threaten to make the sky crash down and destroy the world she had created, she had borne the sun god Ra and moulded humans into being. Almost all early female royals bear her name, and male kings are hailed as the 'son of Neith'; on an inscription found beside the Sphinx at Giza, the warrior king Amenhotep II called himself 'The one whom Neith fashioned.'

Although Neith is certainly the most appealing of the great creators, ancient Egypt's multi-faceted religion had at least three more creation myths. In the most graphic version, the sun god Atum masturbated to produce two children, Shu and Tefnut, although in some versions he simply sneezed out his appropriately named son – 'Shuuu!' The sun god's two children were also perfect role models for the king and queen, and Akhenaten and Nefertiti were shown as this god and goddess duo in their 'grotesque' statues from Karnak. And, as daughter of the sun, Tefnut was often merged with Sekhmet, whose destructive powers she shared.

The Egyptian acknowledgement of the female capacity for violence was not, however, restricted to goddesses. In a range of artistic representations, female town dwellers stab invading male soldiers, a female pharaoh fires arrows at a male opponent, Hatshepsut carries a mace when still a queen, Tiy attacks the enemy as a sphinx and Nefertiti executes prisoners with her scimitar. Although such scenes are usually brushed aside as fictitious or ritual events, they can all be supported by literary and archaeological evidence, which is less easy to ignore. Some women were sufficiently threatening to be listed as enemies of the state; Hatshepsut is named as 'She Who Will Be a Conqueror'; whilst the earlier Queen Ahhotep rallied Egypt's troops and was buried with full military honours and splendid weapons. Indeed, stone maces and daggers have been discovered in female graves dating back to the days before the country was even unified into a nation state c. 3100 BC.

Though by no means a race of Amazons, Egyptian women still enjoyed a degree of power and self-determination in a world where other ancient cultures regarded the female sex as just another category of inferior being, to be ranked alongside foreigners and slaves. Making much of male power and strength, as if acknowledging that the same in women would make them less able to fulfil their expected roles as wife and mother, Greek visitors seem to have been genuinely shocked by the relative freedom of Egyptian women. On a visit in 450 BC, the traveller Herodotus was amazed to see women 'attending market and taking part in trading whereas men sat at home and did the weaving'. So different was their society that he commented on how 'the Egyptians themselves in their manners and customs seem to have reversed the ordinary practices of mankind'.

And Egyptian women throughout society did operate in a very public way, unparalleled in some parts of the world even today. They are depicted side by side with men in the workplace: both sexes labour in the fields, buy and sell produce, work in the temples, brew, bake and do housework – although only men appear doing the laundry. Surviving accounts also show that men and women seem to have received the same pay rations for doing the same work, a situation that much of our modern world has yet to achieve, for all its equal-pay legislation. Some royal women are known to have controlled the treasury as well as owning their own palaces, estates and workshops, and women, as independent citizens, could own property, buy and sell it, make wills and choose which of their children would inherit from them.

Since an individual's social status was usually a direct result of their relationship with the king, the most influential women at court were inevitably his mother, sisters and daughters, some of whom might also be designated 'wife'. The practice of inter-marriage has often been seen as a way of keeping power within the ruling house, and it also reflected the way in which a goddess such as Hathor could be, at any one time, the mother, wife and daughter of the sun god.

Yet it should also be stressed that royal women held titles that demonstrated their relationship to the king, regardless of which monarch happened to be on the throne. It seems that once a king's daughter, always a king's daughter – a practice which explains why elderly queens were still named 'King's Daughter' along with their other titles when their son or even grandson was on the throne. So the situation existed where a great queen such as Ahmose-Nefertari could be King's Daughter, King's Sister, King's Wife and King's Mother all at once – not referring to the same king, but simply stressing the female link between several generations. Some kings also promoted their mothers retrospectively, making them Great Royal Wives during their own reigns, whilst not, of course, marrying them themselves. But as you might imagine, it was a tradition that did cause a certain amount of confusion for some of the early Egyptologists. With imaginations working overtime, the Victorians seemed to have liked nothing better than to contrast their God-fearing biblical heroes with the idol-worshipping delinquent Egyptians for whom incest was merely an extension of an already depraved repertoire. Although royal intermarriage is known sometimes to have resulted in children, this was usually the task of minor wives unrelated to the king, and royal incest between full siblings really only became policy with the later Ptolemaic pharaohs, who were in fact European.

Women were honoured with the official title 'Mother of the King' should their son be made pharaoh. But succession did not automatically pass to the eldest son, and inevitably there was a great deal of intrigue and plotting, the most famous case being the so-called Harem Conspiracy in which a wife of Ramses III and seven other women conspired with government officials, army officers and guards to have the king deposed and her son made king. There was even something of a scandal during the trial, when five of the judges were caught drinking with the accused women in a local alehouse. Although the plot seems to have been discovered in time and the perpetrators executed or allowed to commit suicide, the number of other plots of this kind which succeeded and changed the course of Egypt's history will probably never be known. Such episodes certainly underline the power and influence of so-called minor wives, who clearly had both motive and opportunity directly to alter the line of succession.

To dismiss these influential individuals with the hideous term 'concubine', as many still do, does not seem right, and the term 'minor wife' is much the best option. Yet even the term 'wife' can be problematic, since there is no evidence for any kind of legal or religious marriage ceremony in ancient Egypt. If a couple fell in love and wanted to be together, the families would hold a big party, presents would be exchanged and the couple would set up home. The man would continue in his profession, which was often hereditary, and the woman would become Lady of the House and produce children. If a wife did work outside the home it would generally be in wealthy households, doing housework, making food or textiles, hairdressing or looking after children.

Those women who had staff working for them also had the opportunity to undertake roles outside the home, the most common title after Lady of the House being Priestess. The top post held by royal women was that of God's Wife, a highly lucrative position which brought tremendous prestige. And as well as her involvement in the usual processions and liturgies, as part of her ritual duties the God's Wife was involved in burning images of the enemy or firing arrows into targets.

Many more women held the title 'Chantress' or were members of the 'khener', a term usually mistranslated as 'harem' which conjures up images of languid women lying around awaiting their lord and master. The khener was in fact a group of predominantly female musicians and dancers who provided the essential musical accompaniments to rituals. The gods – especially Hathor, patron deity of music and dance – were said to love this form of entertainment. She was regularly honoured with musical performances from her devotees, and the awesome powers they were able to summon up from her could be harnessed for all manner of things, from protecting the king to raising the dead.

Employed as professional mourners at funerals, women were also regarded as the ones able to contact the dead. Those referred to as 'the woman who knows' or the local 'wise-woman' were felt to possess the intuitive powers necessary to communicate with unseen forces.

Beyond the religious sphere, some women are also known to have functioned in an official capacity. Although it is generally assumed that there is no evidence for Egyptian women being able to read and write, some are shown looking at documents whilst one in every seven of the almost five hundred letters found at the workers' village of Deir el-Medina was written by or to a woman. Although it has been assumed that women paid a male scribe to write on their behalf, this seems hardly likely for what are often simply notes and reminders: one woman, for instance, sent her sister greetings and asked her to weave her a shawl, with a further request for what may be some sort of sanitary towel. Other letters reveal that at least some women must have been able to read. For example, a scribe writes to a chantress of Amen and says that as soon as she receives his letter she must send him beans. When one man was away on business his wife seems to have acted in his place, telling him that 'the vizier has written to me', presumably expecting her to be able to read the letter – otherwise her husband would surely have appointed a male colleague to act on his behalf. And women must have had to consult written records when working in certain professions. Although the vast majority of officials were men, women did occasionally hold office as governors, as overseers of workshops and even in the medical profession. A woman named Peseshat worked as an 'overseer of doctors' four thousand years before her modern counterparts achieved the right to practise medicine in the West. Two women also achieved the rank of vizier, the highest administrative post and second only to that of pharaoh.

The first Egyptian royal woman can be traced back to around 3150 BC, before Egypt even existed as a nation state. She appears on the huge limestone macehead of King Scorpion found at

Hierakonpolis, and whilst the king wields a hoe and gets his hands dirty at an agricultural fertility ritual, 'Queen Scorpion' remains seated in her carrying chair. With Scorpion's southern-based successors vying for supremacy with their rivals in the north, the two feuding states were finally united under a single king when Narmer triumphed over the forces of Lower Egypt around 3100 BC. The moment is captured on the so-called Narmer Palette, a great piece of carved slate and venerated piece of history which is actually a glorified make-up palette. Discovered in the foundations of the Horus temple at Hierakonpolis, the palette depicts Horus only once, whereas the goddess Hathor appears no fewer than eight times, her four great cow-horned heads at the top of the palette and her protective image on Narmer's kilt as he prepares to bring down his mace on his unfortunate enemy's skull.

To judge from a second piece of Narmer memorabilia, the so-called Wedding Macehead, the new king seems to have married his dead enemy's daughter to seal the country's unification. Again seated in her carrying chair, the unnamed queen faces Narmer beneath the protective outspread wings of the vulture goddess Nekhbet.

Their son Aha, the Fighter, married a northern princess named Neithhotep, whose name, meaning 'Neith is satisfied', was written in the same form of early cartouche as the king. Following Aha's death she became regent, and when she herself died was honoured with a truly king-size tomb near Nagada, boasting no fewer than twenty-one separate chambers.

Aha and Neithhotep's successor, Djer, is believed to have had several northern wives, and his tomb at Abydos was identified by later generations as that of Osiris himself. Along with masses of hair fragments, Petrie also found at the site jars of cedar perfume and Egypt's oldest royal remains, a mummified arm which he believed to be that of 'Djer's queen' because it was covered in jewelled bracelets. The jewellery was retained by the Cairo Museum, but the arm was unfortunately 'discarded'.

Raised within a sophisticated court, with links as far afield as Palestine, Libya and beyond, Djer's daughter Merneith, who lived around 3000 BC, became the second woman to rule the country in only a few decades, and through her control of the royal treasury held the country's purse strings. Her name, written with the shield and crossed arrows, was enclosed within a kingly cartouche and appears in an official list of the dynasty's rulers. She was buried at Abydos in a grand tomb of kingly proportions, which was marked by two great stone stelae. These were published by Petrie as the stelae of 'King Merneith', one of his colleagues stating that 'it can hardly be doubted that Mer-neit [sic] was a king'. 'Hardly doubted', that is, until it was discovered that he was a she and her position then subtly demoted to that of 'regent'. A familiar story.

By the testosterone-fuelled Pyramid Age, women mainly appear as wives, mothers and daughters, although ironically the earliest of any royal remains to have survived seem to be those of a royal daughter. Skeletal remains of a sixteen- to seventeen-year-old woman from the burial chamber of King Djoser's Step Pyramid date exactly to the king's reign, and are thought to be those of one of his three daughters, possibly Princess Hetephernebty.

With pyramids now the accepted form of tomb for the pharaoh and his family, the greatest pyramid builder of all was King Sneferu (2613–2589 BC). Much venerated by later generations, one of the most poignant images from ancient Egypt is a small fragment from the walls of one of Sneferu's pyramid temples, the king closely embraced by the lioness goddess Sekhmet who stands nose to nose to give him the breath of life.

Something more of their relationship may be found in one of the so-called 'Tales of Wonder', a collection of stories popular in ancient times, in which Sneferu is accompanied on a sailing trip by twenty female courtiers. Although usually interpreted as a lurid tale of a lascivious old man seeking dubious amusement from a rowing crew of semi-naked women, there appears to be rather more to it than that. It seems in fact to be some sort of allegory, with the king as sun god propelled across the heavens by representatives of the goddess Hathor, all exhibiting her divine attributes of well-dressed hair and prominent breasts.

Sneferu was buried inside Egypt's first smooth-sided pyramid at Dahshur, but the burial of his wife, Queen Hetepheres I, was transferred to Giza, close to the Great Pyramid tomb of their eldest son, Khufu. Some think Khufu wanted his mother close by to ensure his rebirth into the Afterlife, but whatever the motivation, Hetepheres' shaft tomb was discovered in 1925 when the leg of the archaeologists' camera tripod sank into a gap in the floor above. With the sarcophagus empty and the queen's mummy already destroyed by robbers, it seems that no one dared tell her son the king, who unknowingly reburied an empty coffin amidst his mother's golden treasures. These included Hetepheres' carrying chair inscribed 'Mother of the king who guides him, she whose every command is carried out', together with her golden bed and chairs, her mosquito net-like canopy, gold vessels, razors and silver bangles inlaid with delicate butterflies in semi-precious stones. Her alabaster canopic chest still contained her mummified entrails which provide the first positive evidence for true mummification, in which the internal organs were removed to prevent putrefaction and preserve the body properly.

Sneferu and Hetepheres also had at least three daughters, whilst their son was married to a woman named Nefret, a name written with the hieroglyph sign 𓄤 'nefer', meaning 'Good' or 'Perfect', sometimes translated as 'Beautiful'. Her pristine statue in the Cairo Museum, complete with a wonderful bobbed wig worn over her own cropped hair, indicates that her name was well chosen.

Via plenty of family intrigue and assassinations, Khufu was eventually succeeded by his second son, Khafra, builder of the second pyramid at Giza and best known as the face of the Great Sphinx which guards his tomb. By adopting the royal title 'Son of Ra', Egypt's kings for ever after identified themselves as direct descendants of the sun god.

Yet Khufu's daughter Hetepheres II presents an even more intriguing character. Not only queen, it appears that she ran the civil service as 'Controller of the Affairs of the Kiltwearers' and was a priestess of Thoth, god of learning. In the Giza tomb scenes of her daughter Meresankh III both women are shown on a large scale and dressed in an extraordinary manner. Hetepheres has bright yellow hair, and although she is actually wearing a yellow wig or headcover her own cropped hair, appearing beneath the front of the wig, is also yellow, as it is on Hetepheres' statuary. Although it was initially believed that this hair colour suggested Libyan blood in the family, her incredibly pointed shoulder pads may give another clue.

Of course, these items may simply demonstrate that she had access to the creative starching and pleating techniques of the royal launderers, but if the queen's yellow hair was meant to suggest solar connections, her head as the sun disc then appears between the horizon's mountain peaks formed by her curious dress. Certainly clothing was used by the ancient royals to suggest similar divine associations: recent studies into Tutankhamen's clothing have revealed that his head was also integrated into the design of particular outfits to reinforce royalty's divine associations. It also shows that there may often be far more to this frocks and cosmetics stuff than at first meets the eye!

The appearance of Hetepheres II's daughter Meresankh III is equally fascinating. As Khafra's queen she appears in a variety of different wigs, and then, standing beside her pointy-shouldered mother, she is shown crop-headed and dressed in the leopardskin costume of a funerary priest. Although this is a post regarded as the preserve of literate men, Meresankh also held priestly titles serving both Hathor and, like her mother, Thoth, god of learning. Since Meresankh's body still lay in her tomb, her bones were sent to Derry, who calculated that she must have been about fifty to fifty-five when she died, around five feet tall and with very worn teeth. The archetypal little old lady, in fact, albeit a very powerful one.

The next king, Menkaure, best known as builder of Giza's third pyramid, had himself portrayed in a series of small statues where he stands beside the protective figure of the cow-horned goddess Hathor, who in every case touches him, holds his hand or places her arm around him. Menkaure's queen, Khamerernebty II, also embraces him, and whilst this pose is generally described as that of an adoring appendage holding on to her big, strong, protective husband, it looks to me as if it is the queen doing the protecting as the embodiment of Hathor.

Although Khamerernebty was once believed to have been buried in one of the small pyramids beside that of her husband, it is now suspected that there may have been a certain amount of marital disharmony, and that she built her own tomb at her own expense elsewhere at Giza. It contained large statues of herself, which she must also presumably have paid for. One of these, at around seven feet high, has recently been identified as 'quite possibly the first large statue of a woman in history', and perhaps the first free-standing colossus of a human, male or female, from Egypt, predating that usually claimed for a male king set up some fifty years later.

Menkaure's daughter Khentkawes must have thought along similarly colossal lines, since her tomb is so huge that it is often referred to as the 'Fourth Pyramid of Giza'. In effect it is a huge bench-like tomb close to the pyramid of her father Menkaure, and the reason for the tomb's size and position is to be found in the inscription carved into its granite gateway, naming 'Khentkawes, KING of Upper and Lower Egypt, Mother of the King of Upper and Lower Egypt, Daughter of the god, Every good thing which she orders is done for her'. Yet even with the inscriptions, which are so necessary to convince the establishment, some experts still managed to find 'an alternative translation which is philologically tenable' and which suggested Khentkawes had not really been a king. The fact that an accompanying figure of Khentkawes wears the false beard of a king and the royal cobra at her brow appeared to pass without comment, as did later legends that a woman, and a blonde woman at that, had ruled Egypt at the end of the 4th dynasty. All that is usually admitted is that Khentkawes was the mother of two successive kings and so may have acted as regent for a while.

Yet it never rains but it pours, and recent excavations have revealed that within a couple of decades a second royal woman, also named Khentkawes, was powerful enough to have her own pyramid complex built at the new royal cemetery at Abusir. Like her predecessor of the same name, Khentkawes II seems to have been the mother of two successive kings, although her titles also include 'King of Upper and Lower Egypt'. Once again, her figure is carved with the uraeus snake at her brow and she holds the great papyrus sceptre in her right hand, and this, combined with the fact that she was worshipped for at least three hundred years after her death, has obliged some scholars finally to concede that quite possibly Khentkawes II may have ruled as pharaoh in her own right.

Although the royal family generally married within their own class, Khentkawes II's granddaughter married the royal hair-dresser, who was then elevated to the lofty position of vizier. The couple were provided with a grand tomb at Abusir close to the pyramid of the king.

As the royal cemetery moved back to Sakkara, queens, like kings, were buried in pyramids now inscribed with magic spells known as the Pyramid Texts. These were filled with evocations of the gods; the sky goddess Nut, for instance, played a key role in protecting the dead and is described as the 'Great Striding Goddess' who scatters the stars like jewels across the night sky, where the souls of previous kings and queens twinkle as the 'Imperishable' ones. Although the only thing which seems to be known about the mother of King Teti was her remedy for baldness – a blend of dog's paw, donkey hoof and date kernels boiled in oil, presumably to make a glue-like mixture – the skeletal remains of two of Teti's wives were found in their pyramids. Sent to Qasr el-Einy with Teti's remaining arm, Queen Iput appears to have been a middle-aged woman with large eyes and a narrow nose, fond of wearing the queenly vulture crown whose outstretched wings formed the sides of the head-dress. Iput also produced the next king, Pepi I, and acted as regent until he became old enough to rule for himself.

Once Pepi I did become king, things got off to a bumpy start when his first wife was involved in a scandal. Her name was removed from every monument and the king's most trusted official was sent to deal with the delicate matter, reporting that 'when there was a secret charge in the [royal household] against the King's wife, Great One of the Sceptre, his majesty made me hear it, I being alone.' Although it is unclear what had gone on – perhaps an assassination attempt, or embezzlement – it was obviously a situation that demanded the utmost discretion.

The king next married a commoner, Ankhnesmerire, and their son, Pepi II, is shown as a small boy on his mother's lap, their hands touching in a gesture of close affection. She acted as regent until he came of age; and at her death she was buried in her own pyramid complex, as was Pepi II's own wife Neith, whose battered, headless mummy was recovered from her ransacked pyramid. Pepi II himself went on to become the longest-reigning monarch in Egypt's long history, clocking up an extraordinary ninety-four years, and after his death at around the age of one hundred the next king was a woman.

There had already been two women named as king and four who had ruled as regent, but it is only with the last king of this dynasty that we finally reach a woman about whose status as ruler there can be no doubt. This was King Neithikret, 'Neith is excellent', better known by the Greek form of her name, Nitocris. She ruled Egypt between about 2148 and 2144 BC, apparently on her own behalf rather than as regent for a son, following the death (maybe murder) of her brother. With the reign of 'Nitokerti' recorded in the ancient Egyptian king list, even the most hard-line traditional Egyptologists are forced to admit that, as a female king, 'her historical existence can therefore not be doubted'. Neithikret also appears in the colour-ful writings of Herodotus, and during his visit to Egypt in 450 BC the priests 'read to me from a written record the names of 330 monarchs' and told him about a woman named Nitocris who had avenged her murdered brother. After constructing an under-ground chamber she invited the murderers to a banquet, then flooded the chamber to drown them all, and 'the only other thing I was told about her was that after this fearful revenge she flung herself into a room full of ashes'.

A few centuries later the Greek scholar Eratosthenes was refer-ring to her simply as 'a woman instead of a man', whilst the priest-historian Manetho says she ruled for twelve years, was the bravest and most beautiful woman of her time, 'with fair complexion [and] who raised the third pyramid', a description which seems to confuse her with the earlier female monarch Khentkawes. King Nitocris can be fleshed out a little more through the obscure work *Tractatus de Mulieribus Claris in Bello*, or 'Women Intelligent and Courageous in Warfare', and although this repeats most of what Herodotus said, it at least showed that Neithikret was sufficiently memorable to be included in a list compiled some two thousand years after her death.

After several centuries of pyramid building combined with a series of bad harvests and famine, the economy had already been weakened to such an extent that some royals had to start reusing old sarcophagi for their burials. As things went from bad to worse, the ancient texts described the chaos when brother fought brother and the land ran with blood. As the world turned upside-down, society was in turmoil as jewels were 'strung on the necks of female slaves. Noblewomen roam the land, ladies say 'we want to eat!' . . . their bodies suffer in rags'. And as the dead lay unburied, the country 'was dying of hunger, everyone eating their children,' so great was the hardship.

After a terrible century of political unrest, sporadic outbreaks of civil war were only ended by the Theban warlords, the greatest hero of whom was unquestionably Montuhotep II (2055–

2004 BC), who reunited the country during his fifty-year reign. Deep in the Theban cliffs behind his funerary temple at Deir el-Bahari, he was laid to rest in a rock-cut tomb whose entrance was guarded by the burials of five priestesses of Hathor. Each woman was also named 'Wife of the King whom he loves' and surviving wall scenes show these women being embraced by him. One of them was Ashayet, whose acquaintance I had made at Qasr el-Einy. I also knew that she had held the additional title 'Great Royal Wife', making her the most powerful woman in Egypt, so it is somewhat irritating that, along with her fellow wives, she is almost always described as a 'concubine'.

Other women buried close to Montuhotep were a five-year-old girl, most likely his daughter, named Mayet, 'Kitten', two more of his queens, and three more female bodies which were heavily tattooed. Two of them, buried with no convenient inscriptions, were immediately dubbed 'dancing girls' by the archaeologists, no doubt using their own opinions of tattooed women to guide them in their identification. Yet, having been buried so close to the king, they were surely important members of the court.

Montuhotep II had put Egypt right back on track, and all went well until King Amenemhat I was assassinated by his own bodyguard in his thirtieth year as king, around 1955 BC, the time of the first mention of the aten. At the precise moment of the king's death his soul left his body and 'flew to heaven and united with the aten, his divine body merging with its maker'. His ghost returned to tell his beloved son Sesostris I to beware of traitors in his midst: 'Hear what I tell you ... Beware of subjects who are nobodies, of whose plotting one is not aware. Trust not a brother, know not a friend, make no intimates ... Had women ever marshalled troops? Are rebels nurtured in the palace?' Yet the new king Sesostris was at least able to trust his sister-wife Neferu, and in a letter to one of his officials wrote that the queen lived and prospered, 'her head adorned with the kingship of the land', which sounds as though the two of them shared royal power in some way.

Their daughters too are mentioned in the literature, and played an active part in court life, carrying the sistrum rattles and menat necklaces sacred to the goddess Hathor, whom they represented. With all manner of gold flowers, rings and jewellery woven into their wigs to resemble the Golden One, royal women throughout the dynasty were also represented as lion-like sphinxes; one such statue was found as far afield as Syria. And accompanying the dynasty's smooth progression of kings named Sesostris or Amenemhat, almost half the royal women had the hieroglyph sign ⧊ 'nefer', 'Good' or 'Perfect' as part of their names.

During the next two centuries of peace and prosperity the royals continued to be buried in pyramid tombs, although the only traces of royal remains are Sesostris II's leg, which Petrie sent back to UCL, and the 'resin-treated bones' of Princess Menet, daughter of the perpetually scowling sovereign Sesostris III. Discovered at her father's pyramid at Dahshur, Menet had been buried along with a dozen or so other royal women whose tombs were ransacked in ancient times. The thieves had, however, missed the jackpot, and some of their jewel chests were still hidden in the floor. When discovered in 1894, they still contained over three hundred necklaces, bracelets, anklets and belts of stupendous workmanship. Some of the royal women had also been buried with cosmetics chests filled with gold and obsidian perfume jars and matching kohl pots, silver compacts for rouge-like mixtures and mirrors adorned with the head of beautiful Hathor; the Princess Ita had even been buried wearing her bronze dagger with inlaid hilt. The same mix of weapons and ornaments were found with the two middle-aged queens of Amenemhat III, who had been buried in his pyramid at Dahshur with their jewellery, perfume pots and a nice selection of granite and alabaster mace-heads.

Their long-lived husband, however, unhappy at the alarming cracks appearing in his pyramid, decided to start again at Hawara, the area sacred to the crocodile god Sobek, symbol of royal might. Here, in the place where the king's own colossal statues showed him wearing a large wig and Hathor's menat necklace, he began a second pyramid complex so large and elaborate that it became known as the Labyrinth. Herodotus raved about it, describing it as better than the Giza pyramids. Apparently it had twelve courts and intricate passages connecting its three thousand rooms. Half of these were set below ground and contained 'the tombs of the sacred crocodiles' mummified at death, with fearsome statues of the crocodile god Sobek also standing at the site beside those of Hathor in a heady mix of beauty and terror.

Early Egyptologists believed that the old king Amenemhat III made both his son and his daughter co-regents with him, but was succeeded only by his son as Amenemhat IV, at which time the daughter, Sobekneferu, seems to have lost her position. When her brother died after a nine-year reign, however, she became king, prompting one scholar to speculate that 'there seems considerable likelihood of a family feud out of which Sebeknofru emerged the victor'.

As Egypt's second female king – even at the most conservative estimate – Sobekneferu ruled for around four years, from about 1799 to 1795 BC, the traditional 'Son of Ra' sometimes switched to 'Daughter of Ra' and her name included on later king lists as a bona fide monarch. With her birth name meaning 'the perfections of Sobek', written with a crocodile and three nefer signs 🐊 𓊹𓊹𓊹 Sobekneferu's own choice for the second name she needed once she became king was Sobekkara. This doubly emphasised her links with this symbol of royal might and seems to have set something of a trend amongst her male successors to be named after the crocodile god.

Three life-size basalt statues and a sphinx of King Sobekneferu were found in northern Egypt, and she also instructed her sculptors to portray her wearing the royal striped nemes headcloth and male kilt, with her name written on her belt buckle just as with male kings. Worn over her otherwise female clothing as a perfect example of cross-dressing, it blends male and female characteristics in a completely innovative way, as does a second unique statue in which she is wrapped in a coronation-style cloak, wearing a round, shoulder-length wig topped by two vultures with outstretched wings and the protective cobra between.

Responsible for a number of temple buildings, she was the one to complete her father's ambitious Labyrinth-style pyramid complex as his dutiful heir, her name occurring as often as her father's on the remaining blocks. When this was achieved she could begin work on her own pyramid, most likely at Mazghuna, just south of Dahshur, where her brother, the previous king, is also thought to have been buried but in a smaller complex.

Although Sobekneferu is usually dismissed as the end of the line, the last resort of a dynasty which had no male contender at that time, the truth is that there was no power struggle and the throne passed smoothly to the next dynasty. The records show that the kings kept doing their kingly thing and the queens likewise continued to do their stuff. But as the turnover of kings began to increase, with some seventy rulers in little more than a century, settlers from Palestine took advantage of the increasing instability. After infiltrating the government they eventually took the throne as Hyksos, meaning 'Rulers of Foreign Lands'. Recent excavations at their capital in the Nile Delta have also uncovered a Minoan settlement, with frescoes of long-haired, bull-leaping figures and the floral and animal motifs typical of Aegean design, proving that there were close connections between Crete and Egypt by around 1600 BC. Yet there seems to have been little overall authority between 1650 and 1550 BC, with intermittent civil war between the Hyksos in the north and their southern rivals, the indomitable warlords of Thebes.

As history repeated itself, the Thebans eventually reunited the country around 1550 BC. Driving the Hyksos right out of Egypt and back up into Palestine, a dynasty of warrior pharaohs went on to create the greatest empire the world had yet seen. Presiding over a true Golden Age when Egypt really did dominate the world, this was the 18th dynasty, the most famous of Egypt's royal families, who traced their line back to a tiny woman born to commoners. The formidable Queen Tetisheri was the Great Royal Wife of the warlord Tao I. And as King's Mother to both Tao II and Ahhotep she was remembered for centuries, her grandson King Ahmose setting up a stela to her at Abydos, centre of ancestor worship. Here he refers to his late grandmother Tetisheri as 'the mother of my mother, the mother of my father', with Tetisheri herself shown seated with the queenly lily sceptre in her left hand to receive honours from her doting grandson. He also built Egypt's last-known royal pyramid in her honour, surrounded by gardens containing a lake. It was built at Abydos as a cenotaph to her memory; the queen herself had been buried in the family plot back in Thebes.

Since the royal family's home town was now the capital of Egypt's growing empire, it was appropriate that the desert cliffs on the opposite bank of the Nile should become the royal burial ground for the next five hundred years. The area's arid conditions were perfect for preserving bodies, mummified using sophisticated techniques which were never surpassed. Their survival in the great caches of royal bodies allows us to look directly into the faces of members of this most extraordinary of families, beginning with Tetisheri herself, the dynasty's female founder. Although her tomb was robbed in ancient times her mummy was salvaged and became part of the great Deir el-Bahari cache: her sparse hair was interplaited with false braids and the distinctive family trait of buck teeth was very much in evidence.

The mummy of her heroic son King Tao II was also found here, his lips drawn back in a grimace reflecting the spasms of death. Even his hair was still matted with blood from the wounds which killed him, quite possibly inflicted on the battlefield while driving out the reviled Hyksos. Because of the shape of the fatal head wounds it has been suggested they were made by characteristic Hyksos weapons, with a dagger thrust behind the ear, a mace smashed into the cheekbone and an axe driven into the forehead.

Following his violent death, his widow and sister Ahhotep, named as King's Daughter, King's Sister, King's Wife and King's Mother, is known to have rallied the troops. An inscription from Karnak Temple states that, 'She looked after Egypt's soldiers and protected them. She brought back its fugitives and gathered its dissidents together. She pacified Upper Egypt [the south] and expelled its rebels.' In short, she picked up the pieces and kept Egypt strong. This extraordinary woman then ruled as regent with full pharaonic powers for her youngest son Ahmose, who rightly lavished honours on her. The same inscription from Karnak also told those who read it to 'Give praise to the Lady of the Land, Mistress of the shores of Haunebu [the Aegean]. Her name is raised above every foreign country, [and she] governs the people. The wife of the king, the sister of the lord [the king] – life, prosperity, health! The princess, the king's mother, the noblewoman, who knows things and takes care of Egypt.' She certainly did that.

Although her amazing achievements are rarely listed in full, Ahhotep was actively involved in running the country; this seems to be confirmed by the contents of her intact tomb discovered near Qurna in 1859. In a rich burial containing some of the most amazing treasures ever found, the mummified body of the queen still lay in her coffin of imported cedar covered in gold, her large curled wig of the goddess Hathor topped by the royal cobra. Unfortunately the tomb was cleared quickly, without super-vision. The contents were taken to a local headman who stripped the mummy of its adornments, threw the body away and sent the remaining four pounds or so of gold to the authorities in Cairo to melt down into bullion. When the Director of Antiqui-ties, Auguste Mariette, heard of the find, in the great tradition of an action hero he jumped aboard his steam boat and headed south, managing to pull alongside the boat with its cargo of treasure coming the other way. Only after issuing a series of dire threats did he manage to rescue the priceless haul, and despite the French Empress Eugénie letting it be known that she quite fancied the jewellery herself, Mariette firmly refused and the treasure ended up safely in the Cairo Museum. Ahhotep would have been proud of him.

As well as the queen's stunning jewellery, mirror and fan, there were items more usually associated with male burials, a large golden staff, an archer's bracer-type armlet, a javelin head and thirteen axes of bronze, gold and silver. One of the axe blades was decorated with an Aegean-type griffin on one side and a sphinx holding an enemy head on the other; similar Aegean-looking motifs also adorned one of the three daggers of gold and bronze, the handle featuring two bulls' heads and its blade a lion hunt. With a loop on the scabbard for attachment to clothing, this could well have been the ultimate stylish accessory for a warrior queen.

Perhaps most significant of all were two sets of military decorations, the Golden Flies of Valour. Based on the relentless energies of this ever-present, persistent insect, these were ancient Egypt's version of the Victoria Cross, awarded for outstanding bravery on the field of battle. Yet traditional Egyptology would have us believe that all these items, both weapons and medals, belonged to the queen's son who had simply placed them in his mother's tomb, and that they had little to do with her personally!

The next royal couple were King Ahmose and his sister-wife Ahmose-Nefertari, whose name is once again written with the ⚱ sign. Like her warlike mother, Ahmose-Nefertari had all the right credentials – King's Daughter, King's Sister, King's Wife and King's Mother, as well as Female Chieftain of Upper and Lower Egypt – and was perhaps the most influential woman not to rule as pharaoh herself.

As the first queen of the 18th dynasty and chief wife of her brother, Ahmose-Nefertari also held important religious office as Second Prophet of Amen, always said to be a male priest's title. She then passed this office on to one of her infant sons following her promotion to the dizzy heights of God's Wife – basically high priestess of Amen himself. It was a lucrative post, carrying the right to pass on her office to her heirs in perpetuity. The queen also set up some sort of training college for Amen priestesses on her estates on the West Bank of the Nile at Thebes. She had a female deputy on hand to fill in for her when busy, and the ancient texts also state that the queen's brother was to act as her steward 'so she may be spared administrative troubles'.

Ahmose-Nefertari certainly seems to have been an active ruler and is credited with taking the lead in restoring temples long neglected under Hyksos rule. As another of the royal women 'who says all things and they are done for her', she shared in the decision-making process with her brother-husband, who is known to have discussed policy with her and sought her approval for his plans. At his death she would have been the one to oversee his elaborate funeral, and was perhaps responsible for the delphinium garland placed on his mummy.

With their surviving son Amenhotep I still a young boy she then acted as regent for around seven years. Even when he had become king in his own right, his mother ruled alongside him as co-ruler, portrayed on one stela as the partner of both her husband and her son.

Ahmose-Nefertari and her son also founded the village of Deir el-Medina to house the workers who built the tombs in the Valley of the Kings. Monarchs, of course, usually began their tombs early in their reign to allow enough time to complete the work, but at his accession Amenhotep I was only a small child and presumably not yet old enough to deal with such matters. It was highly likely, therefore, that his mother, ruling on his behalf, gave the order for the preparation of her son's burial site. And if this is the first royal tomb in the valley, there's a very good chance that the Valley of the Kings was founded by a woman. Tomb KV.39 does seem to be the most likely candidate for the tomb created for Amenhotep I; and after he 'joined with the aten's disc', around 1504 BC, his elderly mother would have been at least partly responsible for his funeral. His mummy was found intact and so perfectly turned out that it has never been unwrapped.

Ahmose-Nefertiti herself seems to have lived to a ripe old age, and, loved by her people, she was worshipped as patron saint in the tomb builders' village for another five hundred years. Her death was even reported in non-royal circles, 'the god's wife having flown up to heaven', and she was buried in a massive coffin over twelve feet long to emphasise her status. Yet the mummy within was that of a tiny old lady, her remaining hair padded out with hair extensions and the family's buck teeth clearly visible.

Her last years must have been taken up with worries about the succession, and since her son had left no obvious heir the throne passed to his brother-in-law, Tuthmosis. Although common-born, Tuthmosis I claimed to have 'come from the Aten', the sun disc now named as a god in its own right for the first time – some 150 years before Akhenaten is supposed to have invented the concept. Also referring to himself as 'Mighty Bull with Sharp Horns', Tuthmosis I spent much of his eleven-year reign consolidating the Egyptian empire up into the Near East and down into Nubia. His wife Queen Ahmose is portrayed with a discreetly rounded belly on her otherwise svelte figure when pregnant with their daughter Hatshepsut, whilst one of the king's minor wives also produced a male heir, Tuthmosis II, who became king around 1492 BC.

Tuthmosis II was married to his half-sister Hatshepsut in order to strengthen his weaker claim, and she, as the real royal heiress, inherited the prestigious and lucrative post of God's Wife of Amen following the death of the ancient dowager Ahmose-Nefertari. Although Hatshepsut gave her half-brother a daughter, Princess Neferure, Tuthmosis II followed in his father's footsteps and produced a male heir by a minor wife. But when the king died soon afterwards, around 1479 BC, his son was still a small child. So the widowed Hatshepsut was made regent and, as the ancient texts state, she 'governed the land, and the Two Lands [Egypt] were under her control; people work for her, and Egypt bowed the head.' And that's when the fun really began!

After six years as regent Hatshepsut evidently decided she was cut out to be pharaoh, and as daughter, sister and wife of kings she had greater legitimacy than the son of a minor wife. So in 1473 BC she put aside her queenly vulture crown and lily sceptre, and, just as Sobekneferu had done three hundred years earlier, took up the traditional kingly regalia of crowns, sceptres, kilt and even the tie-on false beard. As a queen taking on full kingly status she needed two more official names, so Queen Hatshepsut transformed herself into King Maatkara Hatshepsut-KhnemetAmen. And with the feminine 't' sign ⌒ added to the word 'Majesty', the Son of Ra was once again a Daughter.

Once she had taken on the trappings of a pharaoh, Hatshepsut could no longer function as the female God's Wife. She therefore handed over this hereditary position to her daughter Princess Neferure, whose own name was written with three nefer signs 𓎢 and the disc ⊙ of the sun god. Supplying the necessary female element that her kingly mother now could not, Neferure also became her mother's queen; this has been compared to the way in which, in modern Western societies, female mayors still require a lady mayoress. Neferure's portraits show her still with her hair in the traditional sidelock of youth, surrounded by the royal diadem and cobra, and with the menat necklace of the goddess Hathor around her neck; in her left hand she holds the queenly sceptre proudly to denote her status.

Some Egyptologists believe Hatshepsut was grooming her daughter to be her successor, since she entrusted the girl's education to the male official Senmut, Chief of All Works and Chief Steward, a self-made man who had a meteoric rise and ended up in charge of much of the day-to-day running of the country. Six of his ten statues show him with the princess on his lap, sometimes wrapped protectively within his cloak, while the accompanying texts announce that 'I educated the king's daughter, I was given to her ... because of my excellence on behalf of the king', in other words her mother, who was then able to get on with the business of ruling.

Under the strong rule of King Hatshepsut, Egypt thrived for almost twenty years. At her coronation it was decreed that she 'seize the chiefs of Retenu [Palestine] by violence, those left over from your father's reign. Your catch shall be men by the thousands.' And sending the army south into Nubia where 'slaughter was made among them' she 'destroyed the southern lands', concluding ominously that 'no one rebels against me in any land'.

More peaceably, Hatshepsut reopened the turquoise and copper mines of Sinai and expanded the temple of Hathor, worshipped there as 'Lady of the Turquoise'. She also re-established long-distance trade networks between Egypt and the mysterious land of Punt on the Red Sea coast. This was the main area of production for the huge quantities of frankincense, myrrh and pistacia resins required for temple ritual, perfume production and mummification. And as well as the raw resins gathered up by the bucketful, her expedition also brought back incense tree seedlings, with 'thirty-one fresh myrrh trees brought as marvels of Punt'. Hailing Hatshepsut as 'Female Sun Who Shines Like the Aten', the Puntites handed over huge quantities of these costly resins which the king then offered to her father, Amen-Ra. She seems, however, to have retained some for personal use, and is described as having 'the best of myrrh upon all her limbs, her fragrance is divine dew, her odour is mingled with Punt, her skin is gilded ... shining as do the stars ... before the whole land.'

The king gathered around her a trustworthy body of officials, headed by Senmut, and rewarded them according to their abilities. The royal architect Ineni, for instance, was able to claim that 'her majesty praised me and loved me, she having recognised my qualities in the palace; she enriched me with possessions, she made me great and filled my humble abode with silver, gold and every good thing of the palace so that I did not say "would that I had" in regard to anything'. And clearly, from the expense Senmut was able to lavish on his elderly mother's burial, he must have amassed even more personal wealth as a result of his royal service.

Hatshepsut also seems to have had the full support of the Amen priests, headed by the high priest Hapuseneb, whom she seems to have worked with during her time as 'God's Wife' priestess. Brilliant at spin, she also made it known that she was in fact the daughter of Amen, who by now had been combined with the sun god Ra to make him twice as powerful, the new and improved Amen-Ra, King of the Gods. Apparently Hatshepsut's divine birth had come about as the result of a night of passion between her mother, Queen Ahmose, and the god, who thoughtfully disguised himself as her husband so as not to alarm her: Amen had

'found the queen in the inner rooms of the palace. When smelling the divine scent, she woke up and she smiled at him. At once he proceded towards her. He lusted after her, and gave her his heart . . . love for him flowed through her body. The palace became inundated by the scent of god, it smelled like in Punt (land of incense). Thereupon the god did what he wished with her. She made him rejoice over her, and she kissed him. She said to him 'How splendid it is to see you face to face . . . your dew is through all my limbs!'

And Hatshepsut was born nine months later, Amen's own child and 'his daughter in very truth', as she says herself.

This story of divine conception, together with details of the trading expedition to Punt, form some of the key events of her reign which Hatshepsut chose to adorn her funerary temple at Deir el-Bahari, meticulously aligned with Karnak Temple opposite across the Nile, which she also redesigned. Together with a new pylon gateway, her Red Chapel was carved with scenes of the king wearing pharaonic garb and performing many of the key rituals associated with kingship. She also erected a series of great pink granite obelisks, having had the idea 'when I sat in the palace and thought of my maker'. Each weighing hundreds of tons, the obelisks took seven months to extract from the granite quarries of Aswan and were then floated north to Karnak on huge barges. Covered in sheet gold to reflect sunlight around the temple, they could, Hatshepsut tells us, be seen on both sides of the river, 'illuminating the Two Lands like the Aten' in yet another appearance by the so-called Amarna sun god.

The indefatigable monarch also created temples at Luxor and Medinet Habu, and further north, at Speos Artemidos near Amarna, commissioned a rock-cut shrine high in the cliffs; its detailed inscriptions declare that she was the one responsible for restoring temples which had fallen into ruin during the Hyksos Period a century later. Though rarely mentioned, this is a real masterstroke of propaganda and deserves greater appreciation:

The temple of [Hathor] was fallen into ruin, and the earth had swallowed its august sanctuary while children danced on its roof. The serpent goddess no longer promoted terror and . . . its festivals no longer appeared. I re-sanctified it after it had been built anew. It is in order to protect her city I fashioned her image from gold . . . Hear you, all patricians and all commoners as many as you are, I have done this by the plan in my heart . . . I made flourish what had been ruined. I raised up what was cut up formerly since the Asiatics [Hyksos] were in the fold of the Delta . . . foreigners in their midst overthrowing what had been made. Unmindful of Ra they ruled, and he did not act by divine command down to the time of my majesty, I having been established on the throne of Ra. I was foretold for an eternity of years as 'She will become a Conqueror'. I have come as the Sole One of Horus flaming against my enemies . . . My command is firm as the mountains and the [Aten] disc shines and spreads rays over the titulary of my majesty, and my falcon is high over [my name] forever and ever.

Sadly, tragedy struck when her teenage daughter Neferure died some time after her mother's eleventh year as king, around

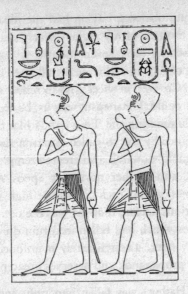

FIGURE 9. Detail of a wall scene from Karnak temple
showing the identical figures of Hatshepsut followed by her
successor Tuthmosis III, both wearing king's crowns and
kilts and holding a royal sceptre in their right hand

1462 BC. This was followed by the death a couple of years later
of her most trusted adviser, Senmut. Hatshepsut then reinstated
her stepson Tuthmosis III as her heir and co-regent: the two
kings are shown dressed identically in blue crown and kilt and
holding the royal crook in their right hand bent across the chest.
When the co-rulers are depicted sailing in Amen's great boat
during the sacred festivals, Hatshepsut stands regally at the bow
whilst Tuthmosis III mans the oar at the stern in a subtle reversal
of old King Sneferu and his female rowing crew.

Over in the Valley of the Kings behind her Deir el-Bahari
temple Hatshepsut had also been busy, building the second of
two tombs. The first, set high in the cliffs to the south of Deir
el-Bahari, she seems to have begun work on while still queen.
Then, as king, she set to work making alterations to the tomb of

her father, Tuthmosis I, originally designed by the royal architect Ineni who had 'supervised the excavation of the cliff tomb of His Majesty alone, no-one seeing, no-one hearing'. It appears that Hatshepsut ordered the burial chamber to be enlarged to accommodate matching stone sarcophagi for herself and her father, with whom she wanted to be buried and 'be eternal like an undying star', as she says rather poetically. The tomb was ransacked in ancient times, and although the mummy labelled as Tuthmosis I was eventually transferred to the great cache of royal mummies found in 1881, that of his illustrious daughter has not yet been discovered – or, if it has, it has not yet been conclusively identified.

Many of the modern accounts of Hatshepsut's reign border on the farcical, as once again her achievements are played down in repeated attempts to cast her as some kind of freak. As the wicked stepmother who seized power from the rightful heir, then masqueraded as a man, this travesty of a woman who flaunted kingly titles also indulged in cross-dressing, and even wore a beard! Since, as a mere woman, she was obviously unable to achieve anything herself, her claims to have done so are often dismissed as 'exaggerations'; and she must have been carrying on an affair with her 'close adviser' Senmut who must surely have been the real power behind the throne. Then, when Tuthmosis III's pent-up frustration finally exploded, Hatshepsut was somehow bumped off together with her fancy man, their fates no doubt well deserved after their presumptuous behaviour, and everything they had built was quite rightly smashed to smithereens the minute they were dead.

Hatshepsut would indeed appear as some sort of anomaly if all her female predecessors had been repeatedly played down, dismissed or ignored. But in fact she was only expanding on the foundations laid by predecessors such as Sobekneferu, Neithikret and Khentkawes with their male garb and false beards, not to mention her own illustrious family of warrior queens who had ruled Egypt and founded her dynasty. Recent research has also indicated that the vandalism to Hatshepsut's monuments did not occur immediately after her reign, and seems at least in part to have been the work of the puritanical kings of the 19th dynasty who did the same to the monuments of Akhenaten and Nefertiti. It is possible that Hatshepsut was in fact something of a role model for Amenhotep III, who seems to have been influenced by the great female king – she was certainly some act to follow.

Tuthmosis III finally emerged from Hatshepsut's shadow around 1458 BC, to become Tuthmosis III, sole pharaoh and Son of Ra. Although there is little evidence to show that Tuthmosis III felt any malice towards his formidable predecessor, it is quite possible he may well have felt a little overwhelmed by this domineering woman who had towered over her stepson in more ways than one. Known in modern times as the 'Napoleon of ancient Egypt', the five-foot pharaoh consolidated the area of Syria-Palestine and stationed garrisons amongst the vassal states there. The children of these regions were taken back to the Egyptian court both as a guarantee of their fathers' continued obedience and also to be educated in Egyptian culture, which they would then take back home when reaching adulthood.

Spending much of his life under canvas, Tuthmosis III led no fewer than seventeen military campaigns, one of the highlights being the ingenious capture of Joppa (Jaffa), in which the Egyptian army infiltrated the stronghold by hiding themselves Ali Baba-style in two hundred baskets. And after the siege and capture of Megiddo, the biblical Armageddon, much of the spectacular plunder – gold, lapis lazuli, turquoise, grain, wine, cattle, horses, male and female servants – was sent back to Amen's priests at Karnak in return for Amen providing the king with victory.

Something of the fabulous wealth which would have continually flooded into Karnak is also reflected in the rewards given to the king's brilliant general, Djehuty. His intact tomb, found at Sakkara in 1824, still contained his gold-encased mummy, thick gold bangles, chunky gold rings, gold and silver bowls and a bronze dagger. The ancient lists of plunder from battles also reveal a sophisticated lifestyle, and whilst the militaristic king was no doubt impressed with the golden chariots, bronze coats of mail and weaponry, the lists also refer to ebony and gold statues with heads of lapis lazuli, walking sticks with human heads, carrying chairs of ebony and ivory worked with gold, and a bed of gilded wood inlaid with costly stones. Many of these luxury items would no doubt have made their way back to the royal palaces.

The foreign campaigns allowed Tuthmosis III to indulge his love of hunting – hippo and elephant hunting in particular. And he also seems to have had something of an interest in botany, revealed by the numerous exotic plants sent back to the gardens of Karnak Temple and carved on the walls of the so-called Botanical Gardens chamber. And like the exotic flowers he so admired, Tuthmosis III collected foreign women; for instance, three of his minor wives, Menhet, Menwi and Merti, came from Syria. Their joint tomb at Thebes, found intact by locals in 1916, was stuffed full of golden treasures, from crowns with gazelle heads, necklaces and bracelets, to superb drinking vessels, mirrors and pots of face cream. Yet, as minor wives, Queen Merti (whose name is the equivalent of 'Martha') and her two compatriots would have taken a back seat to the king's Egyptian wives, the most influential of whom, named after her illustrious predecessor, was Queen Meryetre-Hatshepsut, God's Wife and mother of the next king, Amenhotep II.

It is clear from their respective mummies that Amenhotep II favoured his mother's side of the family. Almost a foot taller than his father, he was rather fetchingly described as 'a beautiful youth who was well developed and had completed eighteen years upon his thighs in strength'. But he did inherit his father's military abilities, and was put in charge of the royal stables while still a young prince. His prowess in chariotry and archery was legendary – a true son of the warrior goddess Neith.

After crushing a rebellion amongst the Palestinian vassal states shortly after his accession, the king personally executed seven of the rebel leaders in time-honoured fashion by bringing his mace crashing down on their heads. Then with their bloody corpses hung upside down from the prow of his plunder-laden ship, he returned home in triumph. After greeting his wife Queen Tia at the administrative capital, Memphis, he sailed on south to present the treasures to Amen's priests at Karnak, together with six of the corpses to be hung from the city walls at Thebes. The seventh was taken even further south, to the Sudanese city of Napata, 'in order to cause to be seen the victorious might of his majesty forever and ever'.

Such swift and vicious retribution clearly made the point and, unsurprisingly, the empire remained loyal for the rest of his reign. Each of the former rebel states tried to outdo the others in the rich gifts they sent to the pharaoh, but this cut little ice for he remembered their duplicity and held them in contempt. Some twenty-three years later, while 'sitting drinking and making holiday' during the festivals celebrating the anniversary of his accession, he was moved to write a letter to his viceroy down in Nubia: 'Now there is brought to you this decree from the king who is great with the sword's stroke, with a mighty arm, and valiant with his forearm, who has subdued northerners and overthrown southerners wherever they are so that there is no longer an opponent in any land.' After a bit of laddish reminiscing about the old days when the two had fought side by side, the king refers to his Syrian vassals as old women: 'Of what use are they anyway?' He also reminds his viceroy, in a kind of PS, 'Don't be at all lenient with the Nubians. Beware of their people and their sorcerers!'

Yet again like his father, Amenhotep II appreciated at least some of the inhabitants of foreign lands, and had an extensive retinue of minor wives from abroad. With 323 daughters of Palestinian princes and 270 female singers and entertainers forming only part of his female entourage, he seems to have been happy with just one Egyptian bride. His Great Royal Wife Queen Tia also held the influential post of God's Wife priestess, and, as mother of the next king, she appears with her son on a superb lifesize black granite statue found at her workplace, Karnak Temple.

The temple treasuries were now filled to bursting point with the mountains of tribute sent to Amen by successive warrior kings, and Tia's colleagues in the priesthood had become so powerful that it was feared they would soon rival the throne. So subtle moves were gradually made to limit their ambitions and balance Karnak's power by placing greater emphasis on the ancient sun god Ra. Focussing on the ancient burial grounds of Giza, whose pyramids were already over a thousand years old, a newly crowned Amenhotep II built a temple beside the Sphinx to whom it was dedicated. He also gave a new twist to this ancient monument, now identified as an image of the sun god himself, by setting up a twenty-foot-high statue of himself between the Sphinx's paws, together with a royal rest house and inscriptions honouring the Old Kingdom pharaohs Khafra and Khufu.

Although all kings since this early time had been named as Son of Ra, there was now an additional emphasis on the sun disc itself, the Aten. First mentioned back in 1955 BC, the Aten wasn't actually portrayed until Amenhotep II decided to give it a recognisable form and had his artists devise a sun disc with a pair of enveloping arms. It was a policy continued under his son Tuthmosis IV, who, according to the royal spin doctors, had been selected as king by the sun god Sphinx himself. The colossal figure had spoken to him in a dream 'as a father speaks to his son', saying, 'I shall give you reign upon earth over the living and you shall wear its white crown and its red crown on the throne of Geb . . . To you shall belong the earth in its length and its breadth, together with that which the eye of the All-Lord illuminates . . . For prolonged years already my face has been turned to you and my heart likewise. You belong to me . . . I know that you are my son and my champion. Approach; I am with you; I am your guide.' Seemingly little more than a far-fetched romantic story carved on the so-called Dream Stela by the Sphinx's great paws, this clever propaganda reveals the shift in the pharaoh's religious allegiance. Neatly distancing Tuthmosis IV and his successors from the influence of the Amen clergy down in Thebes, it clearly linked the pharaoh with the sun god, worshipped as both Ra and the Aten.

Although he only had a ten-year reign, from about 1400 to 1390 BC, Tuthmosis IV packed a lot into his life. Something of a dandy with his shoulder-length dyed hair, long fingernails and pierced ears, the fourth Tuthmosis nevertheless laid solid foundations for the next four decades' achievements. A clear supporter of the sun god, he realised the need to keep Amen's priests happy too, adding new buildings to Karnak and finally getting round to setting up the golden obelisk begun by his grandfather, Tuthmosis III. As he says himself, 'the obelisk had 'spent thirty-five years lying upon its side in the hands of the craftsmen, on the south side of Karnak. My [grand]father commanded that I should erect it for him, I, his [grand]son, his saviour.'

Apart from two Great Royal Wives Tuthmosis IV had a number of minor wives, some of whom were from outside Egypt. With foreign nations mindful of rotting corpses on the battlements, they decided to give peace a chance while Tuthmosis IV did his bit for international relations through diplomatic marriage. His alliance with Egypt's former enemy Mitanni in Syria, sealed by marriage to a daughter of the Mitannian king, represented a milestone. Tuthmosis also had a woman named Mutemwia in his retinue, named after Amen's consort goddess Mut and described as 'well-disposed and sweet of love'. Her precise origins remain a mystery, but she did produce the next king. Tuthmosis IV is known to have had a number of children by his various wives, and after the premature death of his eldest son, Amenemhat, the king went against royal tradition and publicly declared young Amenhotep to be his heir. Although royal daughters were always seen as an asset and added to the high-profile retinue of royal women surrounding the male king, royal sons were rarely given an official mention during their father's lifetime.

Only a couple of years later, in about 1390 BC, Tuthmosis IV himself was dead, his beautifully prepared mummy laid to rest in his tomb (KV.43) in the Valley of the Kings together with the bodies of his son and a daughter who had predeceased him. The walls were adorned with figures of Hathor clad in a range of gorgeous outfits, and the tomb was now filled with all the items deemed essential for the royal Afterlife, from canopic jars of royal entrails to funerary statuettes, glazed ankh ☥ amulets, gilded statues and model boats. The king's weapons, golden chariot and gold-covered throne were also buried with him, and the sumptuous nature of court life was reflected in other artefacts such as glassware, feathered fans, finely embroidered textiles and jewellery, and even riding gloves of red and green leather.

The new king was a boy of no more than twelve, so his mother Mutemwia acted as regent. In a superb wall painting now in the foyer of Luxor Museum, Mutemwia is literally shown as the power behind the throne as she holds her son's shoulders to guide him through the maze of protocol following the death of his father. Given his age, she would have been involved in selecting his official names and titles, 'The Horus, Strong Bull, Appearing in Truth, He of the Two Ladies, who establishes the laws and pacifies the Two Lands, the Golden Horus, Great of Strength, the Smiter of the Asiatics, the King of Upper and Lower Egypt, Nebmaatra, the Son of Ra, Amenhotep, Ruler of Thebes'. Little wonder royal names can cause so much confusion! After a traditional coronation at Memphis the king would have rounded off events at Giza, following in the footsteps of his innovative father and grandfather to stand before the Great Sphinx and undergo the transference of royal power at the feet of the ancient sun god. Under the watchful eye of his mother, Amenhotep III started as he meant to go on, and as his dazzling reign unfolded the Amarna Period was brought into being.

8

THE DAZZLING GOLDEN AGE

In 1390 BC, a year full of grand state ceremonies, a royal funeral and a coronation were followed by a royal wedding when the boy king took a young girl as his Great Royal Wife. After listing the new king's names and titles, the public announcement sent out across the empire stated that 'the Great Royal Wife is Tiy. Her father's name is Yuya, her mother's name is Tuya, and she is the wife of a mighty king.' Mighty or not, he was still only a boy and it was unlikely to have been love at first sight. The choice of bride may well have been made by the regent, Mutemwia, who 'put oil on the head of the girl' to signify the choice.

Although Tiy is usually dismissed as a commoner, it seems unlikely that an unknown quantity would have been plucked from obscurity to perform the vital role of Great Royal Wife. Maybe Mutemwia looked within her own family, and some have suggested that Yuya was Mutemwia's brother, which would make Tiy her niece. It would certainly explain how Tiy immediately attained great influence. It has even been suggested that Tiy was descended from the illustrious Ahmose-Nefertari, since it has been suggested that her name is a shortened form of Nefertari and its variant Nefertiti, sometimes spelled Nefertitiy.

Whatever the reasons for the choice, Tiy's family is certainly a fascinating one. As the marriage announcement stated, she was the daughter of Yuya and Tuya, or, as it is occasionally written, Tuya and Yuya, with her mother's name given precedence. Early Egyptologists believed the couple to have been Syrian, but in fact the family came from Akhmim, a town between Amarna and Thebes. Akhmim was cult centre of the potent fertility god Min: Tiy's father was one of his priests and her mother also worked for the god as Chief of Entertainers. Following their daughter's nuptials, the family moved to Thebes and were promoted by their new son-in-law. Yuya was made Master of the Horse and His Majesty's Lieutenant-commander of Chariotry, whilst his additional priestly title of God's Father is often interpreted as 'father-in-law'. As for Tuya, Royal Mother of the Great Royal Wife, she became Chief of the Entertainers of Amen and was a singer to both Amen and Hathor. Even Tiy's brother Anen was elevated to high office when he was made 'second prophet', or deputy high priest of Amen at Karnak Temple, presumably to keep tabs on what was going on there. To symbolise his role as temple astronomer, his priestly panther skin robe was spangled with gold stars. Tiy's other brother is believed to have been Ay, who later held much the same titles as Yuya including that of God's Father.

Supported by an increasingly influential family, and with her name twinned with that of her husband, she appears alongside Amenhotep throughout his entire reign. Although she never ruled in her own right she certainly took an active role in politics, corresponding with foreign dignitaries who clearly respected her wise counsel and sent precious gifts in an attempt to win her favour. There is a strong suggestion of her determined, tenacious character in the pouting features and concentrated expression found in her sculpture, and she seems to have achieved greater prominence than any other royal wife before her.

Tiy is regularly depicted with all the attributes needed to protect and sustain the king, and wore crowns incorporating the goddesses' horns, sun disc, feathers and vulture head. She is also shown wearing a superb robe of feathers as homage to the vulture goddess Nekhbet, the one who helped the sun god through the sky in the same way that the queen helped the sun king through his reign. As goddess queen to his god king Tiy was the incarnation of the sun god's female relatives, and as Hathor, goddess of beauty and sexual love, she was known as 'the one who fills the palace with love, the one who fills the palace with beauty'. Yet Hathor's alter ego was of course Sekhmet, known as Great of Fearsomeness, and so the queen appears as a sphinx, guarding her husband's names and trampling the enemy, the defender of king and country in the same way that the goddess defended the god.

As Great Royal Wife Tiy was not alone, since the king had also awarded the title to his mother, Mutemwia, and later in his reign would do so to his two eldest daughters, Sitamen and Isis. And then of course there were all the king's minor wives, from home-grown talent to the mail-order brides who arrived throughout the reign as tribute from across the empire.

At this time Egypt was without question the most powerful nation in the ancient world, with a vast empire reaching from the Euphrates (in modern Iraq) down into the Sudan. Nubia and the Sudan were controlled by the king's viceroy, who also kept a firm grip on the region's goldmines. To the north, the vassal states of Syria-Palestine were divided into three areas. Each of these was ruled by an Egyptian governor supported by a military garrison, and it was their job to keep an eye on the local leaders, who remained in place provided they were loyal and sent annual tribute. This could include their own women and children, and, as one vassal wrote, 'Say to the king, my lord, my god, my Sun! Message from Satiya, the ruler of Enisasi, I am your servant, the dirt beneath your feet! I send my daughter to the palace, to you the king, my lord, my god, my Sun.'

Pharaoh also laid claim to the Aegean, and the bases of some of his statues were carved with the names of sites such as Knossos, Rhodes and Mycenae. Hailed as the 'Star ✳ of Egypt', Amenhotep III and 'King's Wife Tiy' were names well known in the region, and appear on imported Egyptian objects such as vases, plaques and scarab seals. Some of these were found within the citadel of Mycenae in the House of Idols cult centre, revealing something of the esteem in which Egypt's king and queen were held. And since Aegean pottery has been found at the Egyptian palaces of Malkata and Gurob, it seems likely that Greek women may also have been sent along as gifts.

The empire also enjoyed good relations with the major powers of Babylonia, Assyria, Arzawa (Western Anatolia), Cyprus and Mitanni in Syria. The diplomatic correspondence which flowed between them would become known as the Amarna Letters, although they actually began in the reign of Amenhotep III. Revealing a wealth of detail about royal life in the fourteenth century BC, their contents give glimpses of actual characters, from the opportunism of the king of Babylon to the warmth of Tushratta of Mitanni and even the hard-headed diplomacy and unexpected humour of pharaoh himself.

Friendly relations between Egypt and Mitanni had already been sealed when the king's father, Tuthmosis IV, married a Mitannian princess, a policy his son Amenhotep III enthusiastically pursued every time a new king succeeded in the allied countries. So when Shuttarna II became king of Mitanni, his daughter Kiluhepa was despatched to Egypt and pharaoh sent out a proclamation dated to his tenth year as king. His names and titles, together with those of Tiy and her parents Yuya and Tuya, are followed by the announcement that there was 'brought to his majesty the daughter of the ruler of Mitanni, Kiluhepa, and the chief women of her household – a total of 317 women.' The king's eyes must have lit up at the arrival of hundreds of women all at once, an event which he describes as 'a wonder'.

Twenty years later, when Tushratta took over as king of Mitanni, he wanted to continue the alliance and told pharaoh that 'My father loved you, and you in turn loved my father. In keeping with this love my father gave you my sister. And who else stood with my father as you did? So I send you six chariots and horse-teams, and as a greeting gift to my sister Kiluhepa I send her a set of gold brooches, a pair of gold earrings, a gold ring and a bottle of sweet perfume.' He also offered his daughter Tadukhepa in marriage, and when the Egyptian delegation went to Mitanni to collect her Tushratta reported back,

Your messenger came to take her to become the mistress of Egypt. I read and reread the tablet which was brought before me and I listened to its words. Your words were very pleasing my brother, and I rejoiced on that day as if I had seen you in person. I made the day and night a festive occasion. I will now deliver her as your wife, mistress of Egypt, and on that day we shall be as one. May Ishtar my goddess, mistress of all lands and of my brother, and Amen, the god of my brother, make her [Tadukhepa] the image of my brother's desire. You will note that she has become very mature, and is surely built according to my brother's desires.

For their wedding ceremony Tushratta supplied his personal statue of the Syrian goddess Ishtar to legitimise the cross-cultural union, as had also occurred at the time of Amenhotep's previous Mitannian marriage. Together with the blessing 'May Ishtar grant you great blessings and exquisite joy and may you live forever', Tushratta gave pharaoh a wonderful necklace of chunky gold and lapis lazuli beads, with the wish 'May it rest on the neck of my brother for 100,000 years.' He also sent him more horses and chariots, weaponry and exotic foreign clothing which the king seems to have appreciated, whilst Tadukhepa was sent jewellery worth around £150,000 or a quarter of a million dollars in today's terms. Such generous gifts from her family must have been a comfort to the new bride in a foreign country. Her father also wrote a stream of letters to pharaoh and Tiy, one of which ends, 'Tushratta is the Mitannian King, Amenhotep the Egyptian King and they love one another exceedingly'.

Pharaoh also opened negotiations with the king of Anatolia, sending his messenger to vet another prospective bride and 'pour oil on her head' to mark their betrothal. The accompanying sacks of gold and precious gifts apparently did the trick, since the Anatolian king wrote back, 'If you really desire my daughter, why should I not give her to you? I give her to you.'

Yet things were rather more protracted when it came to dealing with the splendidly named Kadashman-Enlil of Babylon.

Having already married the king's sister, pharaoh requested another alliance. But the Babylonian king wrote back: 'Now you are asking to marry my daughter, but my sister whom my father gave you is already there with you, but no one has seen her to know if she is alive or dead. You received my messengers when all your wives were there, saying "Here is your mistress who stands before you." But my messengers did not recognise her and didn't know if it was my sister who was at your side.'

Clearly Amenhotep read the rest of the long letter carefully, since he replied point by point:

I have just heard what you wrote to me about. But have you ever sent one of your officials who actually knows your sister, who could speak with her and identify her? No. The men whom you sent here do not count. One was a nobody, the other a donkey herder ... As Amen is my witness, your sister is alive. I have made her a Mistress of the Household. And as for you writing to me to make yourself wealthy, you only sent me a single present. Are we to laugh?

Sensing that pharaoh was none too pleased, Kadashman-Enlil finally agreed to his request, conceding that since 'my daughter about whom you wrote me in view of marriage is now a woman, you can send a delegation to fetch her'. Yet the arrangement was strictly one-way, and when the Babylonian king asked for one of Amenhotep's daughters he was turned down flat. When he then asked why not, since 'You are King, You can do as you please,' pharaoh remained adamant and told him straight, 'From of old a daughter of a king of Egypt has never been given to anyone.' And that was the end of it.

Whilst Amenhotep was building up international relations, his allies' prime objective was gold, since it was widely believed that 'gold is like sand in Egypt, you simply pick it up'. The king of Babylon was especially keen, and had written:

Now as to the gold I wrote to you about, send me whatever is available so I can finish the work I am doing this summer. If you send the gold I will give you my daughter, so please send it. If you do not, and I cannot finish the work, what would be the point sending it later? Then you could send me 100 tons of the stuff and I wouldn't accept it. I would sent it back, and wouldn't give you my daughter in marriage.

None too impressed by this attitude, pharaoh had told him, 'It's a fine thing when you give your daughters simply to acquire a nugget of gold from your neighbour.'

One of the letters, written in Babylonian script, even preserves the words of one of these women; although sadly anonymous, she said, 'Tell my lord so speaks the princess: may the gods accompany you. In the presence of my lord I prostrate myself. My messenger brings you a gift of coloured cloth. May all go well with your cities and your household, and do not worry or you will have made me sad. I would give my life for you.'

The five or more foreign wives from Mitanni, Babylonia and Anatolia were accompanied by hundreds of female attendants and ladies-in-waiting. There were more than 600 Mitannian women alone, 317 accompanying Kiluhepa and another 270 sent later with her niece Tadukhepa. And Amenhotep III was always on the look-out for those little extras. In the days when 'beautiful female cup-bearers without defect' could be bought for the bargain price of around forty shekels each, the king wrote to one of his Palestinian vassals saying, 'I am sending you my official to fetch beautiful women, in whom there is no defect. Then the king your lord will say "this is excellent".'

A great many children were also sent to Egypt to be raised at court, no doubt acting as convenient bargaining counters in the diplomatic game. Referring to the large numbers of foreign women and children he housed on the West Bank of Thebes, the king described buildings filled with servants and 'the children of every foreign country . . . It is princes surrounded by Syrian settlements inhabited by the children of princes'. Although incredibly cosmopolitan it must also have been a pretty noisy environment, filled with the chatter of voices from across the ancient world.

Music-making was one of the main occupations of the women surrounding the king. Performed for their own amusement as well as that of the court, song and dance also played a vital part in state ritual, led by the royal women and the wives and daughters of his high officials. At investitures, award ceremonies and festivals to replenish royal powers, voices were accompanied by hand-clapping, finger-clicking and the playing of small harps, lutes, drums and the newly invented tambourine. There were also small clappers of wood or ivory; one surviving delicate pair in ivory carved into a pair of tiny hands is inscribed with the name 'Great Royal Wife Tiy'.

Then there were the cult symbols of the goddess Hathor carried by her priestesses as a badge of office. The menat was a heavy necklace made up of thick rows of beads, and, though not strictly speaking a musical instrument, it was held by its metal counterpoise and shaken to produce a percussive rattling sound. A superb example, found in Queen Tiy's royal apartments, was made of thousands of tiny blue beads customised with semi-precious stones and amulets, and clear signs of wear and tear show that it had seen long service. The menat was generally accompanied by the sistrum, the sacred rattle. The goddess's devotees sang, shook their tinkly sistrums and rattled their menats to summon up her powers for the king's benefit, telling him in song to 'Reach out to the beautiful one, to the ornament of Hathor, lady of heaven.'

The hymns also convey something of the festive atmosphere of wine, women and song which carried on late into the night as the drink helped her devotees commune with the Lady of Drunkenness. 'Come, Golden Goddess,' ran the words of one hymn, 'the singers are chanting and it is good for the heart to dance! Shine on our feast at the hour of retiring, and enjoy the dance at night. The procession begins at the site of the drunkenness, the women rejoice and the drunkards play tambourines for you in the cool night, and those they waken bless you.'

Since the women were the earthly representatives of the beautiful goddess their appearance was vital, and, headed by Tiy, 'splendid of ornaments', they would have spent a great deal of time beautifying themselves and each other. Their robes were made of the very highest-quality linen, its degree of fineness – gauze-like almost to the point of transparency – indicating the status of the wearer. Garments could also be embellished with dyes, embroidery, feather effects, gold sequins and elaborate beadwork, and some were made entirely of precious materials. Other costumes featured flexible pieces of cloisonné work in gold, carnelian, turquoise and lapis lazuli, whilst some net-like dresses were made entirely of beads, their modern equivalents worn by some of the big-name belly dancers and still sold in Egypt's tourist markets.

Like their men, royal women wore huge quantities of jewellery, although the difference between ornament and amulet was often indistinct. Much Egyptian jewellery was made of brightly coloured glazed pottery or coloured glass, but the most elite wore gold and precious or semi-precious stones such as carnelian and amethyst, lapis lazuli from Afghanistan and turquoise from the mines of Sinai. Much of this jewellery would be presented to them by the king as a sign of favour, the large gold beads known as 'gold of honour' given to officials of both sexes, as were the Gold Flies of Valour which at least one of Tiy's predecessors was awarded. Although many of the king's foreign wives brought their own jewellery with them, it was sent to the Egyptian court by foreign potentates as keen to demonstrate their country's wealth and sophistication as the recipients were to set new trends with foreign fashions.

Necklaces were almost de rigueur; they included gold chains suspending large cloisonné-style ornaments, and broad collars made up of multiple rows of beads and amulets. Narrow waists and desirably wide hips could be accentuated with jewelled and beaded belts, whilst arms glittered with gold and silver bangles and bead bracelets set with large plaques of semi-precious stones; several carnelian examples show the king, queen and their daughters, and an open-work example in purple-brown sard stone features Tiy as a winged sphinx guarding the king's name. Rings were also very popular, from great gold signet rings to seal stones carved with the name of the owner or those of the royal family; in fact, a century after his death Theban women were still being buried in rings carved with the name of Amenhotep III. With the increasing cosmopolitan nature of Egyptian society, earrings were catching on. Amenhotep III's father had set the trend for pierced ears, and the large holes found in the ears of mummies were needed to support the elaborate designs worn by men and women, the royal women in particular favouring huge gold hoops or discs.

The right to wear the cobra or vulture over their brow was restricted to great royal wives, so minor wives and court ladies contented themselves with gazelle heads on their diadems. Magnificent golden head-dresses made up of lengths of cloisonné rosettes were found in the tomb of Tuthmosis III's three Syrian wives and, although their weight would have caused some serious headaches if worn for too long, they must have looked amazing in the sunshine. Their form resembled the queenly vulture crown with extended wings which Tiy wore, together with her head-dress of tall ostrich plumes which incorporated a gold sun disc to emphasise Tiy's divine connections. For more lightweight informal wear, gold rosettes, beads or tubes were threaded directly on to the hair to form a kind of chequerboard pattern, or small amulets, beads or discs could be attached to the ends of braids to cause them, thus weighted, to swing artfully. Otherwise a simple headband of gold or coloured linen, or even just a circlet of fresh flowers, kept the hair in place.

Hairdressers and wigmakers were depicted at work with their hairpins, combs and dextrous fingers. The most fashionable hairstyle of the day was the long, voluminous coiffure or 'enveloping wig', incorporating as many crimped braids as possible in order to pay homage to Hathor as Lady of the Locks. The women of Amenhotep III's court are shown with so much hair that it spills down over their shoulders and even hangs seductively over their eyes. Extensions were used to create this 'big hair', and could also of course be used to conceal thinning hair on older ladies keen to keep up the appearance of youthful vigour. Others resorted to various types of hair restorer, rubbing lion fat into the scalp in the hope of inheriting the animal's splendid mane, or, following the same logic but referring to the creature's fine collection of bristles, used hedgehog fat. Castor oil was another ingredient long prized in hair treatments, prescribed 'to cause a woman's hair to grow if she rubs her head with it' while also keeping it in good condition in the hot climate. Grey hairs could be concealed using henna-based dyes, and there were even recipes to prevent dandruff and head lice. Alternatively, the hair could be cropped or shaved off altogether, keeping the lady louse-free and cool beneath a wig usually stored overnight on a wooden mount. Carved in the form of a woman's head, many of these ancient wig stands are just like the polystyrene examples still found in the windows of old-fashioned ladies' hairdressers.

As the court women peered out from behind curtains of usually false hair, their faces really were their fortune and so needed to be well cared for in the hot, dry climate. Vegetables oils were used to cleanse and moisturise the skin and, mixed with lime or natron soda, made the type of 'cold cream' that was found in over thirty large jars buried with the three foreign wives of Tuthmosis III. The ancient texts also list numerous preparations 'for beautifying the face', one rejuvenating oil entitled 'Instructions to make the old young again'. Daily bathing was standard practice at court and the Egyptians were the first people to use deodorants: as 'a remedy to prevent odour in summer', pellets made of incense and dough were applied 'to the places where the limbs join'.

Nature could always be given a helping hand with cosmetics, which the Egyptians used by the sackload. Eye paint is, of course, the best known, and although it was used principally to make the eyes appear larger its application around the delicate eye area also acted like sunglasses, reducing the glare of the sun off the desert. The antiseptic qualities of certain blends also provided relief from eye complaints aggravated by sandstorms and disease-bearing flies, so it was something of an all-round product.

The most popular eye paint was black kohl, made from the crushed lead ore. This was mixed with water or, as our recent analysis has shown, date palm oil, and then stored in pots or tubes. Some of these list their contents as 'eye paint for every day' or give specific dates by which the product should be used, rather like modern medicine bottles. Many even carry the owners' names or those of the royal family, and would have been handed out as gifts at festivals and court functions. Applied with the same thin bronze applicator sticks that Egyptian women still use today, eye paint was worn by both sexes; however, only women seem to have coloured their lips and cheeks, using crushed red ochre or plant juice.

The cosmetics themselves were prepared in dishes of polished alabaster and wood, with leaping felines or swimming girls a favourite motif for handles. All were stored away in elaborate make-up chests, with pull-out drawers and separate sections for the kohl pots, silver compacts, jars of setting lotion, tweezers and razors, combs adorned with kneeling ibex, decorative hair-pins and mirrors with blue- and green-glazed handles so popular amongst the king's women.

Those not wanting to make up their own faces could call on the skills of professional make-up artists, whilst the royal manicurist was on hand to file finger- and toenails and stain the nails, hands and feet an attractive red-orange using henna dye. More permanent forms of adornment could be achieved using small bronze pins to prick the skin in whatever pattern was desired and then rubbing in soot or pigment to create the finished design. Tattoos seem to have been worn only by women, and, arranged in patterns of dots or featuring small images of the household god Bes, were usually concentrated on the breasts, abdomen and thighs. They are usually interpreted as charms against sexual diseases or as the marks of prostitutes, although it seems far more likely that they were permanent forms of the amulets needed during the dangers of pregnancy and birth.

The ancient Egyptians were also fully aware of the hidden powers of perfume – the stronger, heavier and sweeter the better – and it was stored in some of the most beautiful scent containers ever devised. Blue-glass bottles feature tiny duck heads with inlaid yellow bills, and hollow alabaster cats represent the cat goddess Bastet, whose name means 'She of the Perfume Jar'. The luscious scent of the native lotus was used to create a happy disposition, and, as a favourite fragrance of both priestesses and, it would seem, Amenhotep III himself, it was also offered to the gods during worship. The heavy, sweet scent of the lily was associated with female spirituality and used in remedies to treat 'female complaints'.

Perfumes also incorporated some of the costly resins and spices imported from abroad, with only tiny amounts needed to create impact. Cinnamon was also used alone as an aphrodisiac, the oil sprinkled over beds and the wood burnt as an incense to scent clothes and surroundings. Myrrh was used in perfumes and as a breath freshener, as was frankincense, which was also used in ancient wrinkle creams just as modern aromatherapists still recommend frankincense oil for the 'more mature' skin.

Often used as aphrodisiacs, perfumes are mentioned regularly in love poems. In one example, a woman reclines with her lover, both drunk on pomegranate wine and sprinkled with perfumed oils. Another woman parading herself before her lover uses every trick in the book: 'I love to go and bathe before you. I allow you to see my beauty in a dress of the finest linen drenched with fragrant unguent. I go down into the water to be with you

. . . Come! Look at me!' It is an invitation followed by the wistful lover's riposte 'I wish I were her laundryman . . . and would wash away the unguent from her clothes.' The same idea is also used in ancient Egypt's version of Cinderella, in which pharaoh's heart was captured by a lock of perfumed hair which fell into his laundry and scented all his clothing. And to underline the importance of perfume in their lives, the wealthy were depicted in paintings and occasionally statues with a cone-shaped lump of semi-solid perfume on their heads, whilst the perfumed oils rubbed directly into the skin were shown seeping through their fine linen garments, which explains the need for regular laundering.

Radiating sensuality on as many levels as possible, the women at the royal court worked hard to look good, smell good, sound good and feel good. The ancient Egyptian ideal of beauty was described as

the Morning Star, shining bright, fair of skin, lovely the look of her eyes and sweet the speech of her lips. With upright neck, shining breast, hair of true lapis lazuli, arms surpassing gold, fingers like lotus buds, heavy thighs yet narrow waist, her legs parade her beauty. With graceful steps she walks, capturing all hearts with her movements, causing all men's heads to turn when they see her. There is joy for him who embraces her, and when she steps out she competes with the sun.

The image would have perfectly characterised each member of pharaoh's hand-picked female entourage, the king being surrounded by such women at formal events and in the more informal surroundings of his private apartments. A cartoon of a lion playing board games with a small gazelle is believed to allude to the Egyptian king in the company of one of these graceful figures, whilst the later pharaoh Ramses III is shown playfully tickling his female companions under their chins.

But this is about as explicit as it gets. By no means a prudish society, to judge from the erections waved around by many a male deity and the number of small sketches and figurines portraying all kinds of sexual activity, the ancient Egyptians were nevertheless reticent about showing the act itself in formal art. Sex was a potentially volatile form of behaviour in which the emotions could not always be controlled, and so, with their great fondness of imposing order on their surroundings, they substituted euphemisms and wordplay to suggest this most intimate of activities.

Looking at the names of Amenhotep III's women in an endeavour to understand something of the nature of his relationship with them, some sound most intriguing: for instance 'She of numerous nights in the city of the brilliant Aten' and 'She who strikes with fury for the brilliant Aten'. Although the latter would seem to reflect the way in which beautiful Hathor was perceived to transform herself instantly into terrifying Sekhmet in order to protect the king, several male Egyptologists have interpreted it as evidence for pharaoh's apparent sado-masochistic tendencies!

Although he used existing royal palaces, such as those at Gurob and Memphis, Amenhotep III decided to build a new one at Thebes, presumably to accommodate his growing entourage. Previous rulers had been based at the traditional capital, Memphis, and usually only came south to Thebes for the big religious festivals, setting up temporary court in palace buildings attached to Karnak Temple. But Amenhotep III wanted an independent palace complex, well away from the watchful eye of Amen's clergy, so began work on the opposite bank of the Nile at the other end of the city. Opposite the king's own temple of Luxor, the site was close to the foothills of the western mountains where the sun sank each evening into Hathor's embrace. Although it is known today by its Arabic name of Malkata, the king himself called it the Palace of the Dazzling Aten. The new palace was his Theban base throughout most of his reign, and he moved the whole court there permanently around year 29.

It was a rambling site sprawling over more than eighty acres, the main areas centred on the king's own apartments in the south-east section, with its audience chambers, large hall for festivals, offices, kitchens and store rooms, its own temple of Amen, desert altars and royal hunting lodge. Then there was Tiy's independent palace complex to the south, and that of their eldest daughter, Sitamen, to the north, together with quarters for the rest of the royal family, the hundreds of court women and of course the retinue of servants that each would require. Large villas housed the king's high officials, and as well as administrative quarters Malkata had its own royal workshop and workers' settlement.

Fronting the palace itself was the mother of all water features, an enormous T-shaped harbour a mile and a half wide, which linked the royal residence to the Nile. Built to handle the heavy flow of waterborne traffic, the harbour allowed the king to reach the temples on the opposite bank of the river, or indeed anywhere else in his kingdom, without ever needing to set foot on land. And he did it in some style in a brand-new, state-of-the-art vessel, the good ship *Dazzling Aten*, on which he and Tiy sailed forth during religious and state festivals.

Pharaoh also had an impressive collection of chariots sent to him from across the empire; as a standard part of royal burial equipment, a complete gold chariot was found in the tomb of his father-in-law Yuya, lieutenant-commander in the king's elite chariot corps. In a world largely at peace, Amenhotep III demonstrated his prowess off the battlefield through high-profile big-game hunting expeditions, including a spectacular wild bull hunt when 'his majesty appeared in his chariot' and captured 96 wild bulls and 102 lions which 'his majesty shot with his own arrows'. His chariots also enabled him to indulge his passion for speed in a great quarter of a mile long stadium laid out just south of the palace harbour.

Like almost every other domestic building in ancient Egypt, the palace complex was built largely from the standard mud-bricks, here stamped with the names of the king. The walls were then plastered over, and the exteriors painted white to reflect the heat. Door and window frames were made of wood or stone, and stone was also used for column bases, steps, drainage systems, en suite bathroom facilities and garden pools with small steps leading down to the water.

Interiors were painted in vivid, even loud, colours enhanced with glazed tiles and bright inlays, and from the thousands of fragments of painted plaster which still litter the site, it is possible to reconstruct much of Malkata's original decor. The royal women's private suites were painted with calves and birds, the floors decorated to resemble the banks of the Nile filled with fish and surrounded by wildfowl. The most imposing part of the palace consisted of a series of rooms incorporating an audience chamber almost 100 feet long. Its high ceilings were painted with repeated images of the protective vulture goddess Nekhbet, supported by columns decorated with wooden lotus flowers, whilst the walls were adorned with figures of the king and his women wearing elaborate head-dresses.

The top end of the hall opened out into the throne room, its floors painted with figures of Egypt's enemies who also covered the throne dais and the footstool placed before the canopied throne. And here sat pharaoh, flanked by fan-bearers and body-guards, to receive reports, diplomatic correspondence and tribute from around his empire. Supervised by the Overseer of the Audience Chamber, foreign dignitaries allowed into the royal presence would have been surrounded by images of their bound countrymen, the same figures on the soles of the king's golden sandals demonstrating that they were indeed 'as dirt beneath his feet'. Even his robes were embroidered with power symbols and hieroglyphs proclaiming him Protector of His Country and Vanquisher of All the Foes of Egypt. It has to be said, however, that it is difficult to imagine him cutting quite such an imposing figure in the 'robe and matching cap of purple wool and shaggy wool leggings' sent as a gift from Mitanni!

The lavish robes of office, crowns and sceptres were stored

in the connecting robing room or House of Morning, in which pharaoh was helped to put on his mantles of state in a daily ritual as old as the pyramids. And in the same way that the priests adorned the gods in their shrines, the divine pharaoh was served by his key officials – even his bathing, shaving and anointing were subject to ceremony in an en suite bathroom just behind the throne room.

At the very heart of the palace lay the brightly coloured royal bedroom, whose ceiling was adorned with the repeated names and titles of the king set between the outstretched wings of the protective vulture goddess designed to watch over the king at night when he was at his most vulnerable. Repeated ankh signs bestowing life and protection decorated the walls and above them danced rows of images of Bes, the household god who carried knives and tambourines for protection and pleasure. Bes would also have adorned the royal bed, an ebony and gold structure with lions' paw feet set on a platform at one end of the room.

The whole place would have been filled with this type of superbly crafted furniture, which was often referred to in diplomatic letters. Amenhotep III wrote to the king of Babylon, for example, 'I have just heard that you have built a new palace, and so I am sending you some furnishings as greeting gifts for your new house: 4 beds of ebony overlaid with ivory and gold and 10 chairs of ebony overlaid with gold, the weight of gold on these things 7 minas, 9 shekels and the weight of the silver 1 mina, 8 and a half shekels. PS: 10 footrests of ebony, overlaid with gold.'

Similarly lavish tableware of gold and silver would have been used to serve food and drink, and amongst the gourmet items consumed by the king and his court were choice cuts of beef, roast duck and geese, dates, beans, honey, milk and oils. Many of them were stored in large pots with a quantity and quality description, the oils termed 'sweet', honey 'clear' and beans 'shelled', whilst items like 'potted meat' and 'fresh lard' were wisely given a 'best before' date. Wine, known as 'irup' as a pun on over-indulgence, was classified on a scale between plain and excellent, using descriptions such as 'sweet', 'blended' and 'wine of becoming', or that still fermenting. There were even instructions about when and where to drink it, from 'offering wine' and 'wine for taxes' to 'wine for a happy return' and 'wine for merry-making'. Although ancient Egyptian wine was made largely from grapes, some kinds incorporated figs, pomegranates and dates, with honey and spices added for sweetness; the resins used as preservatives also produced a Malkata version of retsina, and a type of sweet barley beer, known as 'sermet', also seems to have been drunk in large quantities at the palace.

The building's original interiors, complete with their ornaments, linens and similarly decorated inhabitants, can only be imagined, although the huge variety of small personal items found at the site does help bring its ancient inhabitants back to life. Fully deserving of its Arabic name, which means 'the place where things are picked up', the site of Malkata was covered with fragments of rings, bracelets and necklaces, favourite amulets, cosmetics spoons, kohl tubes, mirror handles, tweezers, perfume bottles and gaming pieces. There were also small faience book plates bearing the names of the king and queen, suggesting that the palace had its own library, literally a 'house of books' such as those found in the temples. Attached to the boxes containing the papyrus roll 'books', the book plates also suggest that horticulture was a subject of some interest, one being inscribed 'the book of the moringa tree' and another 'the book of the pomegranate tree'. And since Amenhotep refers to ornamental flowers and plants as an important feature in his numerous building projects, it seems that the sun king was something of a gardener himself.

Writing equipment included a palette with six oval blocks of coloured paints bearing Amenhotep III's name, and hundreds of clay sealings from rolls of official papyrus documents, some bearing the names of previous rulers, including the great

Hatshepsut. Amenhotep's interest in all matters antiquarian was confirmed by the discovery of a predynastic palette which was already a great antique at almost two thousand years old when the king had it reinscribed with a figure of Tiy.

Possessing a keen sense of tradition, the king also ordered research into the way things were done in the good old days of the Pyramid Age.

Amenhotep III's most trusted official, another Amenhotep, son of Hapu, was remembered for centuries as the one who knew the power 'to be found in the words of the past which date to the time of the ancestors'. With 'his majesty doing things in accordance with the ancient writings', the temple archives were checked and officials such as the royal scribe May were sent to Medum to 'examine this very great pyramid of Sneferu' together with the temples and tombs of Abusir, Giza, Sakkara and Abydos. Quite possibly Egypt's first archaeological conservator, Amenhotep III ordered many of these ancient sites to be restored, and where buildings were enlarged or enhanced he was keen to stress that he did so 'without damaging what had been done before'. Particularly inspired by the reign and achievements of his illustrious predecessor Hatshepsut, he adapted her legend of divine conception, adding to her foundations to create Luxor Temple and carrying out her plans to link Luxor to Karnak with a sphinx-lined road.

Right at the start of the reign he had reopened the ancient limestone quarries near Giza, and now began quarrying at sites throughout the country to obtain the necessary quantities of building stone needed to achieve his architectural ambitions. New temples to deities associated with sun worship in both Egypt and Nubia included the first temple to the Aten built at the sun god's traditional cult centre, Heliopolis, and much of Thebes was also re-modelled according to the king's instructions. Living close to the palace in their own village to the south, his craftsmen in the royal workshops produced exquisite items both for home consumption and for export as far afield as Babylon and Mycenae. Malkata also housed Egypt's oldest-known glass factory. Since 70 per cent of the glass and glazed faience ware found at the palace was deep purple-blue one leading expert has calculated that this was the king's favourite colour, often combined with a tasteful copper sulphate-blue trim.

Following custom, Tiy had her own independent complex in the southern part of Malkata, built with bricks stamped with her name. The interior was decorated and furnished in the same lavish way as her husband's quarters, and something of her original surroundings is reflected in a scene showing her seated on a gilded ebony chair with lions' paw feet, decorated with rows of inlaid cobras. Her feet rest on a plump red cushioned footstool, her pet monkey leaps around, and her stripy cat appears beneath her chair. Tiy had a large household of attendants and servants, including a steward, chef, head weaver and costume designer. A small army of servants and workers produced luxury goods such as jewellery, perfumes and textiles, and many of the provisions she would need came from her own estates dotted throughout the country.

Tiy's appreciative husband embellished one of these properties in his eleventh year as king, the main event of which was 'the making of a lake for the great royal wife in her town of Akhmim. Its length is 3,700 cubits and its width is 600 cubits, and his majesty celebrated the festival of opening the lake when his majesty was rowed across it in the royal barge.' For many years this was imagined as little more than a glorified boating lake, presumably as a diversion for the queen while her husband was otherwise engaged with his latest foreign bride. Yet the suggestion that it was an elaborate irrigation scheme designed to increase revenue on the queen's lands seems far more likely – a public way for the king to honour his chief wife.

Tiy's main role was to perpetuate the royal line. This she certainly did, giving Amenhotep III five daughters and two sons. Although there are hardly any ancient Egyptians whose dates of birth are known, their eldest daughter seems to have been born fairly early in the reign – meaning the royal couple would have been expected to start reproducing as soon as possible. Named Sitamen, 'daughter of Amen', she seems to have been a chip off the old block, as formidable as her mother and also close to her maternal grandparents, Yuya and Tuya. Her youthful figure decorates two of their gilded chairs, on the first as a young girl in a short linen kilt who is named as king's daughter and a Singer of the King, holding out a lotus bouquet to her mother Tiy who sits with the family cat beneath her throne. The second of her grandparents' chairs shows Sitamen described as 'the great one, his beloved daughter', and although her hair is still in the sidelock of a princess and she still wears the gazelle crown, she sits enthroned to receive trays laden with golden tribute. When she was eventually made a Great Royal Wife around 1360 BC, as part of her father's first jubilee rites, held according to tradition after 30 years' rule, the king was surrounded by three generations of royal women, reflecting the way Hathor was mother, wife and daughter of the sun god. Occupying her own palace complex at Malkata, Queen Sitamen was also given generous estates and the services of the king's favourite official Amenhotep, son of Hapu, as her overseer.

Amenhotep and Tiy's second daughter, Isis, was also made a Great Royal Wife a few years later. One figurine shows her dressed in a robe of finest linen, wearing a broad golden collar and with her hair set in the fashionable long, thick sidelock of the time. She also appears large-scale to the left of her parents' colossal figure in the Cairo Museum, in the centre of which stands their third daughter, Henuttaneb, wearing the queen's vulture crown over her long, full wig and clutching her sacred menat necklace to her chest. Although not an official Great Royal Wife, Henuttaneb clearly held high office and is the only princess to have been given the queenly title 'Consort of Horus [the king] in His Heart'. The couple's fourth daughter, Nebetah, is rather more shadowy, and only seems to appear on the right side of the Cairo colossus, whilst their final girl, Beketaten, is only shown after her father's death in the company of her mother Tiy.

Following tradition, the couple's two boys were named Tuthmosis and Amenhotep. But, again in accordance with tradition, these royal sons were hardly mentioned during their father's reign. As the elder of the two, Prince Tuthmosis had been groomed for the succession since birth by a father who himself had become king at around the age of twelve, and was given a series of high-ranking official positions to prepare him for his future duties. The title 'King's Son, Troop Commander Tuthmosis' on a whip handle demonstrates that the king was keen to make a man of him, no doubt remembering his own experiences hunting wild bulls as a young teenager to prove that he had what it took to be king despite his youth.

Prince Tuthmosis seems to have spent much of his time in the northern capital, Memphis, where he was appointed Overseer of All the Priests of Egypt and high priest of Ptah, the great creator god of the city. Heavily involved with the cult of the Apis bull, the animal thought to contain Ptah's spirit, it was Prince Tuthmosis as high priest who accompanied his father in the elaborate ceremonies of the first Apis burial at Sakkara. With its mummy buried in an enormous granite sarcophagus and its entrails packed in canopic jars the size of dustbins, the young prince was shown reading aloud the ritual texts, dressed in his pantherskin robes of office and with his hair in the sidelock of youth. Apart from being symbolic of children, and royal children in particular, it was also the badge of office of Ptah's priests, and as the prince's signature hairstyle it appears on all of his known statuettes.

Very much a cat-lover, like his mother, Prince Tuthmosis is best known for the small limestone sarcophagus in which he buried his pet cat Ta-miu, 'Lady-Cat'. Her name features the ancient Egyptian word for cat 𓄿 'miu', based on the noise made by the animal. Ta-Miu herself appears on her sarcophagus in an ornamental collar, seated on a plump cushion before a large roast duck, and then is shown in mummified form protected by the gods.

As for Tuthmosis' younger brother, named after his father, the only reference to him during his father's reign seems to be a single jar inscription referring to 'the estate of the king's son Amenhotep'. He was believed to have lived in the Middle Palace at Malkata, and it is interesting that here was found the only weapon from the entire site – a javelin head made of highly prized iron, suggesting that it may perhaps have belonged to the prince himself.

Some time prior to the king's first jubilee in 1360 BC everything changed when Crown Prince Tuthmosis died suddenly of unknown causes. The king and queen must have been distraught, and with their private world turned upside down chaos temporarily replaced the natural order of things as son predeceased father. The entire nation would have joined with the royal family to mourn the death of the heir to the throne as his body underwent the standard seventy-day mummification process.

His body decked out in the sumptuous finery befitting his role, a small steatite stone figurine shows the prince's mummy laid in state on a bier with lions' paw feet, his hair dressed in his characteristic sidelock style and his chest covered by a jewelled collar and human-headed bird amulet. With its wings spread protectively over his chest, it represents his soul fluttering above him as the funeral priests recite the words of Spell 89 from the collection of funerary spells known as the *Book of the Dead*: 'Let my soul come to me from wherever it is! Come for my soul, O you guardians of the heavens! May my soul see my corpse, may it rest on my mummified body which will never be destroyed or perish.' The spell was 'to be spoken over a human-headed bird of gold inlaid with precious stones and laid on the breast of the mummy', and Amenhotep III would surely have provided his beloved child with the finest example his craftsmen were able to produce.

Although it is uncertain where the prince was initially buried, it was almost certainly somewhere within the royal cemetery at Thebes. It may even have been in the Valley of the Queens a few miles north-west of Malkata – a smaller version of the Valley of the Kings, where princes and queens were both buried. The great chasm at its head was sacred to Hathor, identified as her womb from which the dead were reborn each dawn, so it was also an eminently suitable site in which to inter the king's mother, Mutemwia, following her death some time in the last decade of the reign. After their own tombs were looted a group of Amenhotep III's minor wives, princesses and noblewomen were reburied around 1000 BC in a rock-cut tomb somewhere close to the Qurna foothills. Although this too was ransacked in ancient times, surviving canopic jars and mummy labels mention one of the king's sisters, a minor wife and a daughter amongst those once buried there.

When the king's closest advisor, Amenhotep, son of Hapu, died around 1356 BC, aged about eighty, pharaoh honoured him with a rock-cut tomb in the Theban hills and even his own funerary temple, a singular honour otherwise reserved for royalty. Tiy's parents, Yuya and Tuya, had died earlier in the reign and were buried with great honour in a small tomb in the Valley of the Kings, and their son Anen also died around the time of the king's first jubilee in 1360 BC. And having already buried his eldest son, his mother, at least two of his sisters, his wife's parents, his brother-in-law and his great confidant and adviser, Amenhotep III must then have turned his thoughts to the matter of his own mortality, god or not. Work on his vast tomb in the western branch of the Valley of the Kings had been underway since the start of his reign, and it seems that goods now began to be stockpiled for his own eventual burial.

Inevitably he then had to deal with the question of the succession and what would happen to Egypt after his death. His remaining son Prince Amenhotep had not been prepared for the role which now lay ahead – indeed, he seems not to have been up to the job during his father's first jubilee celebrations and the elderly Amenhotep, son of Hapu, had been brought on as last-minute stand-in. This may, of course, have been due to the prince's young age, although he would now have to grow up fast if he was to rule as pharaoh. As crown prince he presumably inherited his late brother's titles and his roles in the north. There is evidence for a palace belonging to him in the sun god's cult centre at Heliopolis, and some scholars think his father may have sent the prince to study with the city's priests. Just as his brother Tuthmosis had been involved with the cult of the Apis bull at Memphis, Prince Amenhotep would have been instructed in the cult of the sun god's sacred bull at Heliopolis.

But of course what the prince needed most was a crash course in how to rule the world's greatest superpower, and it has been suggested by one eminent Egyptologist that his capable elder sister, Sitamen, may have acted as his mentor after being made a Great Royal Wife at the king's jubilee in 1360 BC. This jubilee was also the occasion when the king declared that he was 'the sun god's living image on earth' and, styling himself 'Dazzling Aten', decked his person in gold necklaces, collars, armlets and bracelets to reflect his new solar persona.

Spending the final eight years of his life as a living god, Amenhotep III was still doing whatever it took to make Egypt ever richer and to consolidate the empire. And even now he was keen to take possession of more wives. As he enjoyed newly married bliss with the young Tadukhepa of Mitanni, the king's statuary showed him wearing decorative fringed robes, possibly influenced by garments sent to him by his father-in-law. Tribute continued to pour in, and Egypt basked in the golden reflection of its pharaoh in an era of peace and prosperity which it seemed would last for ever.

Plans to extend the already sprawling palace at Malkata were well underway, no doubt to accommodate Tadukhepa's entourage of 270 women and 30 men and an ever-increasing household of women and children. In addition to his seven children by Tiy, Amenhotep presumably had many more born to his numerous minor wives and court ladies, and young women simply named as 'daughter of the king' were portrayed in tomb and temple scenes throughout the reign.

Since the king's powers needed regular replenishment it seemed timely to top them up with another jubilee festival, his third and final one, in 1353 BC. Following frantic preparations, when huge amounts of food, drink and perfumes were sent as gifts to the palace, everyone learned their lines and finalised their costumes. With the high officials decked out in their finest robes and specially decorated headbands, the king put on the knee-length jubilee robe, decorated with a blue and red diamond pattern skilfully executed in beadwork. Decked out in full regalia, Queen Tiy presided over the proceedings followed by a line of sixteen unnamed princesses – 'children of the king' and presumably some of her husband's daughters from his numerous minor wives. Each beautifully dressed in the finest of transparent linen robes and gold collars, their hair set in thick, crimped sidelocks, they poured out pure water from golden vessels, shaking their sistrums to encourage the pharaoh as he undertook the traditional rites to prove his ability to rule.

As the king raised the maypole-like ceremonial pillar and ran the ceremonial race 'according to ancient tradition', his efforts were encouraged by the female performers' ritualised gestures and carefully choreographed dance steps. One group, dressed in short skirts based on fashions worn a thousand years before, raised their arms above their heads as a second troupe in long gowns, brought in specially from the distant oases, clapped and played tambourines. Like the male performers these had cropped hair, whereas a further group of women wore long wigs which they swished around to great effect as they gyrated to the rhythm of the music.

Then, to reinvigorate the king with Hathor's great powers, the women sang songs 'to the Golden One, so she will cause the king to endure! Appear in your glory, Lady, come and protect the king! Make him healthy in the eastern sky, so he is happy, prosperous and healthy in the horizon. If you desire then make him live for millions of years without end.' Following this, the king was rowed across the waters in his golden boat, infused with the goddess's vitality and reborn as the living image of the sun god on earth, the dazzling Aten, eternally young.

Yet his onerous duties as living god inevitably took their toll, and Amenhotep III died seven months into his thirty-eighth year as king, probably some time in January 1352 BC, aged almost fifty. It had been a good innings when the average lifespan was around thirty-five. According to official protocol, it was announced that 'the god has ascended to his horizon' and, as the palace fell silent 'the great portals were closed as courtiers sat with their heads on their knees and people groaned, their hearts grieved'. As his subjects mourned the death of their king and the loss of their god, the news spread abroad like wildfire. Tushratta of Mitanni was moved to write to the widowed Tiy: 'When I heard that my brother had gone to his fate, on that day I sat down and wept. On that day I took neither food nor water and simply grieved.'

As soon as possible after death, the king's body was taken in state along the causeway to his massive funerary temple to enable the mummification process to begin. At this period the techniques were at their most effective and could produce a very life-like mummy; but the king seems to have left orders for something quite different, and, using vast quantities of resins, his body was transformed into a statue-like figure. No doubt decked out in staggering quantities of gold from head to toe, and wrapped in the finest of linens woven by the women of his court, his mummy would have been placed inside a nest of gold coffins inlaid with a feathered design which was then put into its golden shrine to await the funeral.

Early one March morning in 1352 BC the highest officials, dressed in plain white robes and headbands, gathered to take the king to his final resting place. Accompanied by his eldest son and heir, Prince Amenhotep, dressed in priestly leopardskin robes, his wife Tiy and daughters Sitamen and Isis would have acted as chief mourners. On their arrival at the king's isolated tomb the heir performed the Opening of the Mouth ceremony to reawaken his father's soul prior to burial. Surrounded by scenes of the dead king greeted into the Afterlife by the gods and embraced by Hathor, his coffins were placed inside a massive red granite sarcophagus carved with the image of the sky goddess Nut and the welcoming words of Osiris.

Although thoroughly looted in ancient times, this most splendid of tombs once contained all the usual paraphernalia, from large gilded shrines, ritual couches and funerary figurines to chariots and archery equipment, furniture, food and wine, and staggering amounts of jewellery. The robbers took almost everything of value, even his great stone sarcophagus. When the broken body was salvaged and rewrapped the king was reburied in one of the side chambers of KV.35 in the main part of the Valley of the Kings.

Having completed all the necessary rituals as legitimate heir, the fourth Amenhotep ascended the throne to become the most powerful king on earth. All Egypt hoped the Golden Age would continue, and foreign powers held their breath whilst the world's greatest nation passed through a period of transition. The Mitannians could only hope that their special relationship would continue. Tushratta wrote: 'When they told me that the eldest son of Amenhotep and Tiy is king in his place, I said "my brother is not dead! His eldest son is now in his place, and nothing whatsoever will ever be changed from the way it was before."' But although the son closely copied the dazzling father in just about everything he did, Amenhotep IV was merely a pale imitation of the man he tried so hard to emulate.

Things got off to a bad start when the new king greatly offended his Mitannian allies by substituting gold-plated statues for the solid gold ones promised by his father before he died. After this inauspicious beginning it was clear that young Amenhotep was going to need guidance every step of the way. Tiy was obliged to act as effective regent, and as Mistress of Egypt worked hard on behalf of a son who had little grasp of political reality. She even took over some of the diplomatic correspondence, telling the king of Mitanni that 'my husband always showed love to your father and maintained it for you, and so now you must not forget your love for my husband, and increase it for our son! You must keep on sending friendly delegations, one after the other. You mustn't cut them off!'

Tushratta responded by reassuring her that he would show 'ten times more love to your son', closing with his best wishes and those of his own wife Queen Yuni, both of them sending Tiy gifts of 'sweet perfume' and jewellery. He also wrote directly to the new pharaoh and reminded him that his mother should be consulted on all matters of state, since she was the only one who knew his father's policies in detail. Tushratta's extraordinary comment 'Tiy your mother knows all the words I spoke to your father. No one else knows them, so you must ask your mother so she can tell you' reveals the extent of the dowager queen's power and abilities.

With Tushratta also referring to 'Tadukhepa my daughter, now your wife, and the rest of your wives', it seems that Amenhotep IV had inherited his own stepmother Tadukhepa amongst the hundreds of other royal women in his father's household. He also continued Amenhotep III's policy of diplomatic marriage, and with a new king now in Babylon, too, it was time to form a new alliance. The king of Babylon confirmed that the Egyptian delegation had arrived and poured oil on the head of the princess to mark her betrothal, but it seems that Amenhotep IV was still cutting corners and the small escort he had sent to bring his Babylonian bride back to Egypt was quite unacceptable to them. 'There are only five chariots,' complained the king. Are they going to bring her to you in only five chariots? Am I supposed to allow her to leave my house in this way? What would the neighbouring kings say? "Look, they have taken the daughter of the Great King of Babylon to Egypt in only five chariots!"

When my father sent his daughter to Egypt, there was an escort of three thousand soldiers with her!' It all seems to have been sorted out in the end, however, and, together with his Mitannian and Babylonian wives, Amenhotep IV continued to receive women as tribute from his empire's vassal states. Forty-six women were sent by the mayor of Gazru, twenty-one from the ruler of Jerusalem, and the mayor of Palestine threw in twenty girls with a shipment of oxen.

Malkata palace was now renamed the Castle of the Aten. The new pharaoh and his entourage resided here for much of the early part of the reign, and apparently spent time there intermittently later on. At first Tiy remained chief queen and played a key role alongside the new king in ceremonial events, carrying the queenly lily sceptre in her left hand and playing the sistrum as her son made offerings of wine and incense to the traditional gods Ra and Maat, Atum and Hathor.

Then, some time in his second year as king, around 1350 BC, and almost certainly with the guidance of his mother, it seems that Amenhotep IV took a wife. His bride made her first public appearance in the tomb scenes of Ramose, the vizier whom the king had inherited from his father. With Amenhotep IV portrayed alongside the goddess Maat, the final scene was carved in the new exaggerated art style and it featured the new royal wife. The couple were depicted standing together at a large Window of Appearances, framed by images of the king trampling his enemies, as the Aten disc shone down blessings on them (Fig. 7). And as the king leaned forward and threw gold collars to his staff, the female figure standing demurely behind him wearing the Nubian wig and clutching the queenly lily sceptre was named as 'Great Royal Wife, his beloved, Mistress of Egypt', Nefertiti.

Despite being one of ancient Egypt's most famous faces, Nefertiti's origins are unknown. A clue, such as it is, might be found in her name, which is almost always translated as 'The Beautiful One Has Come'. Using the hieroglyph sign 𓄤 'nefer', which actually symbolises a cow's entrails, heart and windpipe, 'nefer' essentially means 'good' or 'perfect', 'happy' and 'beautiful'. With the feminine 't' ⌒ sign added to make it a female name, this is followed by the curious-looking 𝄞 sign, a combination of the flowering reed 𝄚 and a pair of human legs ⋀ to spell out the verb 'to come'. Basing the argument on this part of her name, it was asserted that Nefertiti had come from a foreign land. Referring to 'the evidently foreign queen Nefertiti', Petrie believed there could 'scarcely be a doubt' that Nefertiti was the Egyptian name given to Tadukhepa, the Mitannian princess who had arrived in Egypt shortly before Amenhotep III's death and had been inherited by his successor.

Others have suggested that she may have been a daughter of Amenhotep III. Given the numbers of women who lived within the royal court, together with the unnamed 'royal daughters' born to women other than Tiy, it is possible that Nefertiti was a daughter by one of his minor wives, either an Egyptian or a woman from overseas. Scenes from Karnak show Nefertiti as queen at the head of a row of women named as 'king's children' and, although she herself is not, she is nevertheless named as 'the Heiress' amongst her titles. As a result, many scholars feel confident about placing Nefertiti within at least a minor branch of the ruling house. Some strongly believe that 'she was descended from Queen Ahmose-Nefertari, the virtual female ancestress of the dynasty whose cult as a Theban divinity had been greatly expanded by one of her descendants Queen Tiy. Nefertiti was doubtless of the same family as Tiy, who was perhaps her aunt.' This view is partly influenced by the women's names, since Tiy has been identified as an abbreviated version of Nefertari and its variant Nefertiti, whilst Tuya is apparently a similarly shortened form of Ahhotep, one of the dynasty's early queens.

Perhaps the most likely scenario is that Nefertiti was the daughter of Tiy's brother Ay, whose title 'God's Father' is often thought to mean 'father-in-law of the king'. Another important clue is the fact that Ay's wife Ty is named as Nefertiti's wet nurse, suggesting that her own mother had perhaps died in child-birth and the infant was then raised by Ay's presumably second wife Ty. Certainly the fact that Nefertiti had an Egyptian nurse must mean that she was raised from birth, or at least from a very young age, at the Egyptian court, and could not have been a foreign princess sent to Egypt at marriageable age.

Although it is not known how old she was at the time she became Great Royal Wife, it seems that her predecessor, Tiy, had been around ten to twelve when she married the similarly young Amenhotep III. Nefertiti's own daughter would in time become Great Royal Wife to Tutankhamen when she was about ten or eleven, and, given the average life expectancy of around thirty-five, it is quite possible that Nefertiti would have been an equally youthful consort.

Another clue to her family connections is that the tomb of Ay and Ty at Amarna is one of the few places which mention Nefertiti's only definitely known blood relative other than her future daughters, her younger sister Mutnodjmet. As a lady-in-waiting in Amarna, Mutnodjmet is usually shown in the company of her two dwarf attendants, Mutefpre and Hemetnisu-weterneheh, and a unique alabaster statue recently discovered in a private collection near Bolton in northern England may possibly represent Nefertiti's sister.

Nefertiti's status as a member of a minor branch of the royal house would certainly help explain her selection as Great Royal Wife, a position unlikely to have been given to someone newly arrived from abroad and unfamiliar with Egyptian ways. It also seems highly unlikely that Tiy would have entrusted her way-ward son to an unknown foreigner. That Nefertiti must have been regarded as a reliable choice is emphasised in the way she began to be portrayed, with growing powers that no Egyptian queen had yet enjoyed – very much building on the trail blazed by Queen Tiy. Known as the 'High and mighty one in the palace and one trusted by the king', she was certainly his confidante.

Several influential courtiers even state the wish that 'she be by his side', presumably to make their job easier in their dealings with a king who seems not to have been the most straightforward of men.

Within a few years of her marriage to Amenhotep IV Nefertiti took a second additional name, Neferneferuaten, meaning 'Exquisite Perfection of the Aten disc'. Demonstrating the way in which she seemed to lead whilst her husband followed, he did something similar by changing his name from Amenhotep to the more familiar Akhenaten, 'One Beneficial to the Aten'.

Concentrating their attentions on the sun god, the couple began to dismantle much of the existing religious and political framework built around the state god Amen, replacing it with their own brand of Aten worship though still acknowledging many of the traditional gods. During the first five years of the reign, the royal steward Apy wrote to the king to tell him that 'the offerings for all the gods and goddesses have been issued in full and nothing held back' at the great temple of Ptah at Memphis. The couple also added a limestone Aten temple within the existing complex, adorned with finely carved wall scenes of Nefertiti in kingly dress and fine statues of red quartzite. Having created other Aten shrines up and down the country the king and queen were also active further south in Nubia, and after completing the wall scenes in Amenhotep III's temple at Soleb a twenty-mile road was constructed to link it to a new Aten temple at Sesebi. Its tall columns were decorated with figures of Akhenaten and Nefertiti worshipping in the open air beneath the shining rays of the Aten disc, and it is intriguing to find them paying homage to the rest of Egypt's pantheon inside the temple's subterranean crypt, having literally taken the traditional gods underground.

The most ambitious ideas, however, were reserved for the empire's religious heartland, Karnak Temple in Thebes. After the new king had carried on his father's work by completing the decoration of two of the pylon gateways with fetching images of himself destroying the enemy and worshipping the falcon-headed sun god Ra, the couple turned their attentions to their own controversial plans for the site. Expeditions were sent to the quarries of Aswan to find granite for new altars and obelisks, though most of the building stone came from the quarries of Gebel Silsilah. The sandstone was cut into small, easy-to-handle blocks known as *talatat*, and then the builders began to assemble a series of temples the like of which Egypt had never seen: the largest would measure nearly 2000 feet by 650 feet. The royal couple would have been able to oversee the construction work from a palace they built adjacent to the vast building site, and must have proved demanding clients. Everything was built to precise royal specifications, and the chief sculptor, Bek, admitted he was simply 'the apprentice whom his majesty himself taught'. This may of course just be standard flattery – or perhaps a subtle way of letting future generations know that the work had nothing to do with him and he was only 'following orders'. Yet if Bek was following the orders of the king, it must have been Akhenaten's wish that Nefertiti be shown on average twice as often as he was himself. Image after image shows the ever-present sun disc shining down on Nefertiti, or the royal couple performing endless acts of worship. Granite altars were inscribed with the offerings to be laid out beneath the sun each morning, with incense and music equally vital ingredients in the ritual mix.

Having apparently thrown away the official guide to royal protocol, the king decided to celebrate a jubilee after a mere three years as king instead of the thirty dictated by tradition. At the 'First Jubilee of His Majesty given to him by the Aten' Akhenaten wore the traditional knee-length jubilee robes and the red crown of the north or the white crown of the south on different days, suggesting the long drawn out nature of the grand ceremonials. With Nefertiti borne aloft in her elaborate golden carrying chair at the head of a procession of royal women, the king sat on his golden throne, surrounded by the major court officials and

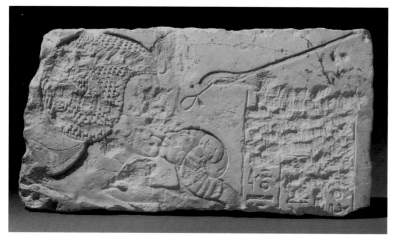

Painted limestone relief scene originally from Amarna showing Nefertiti in a short wig and diadem kissing one of her daughters, possibly Meritaten, as an arm of the Aten sun disc reaches down to bless them with an ankh sign.

Limestone stela featuring the Amarna royal family beneath the Aten, Akhenaten kissing his eldest daughter Meritaten whilst younger sister Meketaten sits with her mother Nefertiti, enthroned on an elaborate seat as the baby Ankhesenpaaten, future wife of Tutankhamen, plays with her crown ornaments.

Red quartzite statuette of Nefertiti, a pleated robe of finest linen with fringed border tied beneath her right breast and revealing her exaggeratedly voluptuous figure.

(*bottom left & right*) A newly discovered alabaster (calcite) statuette of a royal Amarna female, possibly Nefertiti's sister Mutnodjmet or one of the royal princesses, the end of a short thick sidelock visible at the right shoulder and fine linen robes again revealing an incredibly distorted body shape.

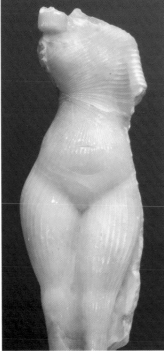

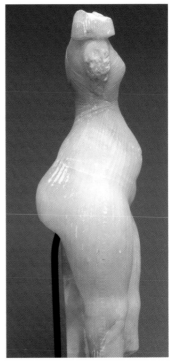

Part of a painted relief scene on a sandstone block from Karnak showing the elongated face of Nefertiti framed by the intricately styled Nubian wig as one of the Aten's hands reaches down to touch her shoulder.

(*above*) Part of a painted sandstone relief scene from Karnak showing Nefertiti with exaggerated facial features, wearing a long tripartite wig, headband and bracelets as she raises offerings to the Aten who in return blesses her with the ankh sign.

(*right*) Part of a limestone column from Amarna carved with figures of Nefertiti and her eldest daughter Meritaten worshipping the Aten, Nefertiti's tall blue crown further embellished with solar disc, double ostrich plumes and a pair of kingly rams' horns.

Limestone statuette of an older Nefertiti from the Amarna workshop of Tuthmose, wearing the royal cap crown and brow band as she strides forward alone as sole ruler.

Gilded wooden statuette from the tomb of Tutankhamen, showing a female pharaoh standing on the back of a leopard and originally discovered wrapped in linen dated to Akhenaten's reign.

One of four small coffinettes of gold and semi-precious stones designed to hold mummified entrails, inscribed with the names Ankhkheperure Neferneferuaten but reinscribed for Tutankhamen.

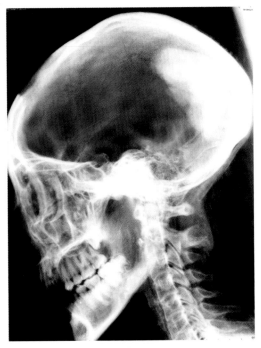

Digital X-ray image of the Younger Woman's skull, revealing intact nasal bones and desiccated brain tissue, the partly erupted wisdom teeth initially suggesting an individual in their late teens or early twenties.

(*below*) Digital X-ray image of the Younger Woman's torso revealing traces of small beads and nefer-shaped amulets (upper left), a slight curvature of the spine, and arthritic traces which, together with the fusion of the long bones, suggest an age of twenty-five up to thirty years.

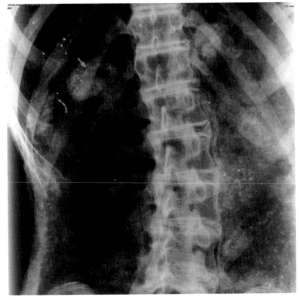

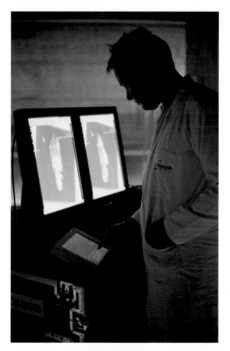

Andy Gaskin of Xograph monitoring the digital X-ray images on the computer screen set up in the burial chamber of tomb KV.35 in the Valley of the Kings.

The flexed female right arm with clasped hand, last reported by anatomist Grafton Elliot Smith in 1907 and recovered from mummy wrappings beside the legs of the Younger Woman in 2003.

Egyptian workmen reseal the side chamber of the tomb in February 2003 following examination of the three mummies by the multidisciplinary research team from the University of York, King's College Hospital and Cairo Museum.

The Valley of the Kings, the world's most famous cemetery, looking down toward the Amarna cache tomb KV.55 (beside the modern rest house in the centre), the tombs of Tutankhamen and Ramses VI (lower left) and the mysterious tomb KV.56 and tomb of Amenhotep II (KV.35) along the path (bottom left).

members of the armed forces, whilst foreign delegates literally kissed the earth at his feet in a gesture of complete submission.

A military theme also figured prominently on the walls of some of Karnak's other Aten shrines: Akhenaten and Nefertiti were both shown as aggressive defenders of their country, executing foreign prisoners. And it may well have been more than posturing, since one of the few letters Akhenaten wrote to his vassals in Palestine declared that traitors would be punished and sent to Egypt in fetters, 'and you and your entire family shall die by the axe of the king'.

Intimidating wall scenes weren't the only innovation. The temple's colonnade courts were adorned with at least twenty-eight huge painted sandstone statues, the so-called grotesque colossi. They portray Akhenaten and Nefertiti as the twin children of the great creator sun god, the three of them making up the divine triad, Akhenaten shown as Shu in his tall feather head-dress and Nefertiti playing the role of his sister, the great creator goddess Tefnut. Like her male counterpart she clutches the kingly sceptres of crook and flail in her crossed hands, and even wears the traditional false beard of kingship just as other female rulers had done before her. Yet, with their existence long suppressed or denied, it is little wonder that Nefertiti's Karnak figures were for so long believed to be those of the king. And in quarters where this is still the case, their distinctly feminine appearance is still regarded as evidence that Akhenaten was a eunuch, hermaphrodite or victim of various medical conditions.

Finally, in the very heart of the new complex, the king himself was nowhere to be found but Nefertiti dominated every scene. However, she was no decorative accessory in male-dominated rituals. Blowing apart centuries of tradition, she was shown leading the daily worship of the Aten centred on the conical benben stone, the ancient cult fetish of the sun god. The benben stone was regarded as the very embodiment of the Aten, but it was Nefertiti who was responsible for invoking the god's spirit down into the sacred stone and 'satisfying him as he rises at dawn' – it was she who kept the divine spark aroused and content through all manner of offerings.

Playing the sistrums, Nefertiti is repeatedly portrayed on immense columns over thirty feet high as she leads the lavish daily rites. She is accompanied by her first-born child, her daughter Meritaten, 'The Aten's Beloved', making her earliest public appearances playing her own tiny sistrum as she stands behind her mother in an all-female line-up praising the Aten at Karnak.

All these innovations and building projects involved a great deal of expense, and with the royal coffers so over-extended more taxes had to be raised. A surviving fragment of a decree issued at Karnak hints at how this was done. Every existing temple in Egypt seems to have been expected to contribute by sending silver, incense, wine and cloth, whilst the mayor of every town was responsible for sending more precious metals together with food and wine.

Ever since the monarchy had started to strongly support the sun god back in the reign of Amenhotep II in the 1420s BC, the priests of Amen had seen their powers slowly eroded by successive kings, and this must have been the final straw. The highly conservative priests had been forced to stand by as their sacred precincts were hacked about and redesigned, and yet the woman who covered their walls and towered over them in sculpted form did not wish to serve Amen as his priestess, but instead served the Aten within parts of the temple that she very much controlled. And whereas previous monarchs had swelled Amen's coffers with tribute, this king and queen were demanding that the flow be reversed! Although details are frustratingly shrouded in mystery, it seems that the Amen priests began to voice their objections openly. On a fragmentary inscription, Akhenaten refers tantalisingly to 'evil words' which had been overheard. He says that

it was worse that those I heard in regnal year 4, worse than those I heard in regnal year 3, or those I heard in regnal year 2 or during my first year as king. It was worse than those which Nebmaatra [Amenhotep III] heard; it was worse than those which Aakheperura [Tuthmosis] heard; it was worse than those which Mankheperra [Amenhotep II] heard; in fact worse than those heard by any king who had ever worn the crown.

In the face of such apparent plotting, the royal couple acted swiftly and began to remove all traces of Amen and his clergy. Beginning with the god's name, Akhenaten had already changed his own name from Amenhotep, and now sent out his agents across the land to chisel out the god's name, wherever it was found, from the tops of columns, statues, obelisks and even the capstones of certain pyramids. As the god was gradually rendered impotent, the royal couple turned their attentions on the many thousands who served him and presumably could not be trusted. After 'a charge was given to May, High Priest of Amen', he was sent off to the remote quarries of the Eastern Desert. Those left behind, from the holiest priest to the lowliest worker, were all made redundant when Egypt's greatest temple was closed down.

As the dissolution of the temples continued throughout the land, settlements were deprived of their civic and religious heart, and thousands were thrown out of work. And as images and inscriptions were defaced, cult statues melted down and their treasuries ransacked, the incalculable wealth of centuries was now laid at the feet of the new gods: the Aten, Akhenaten and Nefertiti.

9

LIFE IN THE ROYAL CITY

In less than five years Akhenaten and Nefertiti had completely upset the long-established balance of power between crown and clergy, and with massive unemployment resulting from the dissolution of the traditional temples public unrest would understandably have been on the increase. So some time around 1347 BC, probably more for reasons of self-preservation than anything else, it was felt best to relocate the royal capital to a different part of the country.

With recent events still fresh in his mind, Akhenaten decided to find a completely new site to which no one had prior claim. As he said himself, he wanted a site which 'did not belong to a god nor to a goddess, nor to a male ruler nor to a female ruler nor to any other people'. Although some have seen the choice of Amarna's windswept plain as a little eccentric, cut off as it is in the middle of nowhere, it was in some ways quite a strategic location. Set almost exactly midway between the northern administrative capital, Memphis, and the southern religious centre, Thebes, it was far enough away from either to avoid any direct conflict, though still being central enough to enable its inhabitants to reach any part of the country by river relatively swiftly.

The royal couple must have first noticed the site as they sailed past between Thebes and Memphis on matters of state, and the spectacular landscape obviously appealed. Witnessing the sun rising up from a gap in its eastern cliffs, they named it Akhet Aten, meaning 'The Horizon of the Aten' – the perfect backdrop for their dream city. The city itself was envisaged as female, and 'the Aten will rise within her, filling her with his rays'. Akhenaten

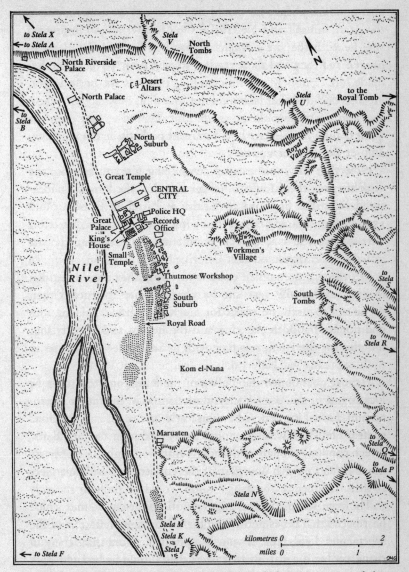

MAP 4. Amarna (ancient Akhetaten) showing the main parts of the city, including its palaces and temples, the Royal Road, the Workmen's Village, the tombs and the boundary stelae on both banks of the Nile

also announced that he would build the city as a memorial to the Aten, himself and Nefertiti – the divine triad. So impressed was he with the site's potential that he raised his hand up to heaven and then and there made a solemn oath 'to the Aten that made him', publicly announcing that this was the perfect spot. He also declared that he would not found his new city anywhere else and no one would persuade him otherwise, 'not even the great royal wife' Nefertiti – a comment perhaps on her considerable powers of persuasion.

Now that the royal treasury was being filled to overflowing with the wealth of Egypt's former temples, the king was accurately described as 'Lord of Wealth and Rich in Goods'. With an almost unlimited budget, the couple put their plans into effect with no expense spared. Taking up temporary residence on site in a lavishly appointed tent described as 'a pavilion of woven stuff', the couple worked out exactly what they would require. Having toured the vast site by chariot, they instructed their architects to draw up plans for a series of grand palaces with apartments for both the king and the queen, and at least four temples for the Aten, together with a 'Sunshade' Temple to be built expressly for Nefertiti.

Having abandoned the Valley of the Kings and the tomb he had begun in the West Valley close to that of his father Amenhotep III, the king ordered a completely new royal burial ground to be established at Amarna. But he wanted it on the East Bank, where the sun rose, abandoning the traditional practice of burying the dead on the West Bank where it set. In a brilliant piece of political theatre the king's tomb would be built in the very valley from which the sun appeared to rise at dawn, and where he decreed that he, Nefertiti and their daughter Meritaten would all be buried together. It was also publicly stated that if any of them were to die in any other place they should be brought back to Amarna for burial in the family vault.

Akhenaten also ordered a tomb be built for the sun god's sacred bull, whose predecessors had previously been buried in

Heliopolis, together with tombs for the priests of the Aten and all the other royal officials, many of which were again modelled on the earlier Theban tombs of his father's officials. And in the same way that his father, Amenhotep III, had described his own buildings on a great stela set up near the Colossi of Memnon, Akhenaten listed on a series of great boundary stelae all the buildings he and Nefertiti had planned for their new city. Carved into the semicircle of cliffs surrounding the site, these stelae defined their city limits, with the first two set at the most northerly and southerly points.

In 'regnal year 5, Month 4, Day 13' – some time in the summer of 1347 BC – Akhenaten and Nefertiti officially founded their city amidst great rejoicing. The decree itself began with the usual list of the king's titles, followed by a fulsome description of Nefertiti as

Heiress, Great One of the palace, fair of face, adorned in the double plumes, lady of joy, at the sound of whose voice the king rejoices, possessor of grace, great of love, whose arrangements please the king, leader of Aten's encourage, who satisfies him as he rises at dawn. Everything she says is done, the Great Royal Wife, his beloved, the Lady of Egypt, Neferneferuaten-Nefertiti, may she live forever.

Quite an impressive resumé.

Exactly one year later, in regnal year 6, the couple revisited their city and its limits and ordered more stelae to be set up in the surrounding hills to further delineate the city's boundaries. Akhenaten was also anxious that each stela should be kept in optimum condition, and ordered that they 'shall not be obliterated, washed out, hacked out, or plastered over' – the very damage his agents were inflicting on Amen's name all over Egypt. The stelae were adorned with figures of the king and queen praying to the Aten disc (see Fig. 1), followed by evidence of their growing family when the toddler Meritaten was joined by a sister, Meketaten, meaning 'She Whom the Aten Protects', some time around her father's fifth or sixth regnal year. As both girls play their small sistrum rattles in the course of worship, Akhenaten states, 'My heart is joyous over Nefertiti and over her children, the king's daughter Meritaten and the king's daughter Meketaten, her children being under the hand of the royal wife their mother, forever and ever.' Nefertiti was soon pregnant again, giving birth to her third child, probably in regnal year 6 or 7. The new baby was named Ankhesenpaaten, or 'May She Live for the Aten', and her tiny figure was squeezed into the available space on the monuments (see Fig. 10).

The representations of the couple with increasing numbers of children have generally been regarded as little more than endearing scenes of family life. But having removed Egypt's complex network of traditional deities, particularly the Theban divine family of Amen, Mut and their son Khonsu, Akhenaten and Nefertiti were simply setting themselves up as the new gods with their own divine children, the replacements for centuries of tradition. Her frequent pregnancies also seem to have reinforced Nefertiti's role as the life-giving creator goddess, her status as a mother being an important part of her ritualised role. She is generally portrayed with huge hips and thighs, and her gowns are often shown open at the front to accommodate her regular pregnancies (Fig. 10), their design fully emphasising maternal attributes admired as early as the Pyramid Age when royal mothers were admired as 'splendid and rounded'.

There are also representations which have been interpreted as Nefertiti breast-feeding her daughters in the same way that female divinities were shown breast-feeding kings. Divine milk was believed to be imbued with all the necessary qualities to strengthen them from birth to death and beyond, and even human milk was regarded as highly potent stuff which featured regularly in medical recipes and magic spells.

On the small stelae set up in the homes of royal officials, the king and queen are shown lifting up their daughters to kiss them in idealised scenes of royal family life. The three girls clamber over their parents' laps, trying to attract their attention by touching their faces, playing with the cobra on their mother's crown or jumping up to reach one of the large beaded earrings their father holds out. In similarly intimate scenes between Akhenaten and Nefertiti, he turns to touch her chin in the same way her daughters do. The couple are even shown nose to nose, sharing the same breath as she leans forward to tie a jewelled collar around his neck, even as they drive together in one of the royal chariots. Although usually interpreted as no more than a romantic interlude in which the couple are described as kissing, it is the same pose found in representations of goddesses giving kings the sustaining breath of life.

Despite all this heavy breathing, symbolic or otherwise, sex was still perceived as too uncontrollable to be shown in official art, although its powers were acknowledged as a means to overcome death through the creation of the next generation. The Egyptians also drew on the powers of sexual orgasm as a means of sparking the beginnings of eternal life with coffin inscriptions describing the moment when 'your contentment is mine whilst I form seed and receive breath'. With the wish that 'you conceive me in the night and give birth to me each morning like the sun god every day', the sky goddess Nut gave birth to the sun amidst the blood-red glow of dawn.

For all the high-flown symbolic imagery childbirth was the most hazardous moment in a woman's life, and whilst it was a trial that Nefertiti successfully underwent six times, at least one of Akhenaten's minor wives was not so lucky and appears to have died in childbirth. Numerous precautions were taken before and after delivery in an attempt to ensure the health of both mother and child – presumably no more so than when that woman was a living goddess and queen of Egypt. A whole array of deities could be invoked to help women during birth, and images of Hathor, Bes and Heket the frog goddess associated with birth were all found on items from royal tombs at both Amarna and Thebes. It seems likely, therefore, that Nefertiti may well have cried out to these traditional powers for assistance during her frequent labours. Hathor was invoked to bring the cooling north wind, whilst amulets of the protective household god Bes were sometimes tied around the woman's head and spells recited over them to 'bring down the placenta'. Some women even chose to be tattooed with protective Bes figures on the top of each thigh, and women attending the birth may well have worn masks to play the role of the gods invoked.

Like all expectant mothers, Nefertiti would almost certainly have been confined within a room specially decorated with papyrus, lotus and convolvulus flowers, symbols of fertility and motherhood. When the time of delivery approached, gravity was allowed to do much of the work, as the woman squatted on birth bricks covered in magical figures to protect both mother and child from the dangers lurking in the darkness. And on a practical level, the bricks raised the woman up to allow her attendants and midwives to take hold of the emerging child, the moment graphically portrayed in the hieroglyph symbol 𓄿 for birth. And it even seems as if men appreciated the degree of pain involved – one claimed his illness was so painful that he 'sat upon bricks like a woman in labour'.

Details of the life-threatening process itself were rarely given, but an early tale of royal birth describes how the sun god Ra sent down four goddesses to act as midwives to a woman about to give birth to three future pharaohs. As they arrived, they were met by her husband who was so distracted that he was wearing his loincloth upside down. 'Oh my ladies,' he cried, 'look, the woman's in pain and her labour is difficult,' to which they replied, 'Let us see her, for we understand childbirth.' Locking themselves in her room, one goddess stood behind to support her and, as the other two provided encouragement, Isis waited as the first child slid into her arms. After washing him and cutting his umbilical cord, they placed him on a soft pillow and went on to deliver his two brothers.

After a successful delivery, a whole series of protective rituals were performed for both mother and child whilst the woman 'cleansed herself' for fourteen days, the traditional two-week period of purification and seclusion following every birth prior to resuming her place in society. If sufficiently wealthy the woman would be pampered and groomed, her attendants bringing her make-up, perfume and a mirror – a vital part of the process in Nefertiti's case, where a pristine, goddess-like appearance was all-important in maintaining the façade of divinity.

It was a cycle of events Nefertiti would be all too familiar with, as Meritaten, Meketaten and Ankhesenpaaten were joined by Neferneferuaten Tasherit, 'Junior', around regnal year 8 or 9. Neferneferura, or 'Perfect One of Ra's Perfection', and the youngest girl, Setepenra, 'She Whom Ra Has Chosen', followed over the next three years. And with all six daughters born by their father's twelfth regnal year, Akhenaten's official, all-female household was complete.

Diplomatic correspondence, however, also asks after his 'wives and sons', and clearly he had wives other than Nefertiti. These included foreign princesses from Mitanni and Babylonia and the enigmatic Kiya, 'the other woman'. Kiya's unique title, 'Greatly Loved Wife of the King', perhaps reflects the feelings she may have inspired in him in contrast to his chief wife, the powerful, intimidating and perhaps none too lovable Nefertiti.

Although nothing is known of her background, some believe Kiya was the Egyptian name given to the Mitannian princess Tadukhepa, sent to Egypt to marry Amenhotep III and then inherited by Akhenaten. In keeping with the way in which women were sometimes named after the animals they resembled, such as Miuwt, 'Cat', written with the 𓃟 determinative sign placed at the end of the word to clarify its meaning or the less flattering Debet � 'Hippopotamus', the name Kiya seems to be derived from 𓃻 'Monkey', hopefully more of a reference to a playful temperament than to physical appearance!

Wherever she came from, Kiya is known to have lived at Amarna, where she had estates and her own sunshade temple. She also had a taste for rather large round earrings, and although she seems to have adopted Nefertiti's favourite coiffure, the Nubian wig, she is never shown with the royal uraeus cobra at her brow. Yet since she is shown side by side with Akhenaten Kiya must have been held in high esteem, possibly linked to the fact that she was the mother of one or perhaps two daughters and, it seems, at least one son, Tutankhaten, later Tutankhamen, described as 'king's son, from his body'. Whilst Kiya's production of a male heir would have greatly endeared her to Akhenaten, Nefertiti's feelings for a woman who had been able to do what she had not would presumably have been rather less enthusiastic.

Although Kiya seems to have been Nefertiti's only real rival, she wasn't Akhenaten's only other woman. As well as his foreign wives, there were beautiful Egyptian courtiers such as 'Royal Ornament' Ipy, 'true favourite' of the king, not to mention the hundreds of women sent as tribute from abroad. It is therefore highly likely that Akhenaten would also have had children by such women, even if details, like so much else at Amarna, have not survived.

As the number of royal children continued to grow steadily, so too did the dimensions of the royal city built to accommodate them all. The huge settlement spread out quickly along some eight miles of open plain in only a few years. The Nile ran along the western edge of the city, bringing constant riverborne traffic carrying goods and communications from around the empire. As endless numbers of people and quantities of materials arrived and departed in all manner of vessels, the great golden barge *Dazzling Aten* inherited from Amenhotep III would presumably have moored here when transporting the royal couple between Thebes, Memphis and Amarna, attended by May, Royal Attendant on the August Barge. In the same way that Tuthmosis IV had travelled 'in his golden ship with sails of bright red and green linen', his grandson Akhenaten made a stately progress, with his wife, in their own golden vessel, 'making Egypt gleam with its beauty'.

River traffic was, however, not the only means of transport, for Amarna also had its own road system. Amarna was the only Egyptian city to be built around a processional chariot way, a 130-foot-wide central route dubbed 'Kingsway' and described by Akhenaten as 'a goodly road'. It ran from the Northern Palace down to the southern end of the Great Official Palace and beyond following the line of the river to the west, with all the great state buildings laid out around it and footbridges allowing the royal family to rise above the hustle and bustle beneath.

The route also allowed the couple to travel at speed around their city. Chariots were always the preferred modes of transport, and their vehicles were covered in gold and electrum. Not only did this show off their wealth and status but it reinforced their solar connections, with Akhenaten described as 'mounting his great chariot of electrum like the Aten as he rises'. Although Nefertiti often travelled with Akhenaten she also drove her own golden vehicle, its highly polished bodywork gleaming in the sun and quite possibly one of six well-preserved examples buried with Tutankhamen.

Since fragments of chariot equipment have been found in every king's tomb from Amenhotep II to Tutankhamen, the royal family must have had a high regard for horses. The young Amenhotep II had loved his horses and was skilled in training them and understanding their ways, whilst his son Tuthmosis IV had sped around between Memphis and Giza 'in his chariot whose horses were swifter than the wind'. At Malkata, Amenhotep III had taken the family's love of horse racing to new heights by building a chariot stadium with a long, straight course which enabled the king and his family to practise their driving skills. The pharaoh was regularly shown driving his own chariot, and a whip handle inscribed with the name of Tuthmosis, quite likely the heir apparent Prince Tuthmosis, suggests that he too may have been something of a horseman. Yuya and Ay were both in charge of the royal horses, and on a large seal stone found at Amarna Queen Tiy is described as 🐎 🐎 'rich in horses'. It has been suggested that this seal was perhaps used to secure the bolts on her stables, and excavations at the estate of Master of the Royal Horses Ranefer had even revealed the cereal chaff fed to horses, together with traces of the houseflies known to thrive in horse manure.

As high-maintenance creatures, horses were really only an option for royalty and their favoured elite, and, generally imported from abroad, they often appear in diplomatic correspondence. Kings began their letters with polite enquiries after the health of their fellow monarchs, followed by that of their family and their horses and chariots, and foreign kings often sent Egypt's pharaohs such exotic gifts as 'fine horses which run swiftly' and 'chariots all of gold'. They even sent the necessary accessories, including 'a set of bridles, blinkers of ivory and a set of reins whose base and straps are overlaid in silver'. This description sounds quite similar to the fancy leather harness of dyed calfskin adorned with large metal studs that was found in Amenhotep III's tomb. Most horses shown in art of the time, often with feathery plumes attached to their headpieces, are a red-brown colour, although the diplomatic correspondence also reveals that white horses were especially prized, the king of Assyria sending two chariots and two white horses to the Amarna court.

It is clear that Nefertiti took advantage of such generous gifts, and as a skilled horsewoman was regularly shown driving her own chariot through the Amarna landscape, wielding her whip to make the creatures go faster (see Fig. 6). For more stately occasions, however, she was borne aloft in a carrying chair as royal women had been since the beginning of Egyptian history. At Karnak she is borne in an elaborate, sedan chair-like creation with lions carved on the sides, whilst at Amarna she relaxes in an open-topped version, 'The Great Royal Wife Neferneferuaten Nefertiti on the great carrying chair of electrum'.

The royal couple used both carrying chairs and chariots to

travel from their various palaces to the temples, where they would officiate on a day-to-day basis as well as in important rituals on state occasions. Prior to their arrival, temple staff would have assembled the masses of fresh offerings on hundreds of individual altars within the open solar courts of the Great Aten Temple, adorned with numerous statues of Akhenaten and Nefertiti. As they performed many of the rituals together the couple are shown side by side, often dressed in the same clothes, holding the same regalia, standing on top of the great ramp before the high altar and pouring out wine over incense-topped offerings. In a text describing the similar dawn rituals undertaken for the sun god at Heliopolis,

great offerings were made before the face of the sun at his rising, white oxen, milk, myrrh, incense and every kind of sweet-smelling flowers. Going in procession to the temple of the sun god, one enters the temple with the prayers of the chief lector priest praising the god, removing all harm from the king. The king climbs the steps to see the sun god in the House of the Benben, where the king is alone.

And after further secret rites, the worshippers 'stretch out on their bellies before the god', a position Akhenaten and Nefertiti both adopt before the Aten with their noses to the ground in the same way that their subjects lie down before them in turn.

Although such rituals were undertaken every morning as the sun rose and every evening as the sun set, the extent to which Akhenaten and Nefertiti were actually expected to attend in person isn't known. And since they employed a high priest whose traditional function was to stand in for the monarch, it seems likely that this must also have happened at Amarna, particularly when the royal couple were not in residence.

Yet, just as at Karnak, Nefertiti would have led her own female clergy in worship. They were presumably hand-picked acolytes, including her nurse, Ty, the high priest's wife, Tenra, and of course her own family, from her sister Mutnodjmet to a growing number of daughters, often shown playing their own small sistrum rattles as they follow their mother. In some cases the three youngest girls are shown with their nurses following, presumably to enable their mother to continue with the complex rites and rituals undisturbed by maternal duties.

Only temple personnel were allowed within the sacred precincts, and all had to bathe in the sacred waters of the Nile. Cleansing her skin with natron salt, Nefertiti is described as 'pure of hands' to indicate the high level of ritual cleanliness needed for handling the Aten's offerings. She would also presumably have chewed natron pellets, which were used to purify the breath before reciting the hymns of praise. With her closely shaven head and robes of finest linen another requirement of ritual purity, she would have 'put on the sacred garments in the robing room, purifying with incense and cold water, taking up the floral garlands from the House of the Benben and receiving the amulets'. The later description of priestesses as 'beautiful in their finely adorned appearance, anointed with myrrh and perfumed with lotus, their heads crowned with flowers' is an equally apt description of Nefertiti and her retinue.

As a key ritual ingredient, huge clouds of perfumed incense were used to purify both the worshipped and the worshippers, its swirling, fragrant smoke adding to the magical and mystical aura surrounding the proceedings, and its sweetness conveniently driving away evil spirits. At Amarna the pale yellow pistacia resin seems to have been most frequently used, imported and stored in the large pottery jars called amphorae and burnt as incense in the city's temples as it had been at Karnak. Crushed frankincense and myrrh mixed with honey, wax or wine were compressed into small cakes and burnt whilst reciting the 'spell for putting incense on the flames', using finely made bronze tongs ending in human hands. Several pairs of these were found at Amarna, together with limestone offering tables containing four small depressions for incense and perfumes. Large bronze incense burners were found inside the Great Aten Temple sanctuary itself – a bowl from the site was still holding its original incense and charcoal when discovered. Nefertiti is shown holding up pairs of such incense-filled bowls in both hands, whilst Akhenaten throws pellets of incense into an arm-shaped incense burner.

Water, wine and milk were offered up in gold, bronze or blue-glazed situlae, bucket-like objects inscribed with the names of Nefertiti, Akhenaten and the Aten, which have also been found at the Great Aten Temple site. Fresh produce was another essential ingredient in daily offerings, and the tomb scenes of the Aten high priest Meryra show the temple store rooms filled to bursting 'with every good thing, much corn and southern grain'. Even the gardens beyond were filled with lush date palms, pomegranate trees and vines; and flowers – lotus, lilies, cornflowers, safflowers and poppies – were essential for making up the thousands of bouquets piled high on altars and offered up by the royal couple.

Described as 'the one who satisfies the Aten with her sweet voice', Nefertiti herself would have sung praises to the god, although the ancient texts reveal that the adoration was not all one-way, since 'the Aten rises to give Nefertiti praise and then sets to repeat her love'. Hymns describe 'the singers and musicians shouting for joy in the court of the benben and in all the temples of Akhetaten', and the women's song would have risen to a crescendo as the Aten's rays reached them.

Temple performers also included groups of elderly blind men who sat in rows on the ground as they clapped their hands and sang, and scenes in Akhenaten's Royal Tomb show a group of trumpeters tootling away as the sun rises. On certain occasions worship also included guest slots by Syrian musicians in their distinctive layered robes, playing lyres, lutes, drums and a harp so large that it had two men playing it from either side. Accompanied by male and female Egyptian performers in a blend of Egyptian and Syrian music, Nefertiti is shown enthroned as she presides over this recital for the Aten.

She herself seems to have been something of a musician,

playing a pair of sistrum rattles using a two-handed technique. Since her instruments are generally shown on a much larger scale than those played by other women, it is tempting to see the two larger-than-average, well-worn sistrums found amongst Tutankhamen's tomb equipment as perhaps having once belonged to Nefertiti herself.

Dance was another form of worship, performed by the temple's musical troupe, that even the royals themselves are known to have engaged in. Later male pharaohs were encouraged to dance and sing for Hathor, and a queen of the 19th dynasty is herself described as a 'dancer of the god', her performance suggested by the lively 𓀟 hieroglyph symbol. It seems entirely possible, therefore, that Nefertiti too may have danced before the Aten.

We have no real idea of the kinds of movements she may have performed, but her temple duties have been described somewhat delicately as 'maintaining the god in a state of perpetual arousal'. And despite the highly secretive nature of the rites able to achieve the impressive results seen on figures of some of the more aroused male deities, royal women are known to have held the priestly title 'God's Hand'. This is a graphic reference to the creation of the world when the primordial deity, all alone in the darkness, 'took his phallus in his fist and ejaculated, giving birth to the twin gods Shu and Tefnut'.

Nefertiti is frequently represented as Tefnut, the daughter of the creator sun god who at Amarna was the Aten. This father-daughter relationship is also found in an ancient story describing how 'the great god spent a day lying on his back in his pavilion, his heart very sore and he was alone. After a long while, [the goddess] came and stood before her father the All Lord. She uncovered her nakedness before him; thereupon the great god laughed', her behaviour having revitalised him and given him the energy he needed. Similarly graphic behaviour was also witnessed by the Greek traveller Herodotus amongst female devotees of the cat goddess Bastet as they sailed to her cult centre. Making music and singing, 'whenever they pass a town on the riverbank, they bring the barge close in shore, some of the women . . . start dancing, or stand up and hitch up their skirts'. A little-known scene from Karnak shows Nefertiti submitting her naked torso to warm caresses from the many-handed Aten disc, so it seems quite likely that she ignited the divine spark through a provocative performance involving the removal of at least some of her clothing.

Judging from numerous portrayals, she clearly used her appearance to great effect and regularly changed her image to suit the occasion, using a huge range of crowns, wigs and jewellery. Among her large retinue of female attendants was her sister, Mutnodjmet, who acted as her lady-in-waiting. Mutnodjmet's own pair of dwarf attendants may well have helped her sister in her choice of costume, dwarves having been associated with the royal wardrobe since the Pyramid Age.

A piece of pottery found near the Royal Tomb, inscribed the 'robing room [or 'inner chamber'] of Neferneferura', Nefertiti's fifth daughter, suggests that each member of the royal family may have had his or her own kind of walk-in wardrobe, rather like the robing room with en suite facilities used at Malkata. 'Bathrooms with mirrors' appear to have been a standard feature of royal palaces for the previous five hundred years at least. Their mudbrick walls were sensibly lined with slabs of fine limestone, and water poured down on to the bather from gold and silver bowls would then drain away down stone drainage channels. Natron and oil were used as cleansing agents before the invention of soap, and both body and head would be regularly shaved by the royal barber using a range of lethal-looking razors. These were generally made of bronze, and a box from Tutankhamen's tomb was labelled 'copper-handled razors, knife-razors, ewers and linen'. A similar range of equipment was no doubt used to shave Nefertiti's scalp and body.

The skin was dried off using incredibly modern-looking towels with looped threads for absorbency, after which the royal person would be anointed with a variety of moisturising oils including sesame or olive. In scenes dating back to the Pyramid Age, royalty are anointed by courtiers holding oil pots; some of them even massage the royal feet.

Various perfumes were added to the oils, and different fragrances were used on different occasions, with myrrh oil favoured for ritual events and lotus employed for its protective and restorative qualities. Although Nefertiti offered generously filled perfume vessels to the Aten's rays, she would have worn such scented oils herself for both ritual and practical purposes. And as the ultimate sun worshipper, spending much of her time performing open-air rituals in full sun, she presumably went through huge quantities of moisturising oils to keep her skin in good condition.

Although Egyptian perfumes were exported, the Amarna royals were often sent foreign perfumes as diplomatic gifts. Queen Puduheba of Ugarit wrote to the queen of Egypt, quite possibly Nefertiti, addressing her as 'my Mistress, I fall at your feet! For my mistress may all go well, and I sent to you a jar of fragrant suurwa balsam'.

Perfumed oils and unguents were made by those named as 'oil boilers' or 'the superintendent of unguents', some of whom worked on palace premises for the various members of the royal family. Nefertiti's eldest daughter even had her own perfume production line headed by one Ramose, 'unguent manufacturer in the house of Princess Meritaten'. Perfumes were stored in exquisite pots made of gold, semi-precious stones and brilliantly coloured glazed ware; glass containers, predominantly blue and yellow, were also popular during the Amarna period. Along with straightforward jars and tubes were novelty examples such as a wonderful blue and yellow glass fish wearing a startled expression, whose wide-open mouth was the means of pouring out the scented contents. A list of gifts that Akhenaten sent to Babylon includes a gold perfume container with a lapis lazuli stopper, coloured ivory pots decorated with ibex or fruit and 'a stone servant figurine with a jar in his hands', exactly like one found at Amarna inscribed with his name and that of Nefertiti.

Having been bathed, depilated, perfumed and moisturised by a retinue of attendants, Nefertiti would have been dressed in robes of the very finest quality. The textile fragments recovered from the re-examination of the Royal Tomb were of a high-quality, fine linen when compared to those worn by the general public elsewhere in the city.

Amongst huge numbers of Egyptian garments sent to the king of Babylon were mantles, shawls, cloaks and pieces of linen including 'a double-sized piece of finest linen to make into a festive garment', presumably so that the Babylonians could make up their own fashions using Egypt's famous linen. Colour and decoration were also appreciated by the Amarna royals. There are descriptions of 'linen garments for the front of the body with fancy borders' and robes of contrasting shades of red. Attempts to recreate these ancient reds have involved a lengthy process blending a plant-based dye with sheep droppings and rancid olive oil in order to attain the desired shade.

Some of the garments buried with Tutankhamen are known to have belonged to his Amarna predecessors, including a garment found draped around the large Anubis jackal statue in his tomb which bore the name of Akhenaten and 'regnal year 7' written discreetly up the lower left side. Made of a single length of linen folded over and sewn up the side, it has fine bands of red and blue vertical stripes and a fringe along the bottom hem. And since Akhenaten and Nefertiti often dressed identically, it is more than likely that she too wore such robes. Another length of linen from the tomb was labelled 'Ankhkheperura', the name of Akhenaten's co-regent and quite possibly Nefertiti herself.

Further tunics from the tomb feature embroidered and woven panels with falcon's wings around the neckline, red and blue rosettes, tapestry-woven ankh ☥ and nefer ♃ hieroglyphs, and hunting scenes. Basing their assertion on the cut, the type of sewing and the nature of the embroidery on one of the tunics, textile experts believe it was made in Syria and came to Egypt possibly as a diplomatic gift. Female musicians living in Amarna's palaces also wore what have been described as 'flounced Syrian skirts', indicating that ethnic minorities living in the city appear to have kept their own customs and costumes, which no doubt influenced Egyptian fashions of the day.

Heavily beaded and sequinned garments were also worn on state occasions, their glittering surfaces designed to catch the sunlight and dazzle onlookers. Those encrusted with gold and beading on both front and back were worn when the monarchs needed to stand, so it has been suggested that those decorated only on the front were meant for the long drawn-out ceremonies when they could be seated – no doubt a relief, given the weight of such sumptuous garments. A heavily decorated shawl from the tomb, decorated with forty-seven small gold discs, again featured the name 'Ankhkheperura, beloved of the Aten'; this glittering, golden garment may therefore once have graced the shoulders of Nefertiti herself at some grand occasion.

Her robes are usually shown worn almost sari-like and knotted beneath the right breast, and sometimes the linen is so fine that only the addition of pleats and fringes show that Nefertiti is wearing any garment at all. In her great Karnak statuary, her plain gown fits so closely that she appears to be naked, whilst other statues show her in pleated robes which leave her breasts and the front of her body exposed. One minimalist garment covers little more than her back (Fig. 10).

During some of her ritual duties she also wore male attire, a male-style kilt with its high back leaving her torso completely naked as she worships the Aten. She is also shown sensibly stripped to the waist to perform the bloody duties of executing prisoners with her scimitar (see Fig. 4), her choice of kingly costume corresponding with an act performed only by a king. Although such kilts could be made of fine pleated linen, one made of coloured beads was found in the tomb of Tutankhamen. Further colour and shape were added with long sashes, worn

FIGURE 10. Side view of one of the sculpted figures of
Nefertiti holding the top of a small stela beside the larger
Boundary Stela A, her three eldest daughters Meritaten,
Meketaten and Ankhesenpaaten carved in relief beside their
mother who wears a finely pleated robe tied across the front
of her body

either just below the breasts or closely around the waist, knotted
at the front and the ends hanging down at the front and flaring
out. Gorgeous sashes were worn by Akhenaten and Nefertiti as
they sped along in their chariots, streaming out behind them in
a rich display of reds, blues and greens, whilst long red versions
known as 'Amarna sashes' were worn only by Akhenaten and
Nefertiti, their daughter Ankhesenamen and Tutankhamen,
whose tomb contained five of them.

Akhenaten and Nefertiti are shown presenting a pair of red
gloves to Ay, and 'a pair of gloves trimmed with red wool' was
sent to them from Mitanni. On a more practical level, skilfully
made riding gauntlets as found in several royal tombs would
have been worn to protect the royal hands when holding the
reigns of their chariots. Equally, the royal feet would have

needed finely crafted footwear, with flip-flop type sandals the commonest and most practical option in the heat. Made of palm leaf, grass, papyrus or leather, those worn by royalty usually had extra decoration in the form of gold leaf, embroidery and bead work, and their soles were decorated with figures of bound enemies, to be crushed at every step.

By the Amarna Period, shoes described as 'enveloping sandals' had just reached Egypt from Syria; highly ornate examples including 'leather shoes studded with gold decoration and lapis lazuli buttons' were sent to the Egyptian court. Such a pair were buried with Tutankhamen along with more than forty others, some of which must surely have been inherited from his predecessors. One pair of leather sandals are particularly fine, and, with thongs of delicate filigree gold, the straps are adorned with small gold daisies, large lotus flowers with lapis lazuli, carnelian and feldspar petals, and tiny ducks' heads which project out and peer around. Etiquette required that sandals be removed in the presence of superiors, and Nefertiti, who of course had no earthly superiors, is usually shown wearing hers, although the royal sandal bearer would be on hand to carry them should she decide to slip them off.

And if the evenings grew chilly she could slip on a pair of linen socks, a gap between the big toe and the rest allowing them to be worn beneath her sandals. Clearly comfort was on the agenda, and an intriguing pair of footwear made of 'purple wood decorated with gold, buttons and lapis lazuli' that were described in diplomatic correspondence sound very much like an ornate pair of carpet slippers.

A markedly relaxed atmosphere can be found in the informal scenes of palace life at Amarna in which groups of women are shown at leisure. Sitting on large floor cushions, they play music, eat, chat and do each other's hair in an all-female environment not unlike that of a modern hair salon. Hairstyles were of tremendous importance to an individual's complete 'look', and were achieved with a wide range of hairdressing equipment.

Decorative hairpins found at Amarna feature tiny pomegranates on the top, whilst fine-toothed combs of bone and ivory stained a variety of colours have handles decorated with kneeling ibex or grazing horses, and there is even reference to an inlaid gold comb sent from Mitanni.

Listed amongst gifts sent to Babylonia are 'twenty-nine implements of silver with boxwood and ebony handles with which to curl the hair', upmarket versions of the small bronze scissor-like implements used to create a variety of small curls on hair and wig styles. Again decorated with animal motifs such as galloping horses or pouncing leopards, such curling tongs often include a sharpened razor-like section which was used to trim the hair.

Apart from guaranteeing her the ritual purity needed to officiate in the temples, Nefertiti's shaven head allowed her to wear close-fitting crowns and a range of beautifully fashioned wigs of human hair. Judging from the wide range of styles she is shown wearing, her clearly impressive wig collection would have been stored in specially constructed wig boxes with internal mushroom-shaped mounts.

In the long style known as the 'tripartite', long straight hair hung down in two sections over the shoulders, whilst a third section hung down at the back. Usually shown as plain black, or in some cases a startling shade of blue to signify her divine nature, Nefertiti's long wig was also sometimes set in rows of tiny, tile-like curls (see Fig. 5), perhaps created with the small bronze curling tongs described above. She sometimes wore the long style when making offerings to the Aten, but is also occasionally shown in a short, rounded-style wig, again set in small curls like the fragments of the wig found in Tutankhamen's tomb.

Yet it is the Nubian wig which became her trademark coiffure, and, although worn by other royal women of the Amarna Period, it was a style that Nefertiti made her own. It was named after the hairstyle of Nubian mercenaries and associated with the military, and Amenhotep II was the first king to wear this pointed shape which was cut high at the back of the neck to fall in points towards the front. Amenhotep III later added more intricate styling to his favourite short round style, adding three overlapping layers of hair to frame his face. This adaptation was enthusiastically adopted by Nefertiti, who added four, five or even six layers of hair to the geometric shape. Wearing it in her earliest-known portrait as a new queen at Thebes (see Fig. 7), she only seems to have worn it at Karnak when Akhenaten wasn't there – although she certainly wore it in his presence at Amarna, where it was her most frequently portrayed hairstyle. Otherwise Nefertiti is shown with her head covered by various crowns and head covers, including the squashy-looking bag-like 'khat' headscarf usually worn by royal men. The numerous linen headscarves from Tutankhamen's burial were made of plain linen apart from a single example dyed a rich blue colour.

Although Nefertiti is also shown with that most manly of attributes, the false beard, its use by this iconic 'beautiful woman' is rarely mentioned, whereas Hatshepsut is almost mocked as some sort of freak-show 'bearded lady' when she is portrayed with this piece of kingly regalia. The fact that Nefertiti often chose to wear crowns and headgear more usually worn by male pharaohs has of course caused much confusion, leading, in the absence of convenient inscriptions, to the assumption that the female-looking figure wearing a pharaoh's crown must be a mysterious young prince. Instead, it is simply Nefertiti wearing kingly regalia, from the khat headscarf and unwieldy atef crown with all manner of additional ritual devices and emblems hanging from it, to the blue khepresh crown and the very neat, helmet-like cap crown. She is also shown with the four-feather head-dress of the creator god Shu, as well as the more common headgear associated with Shu's sister-wife, the goddess Tefnut, whom she often represented.

Although Tefnut wears a tall, flat-topped crown in her guise as a lion-like sphinx, similar forms of headgear were worn by

Minoan women as early as 1500 BC. Egypt was known to have trading links with the Aegean world at this time, and Queen Tiy appeared in such a crown, as did Nefertiti's sister Mutnodjmet when she herself eventually became queen. But it was Nefertiti who very much made this tall crown her own, and, accentuating as it does her long, graceful neck, it has become her most recognised form of headwear courtesy of the famous bust now in Berlin. This sculpture clearly shows the way it was worn, over a tight-fitting gold brow band and with a colourful striped ribbon tied around the crown's centre.

First adopted by Nefertiti just before she moved from Thebes, this imposing crown was clearly a comfortable piece of headgear because she wore it to all manner of events, from making offerings to the Aten and handing out honours to courtiers to executing prisoners and mourning the dead, and even when relaxing at home. Although usually represented with a smooth surface perhaps suggesting dyed stretched leather, the crown is also shown in the Royal Tomb with an elaborate bead-like surface. With its height extended even further on occasion by a pair of ram's horns, or the cow horns of Hathor, the addition of a central polished gold disc to represent the sun demonstrated Nefertiti's goddess-like relationship with her divine father the sun god, and must have looked amazing when it caught and reflected the bright Egyptian sunlight. And as if all that wasn't enough embellishment, her headgear also featured two tall ostrich feathers. Described as 'adorned in the double plumes', her feather crown makes her taller than the king, although its height must have proved problematic when manoeuvring through standard-height doorways.

Her crowns and wigs were kept in place with a tight-fitting gold brow band as a sign of her regal status, and the rearing cobra fixed over her forehead coiled up in wait to spit its fiery venom into the eyes of her enemies. Yet Nefertiti sometimes sought extra protection by increasing the number of cobras over her brow to two and even adding a further pair at each side of her face in the form of two snakes rearing up from the ends of ribbons hanging down from her gold diadem and giving her baby daughters something else to play with.

Another key element in the royal regalia were sceptres, with the drooping lily sceptre the first piece of royal equipment that Nefertiti carried in her left hand when still a young queen (Fig. 7). Yet within a couple of years her image on the colossal statuary at Karnak was firmly grasping the blue and gold crook and flail with both hands – the crook in the left and the flail in the right was the traditional way. She also holds the two sceptres like this in the small fragment of a funerary figurine found at Amarna, although sceptres could officially be held in the right hand only. Kings such as Hatshepsut and Tuthmosis III are shown holding only the crook in their right hand (Fig. 9), whereas Akhenaten holds both crook and flail together in that hand. A wooden figurine of an unnamed, somewhat feminine-looking Amarna pharaoh likewise has the right arm only bent up to hold a sceptre.

For the finishing touches, the Amarna royals' jewellery meant lots and lots of gold. Clearly associated with the sun, gold and its silver-mixed variant electrum were loved for their ability to reflect and mimic the solar glow. Amenhotep III had set the standard, and, wearing increasing amounts of gold as his reign progressed, his eventual merger with the Aten in his thirtieth regnal year meant that he spent the rest of his life tottering around under all manner of gold adornments attached to just about every bit of his body. With the 'gold of honour' dished out to deserving courtiers, making them 'people of gold', Akhenaten and Nefertiti rewarded their high priest by ordering their attendants to 'put gold at his neck and on his body and on his legs'.

Nefertiti herself is regularly shown wearing numerous Aten cartouches suspended from necklaces and bracelets so fine that the cartouches appear to be attached directly to her body. Several pendant cartouches naming Nefertiti herself have also been found at Amarna, and an idea of the kind of jewellery that the city's workshops produced is found in diplomatic correspondence. Amongst the hundreds of costly items sent to Babylon were 'gold necklace plaques', in response to which the king of Babylon sent Akhenaten ten great lumps of lapis lazuli and Nefertiti '20 crickets of lapis lazuli', which she possibly had made up into a necklace.

A similarly elaborate piece of jewellery connected with Nefertiti is an opulent pectoral ornament from Tutankhamen's burial, originally inscribed with Nefertiti's second name, Neferneferuaten. This gorgeous object features the great sky goddess Nut, raising her arms to extend her protective wings of blue glass and carnelian against a gold background. Although such pieces were usually worn suspended over the chest, small attachments at the sides of this Nut pendant have suggested that it may well have been worn as a belt or girdle, perhaps around the queen's narrow waist.

One of her favourite forms of adornment was the broad collar. Made up of multiple rows of amulets and beadwork, the famous example she wears on the Berlin bust features colourful layers of petals and small fruit, and similar examples were found in both the Royal Tomb at Amarna and tomb KV.55 in the Valley of the Kings. In a small fragmentary scene Nefertiti is even shown tying one of these collars around Akhenaten's neck with her nimble fingers.

With both members of the royal couple clearly fond of armlets, bangles and bracelets, Nefertiti is shown with dozens of jangling golden bracelets on her wrists, elbows and upper arms; bangles naming Akhenaten and Neferneferuaten were also found in Tutankhamen's tomb. The diplomatic correspondence refers to 'very wide gold hand bracelets strung with stones', and matching pairs of gold 'foot bracelets'. Large gold, silver and bronze signet-type rings were made both for domestic consumption and for export as far afield as Cyprus, and amongst several gold examples from the Royal Tomb was a large gold knuckleduster naming Neferneferuaten-Nefertiti, her enthroned figure also engraved on a chunky ring of electrum.

Earrings had become incredibly fashionable by the Amarna Period. Some of the royal women had not one but two holes pierced through each lobe, a feature found on the mummy of Tiy's mother Tuya, and in sculpted portraits of Nefertiti and one of her daughters. Nefertiti herself tended to wear large plain gold disc earrings, and a gold example decorated with tiny gold granules, from the Amarna Royal Tomb, is thought to be a Mitannian import. Some truly amazing earrings were also found in Tutankhamen's tomb, their pendant beads closely resembling those worn by his half-sisters, the royal princesses. Mushroom-shaped ear plugs were also popular, and were generally made of brightly coloured glass or glazed ware. The earliest examples are a pair of gold marguerites, again found in the Royal Tomb, and their relatively small size suggests they were made for one of Nefertiti's young daughters.

A clue to how important such adornments were to the Amarna royals can be found in a scene from the Royal Tomb which showed some of the original burial equipment. Although badly damaged, enough remains to make out earrings, necklaces, large storage jars likely to contain perfume, and what looks like an eye paint container and applicator stick, together with the all-important mirror.

Cosmetics were part of the daily life of men and women throughout society, and both Akhenaten and Nefertiti used generous quantities of make-up, particularly black eye paint. Nefertiti herself used black eye paint around the rims of her eyes and, by extending the line only slightly at the outer corners, achieved a very modern look as opposed to the more exaggerated eye line favoured by her contemporaries. And with her eyebrows neatly plucked into shape using small bronze tweezers, eye paint was again used on the brows to give more emphasis to her expression, which she no doubt used to great effect.

Kohl was made from the dark lead ore galena, and green copper carbonate, known as malachite, was also available. Although no longer the height of fashion as it had been in the

Pyramid Age, green eye paint was still required for ritual purposes, its vivid green hue linked to renewal and new life. Jar
sealings from Amarna refer to 'green malachite of the house of
the Aten', and it may have been worn by Nefertiti when under-
taking her religious duties. Eye paint was stored in small pots
or tubes bearing royal names, and clues that Nefertiti was not
Akhenaten's only wife first came from humble cosmetics pots
and eye paint tubes which named Kiya as 'greatly loved wife of
the king'.

The Berlin bust also demonstrates Nefertiti's deft use of lip
colour, specifically her trademark siren red shade possibly made
from ground-up red ochre. Although she may well have used
the services of a professional make-up artist, known in ancient
times as 'Painter of the Mouth', Nefertiti is likely to have spent
much of her time checking her own appearance and may well
have applied her own cosmetics using a hand mirror.

Hundreds of bronze mirrors were sent as diplomatic gifts
abroad, but there were also more upmarket models: one was
described as 'a silver mirror set with stones', and others were
made of silver and gold, just like the stunning examples with
discs of highly polished silver and gold known to have survived
from the burials of royal women. The mirrors placed in Tutankhamen's tomb were stored in their own ☥ ankh-shaped cases
to protect them from scratches, and mirrors were also stored in
specially made compartments of cosmetics chests, amongst the
most common type of furniture used inside ancient Egyptian
homes and palaces.

Although by modern standards these were sparsely furnished,
the lavish use of brightly coloured inlays of stone, faience and
glass in the wealthier homes would more than make up for
somewhat minimalist interiors, with gilding de rigueur for
palatial decoration. A rare glimpse behind palace doors is found
in a description of a 'prince's house' from around 1900 BC,
containing 'luxuries, a bathroom and mirrors, riches from the
royal treasury and clothes of royal linen, myrrh and the favourite

perfumes of the king and his favoured courtiers in every room'. Amarna's palace interiors are also portrayed in tomb scenes at the site, their tall columned rooms provided with high grilled windows and roof-top vents for ancient air-conditioning.

What furniture there was would have been superbly crafted, comparable and perhaps even identical to that buried with Tutankhamen. His famous gold throne was recently reidentified as most likely having belonged to his predecessors Akhenaten and Nefertiti; she is certainly shown sitting on a similar-looking seat decorated with the same heraldic plant designs and lions' paw feet. Sometimes fitted with seat covers – described by one disapproving scholar as 'irritating drapery' – such chairs were usually well cushioned for royal posteriors, whilst Nefertiti and her daughters are also shown relaxing on large red patterned floor cushions. There were also cross-legged stools made in ebony and ivory to replicate black-and-white animal hide, and footstools decorated with repeated images of bound captives, recalling the way Nefertiti's throne dais at Karnak was adorned with a long line of kneeling captives.

In a country where most people slept on mats on the floor, and in places still do, beds were clearly a status item for wealthy homes. The six beds buried with Tutankhamen were mostly of gilded ebony, and, like that from the tomb of Yuya and Tuya, some were decorated with protective figures of the household god Bes to keep the sleeping occupant safe from demons in the night. Although surviving examples have the same lions' paw feet, Akhenaten describes an unusual variation, 'a bed overlaid with gold with female figures for its feet', which he sent to one of his fellow monarchs overseas. He also sent along matching gilded headrests. Royal examples were also made of tinted ivory and turquoise glass with smart gold trim, and these unlikely-looking objects, once well padded with linen, supported the neck in place of a pillow and are apparently still used in the Far East.

Clearly comfort was a top priority. Surviving royal beds were sprung with webbed mattresses to ensure a good night's sleep, and the beds in Amarna's royal palaces were shown as particularly soft and well padded. Cocooned in the finest linen sheets covered with bedspreads described as 'large cloaks for the royal bed', Nefertiti would have passed her nights in sumptuous comfort.

Small bedside table-stands held the queen's cosmetics pots and jewellery, with larger jewel caskets, wig boxes and cosmetics chests stored on built-in wooden shelving or on the floor. Nefertiti's rooms would also have featured decorative vessels of alabaster, glass and brightly glazed pottery, many of them in a combination of white with cobalt blue which one leading scholar has suggested was her favourite colour scheme.

Generously filled vases of flowers would have filled the rooms with their scent, and cinnamon oil, a favourite Egyptian fragrance was recommended for sprinkling around the bedroom. And as darkness fell, servants would have lit the linen wicks of exquisitely fine alabaster oil lamps, and placed candles in ☥ ankh-shaped candlesticks on tall lamp stands in order to illuminate the shadows. If the heat became too oppressive and the royal fan-bearers were temporarily off duty, a personal hand-held fan would be used. Some long-handled ceremonial examples were placed in Tutankhamen's tomb, one of them still inscribed with Akhenaten's name, but in the same place a much smaller, hand-held fan of ivory and ostrich feathers was found in a wooden box labelled 'the procession of the bedchamber'. It was almost certainly used by a member of the royal family to keep cool within their private quarters.

When trying to work out where the royals actually lived at Amarna, it seems that Nefertiti, like Akhenaten, divided her time between the four main palaces – the Great Palace, the King's House, the North Palace and the Riverside Palace – all built along the Kingsway royal road to allow easy access. At the city's heart lay the Great Palace, a massive part-stone structure covering over fifteen thousand square metres on the west side of Kingsway and extending down to the river. With its combination of royal and administrative buildings this seems to have been the royals' official residence, set around a great open-air court lined with statues of the king and queen and resembling a parade ground.

Although in public the royal family were attended by their fan-bearers and even the royal parasol-bearer, and are generally shown enthroned beneath canopied awnings of the sort found in Tutankhamen's tomb, it appears that visiting ambassadors were sometimes kept waiting in the blazing sun within such courtyards. Any benefits derived from the Aten's solar powers appear to have been lost on them, and an Assyrian delegation grew so fed up that they complained to their king who then wrote to Akhenaten to object: 'Why should my messengers always be kept outside in the sun where they will die? If staying in the sun is so profitable for the king, then let *his* messenger stand out in the sun and die.'

Such ambassadors must also have been struck, indeed been alarmed, by the great expanses of floor painted with repeated images of their bound countrymen, enemies whom the royal couple would then symbolically trample as they finally arrived to grant audiences within their imposing throne room. At the southern end was a great hall with over five hundred brick columns, its palm leaf capitals inlaid with red- and blue-glazed chevrons set between ribs of gilded stone. Built for Akhenaten's successor, Smenkhkara, its walls and floors embellished with sumptuous glazed tiles depicting daisy-like flowers, fish and wild-fowl, it may well reveal something of Nefertiti's tastes once she became sole ruler. The more private suites of rooms set around columned halls and open courts were decorated with gentle scenes of the river bank, whose floral motifs were echoed in the palace's extensive walled gardens filled with mud-lined tree pits and raised flowerbeds built around a stone-lined pool.

Connected to the Great Palace via a thirty-foot-wide foot-bridge crossing Kingsway was the King's House, where the couple could rest in more relaxed surroundings between formal engagements. With a courtyard for chariot parking at the side, a separate wing of servants' quarters and extensive store rooms for the refreshments handed out at official events, this relatively small palace seems to have been built on two levels. The royal couple would presumably meet their key officials here, a large Window of Appearances framed by images of foreign captives allowing them to appear Buckingham Palace-style before their subjects, making proclamations and rewarding officials with gifts from the adjoining store rooms. The rubbish dumps near by reveal something of the types of gifts handed out, from brightly coloured glazed rings naming members of the royal family to small bottles of coloured glass and imported Aegean pottery.

Beyond lay private suites, including bedrooms for the occasional night's stay, dressing room and en suite bathrooms complete with limestone shower trays and matching toilet seats set over sand-filled containers. A seat from Amarna currently hangs in the Cairo Museum and reveals the high standard of living available to the city's richest inhabitants.

Brightly painted walls featured heraldic lotus and papyrus plant borders and intimate scenes of family life, with Nefertiti lounging on a large red cushion opposite Akhenaten while two of their baby daughters play beside her and the three eldest girls stand close by with their arms around each other. It also seems that a room in the King's House functioned as the princesses' day nursery: traces of yellow, red, blue and green paints were found daubed across the lower sections of the walls. Small paint-brushes were also found nearby, and rectangular ivory plant palettes belonging to both Meritaten and Meketaten found elsewhere still contained their original oval blocks of coloured paints.

Right next door stood the Small Aten Temple, a scaled-down version of the Great Temple which, being about half a mile long from front to back, would have involved something of a hard slog if used on a daily basis. So it seems likely that this small, user-friendly version acted as the couple's 'chapel royal', its ritual purpose emphasised by its alignment to the great valley in which the Royal Tomb was built and where at certain times of the year the sun was seen to rise.

A number of other, smaller temples were dotted about the city; they housed statues of the royal family together with a number of desert altars and shrines known as 'maru' or 'viewing temples' which were dedicated to the royal women. Based on one built at Malkata, they included a large stone-built temple at Kom el-Nana in the south of the city believed to have been dedicated to Nefertiti, with another built for Queen Tiy being completed around regnal year 9, c.1343 BC. Scenes of its consecration show Akhenaten leading his mother Tiy by the hand, captioned 'Taking the great royal wife and queen mother Tiy to let her see her sun shade'. The temple's open-air courtyards were thoughtfully adorned with statues of herself and her late husband, Amenhotep III.

A third such temple at Maru-Aten in the south was originally built for Akhenaten's 'greatly loved wife' Kiya, then later rededicated to Princess Meritaten. Painted with the standard naturalistic scenes, these temples were surrounded by lush water gardens and tree-lined avenues, and were in some ways the ancient equivalent of a New Age health spa. The discovery of large numbers of food and drink containers also suggests that they were summerhouse-type structures where meals could be enjoyed in beautiful surroundings – places very much designed for 'getting away from it all'.

The North Palace, again something of a country retreat, was set behind large gateways and windows bordered by shutters. It had formal reception halls, quite possibly another Window of Appearances, large royal statuary and a throne room, and the bedroom and bathroom facilities were connected to a sophisticated drainage system. The usual palatial interiors were decorated with richly gilded walls and exquisite murals, the so-called Green Room especially attractive with its black-and-white kingfishers darting in and out of the river beside plump doves alighting on papyrus stalks. These particular scenes incorporated recessed nesting boxes in which the actual birds are thought to have lived side by side with their painted counterparts in a kind of living tableau. The zoological gardens beyond were filled with wild and domesticated species including cattle, gazelle and ibex which fed from large carved limestone feeding troughs.

Providing a living backdrop for some of the royal couple's ritual activities around an open, solar court and central altar – complete, perhaps, with a ready supply of sacrificial animals – it was also a place where the family could relax within their own self-made version of creation. The young princesses are shown holding their pet gazelles, and the entire palace was given to the eldest daughter and heiress, Meritaten, when she came of age.

Yet it is the Northern Riverside Palace complex, set far away from the bustle of city life, which is thought by the current excavators to have been Akhenaten and Nefertiti's main residence. Their only neighbours here, where they lived and slept in splendid isolation, were the royal inhabitants of the large, well-appointed villas over a footbridge on the other side of the royal road. Queen Tiy is known to have had a house at Amarna and her own staff, and her name was found on one of the villas' door jambs and in one of the alabaster quarries in the eastern hills, which may have supplied the stone used for her buildings.

Following an ambitious ground plan comparable to that used at Malkata, the Riverside Palace was surrounded by double-thickness security walls and a huge fortified gateway; well-manned barracks housed the royal bodyguard. This complex was accurately described as having the most remote, most secure and most beautiful setting for a royal palace, and the overhanging cliffs just to the north provided a sharp contrast with the vast expanse of well-manicured palace gardens sloping down to the Nile.

When 'in residence' Akhenaten and Nefertiti travelled down Kingsway by chariot, flanked by their usual large armed escort in an impressive display of royal power which has vividly been compared to the presidential limousine of today with its motorcycle outriders. Sweeping down to the city centre temples to perform their regular ritual duties, the royal couple would then travel on to the Great Palace to deal with matters of state concerning Egypt and its empire. Yet when trying to find out what Nefertiti may have done in her leisure time, it is possible to suggest at least a few things which didn't involve making offerings, appearances or babies.

Although music played a key role in temple worship, it was also enjoyed for its own sake; Egyptian and Syrian women performed within the palace for one another's amusement. Some of them played large harps, lyres and lutes, whilst others jumped up to dance in the relaxed environment. Since musical instruments hung on the walls in adjoining chambers, it appears that there were rooms within the palaces set aside for such informal musical performances. Crowds of women usually described as 'street musicians' are also shown in various parts of the city playing tambourines and throwing up their arms as they make merry, giving a real feeling of joy to their impromptu performances and suggesting that Amarna was quite a lively place. Nefertiti is known to have played sistrums herself, and a fragmentary scene shows an unnamed royal woman, perhaps one of the princesses, playing the lute in a riverside setting. Music was played by the palace band at mealtimes, and since it was so closely associated with love women are shown playing musical instruments when sitting beside their husbands in the confines of their bedrooms. A number of sketches show women vainly trying to hold on to their instruments during love-making, the erotic power of their music apparently making it impossible for the poor men to hold out any longer!

Men and women, including kings and queens, are also shown enjoying rather more sedate board games including the great favourite, senet, a game for two in which players would move their pieces ('dancers') after throwing a knucklebone, dice or marked stick. Senet's popularity amongst the Amarna royals is reflected in the four senet boards buried with Tutankhamen, the largest a de luxe model in ebony, ivory and gold mounted on lions' paw feet with a secret pull-out drawer for the gaming pieces. The three smaller boards are more like travel-size versions. A later queen plays senet on the walls of her tomb in the Valley of the Queens, and the pharaoh Ramses III plays the game with one of his minor wives while embracing another, his exasperated opponent appearing to wave her hand to make him concentrate on the game.

As a similarly sedate form of relaxation, reading seems to have been a popular pastime for both royalty and a small educated minority, with private citizens known to have owned collections of popular stories, poems and self-help texts. Bookplates found at Malkata suggest that the palace had its own library, and it seems likely that Akhenaten and Nefertiti would have incorporated such a feature into their own palaces at Amarna. Certainly some of the cuneiform tablets once believed to be diplomatic letters are actually stories sent to Egypt from abroad, revealing a taste for foreign literature. Two are part of an epic tale about King Sargon of Akkad, and another recounts the adventures of a Mesopotamian superhero in the myth of Adapa and the South Wind: red dots have been added throughout the text, perhaps helping to give emphasis to the right words when reading the story aloud to an audience. Even part of a phrase book was recovered from one house in the city, giving the cuneiform and Egyptian words for 'house', 'chair', 'bed' and so forth, and highlighting the cosmopolitan nature of city living.

Taking an interest in their own ancestry, Egyptian royalty are known to have collected antiques and passed items down through the generations. An alabaster jar naming Hatshepsut, with the name of Amen removed, was found in the store rooms of the King's House, and the lapis lazuli bases of a couple of Tuthmosis I's sceptres were discovered in the city's government offices. Small seal stones naming such kings were found around the city. Ancient heirlooms were also part of the burial equipment placed in the Royal Tomb, for example a steatite and gold scarab seal ring and a diorite bowl both naming Akhenaten's great-great-grandfather Tuthmosis III and describing him as 'beloved of Ra and Hathor'. There was even a bowl naming Khafra, builder of the second great pyramid at Giza and the model for the face of the Sphinx. Since it was already more than 1200 years old, its presence there was rather like a piece of Anglo-Saxon or Viking art appearing in someone's antiquities collection today.

Akhenaten's mother and elder brother were known to have had pet cats, and pairs of seated cats flank the goddess Hathor on an alabaster bowl again found in Amarna's Royal Tomb, whilst amulets of cats and kittens were found throughout the city. Two of Nefertiti's daughters kept tiny gazelles as pets, and as another popular addition to the home a small monkey is shown beneath the throne of Queen Tiy. A large number of monkey figurines found at Amarna show them caring for their young, eating and drinking, playing the harp and even riding in chariots, and it has been suggested that these images may have been made to satirise Akhenaten and Nefertiti, who made such show of travelling around the city in this way. Dogs were kept both as pets and for more serious purposes: the police chief Mahu's dog helped him track down criminals, and the animals were also used on hunting expeditions.

Hunting was very much a sport of pharaohs, and Nefertiti is shown with all the accoutrements necessary to undertake such a pastime, her impressive personal arsenal including scimitars and the bows and arrows carried in the weapons case attached to her chariot. Judging from the drive-by shooting technique employed by an unnamed female pharaoh sketched on a piece of limestone, Nefertiti may have been able to fire arrows directly from her chariot. It is fascinating that the most impressive bow amongst the fifty or so found in Tutankhamen's tomb was a lavishly gilded weapon described as 'a work of almost inconceivable fineness' which originally bore the name 'Ankhkheperura'. The tomb also contained an impressive collection of daggers, swords, clubs and the throwsticks used to catch wildfowl by the river. Part of a model throwstick found at Amarna was inscribed 'Neferneferuaten Nefertiti'.

These activities were obviously a means of relaxation as well as sport: the hunting lodge built by Amenhotep II close to the Great Sphinx at Giza was enjoyed by several generations of royals, whose empty wine jars suggest a convivial end to a hard day in the hunting field. A means of demonstrating royal prowess away from the battlefield, hunting also produced game and wild animals for consumption: the royals are shown hunting ibex, oryx, ostriches, ducks, geese and ostriches, and Amarna's desert fringes teemed with gazelles and wild hare.

And it was during the Amarna Period that food is shown being eaten, rather than simply piled high on tables, tantalisingly close but never actually consumed. Nefertiti, more than any other royal female, is depicted enjoying her food, putting it away with relish (see Figs. 11 & 12). Food consumed by the royal family ranged from the bowls of food and drink placed on small tables in the palace bedrooms, presumably as breakfast or for late-night snacking, to more formal meals taken in the columned dining rooms of their palace.

Nefertiti had her mother-in-law, Tiy, as a dinner guest on occasion (Fig. 12). Perhaps acting as royal food tasters, some of the high officials were honoured with food from the royal table; the newly appointed high priest Meryra was told that 'you shall eat the food of the king, your lord, in the house of the Aten'. Tiy's steward, Huya, also asked if he 'may partake of things which issue from the royal presence, may I eat loaves and pastries, jugs of beer, roast meat, hot food and cool water, wine and milk'.

To the strains of the palace musicians, the family would have been waited on hand and foot by male servants who came and went silently through sets of side doors, carrying in food prepared in kitchens whose window grilles, still coated in soot when discovered, reveal something of their unpleasant, smoke-filled interiors. Men are also shown setting tables, putting out the food and drink, serving the meals and sweeping up afterwards, sprinkling water as an effective way of keeping down the dust as is still done in modern Egypt.

The ideal mealtime experience is described as being enjoyed within a beautiful villa

where you fill your mouth with wine and beer, and with bread, meat and cakes. As the oxen are slaughtered and the wine is opened, beautiful singing surrounds you. Your servant anoints you with perfume, your farm manager brings you flower garlands, your chief hunter brings you ducks and your fisherman brings you fish. Then your ship comes in, laden with all kinds of good things from Syria.

Yet things are not always quite so relaxed, at least for Nefertiti. In one image of her eating with Akhenaten and three of their young daughters, he gets on with his dinner whilst she performs the typical maternal juggling act, balancing one of the girls on her lap as she tackles her food, in this case spare ribs 'of formidable proportions' (Fig. 11).

Meat was regularly enjoyed by the wealthy, and the eight guests at Tutankhamen's funeral enjoyed a sumptuous banquet of nine ducks, four geese and choice cuts of beef and lamb. The beef often came from oxen fattened in their stalls through force-feeding, and certain priests were allowed to 'finish off' meat offerings each day once the gods had been sated. In fact they had such a high meat intake that it damaged their health: recent examination of one priest's mummy revealed that furred-up arteries were something of an occupational hazard.

Although hens, described as miraculous birds which 'give birth every day', were newly imported from Syria, chicken hadn't really caught on and ducks and geese were the birds of choice. They were caught down by the Nile by beaters using nets. Akhenaten is shown wringing a duck's neck as an offering to the Aten; elsewhere he joins Nefertiti and their daughters as they tuck into whole crispy duck, which they eat with their fingers.

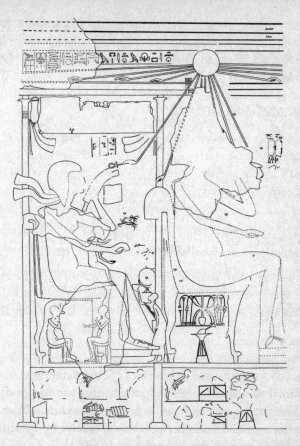

FIGURE 11. Wall scene in the Amarna tomb of Ahmes
showing the royal family dining, Nefertiti on the left in the
Nubian wig balancing one of her daughters on her lap as she
eats a large cut of meat and a servant passes her a drink

Yet it seems that the royals did have access to at least some
form of cutlery: a set of gold knives decorated with small pomegranates on their handles was sent by Akhenaten as a gift to
the king of Babylon.

Meat could also be processed into potted meat, and jar labels
from Amarna refer to 'good potted meat of Nubian cattle made

FIGURE 12. Wall scene in the Amarna tomb of Tiy's steward
Huya, showing Tiy on the right dining with her son
Akhenaten and Nefertiti, shown on the far left wearing the
Nubian wig whilst eating a whole duck

in the processing house of pharaoh'. Some batches were made
for special occasions, such as 'potted meat for the Festival of
Everlastingness', and Nefertiti in particular seems to have quite
a taste for it, since a number of labels also refer to 'potted meat
of the king's wife which the butcher made'.

Often salted, or dried kipper-style, fish made an important
contribution to the royal diet. Fishermen plied the Nile in canoe-
like boats and landed their catch with dragnets, or caught them
on the ends of rods fitted with the small bronze fish hooks found
in the city.

Over the river on the West Bank were the extensive fields
supplying Amarna's grain. Granaries were situated right across
the city, the one attached to the king's house covering an area
of around 20,000 square feet. Bread, the staple diet of most
ancient Egyptians, was made of stone-ground emmer wheat and

barley. A small amount of sand was sometimes added to ease the grinding process, although it did nothing for the teeth. The flour was blended with water and sometimes enriched with eggs, butter or milk, and variety was created by the addition of nuts, spices and seeds. Modern reconstructions of the dense loaves mass-produced in pots for manual workers have shown them to be laden with energy-giving calories, whilst the more refined bread made for the elite was referred to as 'white' bread. Amarna's palaces and temples had their own bakeries to give a constant supply of fresh bread. One hundred domed baking chambers were needed to mass-produce the thousands of fresh loaves required each day in the Aten temples. They were made in a wide variety of shapes and sizes represented by different hiero-glyph symbols, from ⊖ the round loaf with the baker's finger mark to the △ conical loaf made in moulds and regularly offered in temples. For special occasions there were spirals and human and animal shapes, not dissimilar to modern gingerbread men.

The main vegetables were onions and garlic, consumed by workers and found in tombs of the time. Much like the modern Egyptian diet, beans, chickpeas, lentils, lettuce, cucumbers and watermelons also featured heavily, with almonds a popular snack at Amarna. To jazz up the royal menu caraway, coriander, aniseed and sesame seeds would have been added to dishes. Both sesame seeds and olives were used to make oil, and olives were offered to the god when still on the branch. Jar seals from Amarna refer to 'good fresh olive oil of the house of the Aten', although animal fats were also part of the diet, described as 'clarified dripping from the breast meat of cattle'.

For most people the sweet course was healthy and fruit-based. Dates, figs, pomegranates and grapes are shown tastefully arranged on small side tables for Nefertiti and her family to enjoy. Such fruit was also used dried as a sweetener, and added to dough to make fruit bread. Honey, obtained from both wild and domesticated bees, was much loved, and a key ingredient in honey cakes and other forms of sticky confectionery. Jar labels found at Amarna list honey amongst the foodstuffs and offerings, and at least two chief beekeepers were employed in different parts of the city.

Beer was the standard beverage enjoyed by rich and poor, adults and children, and even the dead, whose spirits requested 'A thousand loaves of bread and a thousand jars of beer' in their tomb inscriptions. Made of barley, the strength of the beer was indicated by the darkness of its colour. Somewhat soupy in consistency, it had to be filtered through a strainer before consumption or else drunk through a specially designed straw fitted with a small filter, an example of which was found in the city.

Given the Egyptian fondness for sweet things, dates and honey were added to beer to produce 'sermet'. It was consumed in large quantities at Malkata, where much of it came from the estates of the royal women – some of the beer jars found at Amarna were inscribed 'good sermet beer of the queen'. Shown imbibing in several images, Nefertiti appears to have been a woman who took her beer seriously and even had her own brewery in the city, where large numbers of beer jars stored a quick-fermenting brew ready to drink after only a few days. Recalling the ancient Egyptian saying 'It is good to drink beer with happy hearts when clothed in clean robes,' it is not difficult to imagine Nefertiti seated on a pile of cushions doing just this.

Wine, however, was the principal royal drink, both imported from Syria and made in Egypt's western oases or in the Nile Delta; that brought down from Memphis was often stamped with the image of the northern cobra goddess Ⳣ Wadjet. To judge from the number of wine jars recovered from the rubbish dumps outside the Great Palace, the royals consumed large quantities. Since the wine jars are often dated with the regnal year of the king in whose reign the wine was produced, these humble artefacts provide some of the most important historical evidence for the whole Amarna Period: Akhenaten's highest regnal year, for instance, is given as 17, with 3 for his shadowy successor.

The labels also show that they appreciated vintage wines, a thirty-year-old wine from Amenhotep III's reign having been found in Tutankhamen's tomb along with younger 'sweet wines'. Pomegranate wine was placed amongst funerary goods in the Royal Tomb at Amarna, where wine is referred to as 'nefer', 'good', or 'very good' or even 'the genuine thing', with jars of 'doubly good wine' supplied to the royal palace. Each member of the royal family owned his or her own wine-producing estates, that from Nefertiti's being described as 'Wine of the house of Neferneferuaten-Nefertiti', 'Good wine of the store-house of Nefertiti' and 'Wine of the house of Neferneferuaten from the Western River'.

Alcohol was an important element of celebrations and one of the commodities offered to the Aten: court ladies are shown drinking at Amarna, and a woman banquet guest in a tomb at Thebes says, 'Give me eighteen cups of wine because I want to get drunk! My insides are as dry as straw.' Another ancient text describes 'the woman reclining with her lover, when they are drunken with pomegranate wine', and since great quantities of alcohol were drunk in Hathor's honour ritual drunkenness was particularly associated with women. The lyrics of a song popular a few years after the Amarna Period graphically describe a drunken woman, sitting outside her chamber 'with tousled hair'. The more unfortunate effects of over-indulgence are shown in scenes in which both women and men are heartily sick. Sleeping it off seems to have been the thing to do, with the drunken goddess Sekhmet sleeping off her hangover in her father's palace. A cautionary tale against the evils of drink contains these admonitory words: 'You stagger about, going from street to street reeking of beer. You strike out and people run away from you. If only you knew how bad wine is you would stop drinking it.'

As if acknowledging the power of the alcohol within, the wine jars were themselves garlanded with flowers and often painted in a delicate shade of pale blue colour associated with divinity in the style of so-called Palace Ware. The wine would be decanted and filtered to remove small bits through a strainer like the one found in Tutankhamen's tomb along with a matching goblet. A very similar lotus-form chalice, perhaps from Amarna, also names Akhenaten and Nefertiti, both of whom are shown quaffing their wine from a variety of stemmed vessels, cups and inlaid goblets of silver and gold which were also made for export. In one scene Akhenaten sits beside what looks suspiciously like a wine cooler, whilst Nefertiti is sometimes shown pouring him a drink – more of a gesture between the couple than a hint that they have too few staff. Indeed, the servants responsible for keeping the royal goblet topped up are shown hovering, with napkins draped over their arm to catch spills.

At Amarna, the royal cup-bearer Parrenefer was known as the one 'whose hands are pure', and each member of the royal family was served by his or her own staff, the superintendent of Nefertiti's household named as Meryra 'the second' to differentiate him from his high priest namesake. They also had their trusted fan-bearers to keep them cool and composed at all times: it wouldn't do for living gods to be seen sweating as mere mortals.

And in the same way that modern heads of state commission official photographers to document aspects of royal life and important state occasions, the Amarna royals employed their own artists and sculptors. These highly trained court servants included the sculptor Bek, apparently trained by Akhenaten himself, and the master craftsman Iuty, Overseer of Sculptors for the Great Royal Wife Tiy. Iuty is shown putting the finishing touches to a statue of Tiy's youngest daughter, Beketaken, in his workshop, which also produced high-quality furniture. Yet it was the Overseer of Works and Sculptor Tuthmose who was single-handedly responsible for the way the Amarna royals are now seen, through a whole series of amazing portraits including Nefertiti's famous bust discovered in his huge villa-cum-workshop complex in Amarna's southern suburb.

Tuthmose's neighbours included the general Ramose, the vizier Nakht and the chief priest Panehesy, all given their houses and estates in return for devoted service to the royal family. Each property was provided with both a main entrance and a tradesmen's entrance, and after reporting to a porter's lodge permitted visitors passed through tree-filled gardens with circular wells to reach the houses. These usually consisted of a central main room with other rooms leading off it, the number of rooms and size of house reflecting the owner's social status.

With the homes of most of the city's other officials located throughout the northern and southern suburbs along the minor roads, rich and poor often lived side by side. Just north of the Great Temple near the river were smaller, more crowded houses without gardens but with a large number of grain silos and store rooms. These were perhaps the merchants' quarter, where goods could be traded on the riverside. Then of course there was the basic housing which made up the workmen's village. Set at a good distance from the posh residential quarters, their sixty-eight small dwellings with a larger one for the boss were surrounded by a wall over which they chucked their rubbish – to modern archaeologists, discarded treasures which reveal how life was lived far away from the luxury of the palaces.

The total population of Amarna has been estimated at up to fifty thousand, and it can be assumed that they originated from various parts of Egypt and simply followed the royal family as the source of wealth rather than from any sense of religious devotion or even loyalty. Yet the recent discovery of the public cemetery in the desert south of the Northern Tombs revealed that the inhabitants who died during the twenty-year occupation hadn't been dug up and taken home after the city was abandoned, as once thought because the only known tombs were those of the wealthy.

In the political climate of the day, and when most of the vast country's 2–3 million population were dispersed among small rural communities, a city with such a large concentrated population would have presented all manner of potential problems. Public order was kept by a well-armed force of men under the chief of police, Mahu, with any wrongdoers apprehended and placed in handcuffs to await the appropriate punishment. The police headquarters in the central city were equipped with a well-stocked armoury, police dogs, cobbled-floor stabling for two hundred horses and a 'flying squad' of chariots, all essential requirements for patrolling such a huge area.

It seems as if the city and its surrounding cliffs and desert were regularly patrolled via a network of routes and pathways, with all traffic in and out of Amarna closely monitored. At the end of the line in the north, where the cliffs curved right round to the river, the Northern Administrative Buildings were cleverly built to straddle the road. Described as a kind of ornamental gatehouse, this would also have been the perfect place to extract the appropriate taxes on traded goods.

Supplied by industrial estates which included areas specialising in pottery and glass production, much of the central city was also taken up with administrative buildings and office blocks. They included the House of Life, near the Great Palace, where official inscriptions were composed and copied out by the scribal workforce within its library-like environment. Next door lay the Bureau for Royal Correspondence, Amarna's Foreign Office, where its staff of scribes and officials worked for the Royal Chamberlain, Tutu, 'chief mouthpiece of all the foreign lands'. Responsible for passing on their communications to the king, Tutu is keen to stress in his tomb inscriptions how well he had done his job, insisting that 'my voice is not loud in the king's house. I do not swagger in the palace. I do not receive the reward in order to repress [truth] falsely, but I do what is righteous to the king. I act only accordingly to what he decrees ... I am straightforward and true in the knowledge of the king.'

One of Egypt's main correspondents was King Burraburiyash of Babylon, who at some stage became one of Akhenaten's fathers-in-law when his daughter was sent to Amarna along with a large dowry. Her father also supplied lapis lazuli and horses in return for gold and the coloured ivory figurines of which he seemed particularly fond. Akhenaten responded with gilded statuettes of himself, Nefertiti and one of their daughters, which at the time must have been the nearest equivalent of a family snap.

King Suppiluliumas of the Hittites sent along a selection of silver vessels, asking directly for 'gold statues, one standing one sitting and two more silver statues of women' after pointedly enquiring about the whereabouts of the presents he'd been promised by the last king. The Assyrians too were writing to Egypt, sending chariots, white horses and lapis lazuli jewellery and again asking for some of the gold which they had heard was as plentiful as dust in Egypt. More horses were sent by the king of Cyprus, together with perfumed oils and a cargo of valuable copper; in return he very specifically requested a gold-trimmed ebony bed with a mattress and lots of Egyptian linen.

Vassal states too corresponded with the Amarna court. Queen Puduheba of Ugarit (modern Ras Shamra) wrote to Egypt's first lady, presumably sending gifts, whilst an unnamed queen from the city of Byblos signing herself 'your maidservant' fell at the feet of the queen 'seven times and seven times' as a sign of her loyalty.

Although most of these letters are undated, making it virtually impossible to work out the exact sequence of events, Egypt's empire was looking increasingly unstable. With so many troops needed at home to guard the royal family and keep the peace, the vassal states soon started asking for military reinforcements. And when hostilities broke out between Mitanni and its northern neighbours the Hittites things really started to disintegrate.

Soon virtual anarchy prevailed in many parts of the Egyptian Empire as the more aggressive states and cities turned on their neighbours. The mayor of Qatna (modern el-Mishrife) reported treason and Hittite-inspired attacks, and with 'everything in flames' pleaded for Egyptian archers to help defend the region. The mayor of Qiltu also asked for troops, the ruler of Jerusalem reported military activity, and the vassal queen Ninurmah, Lady of the Lions, wrote twice to tell pharaoh of further unrest and fighting. And as the faithful Rib-Hadda of Byblos repeatedly pleaded for Egypt's military help his subjects, his household and even his own wife wanted him to save his own skin and go over to the enemy.

But still Akhenaten seems to have done nothing. Even when Egyptian mercenaries broke into the palace of the prince of Jerusalem and attacked him, and Egyptian governors robbed a Babylonian delegation crossing Canaan, pharaoh seems to have turned a blind eye. Many of his vassals' pleas he seems to have answered with mail-order requests for glassware! And the mayors of Tyre, Asqaluna (biblical Askelon), the rulers of Akka (biblical Acco) and Yursa (location uncertain), all responding with the requested shipments, the mayor of Lakisa (modern Tell ed-Duweir) having promised to send 'whatever glass I may have on hand' despite more pressing matters. And just as Nero fiddled while Rome burnt, the Egyptian Empire seems to have been teetering on the brink of destruction while pharaoh was collecting decorative tableware.

In their frustration, the vassal rulers started to bypass pharaoh and wrote directly to the Royal Chamberlain Tutu to give him details of the increasing chaos and to warn of the growing powers of the Hittites in the north. They had already conquered Egypt's old ally Mitanni, and without this first line of defence Egypt and its weakened empire were now prime targets. It is impossible to know to what extent Akhenaten was aware of the trouble but chose to ignore it, couldn't deal with it, or was simply kept in the dark by Tutu and his staff. But whatever the truth, it seems he was still letting others deal with such vital communications rather than dealing directly with them as his father had done. It was clear that something had to be done. But rather than sending out the troops who were needed at home, it was decided to go down a different route. Inviting envoys from every corner of the empire to come and pay homage at a great state reception, Egypt would demonstrate its power and wealth amidst the splendours of its new royal capital, with everything directed to the greater glory of the Aten and his twin representatives on earth, Akhenaten and Nefertiti, whose own regal powers were about to be confirmed in the most public way possible.

10

THE SETTING SUN – THE END OF THE AMARNA PERIOD

In regnal year 12, about 1340 BC, the main features of their grand city were complete and the royal couple decided to hold their Great Reception. The summons went out across the ancient world to the lands of Syria and Palestine, to Punt, Nubia and Libya, to the Aegean and even to the troublesome Hittites.

According to diplomatic correspondence, the king of Cyprus does not seem to have received an invitation to 'the festival' and so did not come. He made up for his absence by sending along a hundred talents of copper and a quantity of perfume, including 'a jar of sweet oil to be poured on your head now that you have sat down upon your royal throne'.

Although his letter bears neither date nor the name of its recipient, it is tempting to see this as a reference to a coronation. And as some Egyptologists have already suggested, it seems quite possible that the reception was held to acknowledge the coronation of a new king. In the fog of uncertainty which obscures much of the Amarna Period, some believe that the coronation was Akhenaten's own following a lengthy twelve-year co-regency with his father Amenhotep III. Yet since Egyptologists are unable to agree whether such a co-regency ever existed, the coronation seems just as likely to have been that of another king – Nefertiti, raised to the status of co-regent with her husband.

Building on an impressive track record in which she was shown in poses and regalia only used by kings, evidence that Nefertiti became Akhenaten's co-regent can be found on the co-regency stela with its clearly female figure, together with the later tradition that a woman ruled as king in the late 18th dynasty. After she had adopted the royal name Ankhkheperura to add to

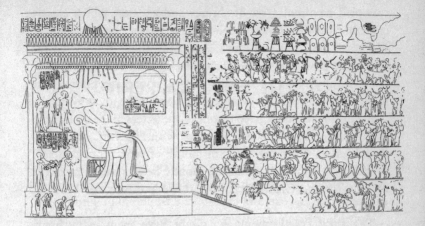

FIGURE 13. Wall scene in the Amarna tomb of Meryra II, the
superintendent of Nefertiti's household, showing Akhenaten
and Nefertiti jointly enthroned and holding hands during the
Great Reception of year 12, their six daughters standing
behind them

her existing name, 'Neferneferuaten', her first year as co-regent
would have coincided with Akhenaten's twelfth as king. Such a
large-scale international event as the Great Reception would
have been the perfect moment to declare Nefertiti official equal
partner to Akhenaten before the eyes of the world. Certainly,
when the couple are shown presiding over the event their overlapping profiles are so close that they almost form a single kingly
entity.

So Egypt's new monarch took her place beside her husband,
enthroned beneath a great canopied and beribboned platform,
with stairs leading up to double thrones. Beneath the full glare
of the all-seeing Aten, the event took place in the dramatic
setting of 'the great desert of Akhetaten'. This location may well
correspond to the great parade ground area discovered between
the North Palace and the Northern Tombs, the so-called 'Desert
Altars' where archaeologists found traces of the columned and

canopied pavilion, a set of shrines and an altar which closely resemble features shown in the tomb scenes of two key officials, Meryra II (Fig. 13) and Huya. And since these men served the two most powerful women at court, Meryra II as steward of Nefertiti and Huya as steward of Tiy, it perhaps hints at the involvement of the two women in planning the great event.

According to a date given on one of the letters in the diplomatic correspondence, Akhenaten, perhaps with Nefertiti, appears to have been in Thebes in the fifth month of year 12, presumably at Malkata. And then, within the month, he was back at Amarna in time for the Great Reception, dated precisely to 'Year 12, Month 6, Day 8'.

The royal couple would no doubt have spent many hours being ceremonially prepared within the confines of their official robing rooms. Having been bathed, anointed and dressed identically in fine linen robes tied with long red sashes, matching sandals and a full range of golden jewellery, the couple donned identical crowns – the red crown of northern or Lower Egypt – before stepping into 'the great golden state palanquin' reserved for state occasions. This huge golden carrying chair, with its protective lion figures, cobras and sphinxes, took fifteen men to lift it. And as the chair was hoisted up on to the bearers' shoulders to begin its stately progress east Nefertiti wrapped her arm about Akhenaten's waist, perhaps in an attempt to steady them.

Accompanied by a full complement of ten fan-bearers, and led by a priest burning purifying incense, the couple were followed by their two eldest daughters, Meritaten and Meketaten, along with their nurses, ladies-in-waiting and the ever-present royal bodyguards, today wearing feathers in their hair to mark the joyous occasion. As the golden procession moved towards the great ceremonial enclosure and the waiting crowds, shouts and cheers in numerous languages would have become louder and louder until the royal couple arrived and stepped out of their carrying chair to ascend the great dais. There they are shown enthroned as identical figures, wearing matching blue khepresh crowns with red ribbons fluttering behind them in the warm breeze.

Before the twin monarchs stood a sea of envoys in ordered rows, all awaiting their turn to pay homage and all arrayed in their distinguishing national dress. There were bearded Syrians in their multi-layered robes, Libyans with their distinctive side-lock and feather combination, Hittites with their characteristic swept-back hairstyles, and long-haired Keftiu all the way from Crete. The large groups of Nubians included both men and women with babies in slings on their backs. Egyptian officials at the head of each line signalled to each delegation when their time came to step forward and approach the throne, prostrate themselves fully on the ground and present their tribute.

For as well as the ancient world's adulation, Akhenaten and Nefertiti also received great quantities of lavish gifts, from chariots and bows to shields and slaves. There were animal skins and ostrich feathers, and spices piled high in the same pyramid and obelisk shapes that can be seen in Egypt's markets today. And similarly there were sacks of gold ingots and rings, together with beautifully crafted vessels of precious metals and even a novelty gold palm tree, typical of the lavish though completely useless gifts that people have always presented to royalty. After the appropriate acknowledgement the tribute was displayed on stands for later inspection, rather like toasters and tea sets at a wedding. Akhenaten and Nefertiti also received living gifts – hounds and leopards on leashes, antelopes, monkeys and even a lion, destined for the royal zoo of the Northern Palace and no doubt greatly appreciated by the young princesses.

The sumptuous offerings were described as 'the tribute of Syria and the Sudan and the West and the East, all the countries there at one time, and the Islands in the midst of the Great Green Sea', the Egyptian name for the Mediterranean; the royal couple had 'received the produce of every land and granted the breath of life'. So Egypt's rulers had acknowledged the existence of those who had travelled so far with so much tribute, by granting them the means to live. It was a pretty good deal, and the couple seemed so pleased with the adulation of the world's masses that it was chosen as one of the main themes in the wall scenes of their Royal Tomb: registers of foreign representatives from the Near East, Libya and Nubia raise their arms in adoration, falling to the ground and kissing the earth.

As for the royal couple themselves, they are clearly shown holding hands throughout the ceremony. But this is no mere gesture to reassure the nervous little wife unused to state ceremonies, since Nefertiti is also shown supporting Akhenaten with her right arm around him in the traditional posture of female protection that dates back to the Pyramid Age.

In a further show of family unity, all six daughters stood beside their parents. Meritaten, as the eldest, pays close attention to the proceedings whilst Meketaten turns to speak to her younger sister Ankhesenpaaten who has been given some pieces of fruit to occupy her. The youngest girls were obviously given things to play with to keep them quiet during the lengthy ceremonies. Neferneferuaten Junior and Neferneferura were even allowed to bring their pet gazelles; the youngest child, Setepenra, is shown reaching out to stroke one.

The grand proceedings were eventually brought to a close with a series of investitures, as the royal couple rewarded with gold those who had organised the event so well. And because it must have been a long day, they declined the stately but slow carrying chair and returned to their Riverside Palace more speedily by chariot.

The scenes portraying these key events suggest something of the celebrations in the streets, no doubt encouraged by the lavish amounts of food and drink handed out. Occasions such as these were generally the only time that ordinary people enjoyed the taste of meat. As one later description revealed, there are all kinds of bread in loaves numerous as sand grains. Oxen abound like locusts. The smell of roast cow, gazelle, oryx and ibex reaches the sky. Wine flows freely through the town like the Nile flood bursting forth . . . Myrrh scattered on the brazier with incense can be smelled a mile away. The city is bestrewn with faience, glittering with natron and garlanded with flowers and fresh herbs. Its youths are drunk, its citizens are glad, its young maidens are beautiful to behold; rejoicing is all around it and festivity is in all its quarters. There is no sleep to be had in it until dawn.

The citizens of Amarna certainly got into the party mood, and are shown clapping, playing tambourines and dancing, even jumping up and down with sheer excitement.

But despite the success of an event in which the twin rulers of Egypt were acclaimed as living gods by the whole of the ancient world, its splendours failed to halt the increasing anarchy and the empire continued to fragment. The Great Reception was also the last time the royal family were shown together, and the final years of the reign were marked by a series of untimely and often tragic deaths.

Lavish tribute wasn't the only thing to arrive in the midst of the royal city, and Amarna had unwittingly opened its gates to an invisible killer. Diplomatic correspondence warned that 'There is plague in the land!' Possibly some sort of cholera or smallpox epidemic, it was raging across the Lebanon, Byblos and Cyprus, eventually spreading north, up into the lands of the Hittites where prayers to the gods would be insufficient to save the life of even the Hittite king.

When he first heard earlier rumours, in his own reign, Amenhotep III had set up more than seven hundred black granite statues of Sekhmet, Lady of Plague, to whom offerings were made morning and night in the hope of warding off a disease she controlled. The physicians responsible for dealing with such ailments were described as priests of Sekhmet, and given their reputation as great healers Egypt's doctors were in great demand throughout the ancient world. Now in diplomatic correspondence, the ruler of Ugarit asked pharaoh to send him a physician, whilst the mayor of Gazru asked for archers and 'myrrh for medication' to deal with the combined threat of war and sickness.

The royal family themselves would have turned to their court physician, Pentu. Using a combination of medicine and magic, Pentu and his staff would have employed the tried and tested remedies from the medical texts of the time. One of these listed 'a spell for the Asiatic disease to be spoken in the Keftiu [Cretan] language', hinting at foreign origins; a fragmentary prescription found at Amarna recommends 'anointing the patient with the fat of cattle'.

Several of the young princesses may have begun to show signs of illness, and some of the ancient spells were designed specifically to treat children. If they had a fever and were 'hot in the nest', it was recommended that they wore a carnelian amulet carved with a small crocodile and hand 'to drive away the disease demon'. Another spell addressed the unseen demon directly, and using a potent blend of garlic and honey challenges it to 'Come out, you visitor from the darkness, who crawls along!' Then asked if it has come to do the child harm, it is told forcefully 'I will not let you!' The desperation of a parent to protect an ailing child from forces unseen is clearly heard in this curiously moving piece of ancient magic.

Yet regardless of such precautions at least three of Nefertiti's daughters disappear from the records around this time, after plague had already claimed the life of at least one of the Babylonian princesses sent to Egypt in marriage. Still little more than babies, the two youngest princesses, Neferneferura and Setepenra, simply vanish, and were quite possibly buried in the city's royal burial ground, perhaps on the south side of the main Royal Valley. Here several large tombs had been begun, and an inscription referring to 'the robing room [or 'inner chamber'] of Neferure' was found on a pot handle in the debris outside one of them. Her name, originally carved into wall scenes in the Royal Tomb, was also at some stage plastered over, suggesting that she had died as the tomb underwent completion.

The fate of the couple's second child, Meketaten, is far better documented. Following her death some time after year 12, perhaps as early as year 13, around 1339 BC, she was buried in the Royal Tomb within one of the side-rooms, dubbed by Egyptologists 'Chamber Gamma'. As she was laid to rest within a great red granite sarcophagus her family and retainers would have provided her with all the necessary funerary equipment including pieces of jewellery, the small size of a pair of gold earplugs found in the tomb suggesting that they were made for a child. The princess would also have been buried with a range of fine linens and pottery vessels containing all the perfumes, food and wines her soul would require in the Afterlife. Specially made miniature pieces of ritual regalia included a tiny gold bucket-like situla used for liquid offerings, inscribed 'The Royal Daughter Meketaten', and a small alabaster vase inlaid with the tiny figure of a princess standing on a lotus flower in the pose of rebirth. Most touching of all is a miniature ivory paint palette with four cakes of coloured paints and small reed pens, its owner named as 'the king's own beloved daughter Meketaten, born of the Great Royal Wife Neferneferuaten Nefertiti', and most probably placed in the tomb by her parents who wanted her to have playthings in the Afterlife.

Certainly their grief at losing up to three of their young children in quick succession must have been intense. And despite the high incidence of infant mortality, such untimely deaths were always times of deep sadness in Egypt, in contrast to other parts of the ancient world where children were rather less valued. A later funeral inscription of one young girl declared: 'Although I am only a child, harm befell me when I was driven from my childhood too early, turned away from my home when still young. The terrifying dark engulfed me while the breast still fed me. I am too young to be alone, I enjoyed seeing people and my heart loved joy. O lord of Eternity to whom all people eventually come, I am a young girl without fault.'

As poignant scenes carved into her tomb walls reveal, Meketaten appears to have died in her bedroom in one of the palaces, where her small body was laid out on a bed whilst her distraught parents stand beside her. Outside the chamber, servants and officials are shown in the most extravagant poses of grief as they support each other or simply fall to the floor in their distress, something that Nefertiti herself would no doubt have done in private.

Following the mummification process, a second scene portrays the Amarna version of the traditional funeral ceremony (see Fig. 3). Meketaten stands upright inside a flower-strewn canopy, often compared to a birth canopy and most likely symbolising the wish for her soul's rebirth into the Afterlife. Although some authorities believe the figure is actually a statue of the princess it may well be her mummified body, anointed in the way the dead were usually shown at their funerals. Only this time it is not the coffin which stands upright but the actual body of the princess, wearing clothing as opposed to mummy wrappings. This may indicate a new form of funerary practice, or it may simply reflect a desire to show Meketaten as if still alive.

In whatever form her body took, the princess is shown being mourned by Akhenaten and Nefertiti, who throw their arms up to their faces in grief, followed by their three remaining daughters, Meritaten, Ankhesenpaaten and Neferneferuaten Junior. And although not shown at their sister's death bed, the girls accompanied their parents to her official funeral ceremony to mourn her along with the rest of the court.

One of the attendants also holds a baby in her arms, and many believe that this was Meketaten's child, the assumption being that the young princess had died in childbirth rather than falling victim to the plague or some form of childhood illness. Yet this seems unlikely, since the princess, herself shown as little more than a baby in family scenes from around her father's fifth or sixth regnal year, could have been no more than seven at the time of her death.

The additional belief that any such child was Akhenaten's also raises the whole question of royal incest, which some Egyptologists think was quite commonplace. Kings often gave the title 'Great Royal Wife' to their daughters, sisters and indeed mothers, but it seems unlikely that in most cases it was anything more than an honorary title. Certainly the eldest daughter, Meritaten, was promoted to Great Royal Wife once her mother had become co-regent. This followed the precedent set by Hatshepsut, who made her own daughter queen when she herself, as pharaoh, could no longer play the female role in state and religious rites. Referred to in some of the diplomatic correspondence, where she was called Mayati, Meritaten's important position as queen was well known far beyond the boundaries of Egypt.

And traditional Egyptologists are quite right when they claim that Queen Nefertiti had disappeared by year 14, to be replaced by Meritaten. But this assertion has often been followed up by the assumption that this meant Nefertiti's disgrace, exile, death or even murder, whilst her husband cavorted with the effeminate-looking 'Prince' Smenkhkara, conveniently married off to the eldest princess as cover for their illicit affair. Yet the feminine-looking figure was surely Nefertiti wearing the crowns of a co-regent. She had put away her trademark tall blue crown and all the regalia needed to play the female role, and instead adopted the khepresh crown and the neat, helmet-style cap crown far more in keeping with her elevated status.

Having already gone through the harrowing process of burying young daughters, Nefertiti would presumably have had to support her husband when his mother Tiy died at Amarna perhaps as late as his regnal year 14, around 1338 BC. Although the original plan seems to have been that Tiy should be buried with her husband Amenhotep III in Thebes, she had outlived him by as much as fourteen years and things had moved on. With Akhenaten no doubt keen to have his mother buried in the new Royal Valley at Amarna Tiy was placed in the Royal Tomb in the company of her granddaughter Meketaten (Fig. 2).

Although so much has been either removed or destroyed, Tiy's mummified body seems to have been wrapped in sheets of gold inscribed with her name, her body no doubt laden with much of the jewellery she wore in life as well as pieces specially commissioned for her burial. Recent research has revealed that she was then placed within a splendid granite sarcophagus decorated with figures of her son and Nefertiti wearing the cap crown, their names accompanied by those of Tiy herself and of her husband, the late king.

Her sarcophagus, thought to have been placed in the main burial chamber of the tomb, was then covered by a lavish cedarwood shrine smothered in gold and decorated with scenes of mother and son making offerings beneath the rays of the ever-present Aten. Presumably she would also have been provided with funerary figurines in alabaster, wood and coloured glazed ware similar to those originally placed in the tomb of Amenhotep III, perhaps as a votive offering.

Still the death toll continued to rise. Its next victim with royal connections was one of Akhenaten's secondary wives, Kiya. Although she had disappeared from view by year 12, the year of the Great Reception, she may well have lived for another four years, since a wine jar label referring to her as 'Greatly Loved Wife of the King' is dated to regnal year 16. She too was quite possibly buried within Amarna's large Royal Tomb (Fig. 2) in one of the side-chambers, known now as Room Alpha. The room certainly once contained a royal burial, since each of its walls features a small niche in which magical bricks and amulets were placed to protect the deceased. To judge from the attention lavished on the sumptuously inlaid coffin and alabaster canopic jars originally made for Kiya and later reused in Thebes in Tomb KV.55, it appears that Akhenaten must have cared deeply for her. A small sketch scribbled on a limestone chipping is believed to be a likeness of Akhenaten, showing him unkempt and unshaven as he weeps with grief, and the wall scenes decorating the room in which Kiya is believed to have been buried again show him distraught beside a woman's body.

Although no names remain with these heavily damaged scenes, originally thought to be a repetition of the death of Princess Meketaten, it is perhaps telling that none of the surviving princesses is shown in these later scenes in Room Alpha. As a leading Egyptologist has suggested, it seems plausible that the woman being mourned here is Kiya, who seems to have died giving birth to the child which an attendant is seen carrying away. And whereas the child in Meketaten's scenes is simply being held by an attendant, the scenes in Room Alpha reveal that this child is being suckled by a wet-nurse and may well be newborn. It has even been suggested that the child is Tutankhaten, the later Tutankhamen, the son of Kiya and Akhenaten born around regnal year 12 or 13, or even perhaps an unnamed daughter that some believe the couple also produced.

Certainly it is interesting to compare the way in which Akhenaten and Nefertiti are represented beside the woman's death bed. Shown bent forward in his grief, Akhenaten reaches out behind him to grasp the arm of the rather more composed Nefertiti for support. It would be interesting to know just how many tears Nefertiti shed at the death of her only real rival, and it has even been suggested that Kiya's death may have been no tragic accident but was engineered by the jealous Nefertiti. Although there is no evidence for this I wouldn't have put it past her.

Whatever the truth, Kiya was certainly unpopular with someone high up in the royal family, and as a result her name and images were systematically defaced throughout the city. On her figures the eyes were gouged out and the mouths erased to deprive her of the breath of life, whilst some were recarved as the eldest princess Meritaten or in some cases her sister Ankhesenpaaten. Once thought to have replaced figures of Nefertiti, the princesses were actually hiding the existence of their mother's apparently hated rival.

It would be quite easy to see the all-powerful Nefertiti as the one who gave the order to the stonemasons to begin rewriting history, watching with satisfaction as Kiya disappeared before her eyes. And as well as her name being removed to render her anonymous, Kiya's Nubian wig was recarved into the more acceptable sidelock worn by the royal daughters to enable Nefertiti to reclaim the trademark style she seems to have regarded as her own.

Although it isn't known exactly when the damage to Kiya's memory was inflicted, it is unlikely that Akhenaten would have stood idly by and let it happen if he'd been in a position to do anything about it. So either Nefertiti really did have the upper hand and continued to guide and even dictate royal policy, or he was unable to do anything physically and may have been suffering from some form of illness.

Akhenaten's last recorded regnal year is 17, around 1336 BC, although just as with those members of his family who predeceased him it is not known exactly when or indeed how he met his death. He may have died from natural causes, from plague, or from one of the various conditions which many think afflicted him throughout his life. Then again, others believe he may have been assassinated – regicide was not unknown in ancient Egypt, and there would have been plenty of people who wished the unorthodox pharaoh dead along with his disastrous policies.

Whilst it would be foolish to imagine assassins lurking round every corner of the palace, scenes in the tomb of the police chief Mahu show the capture and interrogation of three men whom some describe as spies or assassins, although frustratingly there are no further details. It is also intriguing that those who believe Akhenaten's son Tutankhamen was murdered generally lay the blame at the door of Ay; if he was Nefertiti's father, could this hint at a family of manipulative, almost Borgia-like characters?

However Akhenaten met his end, power would be firmly in the hands of his co-regent, Ankhkheperura Neferneferuaten. So, having already ruled jointly for several years, she would have been the obvious choice for pharaoh, finally taking the kingly name 'Ankhkheperura Smenkhkara' as her eldest daughter Meritaten continued in her role as her mother's Great Royal Wife.

Yet Akhenaten also had a son, Tutankhaten, and although still a small boy he would have been very much part of Nefertiti's plans. Well aware of her own mortality in the light of so many royal deaths, she had already started work on the succession. Both strands of the royal house were brought together when her second surviving daughter, Ankhesenpaaten, was made Great Royal Wife to her slightly younger half-brother. Guaranteeing that Nefertiti's blood as well as that of Akhenaten would continue to flow through the veins of the royal house, Egypt's new monarchy may well have appeared somewhat unorthodox – a woman accompanied by a small boy and two girls as opposed to the standard male pharaoh and his queen. Yet correct protocol would have been observed as Nefertiti initiated Akhenaten's funeral arrangements while his body underwent the mummification process.

After his internal organs had been removed and preserved separately within alabaster canopic jars, Akhenaten's eviscerated corpse, supported on plain rectangular bricks, would have been dried out in natron for the standard forty days. Then, coated heavily with precious resins to make the skin glisten, his embalmed body would have been covered in all manner of protective amulets, a gold death mask, and sheets of gold to mark him clearly as the Aten's own.

Although few written details exist, an inscription on one of his courtier's funerary figurines reveals the continued importance of bodily preservation in order to make it through to the Afterlife Amarna-style. Despite the fact that Osiris was no longer there to meet and greet the deceased into his gloomy Underworld kingdom, the Aten was, as always, waiting with open arms. In a wonderful evocation of the new paradise the short text states: 'May you breathe the sweet breeze of the north wind and go forth into the sky on the arms of the living Aten, your limbs protected and your heart content. No evil can affect your limbs, you remain whole and your body will never putrefy as you follow the Aten as he rises at daybreak.'

As Akhenaten's earthly remains were being prepared, final preparations would be made to ensure that he had all the funerary equipment necessary for his burial. While last-minute details were being added to the Royal Tomb's wall scenes the sarcophagus was at some stage hauled into position. Using hemp ropes and plenty of brute force, it was manoeuvred slowly down the steeply sloping, 100-foot entrance passage to be set up on the raised rectangular platform in the middle of the main chamber's floor to await final interment. Then other heavy items would have been arranged around it before the actual day of burial.

With Akhenaten's mummified body placed within its nest of gold and inlaid coffins, Nefertiti and the young Tutankhaten must have led the elaborate royal funeral ceremony. The female pharaoh, dressed in kingly regalia, would have made sure the young boy as son and heir wore the appropriate garments in miniature, including the child-size pantherskin robe found in his tomb and which has recently been suggested as the garment he wore at his father's funeral.

Setting out from the city up into the Royal Valley, presumably making the four-mile journey by carrying chair rather than on foot, the procession would have included surviving members of the royal family: the king's daughters and royal wives Meritaten and Ankhesenpaaten, Nefertiti's sister Mutnodjmet and their likely relatives, the courtiers Ay and Ty. There would also have been key officials such as the vizier, the high priest of the Aten and his retinue including incense-bearers, female mourners in the required state of melodramatic hysteria, fan-bearers and the royal bodyguard, not to mention the army of bearers needed to carry chests full of the smaller burial objects such as funerary figurines, gilded statuettes, linen robes, jewel caskets, fans, stone vessels, jars of food and fine wines.

By the light of flickering torches, the burial party would have stood by and watched through a haze of sweet, heavy incense as Akhenaten's mummified body within a nest of golden coffins was laid to rest within his great sarcophagus, the pink granite box and contrasting grey lid covered in a fine linen pall studded with gold rosettes. Although the sarcophagus itself was carved with his names and those of the Aten, the figure who dominated was Nefertiti, appearing in place of the traditional goddesses on each of the four corners, and stretching out her arms to give maximum protection to the dead pharaoh (Fig. 5). Her role of safeguarding his eternal future reveals the tremendous power Nefertiti must have wielded both in this world and in the next. Indeed, the name found most often in the entire tomb is that of Nefertiti, causing at least one earlier scholar to suggest that this must have been her tomb.

Yet it seems she was never actually buried here. The large suite of king-sized chambers halfway down the entrance corridor, thought to have been intended for Nefertiti, was left unfinished and was apparently never used. The frequency of her name may instead reflect the fact that she was the one responsible for sealing up the tomb once and for all, since she, it seems, had other plans. Unsurprisingly, she wanted her own tomb, so elsewhere in the Royal Valley an impressively proportioned vault was begun which features a similarly steep entrance, although its descending corridor goes down a staggering 130 feet into the bedrock, 30 feet further than that of the Royal Tomb itself. Obviously built for royalty, it is likely that this was the tomb Nefertiti began for herself; another tomb, begun near by, may well have been intended for Tutankhaten.

With her duties to her husband and predecessor completed,

Nefertiti could begin the task of ruling the country as Ankhkhep-erura Smenkhkara, and although her reign may have lasted little more than a year or so it could certainly have laid the ground-work for her immediate successors. A small limestone statue in Berlin shows her as sole monarch standing alone and wearing the sober cap crown befitting her rank. She is dressed in a gown of finest linen, broad collar and a pair of circular stud earrings, her eyes and eyebrows outlined in her usual subtle black eye paint whilst her somewhat down-turned lips are painted her trademark shade of red. It is a vivid portrayal of a woman who has been described as 'past her youth but not old': her slightly sagging breasts are evidence of repeated childbirth, and she seems to carry the weight of the country on her slim shoulders.

And it was a country close to ruin following all the political and religious upheavals of the previous seventeen years. With unrest growing steadily at home amongst a disaffected popu-lation headed by the priesthood, Egypt's empire continued to crumble. Realising the difficulty of controlling the situation from such an isolated capital, the pragmatic Nefertiti seems to have decided to cut her losses.

Although Amarna was not abandoned immediately, there was certainly some sort of return to Thebes and an attempt to reach an understanding with the old order. In trying to win back both priests and people, she would no doubt have been assisted by close advisers including Ay, her putative father, who continued to play an important role at court. Then there was his military colleague Horemheb, who may have started his career at Amarna as the young recruit Paatenemheb, later removing the 'Aten' element and changing his name to the more socially acceptable Horemheb. As things gradually started to calm down at home fewer troops would have been needed to keep order, and so plans were eventually put in place to try to win back the lost regions of Egypt's empire under Horemheb's more than capable military leadership. The threat from the Hittites certainly needed to be dealt with, and although her reign was brief, a shipwreck off the coast of the mighty Hittite Empire was found to contain a cargo of goods accompanied by a single royal name, Nefertiti, inscribed on a golden scarab. Revealing the extent to which Nefertiti's name had spread out across the ancient world the name of her daughter, the next queen, Ankhesenamen, turned up as far away as Poros in Crete.

In an attempt to reverse the decline in the country's fortunes it may even be possible that Nefertiti returned to Thebes on a more permanent basis earlier, during Akhenaten's last years, and that while he stayed on at Amarna she ruled as co-regent Ankhkheperura from Thebes. However the power-sharing worked out, co-regent Ankhkheperura was certainly amenable to dealing with the traditional priesthood, and in a complete U-turn in policy it seems that the priests of Amen were given permission to resume operations.

A piece of graffiti tucked away in the Qurna tomb of one such priest is about the only surviving clue to what was going on during these chaotic years. It is dated to the third year of the reign of Ankhkheperura Neferneferuaten, 'Beloved of Akhenaten', which may well equate with Akhenaten's fourteenth regnal year, some time around 1338 BC. Written by a certain Pawah, 'priest and scribe of Amen's offerings in the temple of Ankhkheperura in Thebes', it takes the form of a prayer which boldly begins with the long-banned words 'Praise to Amen!' He then goes on to confess that it is

my wish is to see you O Lord, to look at you, so my heart may rejoice. O Amen, protector of the poor! It is good to speak your name! It tastes like life, like bread to a child, like cool food in hot weather. You are like the taste of favour from the king, the breeze of freedom to the prisoner, peace to the troubled. Come back to us, Lord of continuity! You were here at the beginning before anything else existed, and will be here when all else is gone. You have brought the darkness as yours to give, make light so I might see you again. As your soul endures and as your beautiful, beloved face endures, come from afar and allow your servant, the scribe Pawah, to see you again! Oh Amen, great lord, found by those who seek him, drive away our fear! Fill our hearts with joy, for joy is for those who see you Amen!

This is a real cry from the heart, begging Amen to return and make everything just as it was in the good old days. The Egyptians clearly wanted their gods back, and as the name 'Amen' was spoken openly for the first time in years an uneasy truce formed between crown and clergy, and a full-scale return to orthodox practice was set in motion.

It was felt that Egypt's declining fortunes could be reversed if only the old gods could be tempted back to their temples. But these were now in a sorry state after their twelve-year closure and would need serious renovation before any self-respecting god would even think of honouring them with their presence. An edict issued within a few years of Akhenaten's death paints a sad picture, describing 'the temples of the gods and goddesses from the Delta to Aswan in ruins. Their shrines had collapsed and were overgrown in weeds and it seemed as if they had never existed. The land had been struck by catastrophe and the gods had turned their back on Egypt. If an army was sent to the Levant they had no success. If anyone prayed to the gods they never came. Hearts were weakened in bodies, for what had been had been destroyed.'

The much-needed restoration work was funded by the crown, the least it could do in the circumstances, and the reopening of the old temples marked the beginning of financial recovery for Egypt. People could resume their employment, be they priests, musicians or dancers, florists, incense makers, those who worked the temple's fields or cleaned out the sacred cowsheds. And with temple revenues restored, moves began to make amends to the noble families traditionally chosen for religious office but snubbed by Akhenaten. As the old power networks of influential families were gradually restored, Tutankhaten (as Tutankhamen) was later able to state that 'I made priests of the children of local princes, each one the son of a noble person whose name is well known.' The crown even met the shortfall of religious personnel by supplying singers, dancers and servants directly from the royal household.

The royal family must also have made frequent journeys between Thebes and Amarna, where Nefertiti and her soon-to-be successors Tutankhaten and Ankhesenpaaten, soon to be known as Tutankhamen and Ankhesenamen, continued to spend at least some of their time. Recent research has suggested that royal sculptures were still being made in the Amarna workshop of Tuthmose, such as an unfinished head of Nefertiti made of the grey-black granodiorite stone, which only appears to have become popular after Akhenaten's death. Her lips are as usual painted red and it has been noted how relatively young and smooth her face still appears – she was, indeed, still a relatively young woman. Yet it has also been suggested that Nefertiti must have died soon after this head was created, probably not very long after Akhenaten himself, around 1336 or 1335 BC.

The dates on jar labels from Amarna suggest that the reign of Ankhkheperura Smenkhkara was brief, although once again it is unclear exactly when and indeed how this king died. Natural causes would not be unexpected, given the fact that she had not only gone through childbirth six times but had supported her useless husband in running the country and then been forced to pick up the pieces after his death. Clearly trauma and stress had characterised her life. Yet there is always the possibility that Nefertiti's death was not at all natural.

There must have been many who wanted her out of the way, tainted as she was by her association with Akhenaten and his disastrous policies. In fact she would have been in a particularly vulnerable position, hated not only by the traditionalists who held her at least partly responsible for getting rid of Amen, but also by the new breed of officials who had been doing very well and would be less than pleased at any attempt to reduce their powers. Then of course there is the Zannanza Affair, stuffed full of fatal court intrigue and plotting.

During the intermittent hostilities amongst Egypt's wavering allies and vassals, and the increasingly strong Hittites, the Hittite king Suppiluliumas I was besieging Carchemish when he learned of the death of pharaoh Niphururiya (the Hittite pronunciation of either Akhenaten's name Neferkheperure or Tutankhamen's name Nebkheperure). In the Hittites' diplomatic archive at their capital, Hattusas (modern Boghazkoy), was a copy of a letter sent by an Egyptian queen named as Dahamunzu, which scholars came to realise was not a name at all, but the Hittite for 'ta hemet nisu', 'the royal wife'. The missive is generally believed to have been sent by Ankhesenamen after the death of Tutankhamen, although some have wondered if in fact this letter may have been sent by her mother. As one eminent Egyptologist pointed out, the unusual use of 'ta', meaning 'the', stresses that this was not just any royal wife, but *the* royal wife, and emphasises the sender's importance.

If this was Nefertiti, then the contents of her letter are dynamite. As she goes on to inform the enemy king, 'My husband is dead and I have no son. But you, people tell me, have many sons, and if you give one of your sons to me he would become my husband, because I will never pick out a servant of mine for a husband. But I am afraid.' This was an astonishing request unprecedented in Egyptian history, for royal women never married foreigners. Nor were foreign royals simply called in to take power, although, if this is indeed Nefertiti speaking, she would probably have expected to continue ruling through her invited prince regardless of any objections he might raise.

The Hittite king was, unsurprisingly, not convinced, exclaiming that 'such a thing has never happened before in my life'. And, given the less than friendly relations between their two countries, he was deeply suspicious and sent an envoy to check the request's authenticity. In her reply she asked him, clearly somewhat annoyed, 'Why did you think I deceived you? If I had a son why would I have written about my shame to a foreign land? You didn't believe me and have said so. But my husband has died and I have no son and I will never take a servant of mine for a husband. I have written to no other but you, and you have many sons. So send me one of them to be my husband and be king.'

Finally convinced by this heartfelt, direct plea, and no doubt mindful of the wealth and prestige his country would gain from such an alliance, the Hittite king sent out one of his sons, the splendidly named Zannanza. But the prince seems to have been little more than a lamb to the slaughter, and although his exact fate is unknown he and his entourage simply disappeared, presumed murdered. So it may have been a trick all along, engineered by the Egyptians or even by Nefertiti herself, in the context of the hostilities between her country and the Hittites. Or perhaps the unfortunate prince was killed by Nefertiti's enemies, unwilling to accept such an outrageous plan. And if so, did Nefertiti share her would-be husband's fate?

Although nothing is known about when, where or how Nefertiti died or was buried, she would have been making plans for the event throughout her adult life. The wealth of funerary equipment already prepared, following standard practice, would have included a gold death mask, one or more golden coffins, canopic equipment for her internal organs, gilded statues and funerary figurines. In her case it would of course be accompanied by all her personal possessions – her lavish jewellery, clothing, wigs and make-up – and all manner of favourite food and drink to sustain her in the Afterlife.

With no evidence to suggest that she was buried at Amarna it seems most likely that Nefertiti was buried somewhere in Thebes, for not only were the city's traditional temples reopened but the Valley of the Kings was reinstated as the royal burial ground. Indeed, recent work in the valley by an international team of archaeologists has revealed that the small rock-cut tomb numbered KV.56 cut into the valley floor may originally have been created in the late 18th dynasty. Clearly designed for royalty, its entrance shaft is the largest in the valley, although the relatively modest size of the rest of the tomb suggests someone who didn't have very long in which to finish the work. Its location may also be a clue as to the identity of the person originally buried there, situated as it is very close to the tomb of Tutankhamen KV.62 and the mysterious KV.55, both of which contained large quantities of funerary equipment made during the Amarna Period for members of the royal family.

Some time after Akhenaten's death, the Amarna Royal Tomb was re-entered and part of its contents removed and brought back to Thebes for reburial in KV.55, which was found to contain 'exact parallels' of pieces found in Amarna's Royal Tomb. This work seems to have been completed under Tutankhamen, whose official seal appears on KV.55's walled-up doorway, although the actual process of dismantling the Amarna burials may well have been begun by Nefertiti. This may also explain the confused picture which emerges from KV.55's contents, in which a male body believed by many to be Akhenaten ended up in a coffin made for his secondary wife Kiya, together with her canopic jars which presumably once contained her internal organs. Although it is hard to imagine Tutankhamen allowing his mother's body to be turfed out of her coffin and reused for his father, it is certainly not difficult to imagine Nefertiti giving orders to dispose of her mummified rival. Yet Kiya's precious inlaid coffin along with other valuable pieces, including Queen Tiy's body and gilded shrine, were all brought back to Thebes, and the unwieldy stone sarcophagi left behind along with some of the smaller, less important items.

The process of sorting through all this material continued under Tutankhamen, but the story took another twist when he himself died unexpectedly, before his coffins and related material were anywhere near complete. So, whilst his body underwent mummification, his funeral equipment was cobbled together quickly from other sources. Some items buried with him, ranging from bracelets, gold sequins, wooden caskets and linen clothing to a paint palette, a fan and a finely made bow, still bore the names of Akhenaten, Nefertiti, Neferneferuaten and Ankhkheperura, as well as those of several of the princesses. And amongst the funerary statuettes found in Tutankhamen's tomb were two gilded figures of kings standing on black leopards. Each wearing the white crown of southern Egypt and a king's kilt, and carrying the royal flail in their right hand, they were found wrapped in linen dated to Akhenaten's third year. So it has logically been suggested that the figures were made early in Akhenaten's reign for his intended burial in Thebes, but following the move to Amarna they were left behind, only to be brought out of storage and dusted down for use in his son's burial.

However, the really astonishing thing about the statuettes is that they are by no means an identical pair. Rather like novelty bookends, one king is male, the other most definitely female, with breasts so prominent that they cannot be explained away as simply a quirk of Amarna art. This is a statuette of a woman with all the regalia of a king. Now who might that be, I wonder?

In fact, many of the most famous pieces from Tutankhamen's tomb seem to have been made for others: the gold throne, for instance, was almost certainly altered from the original figures of Akhenaten and Nefertiti to show Tutankhamen and Ankhesenamen. Even the face of Tutankhamen's famed gold death mask has been said to show signs of alteration from an earlier version, and at least one, if not two, of his three gold coffins do not seem to have been made for him either.

The outermost coffin has the ends of a long tripartite wig hanging down from its royal head cover in a similar combination to that found on the Karnak colossi of Akhenaten and Nefertiti. And whilst the head covering is decorated in gold leaf, close inspection reveals that the face is made of thicker sheet gold of a much paler colour, and may well have been added at a different time. The second coffin remains much as it was originally made, its face quite different from that on the other two coffins, and, as one leading Egyptologist has commented, 'there is every reason to believe, as with other objects from the burial furniture, that Tutankhamen was not its intended owner'.

This is again true of the gorgeous strips of inlaid gold known as mummy bands which were laid over Tutankhamen's mummy, originally inscribed for Ankhkheperura and later cut down to fit their new owner. The same goes for the canopic equipment used to store Tutankhamen's mummified entrails, for not only do the faces of the jar stoppers resemble that of the second coffin, but the miniature gold coffinettes which went inside the jars and held the actual organs still bore the royal name Ankhkheperura.

Given that so much of Ankhkheperura's – Nefertiti's – lavish funerary equipment was apparently reused in the tomb of Tutankhamen, there seem to be two possible scenarios. Either Nefertiti's body was ruthlessly stripped of its wealth only a few years after her death, or the great woman was given a cut-price funeral and her unused treasures simply stock-piled for another. As for her body, it was either placed in temporary accommodation alongside other rifled royals before finding refuge in one of the royal caches, or else it was damaged or even destroyed by the following dynasty. Military-minded, puritanical pharaohs, they were responsible for tearing down Amarna's legacy and removing all trace of the hated 'criminal' and his family. Akhenaten's coffin ended up on the floor with its face torn off when KV.55 was re-entered some time around 1110 BC, so did Nefertiti share her husband's fate at the hands of the new orthodoxy?

It's a very messy scenario, and with the bodies of the Amarna royals and their treasures dragged from pillar to post with considerable regularity, it makes things very confusing for anyone trying to work out exactly what happened. And although we may never know for certain, this intriguing puzzle has been challenging minds far greater than mine for years. But was there any point in chasing the same pieces of information round and round? New evidence was what was required. And that was precisely what I hoped to find that hot day in June 2002 when I finally looked into the faces of three long-dead mummies in the side chamber in the Valley of the Kings.

11

THE FIRST VISIT INTO THE SIDE CHAMBER

As I stood on the threshold of the tomb's side chamber the torch cut through the blackness in front of me, lighting up three mummified faces in turn. And what serene and dignified faces they were – it was impossible not to feel apologetic for intruding in such an abrupt manner. Just as the sun god's life-giving rays were thought to penetrate the darkest recesses of the Underworld and resurrect all they touched, the torchlight fell upon each one in turn, and myth and reality briefly seemed to merge. It was a moment I'd thought would never come.

But there was little time to stand and stare. The headman was keen to continue removing the rest of the wall in time for the arrival of his boss, and from the animated activity going on behind us it was clear that Egypt's head of antiquities, Dr Zahi Hawass, and his entourage were fast approaching up the Valley. This posed something of a dilemma. Should I tear myself away from the three mummies and go up to the tomb entrance to await his arrival, or should I stay put? What was the protocol? Fortunately the decision was taken out of my hands when the growing buzz of conversation and noise of footsteps heralded his imminent arrival. Wearing his trademark hat, he emerged into the burial chamber surrounded by a crowd of staff, inspectors and his 'people'.

After the standard introductions and handshakes we waited while the workmen removed the last of the bricks. Then Dr Hawass gestured me forward.

'Please,' he said, 'after you.'

Although I longed to accept his courteous invitation, something stopped me. After all, who was I to take precedence? 'No, no, after you,' I heard myself say.

Climbing over the rubble-strewn threshold, he disappeared momentarily into the darkness.

'Can you see them?' I asked, craning forward.

'Yes, all of them.'

Remembering their faces, I couldn't help remarking how beautiful they were.

'Yes,' he agreed as he looked round with a torch, taking in the sight.

'Do you want to come in?' he asked, extending his hand out through the entrance to help me.

As I climbed very slowly into the chamber, one of very few people to have been given this privilege, I was aware that one false move could prove disastrous. The bodies lay very close to the entrance and I didn't dare imagine what any accidental clumsiness of my great desert boots could do to such precious remains. Not only that, but the moment was being preserved for posterity by a film crew – imagine the headlines.

I made it into the small chamber, and as I gazed down on the three bodies it was immediately obvious that they were royal. The mummy nearest to us was an adult woman, the so-called Elder Woman whose noble profile made me feel as though we'd been granted an audience. She looked just as she had in the black-and-white photograph taken almost a century before, her long hair streaming down and her left hand still clutching a long-vanished sceptre which had once lain across her chest. Despite the extensive damage to her torso, she remained in amazing condition as a superb example of the embalmer's art.

Clearly impressed, Dr Hawass looked closely at the Elder Woman. 'The face is very impressive', he remarked, agreeing that it was also a very proud face. Then, pointing to the slightly wrinkled skin on her face, he commented that she must have been quite old at death, unlike the young boy at her side. Still fresh-faced and incredibly appealing, with his thick sidelock of hair cascading around the right side of his head, could he really be a son of Amenhotep II, as so many thought? And finally there she was, the enigmatic Younger Woman, at the end of the row on the other side of a boy. But who was she?

Face to face with her at last, I could see nothing to make me doubt my original belief that she might well be one of the most important of all Egyptians. As I stared at her, trying to take in every detail, I had to force myself to remain clear-headed and objective. This, despite all the emotions spinning through my head, not to mention the cameras, able to catch every nuance, every gesture and, I could swear, everything I was thinking.

She was so like that famous piece of sculpture – the resemblance was quite extraordinary. But before I could voice my thoughts I noticed that something was not quite right. Looking down at her, I could see no sign of the bent right arm that Smith had clearly described on his visit of 1907. Instead, beside the body lay an extended, handless limb. What was going on? If her right arm had not in fact been bent up in the traditional pose of a pharaoh this certainly detracted from the idea that she could have ruled as king. Perhaps the body wasn't hers after all. I was engulfed in a wave of disappointment.

Then I remembered that there were other clues. Whoever this woman was, she had been buried with a short wig, most likely set in the distinctive Nubian style. Across her smoothly shaven head was the clear impression, even more visible than it had been on the old photograph, of something having once fitted tightly across her brow – a crown, perhaps? All these were clues pointing to an Amarna female, but to which one? Was she one of Nefertiti's daughters? Or a daughter of Tiy and Amenhotep III? Or someone else altogether?

As I attempted to work through all the possibilities and permutations, I realised that a lot more scientific evidence would be necessary before we could find out exactly who this woman was. I needed to know how old she was, how she had died, how she had been mummified and if she was related to the other two, both of whom I also wanted to know much more about.

Unable to provide the answers myself in such a short space of time, I would need to ask the experts.

The temperature in the small chamber had passed 100 degrees Fahrenheit, with humidity running at 90 per cent. So when the archaeologist Arthur Weigall had described the 'Turkish-bath like' temperatures while he was working in the Valley's tombs he had certainly not been exaggerating. Dr Hawass adjusted his hat and tissues were passed through the gap in the wall in a vain attempt to stem the tide of perspiration as we discussed the three mummies further.

When the time came for him to leave I was given permission to remain there with the inspectors and film crew until the end of the day, when the wall would have to be sealed up again. That gave me a few more hours – this time with powerful lighting, tape measures, camera, magnifying glass and the skills of leading mummification specialist and archaeological chemist Dr Stephen Buckley.

Although we were not allowed to touch the mummies we were allowed to study them as closely as possible, which often meant only a few inches away. I was glad I'd remembered to pack face masks – a good idea given the thick layer of grey dust on each of them, and we didn't want to contaminate them by breathing on them either.

I settled down on the hard, bumpy stone floor which put me on the same level as the bodies, each laid out with its legs pointing down to the space just below the entrance. They still lay on the wooden boards that Loret had made for them back in 1898, the boards' padded covering far more suitable than the bare stone floor on which the three had originally been left and where I now sat. Not the most comfortable place to spend eternity, I had to admit.

When Maspero ordered Carter to display the three to the public he had placed a small wooden trestle beneath the top of Loret's boards which explained the mummies' semi-reclining position. With the lighting rigged up – another debt to Carter, who had brought electric light to the Valley exactly a century before – Stephen was able to begin his detailed examination of the mummification methods used on the three bodies. And while he looked for any similarities in embalming techniques, I was able to get down to what I love best. Pulling out my magnifying glass, I started to scrutinise their hairstyles.

Beginning with the Elder Woman, identified in the 1970s as Queen Tiy, I examined her wonderful long wavy brown hair, falling from a centre parting to hang in small curls about her shoulders. Just as I'd been told back in 1990 at the Valley of the Kings conference her hair was indeed all her own, with no evidence of any false braids having been tucked in to pad it out. Yet I did wonder about the waves. They seemed too wide to have been made with the usual small bronze tong-like instruments, and the effect may have been created by plaiting the hair when wet and loosening it once dry, the same style found in many of the tomb scenes of Amenhotep III's courtiers.

In the strong electric light the hair also had a definite red sheen, almost a glow, and whilst only dye analysis could give a conclusive answer it may well have been achieved with a henna rinse applied by the royal hairdresser. Knowing from personal experience just how messy this stuff is to apply, I tried to imagine the great queen in life, impatiently sitting on her gilded chair while the gloopy green mixture was applied to her hair. And then there amongst the tresses, right at the front above her right eyebrow, was the empty egg case of a head louse. The great queen, consort of the sun king and icon of royal style, had suffered from head lice, although this perhaps was to be expected, given the fact that it was her own hair.

Beneath her crowning glory, the Elder Woman's wonderfully imperious, indeed proud, face had great bone structure. The dark brown mummification resins applied to preserve her features had darkened the skin in places, and we also noticed small amounts of white, waxy material on her face. Their splash-like patterns may well have been the result of early attempts to light the chamber before it was wired for electricity in 1902, although Loret's original candle-lit examination of the three bodies may also have left this tell-tale clue as he bent over each mummy in turn, sputtering candle in hand.

Closer examination of the Elder Woman's face revealed that her skin seemed to be covered in some sort of rash or pitting, resembling that on the face of Ramses V who had been buried in the other side chamber and was now in the Cairo Museum. When his facial pustules had been investigated some time back it was suggested that this was evidence of smallpox, and Stephen and I agreed that this would be one to ask Don Brothwell about back at the University of York. We also noticed that a small amount of the original linen wrappings still covered her left eyelid, explaining why her eye is partly obscured in the old photographs. Stephen then began to work his way down the body in meticulous detail.

The right arm had been laid straight down along the side with the hand resting on the thigh. Fragments of the original high-quality linens were still stuck to the shiny black resins that the embalmers had originally brushed over the corpse 'to give it that Ronseal finish', as Stephen described it. The hand itself was covered in a thin layer of resin and her middle finger was missing, perhaps the result of an attempt by tomb robbers to pull off the precious gold rings which once embellished each of her fingers, and quite possibly carrying the names of her husband. The same fine layer of resin with more small fragments of linen also covered her left hand, although this lay in a quite different position, resting close to the collar bone, since the embalmers had prepared her body with the left forearm bent up in the pose of a queen. As we already knew from the original black-and-white 'head-shots', the fingers of the left hand were still clutched to form a fist, presumably to hold a sceptre – most likely the lily sceptre that queens regularly hold when depicted in statues and wall scenes. And the royal manicurist had presumably been at work here, since her remaining nails appeared to be well manicured and stained with henna.

Thick layers of linen still covered her neck, where the black resin coating was clearly different from the brownish-red shades of the materials applied to other parts of her body. Many of these seem to have been chosen for various symbolic reasons, and Spell 42 in the *Book of the Dead* reveals that each part of the body was protected by a different god or goddess. Since certain deities could be represented by their signature oil or perfume, we wondered if this was what we were seeing here.

All manner of protective amulets would also have been placed over various parts of the body and, despite the idea that the Amarna royals did away with all gods but the Aten, the amulets found in the Royal Tomb show that they too had relied on such traditional methods to protect their remains. So in addition to the large Heart Scarab placed over the heart, which always remained in the body as the seat of all wisdom, the classic Eye of Horus 𓂀 amulet was provided for 'your protection, spreading its protection all around you and overthrowing your foes'.

Yet such protective powers had not been sufficient to save the Elder Woman from severe treatment. For although her wonderful face remained intact, there was precious little left of the front of her torso, from the chest right down to the abdomen. Fragments of gold winding sheets inscribed with Tiy's name are said to have been found in the Amarna Royal Tomb, and we wondered if pulling them away from a body covered in glue-like resins could have caused such destruction. Something similar certainly seems to have happened when the wrappings and gold sheets had been lifted from the mystery mummy found in KV.55. However it had happened, it was major damage.

But there was a plus side too: it did allow us to examine the way her body cavity had been treated after her internal organs were removed during the mummification process. The cavity itself had been filled with some kind of granular packing. And although the actual incision made to pull out the entrails was located as usual on the left side of the abdomen, its position did not seem to match either of those originally set down by Smith as either 'before Tuthmosis III' or 'after Tuthmosis III' – one of the ways mummies are usually dated. So was this a new and different means of removing the organs, pointing to a different form of mummification?

A thick layer of resin covered what remained of the lower abdomen, and the left leg was largely exposed. The right leg, however, was covered in many of the original wrappings, still in a tangled mass where the ancient robbers had left them. But some time after Loret had had the bodies sketched, and before Smith had examined them, both feet had been broken off. The left foot, which had been retrieved at some time and placed between the thighs, had the tip of the big toe missing and what Smith had described as an ulcer visible on her left heel. If this was indeed an ulcer it would certainly have made walking painful. This was something else we would have to check with Don.

We paused for a moment to look at our surroundings, and saw that the roughly hewn walls of the small, square, rock-cut chamber had never been finished off, and certainly never decorated. Stephen noticed the occasional blob of red paint like ones he'd seen in other tombs earlier. Having analysed them he knew that they were ancient, almost certainly the original guide marks used by the stonemasons when the chamber was being created. The ceiling was also soot-blackened in places, presumably from the flaming torches used by those building the tomb, preparing the burial equipment, and perhaps even those who had stripped the dead of their wealth.

In the far corner against the wall lay the only object remaining with the mummies, a long, plain, brown, body-shaped coffin whose flimsy appearance was due to the fact that it appeared to be made of *cartonnage*. According to the original reports, none of the three mummies had been found in a coffin, nor was there any mention of such a thing being found anywhere in the chamber. But on reflection we realised that the tomb owner, Amenhotep II, had been reburied in ancient times in exactly this type of coffin after his original, presumably golden, versions had been stolen, and was then returned to his stone sarcophagus in the burial chamber outside. When his mummy was finally removed to the Cairo Museum in 1931, it appears that his bargain basement replacement coffin was left behind, along with the three mummies, and walled up with them in the side chamber.

Time was now running out, so we moved along to the boy. Although he too was a very well-preserved mummy, we knew from the old photographs that he'd suffered some severe damage to his chest in ancient times. As I gazed down at his sleeping face, with its wonderful long, curly eyelashes still intact and a splendid hairstyle, it seemed obvious that this was a royal prince. But why would a son of Amenhotep II be left unwrapped on the floor of his father's tomb between two anonymous women who almost seemed to be protecting him? Surely he was in some way connected with them, we thought, as we began to look for clues.

Smith had long ago commented on the boy's 'beloid skull' and his 'exceptional brachycephalism', a reference to the fact that his head is nearly as broad from side to side as from front to back. This was accentuated by the fact that his head had been shaved perfectly smooth except for a long sidelock of hair, the mark of young princes, on the right. Although the hair was now very dry and brittle, the length and thickness of the lock was of the type fashionable in the mid-18th dynasty, the early Amarna Period. This was also true of the large hole in each of his earlobes, since earrings had only become fashionable for royal males from the reign of Tuthmosis IV onwards.

The top of his bare head was darkened with the same resiny mixture we'd seen on the head of the Elder Woman next to him, no doubt applied during the last rites, and the right side of his skull had been punctured, causing a large, sharp-edged hole of the sort found on a number of other royals from the tomb. It looked as if he, like them, had received a violent blow to the head during tomb robbery and the fragments of bone had fallen down inside his skull.

The size of the hole enabled us to check for any trace of the brain. Although Smith had suggested that the ancient embalmers had removed it through the prince's nose, Stephen was suspicious. He'd been studying the work of Alfred Lucas, the chemist who had examined samples from the royal mummies on Smith's behalf – samples which had included an extraordinary 80g of the boy's brain.

As far as we knew from our own experiences, a dried-out three thousand-year-old brain could hardly weigh much more than this when complete, so it seems that the prince's skull had not been cleaned out after all. But this struck us both as curious, since brain removal was standard procedure in the mummification process, especially when achieving such high-quality results as we were seeing now. So was this yet another clue that we were looking at a new form of mummification?

Beneath partly visible eyebrows, the prince's eyes with their long, curly lashes were wide-set, and a slight smile seemed to hover about his broad lips. Looking at him from the side, he shared something of the Elder Woman's profile, especially the shape of his nose. Parts of his face were similarly discoloured by the use of preservative resins, and again small splashes of candle wax could be seen on his skin.

Although the prince had both his hands modestly arranged over his genitals, Smith had been able to work out that unlike most of the Egyptian male elite, he had not been circumcised. His left hand was clasped, although the thumb was extended, whilst the right hand lay below, fully extended with the little finger bent back, suggesting that he had been holding something. But what?

Since his torso was covered only in a thin layer of resin no more than a millimetre thick, the strong lights were able to reveal the slight imprint of some sort of regalia or costume once worn close to the skin. The shapes of the imprint suggested perhaps some sort of jewelled garment resembling the military-style corselet of semi-precious stones set in a layered feathered design which had been found in the tomb of Tutankhamen. So perhaps our prince had been sent off into eternity wearing a similar type of glittering garment? It would certainly help to explain the severe damage to the upper left side of the chest area, an area traditionally festooned with all manner of protective necklaces and amulets of precious materials, and the place most frequently targeted by tomb robbers.

Looking down the left side of the body, Stephen noticed that the boy's embalming incision did not match either of the standard positions given by Smith. Instead it resembled that of the Elder Woman, suggesting that the two bodies may have been mummified by the same technique.

Along with pieces of original linen wrappings still sticking to his torso, resin-soaked linens had been used to pack his chest and abdomen, and the lower part of the body too was packed with what appeared to be mud. This was an ingredient used to pack many royal mummies, but it still seemed a rather strange material to use side by side with so much gold – unless the mud had come from the Nile. Believed to be the source of life, with miraculous regenerative qualities, this highly potent material would have been a most appropriate ingredient to use in the mummification process.

Looking at the lower limbs, the right leg seemed a little shorter than the left. Once again both feet had been broken off after the bodies were discovered in 1898 and some of the toes were missing. In the increasingly suffocating heat a fine layer of dust had begun to stick to our sodden faces. Silently we cursed the ineffectual fans which whirred away at the other side of the wall. Nevertheless we had to press on, as time was running short.

Finally passing on to the third body, subconsciously having left the best until last, I forced myself to suppress any feelings and tried to switch into 'detached scientist' mode as we began to study the body of the Younger Woman which I found so intriguing. A well-preserved mummy, she had nevertheless managed to fool the early archaeologists who had considered her male simply on account of her shaven head. Not the most reliable way of sexing a body, it has to be said, and with no sign of male genitals she certainly appeared female to us.

Her face was beautifully proportioned. The line of her profile, from her forehead to the tip of her nose, followed a perfectly smooth line, just as I'd seen in Smith's photographs and just as in the famous bust, with no sign of the usual indentation or ridge at the top of the nose. Her eyes were closed beneath the faint traces of her eyebrows, and the contours of her face had been preserved with a very thin layer of embalming resin. The same resins had also preserved the distinct impression of something worn tightly around the forehead above the ears, and although the right ear was missing, broken off long ago, the left was intact. Much to my surprise, its lobe was pierced with two large holes, far larger than the 'small perforations' Smith had described. As large as those in the boy's ears beside her, the holes were big enough to have taken some very large earrings.

I tried to imagine her in all her finery, jewel-encrusted earrings swinging from delicate lobes peeping out from the bottom of the short wig Loret had originally found beside her. Beneath this her head was completely shaven, her lack of hair certainly accentuating her face and long, thin neck. Her head was so perfectly shaven that I could find virtually no trace of stubble. Yet the skin was covered in the same thin layer of mid-brown resin used on the other two individuals, and a hole in the front of her skull, once again caused by robbers, allowed us to check if the brain had been removed. And much to our surprise it hadn't, suggesting a link between the Younger Woman and the boy.

Sadly, as I knew only too well from Smith's photographs, the hole in the skull was not the only damage that had been inflicted on this mummy. Her face had been bashed in, the mouth so severely damaged that many of her teeth were missing. Why would thieves attack the mouth, where nothing of value was ever placed? It just didn't make sense, unless it had been done maliciously. And it certainly looked malicious to us, not only disfiguring the woman's face but, even more seriously, preventing her breathing in the Afterlife.

Who would have inflicted such terrible damage? It may have been those responsible for reburying the royal dead, the priests of Amen. If this was Nefertiti, they would have had good reason to despise someone who had played such a leading role during the tumultuous Amarna Period. I could well imagine them trying to destroy her chance of an Afterlife through violent methods which stopped short of destroying the body, which would have jeopardised their own souls when facing the Final Judgment.

The damage to the chest was far more understandable. Both Stephen and I, like Smith before us, assumed it to have been the work of tomb robbers, hacking the mummy about in their search for valuables in the customary neck and chest area. Their handiwork had also exposed the internal packing of linen, once again overlaid with mud. Her abdomen was densely packed with many rolls of linen padding, the area inside and beneath the embalming incision packed with more mud and what appeared to be small pieces of limestone. Thinking that this might be debris from her original place of burial, we discussed what kind of information geological analysis of the rock type might be able to reveal.

There was damage to her protruding left hip, which had clearly been struck with some sort of blade, perhaps by thieves searching for the gold embalming plates sometimes used to cover the incision, as in the case of Tiy's father, Yuya. Given all the other similarities between these three bodies and those of Tiy's superbly mummified parents, it was a distinct possibility that these three too had had gold plates applied over their embalming incisions. And the incision in the Younger Woman, in the same unexpected place as those we'd seen on the Elder Woman and Boy, again suggested a different way of doing things during the vagaries of the Amarna Period.

Now it was time to tackle the enigma of the arms. Covered

in the thinnest coating of resin and fine linen, the Younger Woman's left arm extended down the side of the body and her hand was laid over her thigh. But as we knew from Smith's report, her right arm had been ripped away or hacked off in ancient times just below the shoulder – something I'd always felt may have been done to remove a sceptre she could have been holding, thus forcibly stripping away her symbols of power.

Just as in his original photographs, we could see the twisted, ragged remnants of dried up muscle tissue on the stump of the right arm. Yet, as I'd noticed earlier that day, there was no sign of the remains of the bent up right arm that Smith had seen on his visit here in 1907; instead, a second right arm that he hadn't mentioned had now appeared. It was completely straight and minus the hand, and the damage made it difficult to gauge its original length, so Stephen measured it and found it was almost 2cm longer than the corresponding part of the woman's remaining left arm. Nor did the fine-textured, resin-soaked linen at the top of this extended loose arm appear to match that remaining on her right shoulder. So this loose limb may not have belonged to her after all. What we really needed in order to work it out were X-rays, which would also be useful in studying her legs, still covered in layers of fine brown linen.

Completely immersed in our work as we examined, measured, photographed, sketched and scribbled notes, we were oblivious to the growing crowd gathering at the entrance to the side chamber. Amidst much throat-clearing and eye-rolling, the inspectors decided that our time was up. With the Valley about to close to visitors, they still had to seal up the wall again and plaster it over. So, with great reluctance and many a backward glance, we slowly and carefully climbed back out into the burial chamber and let the workmen move in.

I suddenly felt incredibly emotional and, when asked that classic if unoriginal question 'How do you feel?' I answered like a child who has just seen fairies at the bottom of the garden. I'd been allowed a glimpse of these incredible people after waiting for twelve years, and now they were about to disappear. Within little more than minutes it was difficult to believe that the wall had ever been removed. As the final coat of plaster was applied, one of the inspectors kindly asked if I'd like to write the date in the top left corner as a record of when the chamber was last entered. Forming my clumsy Arabic numerals into the wet plaster, I thought about the countless tomb doorways which had been sealed and inscribed in this way elsewhere in the Valley during the last three and a half thousand years, and felt incredibly privileged. Crossing the Nile that evening as the sun set behind us, the feeling of disbelief was replaced by a huge rush of adrenaline-fuelled excitement. It had been a truly phenomenal experience.

Having examined the mummification techniques used on all three bodies for himself, Stephen was convinced that they all dated to the second half of the 18th dynasty. I'd also been able to add my own observations to everything Smith had seen – except of course for the arm, whose disappearance was a mystery. Our animated discussion about brain removal, embalming fluids and hacked-off limbs continued for hours in the hotel bar, and anyone listening in must have wondered what they'd wandered into.

We were now both convinced that the three were not members of Amenhotep II's family, as had been so often assumed. Because they resembled so closely the mummies of Tiy's parents, Yuya and Tuya, the three were surely linked to this later branch of the royal house. And as had been suggested back in the 1970s, if the Elder Woman was Tiy, then the young prince could just be her eldest son, Prince Tuthmosis. This would give us Akhenaten's mother and elder brother, side by side with the Younger Woman who had been embalmed in a very similar way and was surely in some way connected with them.

If only we'd had more time, or the means of finding out their ages and possible cause of death or whatever other secrets they might have held. But, to quote Howard Carter, it had certainly been 'the day of days, the most wonderful that I have ever lived through, and certainly one whose like I can never hope to see again'. Or so I thought at the time.

Back in the UK we began to talk through our findings with a small group of trusted colleagues, and as hundreds of emails flew between Yorkshire and Ohio, I discussed many of the mummies' unusual features with my colleague Earl Ertman. We were both intrigued that the double-pierced lobe seems only to appear on some of the statues of Nefertiti and one of her daughters, and on the mummy of Tiy's mother, Tuya. And Earl's work on Amarna crowns, dating back to the 1970s, suggested to him that the impression on the Younger Woman's forehead had been caused by a gold brow band, a piece of regalia only worn by reigning kings and their chief wife. After long deliberation, we also spoke with the American television company Discovery who were funding our work, and decided we had nothing to lose by putting together a proposal in the hope of getting permission to go back into the tomb with a team of experts, led by our York colleague Don Brothwell.

Needing to carry out full X-rays of all three bodies, we approached King's College Hospital in London and the King's centre for the Assessment of Radiological Equipment (KCARE). Advisers to the National Health Service since 1979, the KCARE team had a wealth of experience using all kinds of X-ray equipment, and so we travelled down to London one rainy autumn day to meet their principal physicist, Alistair Mackenzie, and superintendent radiographer, Andrea Bates. We needed to know if it would be possible to take the X-rays *in situ*, and they suggested the newly designed digital X-ray detector with a portable X-ray tube made by Canon. This was ideal for imaging in restricted spaces such as the tomb's small side chamber. The most impressive part was that Canon's equipment incorporated digital imaging, which gave an instant X-ray image on the computer screen. It was all a far cry from the days when the film had to be taken off to the nearest suitable place for development, which in the case of the X-rays of Tutankhamen's mummy taken in 1967 was a 'commodious bathroom' at the Winter Palace Hotel!

But what if the equipment was unsuited to the unusual conditions? Before any such cutting-edge technology could be flown to Egypt, sent across the Nile and manoeuvred into position in a small rock-cut chamber in the remote Valley of the Kings, we'd have to organise a trial run closer to home. We needed to work out the optimum dimensions of the metal support arms which would hold the X-ray camera in place within the limited space of the side chamber, and we also needed to test the kinds of results we'd get from a mummified body rather than a live patient.

So we went to see our long-time colleague Angela Thomas, curator of archaeology at Bolton Museum, to ask her somewhat tentatively if it would be possible to 'borrow' one of her mummies. And could we also bring along a team of scientists, radiographers, engineers, computer operators and technicians, and the TV crew who would be filming it all?

'Of course,' she replied, never batting an eyelid. Now that's the kind of curator you don't find every day!

The subject selected was the unwrapped mummy of an anonymous, shaven-headed man. His rigid body was carefully lifted out from its painted coffin and delicately placed on top of the protective glass cover of his sarcophagus. Then the digital detector was gently slid underneath his head while the X-ray machine was swung into position, the red light beam from the machine highlighting his ancient features. As Andrea donned her lead apron and stood by the body, we all stepped a safe distance away before she pressed the button to take the first shot. Within a second it had appeared on the nearby computer screen – a crisp, high-quality image revealing the internal workings of one of Bolton's very own ancient Egyptians. We were all delighted with the quality of the image. As a series of others were taken and assessed for technical and positioning details we behaved like a group of children with a new toy as we crowded around the monitor, able to magnify parts of the image in order to concentrate on specific details.

Much to our amazement, we eventually received official permission from the Egyptian authorities to go ahead with our unusual project, the first time in more than a quarter of a century that such a large-scale expedition had been allowed into the world's most famous graveyard. And with everything ready to go for February 2003, it was with a real sense of anticipation and not a few nerves that I set off to Egypt once again.

This time I'd be getting answers from an entire team including some of the world's leading experts in their field. And although I was happy to give them the historical background and fill in as many of the blanks as possible I didn't want to colour their judgement, so simply stated the facts as they existed at the time – that many authorities thought the three were relatives of the tomb owner, Amenhotep II, and the suggestion that one might be Queen Tiy had not been completely accepted.

There were no guarantees that we'd be able to prove the Younger Woman was who I thought she might be, but it would certainly be exciting to discover all we could about both her and her two companions. It was going to be interesting. Completely and utterly nerve-racking of course, but interesting none the less.

12

THE SCIENTIFIC EXPEDITION
AND ITS AFTERMATH

As we waited by the entrance to the tomb, a long line of men advanced up the Valley towards us in a modern-day version of the ancient funerary procession that brought all the equipment the deceased would require in the Afterlife. But this time there were no coffins, no funerary figures or jars of food and drink, no ostrich feather fans, perfumes, wigs or jewels. Instead, the large red chest contained computer equipment and the metal boxes housed the X-ray machine; the wooden crates were filled with bright blue lead aprons and the long lengths of metal would support a camera rather than a funeral pall. And then of course came all the lights, the wires and the strange-looking bits of kit the television crew and still photographers would be needing over the next few days as they scrutinised us scrutinising the mummies.

In fact it took a total of twenty-two men to deliver everything our team would need down to the burial chamber, and once there, everything had to be set up before the wall could once again be pulled down. Accompanying the long line of porters were Neil Staff and Andy Gaskin from the Xograph company, who would be operating the cutting-edge imaging equipment that had been so carefully adapted for the task ahead. While they were hard at work putting together all the computers beneath the star-spangled ceiling of the 3500-year-old burial chamber, the rest of us waited in the shade of the tourist shelter outside the tomb entrance.

Don, Stephen and I discussed the logistics with Alastair and Andrea, and I tried to set the scene with the help of the tomb plans provided at the entrance for tourists. Pointing out where the three mummies were in relation to the rest of the tomb, I answered their questions as best I could without giving too much away, explaining why the three were still in there and what their relationship was to the tomb owner. Summing up the mummies' convoluted history over the last three thousand years, not to mention trying to explain why I was so interested in them, required considerable mental gymnastics while trying to remain as objective as possible.

Far more used to working with the living, Alistair and Andrea saw the prospect of X-raying three long-dead Egyptians in the Valley of the Kings as something of a change. And whilst Don had been studying ancient bodies from all over the world for the last forty years, he too was visiting the Valley of the Kings for the first time.

As we waited in the rapidly shrinking shade we were joined by a very glamorous lady in a fur-trimmed jacket, lipstick and wonderful earrings. Samia el-Merghani, conservator at the Cairo Museum, was a key member of our expedition, sent by Dr Hawass to ensure that the project was 'undertaken under the full control and supervision of the Supreme Council of Antiquities'. Although we would simply be taking X-rays, a technique which causes the minimum disturbance to the mummies themselves, it would still be necessary for Andrea to place the digital detector plate beneath each body. Samia would be there to oversee the delicate process.

As Andy and Neil completed the fine-tuning of the state-of-the-art equipment we went down into the burial chamber and took in the scene, the two of them in lab coats standing behind a bank of computers flanked by ancient images of Amenhotep II and the gods. Even they, for all their mystical powers, had surely seen nothing like this! The temperature had already begun its inexorable rise to over 100°F, and we all watched and held our breath to see if the heat and humidity, or indeed the long journey, had had any effect on the delicate balance of the equipment. But as the power was switched on, the computer screens suddenly lit up and whirred into life. They seemed not to mind their unusual surroundings in the slightest, much to our relief. Since the Valley's electricity supply was somewhat erratic – surely little different from the day it was installed a century earlier – an extra generator had been brought in to ensure that the power source would not cut out part way through the work.

Then it was time to repeat that moment when the wall came down bit by bit and the black hole began to grow. Delighted to see the mummies again, I was also keen to have the team's first impressions of the three extraordinary individuals who awaited us.

'Who wants to come and have a look?'

As a man who lives and breathes human remains, Don was there like a shot. Taking it all in, he agreed that although all three were rather dusty, they were in a very good state of preservation.

We put on our lab coats and face masks, and Samia led the way as we began to brush away the fine grey dust which clung to the three mummies. Carefully working our way down each one as the dusty layers of centuries gave way to hidden features, we finally arrived at the mass of linen wrappings which still surrounded the Younger Woman's legs. Samia held a section up to the light, appreciating its fine, semi-transparent quality. It was obvious that it was incredibly high-status linen.

'Only for kings,' she pointed out.

Then, as she picked up another section, we noticed something lying underneath the wrappings, close beside the right leg.

'What's that under there?' I asked her. 'Fingers! There are some fingers here.'

And as she gently pulled away the linen, the right arm was slowly revealed in a fine haze of mummy dust swirling gently up into the light. Lost for almost a hundred years, here was the missing limb. I was so delighted I hugged her!

So Smith *had* seen it back in 1907, a right hand and forearm just as his report said, with flexing at the elbow and the hand in a clasped posture, still clutching at a long-gone sceptre. Having been hidden in the wrappings for a century it was far cleaner than the dust-covered bodies surrounding it, and there seemed to be a reddish stain, maybe henna, around the nails. Don believed from the proportions that it was a woman's arm, and since the original bent up position described by Smith was indicative of a pharaoh the importance of the find was self-explanatory.

But it also meant our Younger Woman now had two right arms, and before getting too carried away we would have to X-ray both this bent arm and the detached extended arm which still lay beside the body to see which one 'fitted' – if indeed either of them did. When the three mummies and their assorted arms and loose feet were finally dusted down it was time to set up the aluminium frame which had been specially made to hold and manoeuvre the X-ray machine over each body in turn. And this was probably the most nerve-racking part of all – one tiny slip and the mummies would be crushed, either by the rig collapsing or by the X-ray machine above them crashing down.

Yet once again Andy and Neil performed their hi-tech duties with great dexterity, as if setting up an X-ray rig over ancient mummies in a hot, cramped tomb was something they did every day. Then, with everything ready to go, the two men came back out into the burial chamber to operate the computers while Andrea, Alastair and Samia put on their lead aprons and climbed into the side chamber with the mummies.

Beginning with the Elder Woman, Andrea and Samia carefully slid the detector plate into position beneath her head and shoulders while Alastair checked the settings on the camera. As the rest of us stood outside, looking in, Andrea lined up the machine directly over the Elder Woman's face and pressed the button. A split second later the image flashed up before us on screen, revealing the superb bone structure responsible for creating such a wonderful face. As Andrea took a further series of X-rays of the skull we crowded round the screens and Don scrutinised each image in turn, commenting on her 'noticeable upper incisor overjet' – the 18th dynasty royals' characteristic buck teeth – together with 'well-defined but small frontal sinuses'.

He then asked Neil to zoom in to the area at the top of the nose, where the embalmers traditionally inserted a long metal probe to break through the ethmoid bone to extract the brain. But there was no evidence of any damage here at all; indeed, Don then pointed out the decomposed brain tissue within her skull cavity. Clearly the Elder Woman's brain hadn't been removed, which was just what we'd seen with the Boy and Younger Woman on our previous visit – a further link reinforcing the idea that they were all exhibiting a break with traditional mummification procedures.

As Andrea continued to take X-rays down the Elder Woman's body, we suddenly noticed a dark object on the screen. What on earth could it be? Some sort of strange amulet, perhaps? We zoomed in and turned the image around, but our excitement soon died down when we realised that this was simply one of the nails that Loret's carpenters had used when building the board to support the body. But there was something else there, too, and as Stephen craned forward he pointed out what looked like small white blobs which had started to appear inside the body and which Don described as a 'snowflake effect'. The quality of the digital images offered clear evidence to Stephen that a distinctive type of embalming fluid had been used to mummify the Elder Woman. And as the images continued down the body, the snowflake effect continued too, raising intriguing questions as to what exactly the embalmers had been trying out here.

Looking at the bones themselves, their condition revealed that this was someone who had suffered no periods of illness or malnutrition – more evidence of a high-status, well cared for individual. And because the long bones had all fused we were certainly dealing with an adult. Since 'the pubic symphysis (the front surface between the two halves of the pelvis) appears to be reasonably flat and the teeth are moderately worn', Don suggested the woman was perhaps thirty-five to forty-five or even older, her middle age 'confirmed by the moderate osteophyte development on the lowest two lumbar vertebrae' – so a bit of back pain in later life, perhaps.

Another useful feature of the digital imaging was that we could take accurate measurements on screen, from the thickness of the bones to the dimensions of various features, including the tops of each arm. The woman's right arm was straight down and her left one bent up, which explained why the head of the right humerus appeared to be almost a centimetre wider than the left, since the bent position of the left arm had presented a narrower angle on the X-ray image.

There was also a certain amount of damage to some of the bones, although this was almost certainly post-mortem damage. Possibly caused during the mummification process, when the embalmers didn't always take the greatest of care with their uncomplaining clients, it may also have occurred during the grave-robbing or when transporting the mummy over some distance.

Yet X-rays of the left foot revealed that the robbers had missed something. As Andrea later noticed, there was definitely something flat and metallic, most likely a piece of gold foil, stuck between the toes. Gold caps were sometimes placed on the individual fingers and toes of the elite to preserve the nails during mummification, although her suggestion of 'foil' also brought to mind the gold mummy wrappings inscribed with Tiy's name and reportedly recovered from the Amarna Royal Tomb, and those which had covered the KV.55 body. So was this an example of the Amarna practice of wrapping dead royals in sheet gold?

As the lead-clad Andrea, Alastair and Samia took a well-deserved break from the suffocating side chamber we continued to pore over the images, completely immersed in our various

scenarios and possibilities. Then, with the rig and camera carefully adjusted over the body of the Boy, the central mummy of
the three, Andrea began the process all over again and the first
image flashed on to the screen.

His exceptionally wide skull was clear to see, its dimensions
really only comparable with those of the skulls of Amenhotep
III, Tutankhamen and the mysterious body from KV.55 that
some believe to be Akhenaten.

Don then turned to his teeth. 'Hmmm . . . erupted permanent
canines . . . second molars almost completely formed . . . partly
erupted, and his third molar crowns only partly formed.' The
dental evidence suggested the boy must have died at around
twelve years old, give or take six months.

But then as Andrea moved down the body we saw that
some of the long bones were close to fusion, suggesting he
might actually have been closer to fourteen or fifteen. Stephen
also pointed out the snowflake effect which could be seen
throughout the Boy's body, so he'd been prepared with the
same type of embalming fluid as the Elder Woman. And, just
as in her case, the ethmoid bone inside the top of his nose was
intact.

As Neil and Andy brought up the stored image of the Elder
Woman's profile side by side as a comparison, Don was suddenly
struck by the remarkable similarity of their profiles.

'Look at that. It certainly suggests a close family relationship.'

'Close enough to be mother and son?'

'Yes, indeed.'

That was amazing. If the Elder Woman was Tiy, this was
most likely her son Tuthmosis, whose death had allowed his
younger brother Akhenaten to take the throne. And if this was
indeed Prince Tuthmosis, how had he died?

There was severe damage to the chest area, which we all
assumed to have been caused by tomb robbers as in the case of
the Elder Woman, but Don seemed more interested in the area
around the top of the boy's right leg. We'd already noticed that

this leg appeared to be slightly shorter than his left, and the X-rays soon revealed why. Zooming in on his right hip, we saw a massive injury. The head of the femur was wrenched out of position and driven right back, and there was no doubt that it had been severely dislocated. Given the small amount of new bone growth around the femur head it seemed that the boy had survived, for a short time at least, although he must have been in agony. Don agreed that this could have been linked to the cause of death.

I wondered if the family obsession with fast horses and chariot racing had had anything to do with the prince's horrific injury. And could the gilded whip handle belonging to 'king's son, troop commander, Tuthmosis' once have belonged to him?

Moving down the narrow legs, we saw that the Boy's feet, like the Elder Woman's, had again been detached at some stage, and both were missing the big toes and several smaller ones. And as we completed our examination of the Boy and Elder Woman I really did want to start calling them by the names Tiy and Tuthmosis . . .

It was closing time in the Valley before we realised. Just as the previous occasion, our one-track conversation continued from the moment we all left the tomb and sailed back over the Nile to the moment we turned in several hours later.

Next day we were up bright and early, ready to get back into the tomb to begin work on the Younger Woman. This was it, the culmination of so much preparation. But what would we discover?

We resumed our places in front of the screens, and Andrea once again began to guide the machine into position. As the image of the Younger Woman's skull appeared before us we noticed some similarities with her two burial companions, although the likeness was not as marked as it was between the Elder Woman and the Boy. Quite possibly we were looking at a member of the family – but not of the immediate family.

The roughly triangular hole in the front of her skull was

almost certainly a post-mortem injury likely to have been inflicted by the same tomb robbers who had damaged the Boy in the same way. The images also revealed that the ethmoid bone inside the top of her nose was again intact, and a mass of desiccated brain tissue was clearly visible within the skull. And with the snowflake effect clearly seen throughout the body, the same kinds of embalming fluid had been used too. So now we had clear evidence of unusual but consistent mummification techniques.

Commenting that the face was 'fairly gracile', Don started looking at the teeth – or at least what was left of them following the severe damage to the mouth. As he peered closely at the image, he pointed out that some of the wisdom teeth weren't fully erupted.

'So the individual's young, or youngish – late teens, early adult.'

I looked at him. 'Early adult, you say?', trying to keep my voice as level as possible.

'Maybe fifteen to nineteen.'

Well, that's it, I thought. I've been chasing an illusion. This can't be who I thought it was. Suddenly everything started to slow down for me. Even taking into account the knowledge that ancient Egyptian women married as young as ten and started to produce children soon afterwards, it was a well-known fact that Nefertiti had had six children over an eight- or nine-year period. It wasn't possible for someone aged between fifteen and nineteen to have done so. With so many other clues pointing unmistakably to a royal female of the late 18th dynasty with links to Amarna, this must surely be a younger woman, maybe one of Nefertiti's children, either Meritaten or Ankhesenamen, the two known to have survived at least until early adulthood.

Oblivious to my mental somersaults as I tried to work out who on earth this could be, Don continued to peruse the teeth. Pointing out that some showed signs of dental caries, he commented that this may have been someone with a sweet tooth, perhaps someone who regularly consumed luxuriously prepared foods and sweetened drinks – an indication of a pampered lifestyle. And again the bones revealed no sign of prolonged illness, suggesting a high-status, well cared for individual.

And then we saw them: small shapes which certainly didn't look like carpenter's nails. Beginning around the jaw area, and then moving down into the ribcage, were a number of little metal amulets, possibly made of gold, and at least twelve small beads.

'Aha! That's not normal packing.'

'Can we zoom in on those?' I asked Andy and Neil. 'That looks like one of the tiny amulets that they used as jewellery – a nefer shape, often worn in profusion around the neck!'

Measuring the ⚱ nefer-shaped amulets on screen, we found they were about 1cm long and almost certainly would have been part of a broad collar consisting of amulets and small beads. In fact such a collar had been found around the neck of the mysterious Amarna royal in nearby KV.55, made up of exactly the same shaped 'gold pendants and inlaid plaques connected by rows of minute beads'. Presumably the amulets and beads we were now seeing on screen must have broken free when tomb robbers ripped the jewellery from her neck, scattering loose beads which had then fallen down inside the damaged body cavities – yet another secret the Younger Woman had kept very much to herself. We had literally found hidden treasure in the Valley of the Kings – a tremendous cliché, but quite a thrill nevertheless.

As Andrea continued to send through image after image, working her way down the torso, Don announced that 'the proximal radius epiphysis appears to have united with the radius shaft'. Now this, when translated, sounded a little more promising. Apparently the general condition of the spine and major joints, and the fact that all the parts of the long bones were fused, suggested an age of about twenty-five, although, as both

Don and Andrea later agreed, she 'could have been as old as thirty'. Then Don pointed out that there was also the possibility of very early arthritis in the vertebrae, again suggesting a fully mature individual.

By this point, my brain felt as though it had been put through a mangle, and as we took a short break I sat on the steps of the burial chamber to think. People came and went, carrying in equipment, moving cables and keeping a constant check on all the electrics in the tomb, as I tried to take stock of everything so far. The teeth suggested youth and the body suggested someone older, which all seemed pretty odd to me. How could there be such a wide range of possible ages with a single body? But, as Andrea told me later, 'there's really no such thing as an average body'.

And, of course, there was the mysterious mummy from tomb KV.55 just across the way, which, as all Egyptologists know, had first been assessed as old, then as young, then as old and most recently as young again. Not only that, but it was first thought to be a woman, then declared male after all. Reminding Don of our recent experience in Hull, when our Egyptian princess had turned out to be a man for all his 'gracile bone structure, delicate brow ridge and wide pelvis', I asked him what he thought about the Younger Woman. Could she too be a man after all, as Loret and others had suggested?

None of us had found any evidence of male genitals, and as the pelvis appeared on the screen Don peered at it closely. Taking in all the tell-tale details, he announced that 'the width, shape and depth of the sciatic notch is consistent with a female', just as Elliot Smith had stated. And Andrea also agreed that this was 'most definitely' a female pelvis. What a relief!

As we now had such a clear image, could we also tell from the pelvis just how many children the woman had produced? Having worked in the past with human remains specialists who had studied the pelvic bones to find out whether the muscles had undergone the strain of childbirth, and if so how many times, I wondered if these were visible in this case. But Don explained that the method had been discredited as unreliable several years ago. A pity, as this information would have added considerably to what we already knew of the woman who lay before us.

As we continued to study the images Andrea was taking in stages down the body we came to the lowest part of the spine, where the last lumbar vertebra appeared 'abnormally angular'. From the otherwise straight position of the rest of the spine and body, Don deduced that this couldn't be the result of the embalmers failing to lay out the body properly during mummification. Instead, he believed it to be evidence of scoliosis, an abnormal curvature of the spine.

'It could well have caused a certain amount of abnormal back posture in life,' he said; and, as I tried to imagine the woman standing or sitting, I remembered that the famous Berlin bust had originally been carved with one shoulder slightly higher than the other until the sculptor had perfected its symmetry with a layer of plaster. Quite possibly a simple coincidence, but curious all the same. Apparently Tiy's mother, Tuya, had suffered from mild scoliosis, and when the elder foetus from Tutankhamen's tomb was X-rayed in the late 1970s she too was found to have suffered from this condition. But with a shoulder deformity and spina bifida too, this tiny granddaughter of Nefertiti would have been quite severely disabled had she lived.

Beneath the piles of fine linen which still concealed most of the Younger Woman's legs, the feet had once again been detached at some stage, as with the Elder Woman and the Boy.

And in the Younger Woman's case, someone had inflicted damage on the arms too. There were a couple of fractures on the upper part of the intact left arm, and Don believed the sharpness of the edges of one of them suggested that the injury had occurred soon before death or perhaps post-mortem, maybe, like that on the Elder Woman, when the body was being moved, or even perhaps when jewellery was being ripped from her arms.

As we already knew, her right arm had been torn off altogether just below the shoulder joint – with considerable force, to judge by the twisted remains of exposed muscle tissue and the jagged ends of the remaining bone, which came up very clearly on the computer screen. But which arm had once been attached to this stump of bone? Was it the extended arm we'd first seen lying there, which certainly looked the part, even if it was a little too long? Or was it our newly discovered bent forearm, the one originally seen by Smith in 1907 and then rediscovered, hidden beneath piles of wrappings? Or perhaps neither?

As Andrea set up the extended arm for X-raying we were keen to compare both loose limbs with the fracture, taking careful measurements as well as checking bone density to compare with the remaining left arm. On the extended arm, the jagged bone at the top certainly looked a promising match to the equally jagged stump remaining. Whichever arm it was had clearly been quite brutally detached, and yet the extended arm had survived relatively intact. This seemed strange – particularly at the elbow, where such force could well have caused it to come apart. Then of course there was the almost-2cm difference in length when compared to the remaining left arm, and the mismatch in the linens and resins used to preserve them. Then we looked at the recently rediscovered bent arm. Don again remarked that the proportions suggested it had belonged to a female adult. But with only the forearm present, and not the upper fractured section, it was impossible to make an accurate comparison without further study and analysis. So we decided to look for other clues, beginning with the way both arms had been mummified.

Using the snowflake effect for comparison, Stephen looked back at the arms of all three mummies and found that this distinctive embalming treatment had been applied to both the upper arms and forearms of the Elder Woman and the Boy. But in the case of the Younger Woman, only her remaining left upper arm had been treated in this way; for some reason, her left forearm had not. Assuming the same should be true of whichever right arm was hers, he was able to demonstrate that the extended arm didn't match but the right forearm did, and of the two it was the one which conformed more closely to her remaining left arm.

But, playing devil's advocate, what if neither of the arms belonged to the body? Could we try to find out, just from the position of the remaining stump, exactly how the right arm had originally been laid out?

Once again the digital images allowed us to compare the arm positions of all three, measuring on screen across the head of the humerus in each case. As we knew in the case of the Elder Woman, the fact that her left arm was bent up had caused the diameter of the head of the left humerus to differ markedly from the measurement across the head of the right humerus, since her right arm was straight down at her side. As for the Boy, with both hands down at the front of his body the measurements across the head of both the right and left humerus should have been identical, as indeed they were. So far, so good.

So then we took the same measurements on the Younger Woman, and got much the same difference as we saw in the Elder Woman – clear evidence that her original right arm had been placed in a completely different position from her left and could not have been laid out straight at the side. The measurements suggested that the Younger Woman's right arm had in fact been bent up at quite a sharp angle, confirming the original belief that she had been laid out in the posture and position of a pharaoh.

Having taken a complete set of X-rays of each of the three mummies in turn, Andrea and Alastair's work was over and the X-ray rig was dismantled. With the side chamber clear again, it was time for Don to inspect the bodies at close range and look for any clues which might suggest a cause of death. I was also keen for him to examine the damage done to the three in ancient times – damage which was generally regarded as the result of tomb robbery but some of which looked malicious.

I followed him round with a small dictaphone so that I could catch his observations and go through them again later. We began, as before, with the Elder Woman. Peering at the pitting to her face, he suggested that this might be some kind of post-mortem skin change caused by the mummification process. I asked him if it might be evidence of some disease she may have suffered in life, in the same way that the marks on the face of Ramses V's mummy were thought to have been caused by small-pox. But without the possibility of taking samples, we could only speculate. An interesting possibility, none the less.

Moving to the extensive damage to her torso, we could find nothing to suggest that it wasn't the handiwork of brutal tomb robbers stripping away the gold. Yet Don doubted Smith's origi-nal belief that she had suffered from an ulcer on the left heel, as he had found no evidence for this in the X-rays. With no evidence for anything particularly sinister having happened to her body, we moved on to the Boy, where a very different picture began to emerge.

Except for a puncture hole in the right frontal area of the skull his face was intact, but there was severe damage to the upper left side of his chest. After carefully examining and meas-uring the area, Don stood back and thought for a while.

'Now this poses some very interesting forensic questions,' he said finally.

Clearly not the single 'large gash' referred to in passing by Smith, it was a real mess. Don believed it to be the result of 'an axe-size weapon being driven into the chest at least five times'. Pointing out where the blows had repeatedly cut clean through the bone, he said part of the chest wall had been dragged away each time the weapon had been pulled back. Yet he could find no sign that the chest had then collapsed or splintered as it would have done if the mummy was completely dried out and rigid at the time of the attack, when the segment of chest pulled back also appeared to have been soft and malleable. As he peered further into the Boy's gaping chest cavity with his torch and magnifying glass, neither of us could see any trace of linen in the cuts, suggesting that the axe damage had been inflicted either before it had been wrapped, or, more likely, after it had first been unwrapped.

Don then asked if it was possible that the body was still being prepared when the attack took place. But, knowing just how good the ancient embalmers were at patching up damage, they would almost certainly have done all they could to restore the prince's torso. Still, why would anyone want to start hacking away at a young lad like this? All I could suggest was that they wanted to get at the wealth of jewellery which would have festooned the boy's neck and chest, the area we were now looking at.

As we had seen from the X-ray profiles, the boy was almost certainly a son of the Elder Woman, who, as Don knew, was possibly Queen Tiy. And if the boy was the royal prince Tuthmosis, his funerary figurine clearly shows a large amulet spread across his chest, described in the *Book of the Dead* as 'a human-headed bird of gold inlaid with precious stones laid on the breast of the mummy'. Certainly a treasure worth stealing, but why with an axe?

This was nothing, however, compared to what we were about to see with the Younger Woman, whose body had been damaged far more extensively than either of her companions. Don looked down at the place where the entire left part of her mouth gaped wide open. Scrutinising the wound closely, he used a metal ruler to demonstrate the way in which someone had stood over her body, just over her left shoulder in fact, to bring down a terrible blow.

'Right here, in fact, an axe or machete-type weapon hacked into the face, cutting clean through the jawbone, carrying away some of the upper teeth and breaking off some lower teeth.' It was impossible not to wince at the ferocity of such an attack.

And, just as we had seen with the Boy, the Younger Woman's face showed no sign of collapse or splintering around the wound. This would have been expected if her body had been completely rigid and dry, as it would certainly have been by the time the mummies had been reburied around 1000 BC, over three hundred years after their deaths. So the damage hadn't been inflicted by those who had reburied them, as I'd first thought, but had happened earlier, and not too long after death. And, with no trace of a single linen thread in any of the cuts, her face could not have been wrapped when the damage was inflicted.

The conclusion was inescapable. Whoever had attacked her body by hacking into her face had been able to see exactly who they were attacking. This had been no accident.

Then, moving down to the side of the body, Don examined a fairly straight cut about 12cm long just below the woman's left breast first pointed out by Samia. He pointed out that there were traces of white body fat (adipocere) visible around the break in the skin, indicating that this was something done either in life or immediately after death. Looking at the position of the wound, he decided it couldn't have been produced by a blow directly to the front of the body, but was the result of an angled stab injury which had glanced off the ribs. Although this seemed to be a flesh wound which had inflicted only superficial damage to the ribs and so hadn't been apparent on the X-rays, they had shown up a fracture on the upper part of her left arm, an injury which Don had already suggested might have occurred close to death. So had this woman tried to defend herself by raising her arms as someone tried to slide a sharp blade into her side? And if so, I asked Don, could it have killed her?

'Well, yes, maybe through blood loss. Having looked at all the wounds, murder can't be ruled out. But it's something that needs further investigation.'

In fact he'd already started to plan experiments that we could carry out back in the lab at York, to simulate the damage we'd seen on the mummies. And that is exactly what happened.

At the end of our fourth day, with all three mummies X-rayed, examined, measured and photographed, the computers were unplugged, the wires and cables taken up and the world's most unusual X-ray machine put securely back in its safe-like box. And as the wall was finally put back, I had the distinct feeling that this really would be the last time I'd ever see the mummies. Although we now had hundreds of photographs, X-rays and hours of detailed footage courtesy of the ever-present film crew, I realised that this was probably the end of the line as far as face-to-face encounters were concerned. A poignant moment.

As the porters returned to take everything back out of the tomb, I hung around for as long as possible before leaving myself. Slowly the procession of equipment made its way back down the Valley, followed by Samia and me. Whilst I looked my usual bedraggled self, she was as glamorous as ever, lipstick intact and earrings dangling beneath her neat hair. I said I admired her taste in earrings, and before I could say anything else she had taken them off and placed them in my hand. Looking down at the two amber and silver treasures in my palm, I remembered the two holes in the Younger Woman's ear and, deciding the impromptu gift was somehow fitting, I accepted her generous gesture.

With addresses exchanged and goodbyes said, we returned to the UK that evening and, back in York, prepared the official report required by the Egyptian authorities on the work we had done, also expressing the hope that further forensic studies could continue on the three bodies. We also continued to work through the great stack of digital images, as did Andrea and her consultant colleagues at KCARE in London.

With all their different specialities, the team were able to shed light on all manner of intriguing details. One of the consultant radiologists, an expert at interpreting X-ray images, studied the X-rays and told us that the Younger Woman's scoliosis was 'fairly minor and would probably not be obvious in life except when seen from behind, becoming more obvious when bending forward. But when fully clothed, it would probably be unnoticeable.'

They also provided plenty of supporting information about her original arm position after we'd made further comparisons between the X-ray images and the departmental skeleton. These revealed that her right arm could indeed have been bent up at an angle, something which would confirm the Younger Woman's possible pharaonic posture.

And then, of course, Don's recreation of the ancient damage through experimental trauma also added greatly to the picture. We gathered in the lab on a very wet Monday morning to begin preparing two dead pigs – the nearest thing to a human body, and regularly used in such experiments. I have to say I was having second thoughts about my role as I began to wind great lengths of linen strips round and round the posterior regions of these dead creatures in the manner of an ancient mummy. One was a fresh carcass and the other had been thoroughly dried out to give the effect of a mummified body. And with half the body wrapped and the other half left unwrapped, it would also be possible to see what effect the wrappings had.

Then the real work began, using blades which closely resembled the ancient weapons. I'd also consulted the colleague who had drawn the profiles of the Younger Woman and the Berlin bust for me way back in 1990, and who now had a PhD on Egyptian soldiers and their weapons. After examining photographs of the mummies' wounds in detail, she agreed that an axe seemed to fit the bill as the weapon which had destroyed much of the boy's chest. 'But as for our "friend",' she added, 'I'd suggest that someone had a go at her with a short-sword, a kind of elaborate dagger with quite a fine blade. The difference also suggests that there was a difference in intent, and rather than her face just being bashed in at random, the use of the short-sword seems to suggest someone more in control.'

So a picture was building up of someone very deliberately

inflicting terrible damage using a sharp metal blade. Metal was a very precious commodity in ancient Egypt, so such blades would not have been available to just anyone, and the use of some sort of dagger-like weapon suggested someone of quite high status.

With a modern version of the ancient short-sword or dagger and a well-sharpened axe, we were ready. And as the blades crashed down repeatedly into the face and body of each carcass in turn, each cut was numbered and a careful note made of the depth and angle. As the blows were then repeated on the wrapped sections of the bodies, we were all astonished to see the way the blades bounced off the linen. In only one case did the dagger-type blade manage to make any headway at all, and when it did the linen threads were pushed deep into the wounds – something we had not seen on the mummies.

After a fascinating day of truly 'hands-on archaeology', it was clear that the bodies of the Boy and Younger Woman had been attacked relatively soon after death, certainly within no more than a generation. More to the point, they had been unwrapped before the damage had been inflicted, and by someone of sufficiently high status to own a dagger-type weapon.

While Don was leading the experimental trauma sessions in York, the digital X-rays of the Younger Woman's skull had been sent to a team of facial reconstruction experts at Nottingham University. Working closely with their colleagues at Sheffield University, they were building up the face using the latest techniques in forensic graphics in the same way that they reconstruct faces of unknown murder victims for the police. And this case would be no different, for they had no idea who this person was – male, female, young, old, European, African, modern or ancient. They were given no clues. As they explained, 'Whenever we do any sort of forensic work we always work as blind as we can. We work with the data we are given and nothing more, otherwise it may affect our judgement on that particular case.'

Having first turned the X-rays into a three-dimensional

computer model, the team had to map out thousands of individual points on the face and head, with markers put in place to indicate the depth of the skin, before the muscles and flesh could gradually be added. Several months later, when they had finally completed their complicated task, I was invited along to Nottingham to see the end result. I was very excited, rather apprehensive and even a little bit scared.

What would she look like? Who would she look like? Would she even look like a she? And of course, the big question – would she be 'beautiful'?

As I sat in the darkened room, with a growing feeling of expectancy combined with the same long-felt apprehension, the computer image was suddenly projected up in front of me and the entire process began to unfold. First the skull appeared, and as it rotated on the screen the muscles began to wrap themselves around, followed by the skin. And as the skin began to cover the contours of the head, an amazing, striking face began to take shape. There, floating in space and staring back at me, was a truly amazing individual. I couldn't believe it. She was perfect, absolutely perfect. Her fine nose and evenly spaced features gave the impression of strength and dignity – no chocolate-box prettiness here, simply the perfect features of an exquisite face. An Egyptian face.

And as the last thirteen years seemed to stretch out for ever behind me, I felt that this was it – I'd finally reached the end of the search. I believed that this was most likely Nefertiti herself.

But the identification would certainly not be accepted by everyone. As soon as the television company broke the story in *The Sunday Times*, we were bombarded by the media for months on end. As I said at the time, 'I've established in my own mind that this is a royal woman of the 18th dynasty – potentially a female pharaoh – and I believe she could well be the great queen Nefertiti.' Yet the comment was regularly edited down to the simple headline 'Nefertiti found', and, believing that we had declared this was indeed the great woman for absolute certain, some people started leaping up and down and haven't really stopped. And in the grand tradition of Egyptology, with its 'oh-no-it-isn't-oh-yes-it-is' approach, our evidence has been accepted by some, reinterpreted by others and dismissed out of hand by many. Some Egyptologists still maintain that the Younger Woman is a man, whilst others claim it's a girl and have brought my own abilities into question. All part of life's rich tapestry, I suppose. At least I've learned to be philosophical.

Yet controversy has always been par for the course, and having surrounded the Amarna Period for more than a century it will no doubt continue to do so for many years to come. There will always be those who see Akhenaten as a gentle poet-king, a harmless dreamer caught up in his own little world, and certainly not the useless politician and dictator-like figure which many now believe him to have been. They are often the same people who think he was succeeded by an enigmatic and somewhat effeminate-looking prince, whilst Nefertiti had simply looked on, doing what she did best, producing babies and 'being beautiful'.

Nevertheless, the evidence shows that a woman ruled as pharaoh in the late 18th dynasty at the end of the Amarna Period, and the Younger Woman appears to have been buried with her right arm arranged in the pose of a pharaoh. She was also buried with a short wig most likely set in the Nubian style, with Amarna-era double ear piercings and gold beads of the type found in the Amarna Period tomb KV.55. Having suffered malicious damage at the time when all traces of Amarna underwent similar treatment, her mummy was then reburied with two individuals who seem to have been members of the Amarna royal family, all three of them prepared using mummification techniques unique to the later 18th dynasty. And then of course there is the facial reconstruction, which speaks for itself. Yet, as Earl Ertman wisely pointed out to me, 'Unless this mummy can sit up and speak to us and tell us who she is, then there will always be those who won't believe it.'

So is the search for Nefertiti over? I believe it is. And whilst others will always continue to look for her themselves, I feel my search at least is done.

BIBLIOGRAPHY

Although the following bibliography represents the majority of books and papers consulted during the search for Nefertiti, it doesn't by any means cover the thousands of publications dealing with the Amarna Period itself; the majority of those published before 1990 are covered in Martin 1991 (below).

The quotes from Howard Carter's unpublished notes are used with the kind permission of the Griffith Institute, Oxford OX1 2LG.

Aldred, C. 1957, Hair Styles and History, *Bulletin of the Metropolitan Museum of Art* 15(6), p.141–7

Aldred, C. 1957a, The End of the el-'Amârna Period, *Journal of Egyptian Archaeology* 43, p.30–41

Aldred, C. 1957b, Year Twelve at el-'Amârna, *Journal of Egyptian Archaeology* 43, p.114–17

Aldred, C. 1959, The Beginning of the el-'Amârna Period, *Journal of Egyptian Archaeology* 45, p.19–33

Aldred, C. 1961, The Tomb of Akhenaten at Thebes, *Journal of Egyptian Archaeology* 47, p.41–65

Aldred, C. 1962, The Harold Jones Collection, *Journal of Egyptian Archaeology* 48, p.160–2

Aldred, C. 1968, *Akhenaten, Pharaoh of Egypt: A New Study*, London

Aldred, C. 1971, *Jewels of the Pharaohs*, London

Aldred, C. 1973, *Akhenaten and Nefertiti*, London

Aldred, C. 1976, The Horizon of the Aten, *Journal of Egyptian Archaeology* 62, p.184

Aldred, C. 1978, Tradition and Revolution in the Art of the XVIIIth Dynasty, in *Immortal Egypt*, ed. D. Schmandt-Besserat, Malibu, p.51–62

Aldred, C. 1980, *Egyptian Art*, London

Aldred, C. 1982, El-Amarna, in *Excavating in Egypt: the Egypt Exploration Society 1882–1982*, ed. T. G. H. James, London, p.89–106

Aldred, C. 1988, *Akhenaten, King of Egypt*, London

Aldred, C. & Sandison, A. T. 1962, The Pharaoh Akhenaten: a Problem in Egyptology and Pathology, *Bulletin of the History of Medicine* 36(4), p.293–316

Allen, J. 1991, Akhenaten's 'Mystery' Co-regent and Successor, *Amarna Letters* 1, p.74–85

Allen, J. et al. 1994, Further Evidence for the Coregency of Amenhotep III and IV, *Amarna Letters* 3, p.26–31

Allen, R. O. 1989, The Role of Chemists in Archaeological Studies, *Archaeological Chemistry* 4, p.1–17

American University in Cairo, 1997, *Description de l'Egypte: publiée par les ordres de Napoléon Bonaparte*, Cairo

Andrews, C. 1984, *Egyptian Mummies*, London

Andrews, C. 1990, *Ancient Egyptian Jewellery*, London

Antelme, R. S. & Rossini, S. 2001, *Sacred Sexuality in Ancient Egypt*, Rochester

Anthes, R. 1958, *The Head of Queen Nofretete*, Berlin

Arnold, D. 1996, *The Royal Women of Amarna: Images of Beauty from Ancient Egypt*, New York

Arriaza, B. 1995, *Beyond Death: the Chinchorro Mummies of Ancient Chile*, Washington

Ashcroft, T. 2001, The History of Tel-el-Amarna, *Past Forward* 28, p.28

Balout, L. & Roubert, C. eds. 1985, *La Momie de Ramsès II*, Paris

Bass, W. M. 1995, *Human Osteology: a Laboratory and Field Manual*, Columbia

Bauman, B. 1960, The Botanical Aspects of Egyptian Embalming and Burial, *Economic Botany* 14, p.84–104

Bell, M. R. 1990, An Armchair Excavation of KV.55, *Journal of the American Research Center in Egypt* 27, p.97–137

Bennet, J. 1939, The Restoration Stela of Tut'ankhamûn, *Journal of Egyptian Archaeology* 25, p.8–15

Bennet, J. 1965, Notes on the 'aten', *Journal of Egyptian Archaeology* 51, p.207–9

Bentley, J. 1980, Amenophis III and Akhenaten: Co-regency proved? *Journal of Egyptian Archaeology* 66, p.164–5

Bietak, M. 1992, Minoan Wall Paintings Unearthed at Ancient Avaris, *Egyptian Archaeology: Bulletin of the Egypt Exploration Society*, 2, p.26–8

Birrell, M. 1997, Was Ay the Father of Kiya? *Bulletin of the Australian Centre of Egyptology* 8, p.11–18

Blackman, A. M. 1917, The Nugent and Haggard Collections of Egyptian Antiquities, *Journal of Egyptian Archaeology* 4, p.39–46

Blankenberg-van Delden, C. 1969, *The Large Commemorative Scarabs of Amenhotep III*, Leiden

Blankenberg-van Delden, C. 1976, More Large Commemorative Scarabs of Amenophis III, *Journal of Egyptian Archaeology* 62, p.74–80

Blankenberg-van Delden, C. 1982, A Genealogical Reconstruction of the Kings and Queens of the late 17th and early 18th Dynasties, *Göttinger Miszellen* 54, p.35–8, 40–5

Boddens-Hosang, F. J. E. 1986, The Death of Akhenaten's Second Daughter, *Wepwawet: Papers in Egyptology* 2, p.37

Bomann, A. H. 1991, *The Private Chapel in Ancient Egypt: a Study of the Chapels in the Workmen's Village at El Amarna with Special Reference to Deir el Medina and Other Sites*, London

Bosse-Griffiths, K. 2001, *Amarna Studies and Other Selected Papers*, Fribourg

Brandon, S. G. F. 1962, Akhenaten: the Heretic King of Egypt, *History Today*, p.622–31

Breasted, C. 1988, *Ancient Records of Egypt II*, London

Brier, B. 1998, *The Encyclopedia of Mummies*, New York

Brock, L. P. 1993, Mummy Business, *KMT: A Modern Journal of Ancient Egypt*, 3(4), p.12–17, 84–5

Brock, L. P. 1995, Theodore Davis and the Rediscovery of Tomb 55, in *Valley of the Sun Kings: New Explorations in the Tombs of the Pharaohs*, ed. R. H. Wilkinson, Tucson, p.34–46

Brothwell, D. 1972, *Digging Up Bones*, London

Brothwell, D. 1986, *The Bog Man and the Archaeology of People*, London

Brothwell, D. 1990, Ancient Calcified Tissue Research: a View to the 21st Century, *International Journal of Osteoarchaeology* 1, p.2–21

Brothwell, D. & Higgs, E. eds. 1963, *Science in Archaeology*, London

Brothwell, D. & Sandison, A. T. 1967, *Diseases in Antiquity: a Survey of the Diseases, Injuries and Surgery of Early Populations*, Springfield

Brussels, 1975, *Le Regne du soleil: Akhnaton et Nefertiti, Exposotion aux Musées Royaux d'Art et d'Histoire*, Brussels

Bryce, T. E. 1990, The Death of Niphururiya and its Aftermath, *Journal of Egyptian Archaeology* 76, p.97–105

Buckley, S. A. 2001, *Chemical Investigations of the Organic Embalming Agents Employed in Ancient Egyptian Mummification*, PhD thesis, University of Bristol

Buckley, S. A. 2002, Les Momies livrent leurs secrets, *Le Monde de la Bible* 145, p.32–5

Buckley, S. A. & Evershed, R. P. 2001, The Organic Chemistry of Embalming Agents in Pharaonic and Graeco-Roman Mummies, *Nature*, p.837–41

Buckley, S. A. & Rose, J. 2000, Chemical Analysis Report, in *Tomb KV.39 in the Valley of the Kings: a Double Archaeological Enigma*, ed. J. Rose, Bristol, p.138–40

Buckley, S. A., Stott, A. W. & Evershed, R. P. 1999, Studies of Organic Residues from Ancient Egyptian Mummies Using High Temperature-Gas Chromatography-Mass Spectrometry and Sequential Thermal Desorption-Gas Chromatography-Mass Spectrometry and Pyrolysis-Gas Chromatography-Mass Spectrometry, *Analyst* 124, p.443–52

Burridge, A. L. 1993, Akhenaten: a New Perspective: Evidence of a Genetic Disorder in the Royal Family of 18th Dynasty Egypt, *Journal of the Society for the Study of Egyptian Antiquities* 23, p.63–74

Callender, V. G. 1990, Queen Hetepheres I, *Bulletin of the Australian Centre of Egyptology* 1, p.25–9

Callender, V. G. 1994, The Nature of the Egyptian 'Harim', Dynasties 1–20, *Bulletin of the Australian Centre of Egyptology* 5, p.7–25

Callender, V. G. 1998, Materials for the Reign of Sebekneferu, in *Proceedings of the Seventh International Congress of Egyptologists*, ed. C. Eyre, Leuven, p.227–36

Campbell, E. F. 1964, *The Chronology of the Amarna Letters*, Baltimore

Capel, A. K. & Markoe, G. E. eds. 1996, *Mistress of the House, Mistress of Heaven: Women in Ancient Egypt*, New York

Carpignano, G. & Rabino Massa, E. 1981, Analisi di un campione di capelli della parrucca appartenente alla moglie dell'Architetto Kha, *Oriens Antiquus* 20, p.229–230

Carter, H. 1902, Report on the Robbery of the Tomb of Amenothes II, Biban el Moluk, *Annales du Service des Antiquités de l'Égypte* 3, p.115–21

Carter, H. 1917, A Tomb Prepared for Queen Hatshepsuit and Other Recent discoveries at Thebes, *Journal of Egyptian Archaeology* 4, p.107–18

Carter, H. 1927, *The Tomb of Tut.ankh.amun II*, London

Carter, H. 1933, *The Tomb of Tut.ankh.amun III*, London

Carter, H. & Mace, A. 1923, *The Tomb of Tut.ankh.amun I*, London

Carter. H. Unpublished Notebook no.17 (VI.2II), Griffith Institute, Oxford

Chatt, A. & Katz, S. 1988, *Hair Analysis: Applications in the Biomedical and Environmental Sciences*, New York

Chiotasso, L., Chiotasso, P., Pedrini, L., Rigoni, G. & Sarnelli, C. 1992, *La parrucca di Merit, Sesto Congresso Internazionale di Egittologia* 1, Turin, p.99–105

Chubb, M. 1954, *Nefertiti Lived Here*, London

Cline, E. 1987, Amenhotep III and the Aegean: a Re-assessment of Egypto-Aegean Relations in the 14th century BC, *Orientalia* 56(1), p.1–36

Cockburn, A., Barraco, R. A., Reyman, T. A & Peck, W. H. 1975, Autopsy of an Egyptian Mummy, *Science* 187, p.1155–60

Cockburn, A., Cockburn, E. & Reyman, T. A. eds. 1998, *Mummies, Disease and Ancient Cultures*, Cambridge

Cohen, R. & Westbrook, R. eds. 2000, *Amarna Diplomacy: the Beginnings of International Relations*, Baltimore

Conolly, R. et al. 1976, Serological Evidence of Tutankhamen and Smenkhare, *Journal of Egyptian Archaeology* 62, p.184–6

Cooney, J. D. 1953, Egyptian Art in the Collection of Albert Gallatin, *Journal of Near Eastern Studies* 12, p.1–19

Cooney, J. D. 1965, *Amarna Reliefs from Hermopolis in American Collections*, Brooklyn

Corteggiani, J. 1987, *Egypt of the Pharaohs*, London

Costa, P. 1978, The Frontal Sinuses of the Remains Purported to be Akhenaten, *Journal of Egyptian Archaeology* 64, p.76–9

Cottevieille-Giraudet, R. 1936, *Rapport sur les fouilles de Médamoud (1932): les reliefs d'Aménophis IV, Akhenaten*, Cairo

Cottrell, L. 1967, *Queens of the Pharaohs*, London

Cox, J. S. 1977, The Construction of an Ancient Egyptian Wig (c.1400 B.C.) in the British Museum, *Journal of Egyptian Archaeology* 63, p.67–71

Cox, J. S. 1989, *An Illustrated Dictionary of Hairdressing and Wigmaking*, London

Crocker, P. 1992, The Use of Space in Amarna Architecture: Domestic and Royal Parallels, *Bulletin of the Australian Centre of Egyptology* 3, p.11–22

Currelly, C. T. 1956, *I Brought the Ages Home*, Toronto

D'Auria, S., Lacovara, P. & Roehrig, C. H. 1988, *Mummies and Magic: the Funerary Arts of Ancient Egypt*, Boston

Daressy, G. 1902, *Fouilles de la Vallée des Rois 1898–1899*, Cairo

David, A. R. ed. 1979, *The Manchester Museum Mummy Project*, Manchester

Davies, B. G. 1992, *Egyptian Historical Records of the Later Eighteenth Dynasty: IV*, Warminster

Davies, N. de G. 1903–08, *The Rock Tombs of El Amarna I–VI*, London

Davies, N. de G. 1921, Egyptian Expedition for 1920–1921, II: The Work of the Tytus Memorial Fund, *Bulletin of the Metropolitan Museum of Art* 16, Supplement, p.19–28

Davies, N. de G. 1923a, Akhenaten at Thebes, *Journal of Egyptian Archaeology* 9, p.132–52

Davies, N. de G. 1923b, The Egyptian Expedition 1922–1923: the Graphic Work of the Expedition, *Bulletin of the Metropolitan Museum of Art* 18, Supplement, p.40–53

Davies, N. de G. 1941, *The Tomb of the Vizier Ramose*, London

Davies, W. V. & Walker, R. eds. 1993, *Biological Anthropology and the Study of Ancient Egypt*, London

Davis, T. M. 1906, *The Tomb of Hâtshopsîtû*, London

Davis, T. M. 1907, *The Tomb of Iouiya and Touiyou*, London

Davis, T. M. 1910, *The Tomb of Queen Tîyi*, London

Davis, T. M. 1912, *The Tombs of Harmhabi and Touatânkhamanou*, London

Dawson, D. P., Giles, S. & Ponsford, M. 2002, *Horemkenesi: May he Live Forever! The Bristol Mummy Project*, Bristol

Dawson, W. R. 1927, Making a Mummy, *Journal of Egyptian Archaeology* 13, p.43

Dawson, W. R. ed. 1938, *Sir Grafton Elliot Smith*, London

Dawson, W. R., Uphill, E. P. & Bierbrier, M. 1995, *Who was Who in Egyptology*, London 3rd rev. ed.

Delaney, C. 1986, *A Son to Luxor's Sand: a Commemorative*

Exhibition of Egyptian Art from the Collections of The British Museum and Carmarthen Museum, Swansea

Derry, D. 1927, Report upon the Examination of Tutankhamen's Mummy, in *The Tomb of Tut.ankh.amen II (H. Carter)*, London, p.143–61

Derry, D. 1931, Note on the Skeleton hitherto Believed to Be That of King Akhenaton, *Annales du Service des Antiquités de l'Égypte* 31, p.115–19

Derry, D. 1942, Mummification: II- Methods Practiced at Different Periods, *Annales du Service des Antiquités de l'Égypte* 41, p.259

Desroches-Noblecourt, C. 1963, *Tutankhamen: Life and Death of a Pharaoh*, London

Dorman, P. 1988, *The Monuments of Senenmut*, London

Drower, M. S. 1985, *Flinders Petrie: a Life in Archaeology*, London

Dunsmore, A. 2002, Pottery from the Royal Wadi at Tell el-Amarna: Burial Equipment or a Workmen's Assemblage? *Akhetaten Sun: Newsletter of the Amarna Research Foundation* 6(1), p.13–15

Eaton-Krauss, M. 1981, Miscellanea Amarnensia, *Chronique d'Égypte* 56, p.245–64

Edwards, A. B. 1889 *A Thousand Miles up the Nile*, 2nd ed., London

Edwards, A. B. 1891, *Pharaohs, Fellahs and Explorers*, New York

Edwards, I. E. S. 1972, *The Treasures of Tutankhamen*, London

Englebach, R. 1931, The So-called Coffin of Akhenaten, *Annales du Service des Antiquités de l'Égypte* 31, p.98–114

Englebach, R. 1940, Material for a Revision of the History of the Heresy Period of the Eighteenth Dynasty, *Annales du Service des Antiquités de l'Égypte* 40, p.133–83

English National Opera, 1985, *Akhenaten – Philip Glass*, London

Ertman, E. 1976, The Cap-Crown of Nefertiti: its Function and Probable Origin, *Journal of the American Research Center in Egypt* 13, p.63–7

Ertman, E. 1990, Another Look at a Relief of King Akhenaten from the Harer Family Trust Collection and the Use of Streamers During the Amarna Period, *Journal of the Society for the Study of Egyptian Antiquities*, 20, p.108–12

Ertman, E. 1992a, Is There Evidence for a 'King' Nefertiti?, *Amarna Letters*, 2, p.50–5

Ertman, E. 1992b, The Search for the Significance and Origin of Nefertiti's Tall Blue Crown, *Sesto Congresso Internazionale di Egittologia I*, Turin, p.189–93

Ertman E. 1993a, From Two to Many: the Symbolism of Additional Uraei Worn by Nefertiti and Akhenaten, *Journal of the Society for the Study of Egyptian Antiquities* 13, p.42–50

Ertman, E. 1993b, More Comments on New Kingdom Crown Streamers and the Gold Temple-band They Held in Place, *Journal of the Society for the Study of Egyptian Antiquities* 23, p.51–5

Ertman, E. 1995, Evidence of the Alterations to the Canopic Jar Portraits and Coffin Mask from KV.55, in *Valley of the Sun Kings: New Explorations in the Tombs of the Pharaohs*, ed. R. H. Wilkinson, Tucson, p.108–19

Ertman, E. 1998, Akhenaten's Use of Bound Foreign Prisoners in Chariot Scenes: a Commemoration of Specific Events, or the King Victorious? *Annales du Service des Antiquités de l'Égypte* 73, p.51–60

Ertman, E. 2001, An Electrum Ring of Nefertiti: More Evidence of Her Co-Kingship? *KMT* 12(4), p.26–8

Ertman, E. 2002, Was King Ankhkheperura's name once placed on Tutankhamun's Golden Throne? in *Eighth International Congress of Egyptologists in Cairo in 2000 Abstracts of Papers*, ed. Z. Hawass & A. M. Jones, p.60

Fairman, H. W. 1961, Once Again the So-Called Coffin of Akhenaten, *Journal of Egyptian Archaeology* 47, p.25–40

Faulkner, R. O. 1969, *The Ancient Egyptian Pyramid Texts*, Warminster

Faulkner, R. O. 1985, *The Ancient Egyptian Book of the Dead*, London

Fay, B. 1984, *Egyptian Museum Berlin*, Mainz

Fazzini, R. 1973, *Art from the Age of Akhenaten*, Brooklyn

Fazzini, R. et al. 1989, *Ancient Egyptian Art in the Brooklyn Museum*, Brooklyn

Filce Leek, F. 1969, The Problem of Brain Removal During Embalming by the Ancient Egyptians, *Journal of Egyptian Archaeology* 55, p.112–16

Filce Leek, F. 1972, *The Human Remains from the Tomb of Tut'ankhamun*, Oxford

Filce Leek, F. 1977, How Old was Tut'ankhamûn? *Journal of Egyptian Archaeology* 63, p.112–15

Filer, J. 1998a, Art or Ailment? The Akhenaten Conundrum, *NILE Offerings* 4, p.28–30

Filer, J. 1998b, Mother and Baby Burials, in *Proceedings of the Seventh International Congress of Egyptologists,* ed. C. Eyre, Leuven, p.391–400

Filer, J. 2000, The KV.55 Body: the Facts, *Egyptian Archaeology: the Bulletin of the Egypt Exploration Society* 17, p.13–14

Fischer, H. G. 1975, A feminine example of w hm.k, 'thy majesty commands' in the Fourth Dynasty, *Journal of Egyptian Archaeology* 61, p.246–7

Fischer, H. G. 1989, *Egyptian Women in the Old Kingdom and Heracleapolitan period*, New York

Flannery, M. B., Stankiewicz, B. A., Hutchins, J. C., White, C. W. & Evershed, R. P. 1999, Chemical and Morphological Changes in Human Skin during Preservation in Waterlogged and Desiccated Environments, *Ancient Biomolecules* 3, p.37–50

Fleming, S., Fishman, B., O'Connor, D. & Silverman, D. 1980, *The Egyptian Mummy: Secrets and Science*, Philadelphia

Fletcher, J. 1995, Ancient Egyptian Hair: a Study in Style, Form and Function, PhD thesis, University of Manchester

Fletcher, J. 2000a, *Egypt's Sun King: Amenhotep III, an Intimate*

Chronicle of Ancient Egypt's Most Glorious Pharaoh, London

Fletcher, J. 2000b, Hair, in *Ancient Egyptian Materials and Technology*, P. Nicholson & I. Shaw, Cambridge, p.495–501

Fletcher, J. 2002, Ancient Egyptian Wigs & Hairstyles, *Ostracon: Journal of the Egyptian Study Society* 13(2), p.2–8

Fletcher, J. forthcoming a, *Ancient Egyptian Wigs and Hairstyles*, Austin

Fletcher, J. forthcoming b, The Decorated Body in Ancient Egypt: Hairstyles, Cosmetics and Tattoos (or How False Hair and Eye-paint Can Speak for the Majority), in *Proceedings from The Clothed Body in the Ancient World Conference*, Oxford

Fletcher, J. & Montserrat, D. 1998, The Human Hair in the Tomb of Tutankhamun: a Re-evaluation, in *Proceedings of the Seventh International Congress of Egyptologists*, ed. C. Eyre, Leuven, p.401–7

Forbes, D. 1992, Cache 35, *KMT: A Modern Journal of Ancient Egypt* 3(4), p.30–3, 86–7

Frankfort, H. & Pendlebury, J. D. S. 1933, *The City of Akhenaten II: The North Suburb and the Desert Altars*, London

Freed, R., Markowitz, Y. J. & D'Auria, S. H. eds. 1999, *Pharaohs of the Sun: Akhenaten, Nefertiti, Tutankhamen*, Boston

Gaballah, M. F. & Walker, R. 1995, *The Derry-Batrawi Collection, Kasr el-Einy Faculty of Medicine, Cairo, Egypt: Introduction and Catalogue*, Douglas

Gardiner, A. 1957, The So-Called Tomb of Queen Tiye, *Journal of Egyptian Archaeology* 43, p.10–25

Gardiner, A. 1961, *Egypt of the Pharaohs*, London

Gera, D. 1997, *Warrior Women: the Anonymous Tractatus de Mulieribus*, Leiden

Germer, R. 1984, Die angebliche Mumie der Teje: Probleme interdisziplinärer Arbeiten, *Studien zur altägyptischen Kultur* 11, p.85–90

Giles, F. J. 1970, *Ikhnaton, Legend and History*, London

Giles, F. J. 2001, *The Amarna Age: Egypt*, Warminster

Glanville, S. R. K. 1929, *Amenophis III and his Successors in the XVIIIth dynasty*, in *Great Ones of Ancient Egypt*, ed. W. Brunton, London, p.103–39

Gohary, J. 1992, *Akhenaten's Sed-Festival at Karnak*, London

Gray, P. H. K. 1972, Notes Concerning the Position of the Arms and Hands of Mummies with a View to Possible Dating of the Specimen, *Journal of Egyptian Archaeology* 58, p.200–4

Green, L. 1988, *Queens and Princesses of the Amarna Period: the Social, Political, Religious and Cultic Role of the Women of the Royal Family at the End of the Eighteenth Dynasty*, PhD thesis, University of Toronto

Green, L. 1998, Evidence for the Position of Women at Amarna, in *Proceedings of the Seventh International Congress of Egyptologists*, ed. C. Eyre, Leuven, p.483–8

Griffith, F. L. 1918, The Jubilee of Akhenaton, *Journal of Egyptian Archaeology* 5, p.61–3

Griffith, F. L. 1926, Stela in Honour of Amenophis III and Taya from Tell el-'Amarnah, *Journal of Egyptian Archaeology* 12, p.1–3

Grimm, A. & Schoske, S. eds. 2001, *Das Geheimnis des goldenen Sarges: Echnaton und das Ende der Amarnazeit*, Munich

Györy, H. 1998, Remarks on Amarna Amulets, in *Proceedings of the Seventh International Congress of Egyptologists*, ed. C. Eyre, Leuven, p.497–507

Habachi, L. 1965, Varia from the Reign of Akhenaten: the Reliefs of Men and Bek at Aswan and a Second Graffito Close by Showing Akhenaten before the Hawk-headed God Aten, *Mitteilungen des Deutschen Archäologischen Instituts Abteilung Kairo* 20, p.84–92

Hall, R. & J. Janssen, 1985, The Egyptian Laundry, *Wepwawet: Papers in Egyptology* 1, p.23

Hamilton-Paterson, J. & Andrews, C. 1978, *Mummies: Death and Life in Ancient Egypt*, London

Hanawalt, R. A. 1998, Did Tut Lie in State? *Akhetaten Sun: Newsletter of the Amarna Research Foundation* 3(2), p.6–9

Hankey, J. 2001, *A Passion for Egypt: Arthur Weigall, Tutankhamun and the 'Curse of the Pharaohs'*, London

Hari, R. 1976, La reine d'Horemheb était-elle la soeur de Nefertiti? *Chronique d'Égypte* 51, p.39–46

Harrell, J. 2001, Ancient Quarries near Amarna, *Egyptian Archaeology: the Bulletin of the Egypt Exploration Society* 19, p.36–8

Harris, J. E. & Weeks, K. R. 1973, *X-Raying the Pharaohs*, London

Harris, J. E. & Wente, E. F. eds. 1980, *An X-Ray Atlas of the Royal Mummies*, Chicago

Harris, J. E., Wente, E., Cox, C., el-Nawawy, I., Kowalski, C., Storey, A., Russell, W., Ponitz, P. & Walker, G. 1978, Mummy of the 'Elder Lady' in the Tomb of Amenhotep II: Egyptian Museum Catalog Number 61070, *Science* 200, p.1149–51

Harris, J. R. 1973, Nefertiti Rediviva, *Acta Orientalia* 35, p.5–13

Harris, J. R. 1974a, Kiya, *Chronique d'Égypte* 97(49), p.25–30

Harris, J. R. 1974b, Neferneferuaten Regnans, *Acta Orientalia* 36, p.11–21

Harris, J. R. 1977, Akhenaten or Nefertiti? *Acta Orientalia* 38, p.5–10

Harris, J. R. 1992, Akhenaten and Neferneferuaten in the Tomb of Tut'ankhamun, in *After Tut'ankhamun: Research and Excavation in the Royal Necropolis at Thebes*, ed. C. N. Reeves, London, p.55–72

Harrison, R. G. 1966, An Anatomical Examination of the Pharaonic Remains Purported to be Akhenaten, *Journal of Egyptian Archaeology* 52, p.95–119

Harrison, R. G. 1978, The Tutankhamun Post-Mortem, *Chronicle: Essays from Ten Years of Television Archaeology*, ed. R. Sutcliffe, London, p.40–52

Harrison, R. G. and Abdalla, A. B. 1972, The Remains of Tutankhamen, *Antiquity* 46, p.8–18

Harrison, R. G., Connolly, R. C., Ahmed, S., Abdalla, A. B. &

el-Ghawaby, M. 1979, A Mummified Foetus from the Tomb of Tutankhamun, *Antiquity* 53, p.19–21

Hart, G. 1986, *A Dictionary of Egyptian Gods and Goddesses*, London

Hassan, A. 1997, *The Queens of the Fourth Dynasty*, Cairo

Hassan, F. A. & Smith, S. J. 2002, Soul Birds and Heavenly Cows: Transforming Gender in Predynastic Egypt, in *In Pursuit of Gender: Worldwide Archaeological Approaches*, eds. S. M. Nelson & M. Rosen-Ayalon, p.43–65

Hawass, Z. 2002, *Hidden Treasures of the Egyptian Museum*, Cairo

Hayes, W. C. 1948, Minor Art and Family History in the Reign of Amun-hotep III, *Bulletin of the Metropolitan Museum of Art* 6(10), p.272–9

Hayes, W. C. 1951, Inscriptions from the Palace of Amenhotep III, *Journal of Near Eastern Studies* 10, p.35–56, 82–111, 156–83, 231–42

Hayes, W. C. 1990a, *The Scepter of Egypt: a Background for the Study of the Egyptian Antiquities in the Metropolitan Museum of Art. I: From the Earliest Times to the End of the Middle Kingdom*, New York

Hayes, W. C. 1990b, *The Scepter of Egypt: a Background for the Study of the Egyptian Antiquities in the Metropolitan Museum of Art. II: The Hyksos Period and the New Kingdom*, New York

Hayter, A. G. K. 1934, Tell-el-Amarna: City of Akhnaton and Tutankhamen, *Wonders of the Past* 47, p.1122–32

Herodotus 1984, *The Histories*, trans. A. de Sélincourt, Harmondsworth

Hollis, S. T. 2000, Goddesses and Sovereignty in Ancient Egypt, in *Goddesses Who Rule* eds. E. Bernard & B. Moon, Oxford, p.215–32

Holmes, E. M. 1888, Note on Two Resins Used by the Ancient Egyptians, *Pharmaceutical Journal and Transactions* 19, p.387–9

Holmes, W. 1959, *She Was Queen of Egypt*, London

Hope, C. 1977, *Malkata and the Birket Habu: Jar Sealings and Amphorae*, Warminster

Hornung, E. 1990, *Valley of the Kings: Horizon of Eternity*, New York

Hornung, E. 1999, *Akhenaten and the Religion of Light*, Ithaca

Hussein, F. & Harris, J. E. 1988, The Skeletal Remains from Tomb No.55, in *Fifth International Congress of Egyptologists, Abstracts of Papers*, Cairo, p.140–1

Jackson, M. ed. 1999, *Egypt's Lost City*, Manchester

James, T. G. H. 1981, *The British Museum and Ancient Egypt*, London

James, T. G. H. 2001, *Howard Carter: the Path to Tutankhamen*, London

Janosi, P. 1992, The Queens Ahhotep I & II and Egypt's Foreign Relations, *Journal of the Ancient Chronology Forum* 5, p.99–105

Janosi, P. 1993, *The Discovery of Queen Ahhotep I*, Journal of the Ancient Chronology Forum 6, p.87–8

Janot, F. 2000, *Instruments d'embaument de l'Égypte ancienne*, Cairo

Janssen, R. M. 1992, *The First Hundred Years: Egyptology at University College London 1892–1992*, London

Johnson, G. B. 1991, *Seeking Queen Nefertiti's Tall Blue Crown*, Amarna Letters 1, p.50–61

Johnson, W. R. 1996, Amenhotep III at Amarna: Some New Considerations, *Journal of Egyptian Archaeology* 82, p.65–82

Jurmain, R. 1999, *Stories from the Skeleton: Behavioral Reconstruction in Human Osteology*, Amsterdam

Kamil, J. 1973, *Luxor: A Guide to Ancient Thebes*, London

Kemp, B. J. 1976, The Window of Appearance at el-Amarna and the Basic Structure of this City, *Journal of Egyptian Archaeology* 62, p.81–99

Kemp, B. J. 1983, Tell el-'Amarna, in *Ancient Centres of Egyptian Civilization* ed. H. S. Smith & R. Hall, London, p.57–72

Kemp, B. J. 1991, *Ancient Egypt: Anatomy of a Civilization*, London

Kemp, B. J. 1994, The Streets of el-Amarna, *Egyptian Archaeology: Bulletin of the Egypt Exploration Society* 4, p.39

Kemp, B. J. 2000, A Glass Case for Boundary Stela A and a New Head of Nefertiti, *Akhetaten Sun: Newsletter of the Amarna Research Foundation* 4(1), p.14

Kemp, B. J. 2001a, Building in Stone at Amarna, *Akhetaten Sun: Newsletter of the Amarna Research Foundation* 5(1), p.2–8

Kemp, B. J. 2001b, EES Field Director's Report Spring 2001, *Akhetaten Sun: Newsletter of the Amarna Research Foundation* 5(2), p.2–15

Kemp, B. J. 2002a Cosmopolitan Life at Amarna, *Akhetaten Sun: Newsletter of the Amarna Research Foundation* 6(1), p.2–7

Kemp, B. J. 2002b, The Discovery of Amarna Talatat Blocks in the Sudan, *Akhetaten Sun: Newsletter of the Amarna Research Foundation* 6(1), p.10

Kemp, B. J. & Vogelsang-Eastwood, G. 2001, *The Ancient Textile Industry at Amarna*, London

Kozloff, A. 1997, The Malqata/El-Amarna Blues: Favourite Colours of Kings and Gods, in *Chief of Seers: Egyptian Studies in Memory of Cyril Aldred*, ed. E. Goring et al., London, p.178–92

Kozloff, A. & Bryan, B. 1992, *Egypt's Dazzling Sun: Amenhotep III and his world*, Cleveland

Krauss, R. 1991, Nefertiti: a Drawing-board Beauty? *Amarna Letters* 1, p.46–9

Lacovara, P. 1997, *The New Kingdom Royal City*, London

Lahren, C. H. 1987, Hair Analysis, in *Se-Ankh: An Interdisciplinary Historical and Biomedical Study of an Egyptian Mummy Head*, ed. J. E. Hamner III, Memphis, p.35–8

Lansing, A. 1918, Excavations at the Palace of Amenhotep III at Thebes, *Bulletin of the Metropolitan Museum of Art* 13(3), p.8–14

Lansing, A. & Hayes, W. C. 1937, The Egyptian Expedition 1935–1936: the Museum's Excavations at Thebes, *Bulletin of the Metropolitan Museum of Art* 32, Supplement p.4–39

Leahy, M. A. 1978, *Excavations at Malkata and the Birket Habu 1971–1974: the Inscriptions*, Warminster

Lehner, M. 1997, *The Complete Pyramids*, London

Lesko, B. 1987, *The Remarkable Women of Ancient Egypt*, Providence

Lesko, B. S. 1998, Queen Khamerernebty II and her Sculpture, in *Ancient Egyptian and Mediterranean Studies in Memory of William A. Ward*, ed. L. H. Lesko, Providence, p.149–62

Lesko, B. S. 1999, *The Great Goddesses of Egypt*, Norman

Lesko, L. H. 1977, *King Tut's Wine Cellar*, Berkeley

Lichtheim, M. 1975, *Ancient Egyptian Literature I*, Berkeley

Lichtheim, M. 1976, *Ancient Egyptian Literature II*, Berkeley

Lichtheim, M. 1980, *Ancient Egyptian Literature III*, Berkeley

Loeben, C. E. 1994a, Nefertiti's Pillars: a Photo Essay of the Queen's Monuments at Karnak, *Amarna Letters* III, p.41–5

Loeben, C. E. 1994b, No Evidence of Co-Regency: Two Erased Inscriptions from Tutankhamen's Tomb, *Amarna Letters*, p.104–9

Loret, V. 1899a, Le Tombeau d'Amenophis II et la cachette royale de Biban el-Molouk, *Bulletin de l'Institut d'Égyptien* 9, p.98–112

Loret, V. 1899b, Le Tombeau de Thoutmes III a Biban el-Molouk, *Bulletin de l'Institut d'Égyptien* 9, p.91–7

Lucas, A. 1908, Preliminary Note on Some Preservative Materials Used by the Ancient Egyptians in Connection with Embalming, *Cairo Scientific Journal* 2, p.133–47

Lucas, A. 1911, *Preservative Materials Used by the Ancient Egyptians in Embalming*, Cairo

Lucas, A. 1914, The Question of the Use of Bitumen or Pitch by the Ancient Egyptians in Mummification, *Journal of Egyptian Archaeology* 1, p.241–5

Lucas, A. 1930, Cosmetics, Perfumes and Incense, *Journal of Egyptian Archaeology* 16, p.42

Lucas, A. 1931a, 'Cedar'-tree Products Employed in Mummification, *Journal of Egyptian Archaeology* 17, p.13–20

Lucas, A. 1931b, The Canopic Vases from the Tomb of Queen Tîyi, *Annales du Service des Antiquités de l'Égypte* 31, p.120–2

Lucas, A. 1932, The Use of Natron in Mummification, *Journal of Egyptian Archaeology* 18, p.125–40

Lucas, A. 1937, Notes on Myrrh and Stacte, *Journal of Egyptian Archaeology* 23, p.27–33

Lucas, A. 1989, *Ancient Egyptian Materials and Industries*, rev. J. R. Harris, London

Luxor Museum of Ancient Egyptian Art 1978, *The Luxor Museum of Ancient Egyptian Art*, Cairo

Luxor Museum of Mummification 1997, *Luxor Mummification Museum*, Cairo

Lythgoe, A. M. 1919, Statues of the Goddess Sekhmet, *Bulletin of the Metropolitan Museum of Art* 14(10), Section 2, p.3–23

Mahfouz, N. B. 1935, *The History of Medical Education in Egypt*, Cairo

Manchester Evening News, 1908, Unrolling a Mummy: Novel Ceremony in Manchester (6.5.08), p.5

Manniche, L. 1987, *Sexual Life in Ancient Egypt*, London

Manniche, L. 1991a, *Music and Musicians in Ancient Egypt*, London

Manniche, L. 1991b, Music at the Court of the Aten, *Amarna Letters* 1, p.62–5

Martin, G. T. 1974, *The Royal Tomb at El-'Amarna: the Rock Tombs of El-'Amarna VII. I: The Objects*, London

Martin, G. T. 1987, A Throwstick of Nefertiti in Manchester, *Annales du Service des Antiquités de l'Égypte* 71, p.151–2

Martin, G. T. 1989, *The Royal Tomb at el-'Amarna: the Rock Tombs of El-'Amarna VII. II: The Reliefs, Inscriptions, & Architecture*, London

Martin, G. T. 1991a, *A Bibliography of the Amarna Period*

and its Aftermath: the Reigns of Akhenaten, Smenkhkara, Tutankhamun and Ay (c. 1350–1321 BC), London

Martin, G. T. 1991b, *The Hidden Tombs of Memphis*, London

Martin, G. T. 2002, The Valley of the Kings: the Amarna Royal Tombs Project, *Akhetaten Sun: Newsletter of the Amarna Research Foundation* 6(2), p.10–14

McDermott, S. B. 1998, A Brief Examination of the Amarna Army, *NILE Offerings* 4, p.32–4

McDermott, S. B. 2002, *Ancient Egyptian Foot-soldiers and their Weapons*, PhD thesis, University of Manchester

McDermott, S. B. 2004, *Warfare in Ancient Egypt*, Stroud

McDowell, A. G. 1999, *Village Life in Ancient Egypt: Laundry Lists and Love Songs*, Oxford

Mejanelle, P., Bleton, J., Goursaud, S. & Tchapla, A. 1997, Identification of Phenolic Acids and Inositols in Balms and Tissues from an Egyptian Mummy, *Journal of Chromatography A*, 767, p.177–86

Meltzer, E. 1978, The Parentage of Tutankhamun and Smenkhare, *Journal of Egyptian Archaeology* 64, p.135

Mendelsohn, S. 1944, The Mortuary Crafts of Ancient Egypt, *Ciba Symposia*, May, p.1795–804

Mims, C. 1998, *When we Die: What Becomes of the Body after Death*, London

Moran, W. L. 1992, *The Amarna Letters*, Baltimore

Morkot, R. 1986, Violent Images of Queenship & the Royal Cult, *Wepwawet: Papers in Egyptology* 2, p.1–9

Morkot, R. 1987, Studies in New Kingdom Nubia I: Politics, Economics and Ideology: Egyptian Imperialism in Nubia, *Wepwawet: Papers in Egyptology* 3, p.29–49

Murnane, W. J. 1995, *Texts from the Amarna Period in Egypt*, Atlanta

Murray, H. & Nuttall, M. A. 1963, *A Handlist to Howard Carter's Catalogue of Objects in Tut'ankhamun's Tomb*, Oxford

Murray, M. A. 1910, *The Tomb of Two Brothers*, Manchester

Murray, M. A. 1930, *Egyptian Sculpture*, London

Murray, M. A. 1963, *My First Hundred Years*, London

Murray, M. A. 1973, *The Splendour that was Egypt*, London

Newberry, P. E. 1928, Akhenaten's Eldest Son-in-Law Ankhkheperura, *Journal of Egyptian Archaeology* 14, p.3–9

Newton, F. G. 1924, The North Palace, *Journal of Egyptian Archaeology* 10, p.294–8

Nicholson, P. 2000, The Amarna Glass Project, *Akhetaten Sun: Newsletter of the Amarna Research Foundation* 4(1), p.8–10

Nicholson, P. & Shaw, I. eds. 2000, *Ancient Materials & Technology*, Cambridge

Nissenbaum, A. 1992, Molecular Archaeology: Organic Geochemistry of Egyptian Mummies, *Journal of Archaeological Science* 19, p.1–6

Niwinska, A. 1984, The Bab el-Gusus Tomb and the Royal Cache in Deir el-Bahri, *Journal of Egyptian Archaeology* 70, p.73–81

O'Connor, D. & Cline, E. eds. 1998, *Amenhotep III: Perspectives on his Reign*, Michigan

Paglia, C. 1991, *Sexual Personae: Art and Decadence from Nefertiti to Emily Dickinson*, New York

Panagiotakopulu, E. & Buckland, P. 2002, Tell el-Amarna, 2001–2002: the Environmental Evidence, *Journal of Egyptian Archaeology* 88, p.17–18

Parkinson, R. 1999, *Cracking Codes: the Rosetta Stone and Decipherment*, London

Parkinson, R. & Schofield, L. 1993, Akhenaten's Army? *Egyptian Archaeology: Bulletin of the Egypt Exploration Society* 3, p.34–5

Peet, T. E. 1925, Akhenaten, Ty, Nefertete and Mutnezemt, in *Kings and Queens of Ancient Egypt*, ed. W. Brunton, London, p.81–116

Peet, T. E. 1930, *The Great Tomb Robberies of the Twentieth Egyptian Dynasty*, Oxford

Peet, T. E. & Woolley, C. L. 1923, *The City of Akhenaten I: Excavations of 1921 and 1922 at El-'Amarneh*, London

Pendlebury, J. D. S. 1934, The New Tell el Amarna Discoveries, *Illustrated London News* 15 September, p.386–8

Pendlebury, J. D. S. 1935, The Heretic Pharaoh's Harem, *Illustrated London News* 5 October, p.564–5

Pendlebury, J. D. S. 1951, *The City of Akhenaten III: the Central City and the Official Quarters*, London

Petrie, W. M. F. 1890, *Kahun, Gurob and Hawara*, London

Petrie, W. M. F. 1891, *Illahun, Kahun and Gurob*, London

Petrie, W. M. F. 1894, *Tell el Amarna*, London

Petrie, W. M. F. 1896, *A History of Egypt during the XVIIth and XVIIIth Dynasties*, London

Petrie, W. M. F. 1898, *Deshasheh, 1897*, London

Petrie, W. M. F. 1900, *The Royal Tombs of the First Dynasty, 1900. Part I*, London

Petrie, W. M. F. 1902, *Abydos I*, London

Petrie, W. M. F. 1915, The Egyptian Museum, University College, *Ancient Egypt* 4, p.168–80

Petrie, W. M. F. 1934, The Gods of Ancient Egypt, *Wonders of the Past* 28–9, p.667–80

Pettigrew, T. J. 1834, *History of Egyptian Mummies*, London

Phillips, J. 1991, Sculpture Ateliers of Akhetaten: an Examination of Two Studio-Complexes in the City of the Sun-Disk, *Amarna Letters* 1, p.31–40

Pollard, A. M. & Heron, C. 1996, *Archaeological Chemistry*, Cambridge

Porter, B. & Moss, R. L. B. 1960–4, *Topographical Bibliography of Ancient Egyptian Hieroglyphic Texts, Reliefs and Paintings* I: *The Theban Necropolis*; II: *Royal Tombs and Smaller Cemeteries*, Oxford

Priese, K. 1991, *Das Ägyptisches Museum: Museumsinsel Berlin*, Mainz

Quibell, J. 1908, *The Tomb of Yuaa and Thuiu*, Cairo

Raisman, V. & Martin, G. T. 1984, *Canopic Equipment in the Petrie Museum*, Warminster

Raven, M. 2001, *The Tomb of Meryneith at Sakkara, Egyptian*

Archaeology: Bulletin of the Egypt Exploration Society 20, p.26–8

Ray, J. 1990, Akhenaten: Ancient Egypt's Prodigal Son, *History Today*, 40(1), p.26–32

Ray, J. 2002, *Reflections of Osiris: Lives from Ancient Egypt*, London

Redford, D. 1967, *History and Chronology of the Eighteenth Dynasty of Egypt: Seven Studies*, Toronto

Redford, D. 1984, *Akhenaten the Heretic King*, Princeton

Redford, D. 1992, *Egypt, Canaan and Israel in Ancient Times*, Princeton

Redford, S. 2002, *The Harem Conspiracy: the Murder of Ramses III*, DeKalb

Rees, J. 1995, *Writings on the Nile: Harriet Martineau, Florena Nightingale, Amelia Edwards*, London

Reeves, N. 1978, A Further Occurrence of Nefertiti as hmt nsw 'ȝt, *Göttinger Miszellen* 30, p.61–9

Reeves, N. 1981, A Reappraisal of Tomb 55 in the Valley of the Kings, *Journal of Egyptian Archaeology* 67, p.48–55

Reeves, N. 1982, Akhenaten After All? *Göttinger Miszellen* 54, p.61–72

Reeves, N. 1988, New Light on Kiya from Texts in the British Museum, *Journal of Egyptian Archaeology* 74, p.91–101

Reeves, N. 1990a, *The Complete Tutankhamun*, London

Reeves, N. 1990b, *Valley of the Kings: the Decline of a Royal Necropolis*, London

Reeves, N. 2001a, *Akhenaten: Egypt's False Prophet*, London

Reeves, N. 2001b, The Amarna Royal Tombs Project, *Akhetaten Sun: Newsletter of the Amarna Research Foundation* 5(1), p.9–11

Reeves, C. N. ed. 1992, *After Tut'ankhamun: Research and Excavation in the Royal Necropolis at Thebes*, London

Reeves, C. N. & Taylor, J. H. 1992, *Howard Carter before Tutankhamun*, London

Reeves, N. & Wilkinson, R. H. 1996, *The Complete Valley of the Kings: Tombs and Treasures of Egypt's Greatest Pharaohs*, London

Reid, H. 1999, *In Search of the Immortals*, London

Roberts, A. 1995, *Hathor Rising: the Serpent Power of Ancient Egypt*, Totnes

Robins, G. 1981a, hmt nsw wrt Meritaton, *Göttinger Miszellen* 52, p.75–81

Robins, G. 1981b, The Value of the Estimated Ages of the Royal Mummies at Death as Historical Evidence, *Göttinger Miszellen* 45, p.63–8

Robins, G. 1986, The Role of the Royal Family in the 18th Dynasty up to the End of the Reign of Amenhotep III. I: Queens, *Wepwawet: Papers in Egyptology* 2, p.10–14

Robins, G. 1987, The Role of the Royal Family in the 18th Dynasty up to the End of the Reign of Amenhotep III: 2: Royal Children, *Wepwawet: Papers in Egyptology* 3, p.15–17

Robins, G. 1993, *Women in Ancient Egypt*, London

Robins, G. 1999, The Names of Hatshepsut as King, *Journal of Egyptian Archaeology* 85, p.103–12

Romano, J. 1979, *Luxor Museum of Ancient Egyptian Art: Catalogue*, Cairo

Romer, J. 1976, Royal Tombs of the Early Eighteenth Dynasty, *Mitteilungen des Deutschen Archäologischen Instituts Abteilung Kairo* 32, p.191–206

Romer, J. 1981, *The Valley of the Kings*, London

Rose, J. 1992, An Interim Report on Work in KV.39, September–October 1989, in *After Tut'ankhamun*, ed. C. N. Reeves, p.28–40, London

Rose, J. 2000, *Tomb KV.39 in the Valley of the Kings: a Double Archaeological Enigma*, Bristol

Rose, P. 2002, Re-excavating the Excavators at Amarna, *Egyptian Archaeology: Bulletin of the Egypt Exploration Society* 21, p.18–20

Roth, A. M & Roehrig, C. H. 2002, Magical Bricks and the Bricks of Birth, *Journal of Egyptian Archaeology* 88, p.121–39

Rowe, A. 1940, Inscriptions on the Model Coffin Containing the Lock of Hair of Queen Tyi, *Annales du Service des Antiquités de l'Égypte* 40, p.623–7

Ruffer, M. A. 1914, Pathological Notes on the Royal Mummies of the Cairo Museum, *Mitteilung zur Geschichte der Medizin und Naturwissenschaften* 13, p.239–48

Ruffer, M. A. 1921, *Studies in the Palaeopathology of Egypt*, Chicago

Ryan, D. 1990, Who Is Buried in KV.60? *KMT: A Modern Journal of Ancient Egypt* 1, p.34–63

Saleh, M. & Sourouzian, H. 1987, *Official Catalogue of the Egyptian Museum Cairo*, Mainz

Samson, J. 1972, *Amarna, City of Akhenaten and Nefertiti: Key Pieces from the Petrie Collection*, London

Samson, J. 1973a, Amarna Crowns and Wigs: Unpublished Pieces from Statues and Inlays in the Petrie Collection at University College, London, *Journal of Egyptian Archaeology* 59, p.47–59

Samson, J. 1973b, Royal Inscriptions from Amarna, *Chronique d'Égypte* 48, p.243–50

Samson, J. 1976, Royal Names in Amarna History: the Historical Development of Nefertiti's Names and Titles, *Chronique d'Égypte* 51, p.30–8

Samson, J. 1977, Nefertiti's Regality, *Journal of Egyptian Archaeology* 63, p.88–97

Samson, J. 1978, *Amarna, City of Akhenaten and Nefertiti: Nefertiti as Pharaoh*, London

Samson, J. 1979, Akhenaten's Successor, *Göttinger Miszellen* 32, p.53–8

Samson, J. 1982a, Akhenaten's Co-Regent and Successor, *Göttinger Miszellen* 57, p.57–9

Samson, J. 1982b, Akhenaten's Co-Regent Ankhkheperura-Neferneferuaten, *Göttinger Miszellen* 53, p.51–4

Samson, J. 1982c, *The History of the Mystery of Akhenaten's Successor*, L'Égyptologie en 1979: axes prioritaires de recherches II, Paris, p.291–7

Samson, J. 1982d, Neferneferuaten-Nefertiti 'Beloved of Akhenaten', Ankhkheperura-Neferneferuaten 'Beloved of Akhenaten', Ankhkheperura Smenkhkara 'Beloved of the Aten', *Göttinger Miszellen* 57, p.61–7

Samson, J. 1983, Evidence and Surmise, *Göttinger Miszellen* 63, p.65–6

Samson, J. 1985, *Nefertiti and Cleopatra: Queen-Monarchs of Ancient Egypt*, London

Samuel, D. 1994, A New Look at Bread and Beer, *Egyptian Archaeology: Bulletin of the Egypt Exploration Society* 4, p.9–11

Sandford, M. K. & Kissling, G. E. 1994, Multivariate Analyses of Elemental Hair Concentrations from a Medieval Nubian Population, *American Journal of Physical Anthropology* 95, p.41–52

Sandison, A. T. 1963, The Use of Natron in Mummification in Ancient Egypt, *Journal of Near Eastern Studies* 22, p.259–67

Schaden, O. 1992, The God's Father Ay, *Amarna Letters* 2, p.92–115

Schulman, A. 1964, Some Observations on the Military Background of the Amarna Period, *Journal of the American Research Center in Egypt* 3, p.51–69

Schulman, A. 1979, Diplomatic Marriage in the Egyptian New Kingdom, *Journal of Near Eastern Studies* 38, p.177–93

Serpico, M. & White, R. 2000, Resins, Amber & Bitumen, in *Ancient Egyptian Materials and Technology*, ed. P. Nicholson & I. Shaw, Cambridge, p.430–74

Seton-Williams, V. 1984, *El-Amarna*, London

Shaw, I. & Nicholson, P. 1995, *British Museum Dictionary of Ancient Egypt*, London

Sieber, R. & Herreman, F. eds. 2001, *Hair in African Art & Culture*, New York

Smith, G. E. 1907, On the Mummies in the Tomb of Amenhotep II, *Bulletin de l'Institut d'Égyptien* 5th serie, 1, p.221–8

Smith, G. E. 1912, *The Royal Mummies, Catalogue General des*

Antiquités Égyptiennes de la Musée du Caire, Nos. 61051–61100, Cairo (republished as *The Royal Mummies* by Duckworth in 2000)

Smith, G. E. 1923, *Tutankhamen and the Discovery of his Tomb*, London

Smith, G. E. 1934, The Wonder of the Mummy, *Wonders of the Past* 23–4, p.549–59

Smith, G. E. & Dawson, W. R. 1924, *Egyptian Mummies*, London

Smith, H. S. 2002, Julia Samson: Obituary, *Egyptian Archaeology: Bulletin of the Egypt Exploration Society* 21, p.44

Smith, R. W. 1970, Computer Helps Scholars Recreate an Egyptian Temple, *National Geographic* 138(5), p.634–55

Smith, R. W. & Redford, D. B. 1976, *The Akhenaten Temple Project. I: Initial Discoveries*, Warminster

Smith, W. S. 1981, *The Art & Architecture of Ancient Egypt*, Harmondsworth

Spence, K. 1999, The North Palace at Amarna, *Egyptian Archaeology: Bulletin of the Egypt Exploration Society* 15, p.14–16

Spencer, A. J. 1982, *Death in Ancient Egypt*, Harmondsworth

Steindorff, G. & Seele, K. C. 1957, *When Egypt Ruled the East*, Chicago

Strouhal, E. & Callendar, G. 1992, A Profile of Queen Mutnodjmet, *Bulletin of the Australian Centre of Egyptology* 3, p.67–75

Strouhal, E., Gaballa, M. F., Bonani, G., Woelfli, W., Nemeckova, A. & Saunders, S. 1998, Re-investigation of the Remains Thought to Be of King Djoser and Those of an Unidentified Female from the Step Pyramid at Saqqara, in *Proceedings of the Seventh International Congress of Egyptologists*, ed. C. Eyre, Leuven, p.1103–7

Taylor, J. H. 1992, Aspects of the History of the Valley of the Kings in the Third Intermediate Period, in *After Tut'ankhamun: Research and Excavation in the Royal Necropolis at Thebes*, ed. C. N. Reeves, London, p.186–206

Taylor, J. H. 2001, *Death and the Afterlife in Ancient Egypt*, London

The Times, 1898, Important Discovery at Thebes, p.12

Thijsse, G. J. E. 1948, Chemical Properties of Human Hair as an Aid to Anthropological Work, *Man* 48, p.64–6

Thomas, A. P. 1988, *Akhenaten's Egypt*, Aylesbury

Thomas, A. P. 1994, The Other Woman at Akhetaten, Royal Wife Kiya, *Amarna Letters* 3, p.73–81

Thomas, E. 1966, *The Royal Necropolis of Thebes*, Princeton

Thompson, J. 1992, *Sir Gardner Wilkinson and his Circle*, Austin

Thompson, K. 2001, Putting Together the Pieces at Amarna, *Akhetaten Sun: Newsletter of the Amarna Research Foundation* 5(2), p.16–19

Thompson, K. 2002, A Visit to Akhenaten's Nubian Aten Temple, *Akhetaten Sun: Newsletter of the Amarna Research Foundation* 6(1), p.11–12

Tiridatti, F. ed., 2000, *Egyptian Treasures from the Egyptian Museum in Cairo*, Vercelli

Titlbachova, S. & Titlbach, Z. 1977, Hair of Egyptian Mummies, *Zeitschrift für aegyptische Sprache* 104, p.79–85

Trigger, B. G., Kemp, B. J., O'Connor, D. & Lloyd, A. B. 1983, *Ancient Egypt: A Social History*, London

Troy, L. 1986, Patterns of Queenship in Ancient Egyptian Myth and History, *Acta Universitatis Upsaliensis Boreas (Uppsala Studies in Ancient Mediterranean and Near Eastern Civilizations)* 14

Troy, L. 1993, Creating a God: the Mummification Ritual, *Bulletin of the Australian Center for Egyptology* 4, p.55–81

Tytus, R. de P. 1903, *A Preliminary Report on the Re-excavation of the Palace of Amenhotep III*, New York

Vandenberg, P. 1978, *Nefertiti: an Archaeological Biography*, London

van Dijk, J. 1995, Kiya Revisited, in *Seventh International Congress of Egyptologists, Abstract of Papers*, ed. C. Eyre, Oxford, p.50

van Dijk, J. 2000, The Amarna Period and the Later New Kingdom, in *The Oxford History of Ancient Egypt*, ed. I. Shaw, Oxford, p.272–313

Vasagar, J. 2003, Turning Heads: Egypt Angered at Artists' Use of Nefertiti Bust, *Guardian* 12 June, p.13

Vergnieux, R. & Gondran, M. 1997, *Aménophis IV et les pierres du soleil: Akhénaten retrouvé*, Paris

Verner, M. 1995, Forgotten Pyramids, Temples and Tombs of Abusir, *Egyptian Archaeology: Bulletin of the Egypt Exploration Society* 7, p.19–22

Vogelsang-Eastwood, G. 1993, *Pharaonic Egyptian Clothing*, Leiden

Vogelsang-Eastwood, G. 1998, The Clothing of Tutankhamun, *NILE Offerings* 3, p.20–3

Vogelsang-Eastwood, G. 1999, *Tutankhamun's Wardrobe*, Leiden

Waldron, T. 2001, *Shadows in the Soil: Human Bones and Archaeology*, Stroud

Watterson, B. 1998, *The House of Horus at Edfu*, Stroud

Watterson, B. 1999, *Amarna: Ancient Egypt's Age of Revolution*, Stroud

Weatherhead, F. & Buckley, A. 1989, Artists' Pigments from Amarna, *Amarna Reports* 5, p.202–22

Wedge, E. F. ed. 1977, *Nefertiti Graffiti: Comments on an Exhibition*, Brooklyn

Wegner, J. 2002, A Decorated Birth-brick from South Abydos, *Egyptian Archaeology: Bulletin of the Egypt Exploration Society* 21, p.3–4

Weidermann, H. G. & Bayer, G. 1982, The Bust of Nefertiti, *Analytical Chemistry* 54(4), p.619.A–628.A

Weigall, A. 1922, The Mummy of Akhenaton, *Journal of Egyptian Archaeology* 8, p.193–200

Weigall, A. 1923, *The Life and Times of Akhnaton, Pharaoh of Egypt*, London

Weigall, A. 1934, The Valley of the Tombs of the Kings, *Wonders of the Past* 49, p.1171–1180

Wells, E. 1964, *Nefertiti, Queen of Ancient Egypt*, New York

Wenig, S. 1969, *The Woman in Egyptian Art*, Leipzig

Wente, E. 1990, *Letters from Ancient Egypt*, Atlanta

Wente, E. 1995, Who Was Who Among the Royal Mummies, *Oriental Institute News & Notes* 144, p.1–6

Wente, E. & Harris, J. 1992, Royal Mummies of the Eighteenth Dynasty: a Biological and Egyptological Approach, in *After Tut'ankhamun*, ed. N. Reeves, London, p.2–20

Werner, E. K. 1979, Identification of Nefertiti in Talatat Reliefs Previously Published as Akhenaten, *Orientalia* 48, p.324–31

White, R. 1992, A Brief Introduction to the Chemistry of Natural Products in Archaeology, in *Organic Residues in Archaeology: their Identification and Analysis*, ed. R. White & H. Page, London, p.5–10

Wigan and District Observer 1936, Famous Egyptian Excavator Visits Wigan: Romance of Ancient Egypt, 10 October, p.1

Wildung, D. 1994, A Gilded Wooden Head in Berlin, *Amarna Letters* 3, p.22–5

Wildung, D. 1998, Le frère aîné d'Ekhenaton: réflexions sur un décès prematuré, *Bulletin de la Société Française d'Égyptologie* 143, p.10–18

Wildung, D. & Schoske, S. 1984, *Nofret – die Schöne: Die Frau im alten Ägypten*, Munich

Wilfong, T. 1997, *Women and Gender in Ancient Egypt: from Prehistory to Late Antiquity*, Ann Arbor

Wilkinson, J. G. 1988, *A Popular Account of the Ancient Egyptians I–II*, (first published as *The Manners and Customs of the Ancient Egyptians*), London

Wilkinson, R. H. ed. 1995, *Valley of the Sun Kings: New explorations in the Tombs of the Pharaohs*, Tucson

Wilkinson, R. H. 2000, *The Complete Temples of Ancient Egypt*, London

Wilkinson, R. H. 2002, The Identity of the Amarna Age Tomb WV.25 in the Western Valley of the Kings, *Akhetaten Sun* 6(2), p.15–18

Wilson, J. A. 1976, Mrs. Andrews and 'the Tomb of Queen Tiyi', in *Studies in Honour of George R. Hughes*, Chicago p.273–9

Winlock, H. E. 1921, Egyptian Expedition for MCMXX–MCMXXI: III. Excavations at Thebes, *Bulletin of the Metropolitan Museum of Art* 16, Supplement, p.29–53

Winlock, H. E. 1926, The Egyptian Expedition 1924–1925: The Museum's Excavations at Thebes, *Bulletin of the Metropolitan Museum of Art* 21, Supplement, p.5–32

Winlock, H. E. 1941, *Materials Used at the Embalming of King Tût-'ankh-Amûn*, New York

Winlock, H. E. 1942, *Excavations of Deir el-Bahari, 1911–1931*, New York

Wisseman, S., Klepinger, L., Keen, R., Raheel, M., Barkmeier, J., Proefke, M., Rinehart, K. L., Lawrance, D., Brady, R., Evenhouse, R., Bohen, B. & Ambrose, S. 1992, *Interdisciplinary Research on the University of Illinois Mummy (3/92), Program on Ancient Technologies and Archaeological Materials*, Urbana

Woolley, L. 1953, *Spadework: Adventures in Archaeology*, London

Zaki, A. & Iskander, Z. 1943, Materials and Methods Used to Mummify the Body of Amentefnekht, Saqqara 1941, in *Annales du Service des Antiquités de l'Égypte* 42, p.223–55

Zivie, A. 1990, *Découverte à Saqqarah: le vizir oublié*, Paris

Zivie, A. 1998, The Tomb of Lady Maïa, Wet-nurse of Tutankhamen, *Egyptian Archaeology: Bulletin of the Egypt Exploration Society* 13, p.7–8

SOURCE REFERENCES

Chapter 2

p.26 'At first I could see nothing': Carter and Mace 1923, pp.95–6

p.29 'their bodies seem deformed': Saleh and Sourouzian 1987, No. 164

p.30 'Pray come immediately': Edwards 1889, p.328

p.30 'one cannot but feel': Edwards 1889, p.50

p.30 'genius and energy': Edwards 1891, p.281

p.31 'There is no one to prevent it': Edwards 1889, p.353

p.31 'and if you could throw': Edwards in Drower 1985, p.127

p.32 'without distinction': Murray 1963, p.151

p.32 'the godless and infidel': Murray 1963, p.152

p.32 'there was still that splendid spirit': Murray 1963, pp.154–5

p.33 'it showed that a man': Murray 1963, p.98

p.34 'the study of ancient Egypt': Murray 1963, p.187

p.37 'ultimate proof of Akhenaten's co-regency': Samson 1985, p.87

Chapter 3

p.40 'sacred writing (hieroglyphs)': Simpson in Parkinson 1999, p.200

p.41 'These grottoes': Wilkinson in Davies 1903, p.3

p.41 'The sculptures are singular': Wilkinson in Thompson 1992, p.68

p.42 'the sun itself': Wilkinson in Thompson 1992, p.68

p.42 'No other deity': Burton in Thompson 1992, p.68

p.44 'beautifully fine': Davies 1908, p.26

p.45 'introduced very heretical changes': Wilkinson I 1988, p.308

p.46 'by nature a poet': Dawson, Uphill & Bierbrier 1995, p.243

p.47 'fragments of a royal mummy': Sayce in Martin 1989, p.1

p.47 'numerous trinkets': Dickerman in Martin 1974, p.37

p.51 'It is an overwhelming': Petrie in Drower 1985, p.189

p.52 'learn something': Drower 1985, p.193

p.52 'Sherlock Holmes': Carter in Reeves and Taylor 1992, p.24

p.52 'a good-natured lad': Petrie in Drower 1985, p.194

p.53 'As regards the work': Carter in James 2001, p.41

p.53 'where the waste': Petrie 1894, p.15

p.54 'A Petrie dig': Lawrence in Drower 1985, p.319

p.54 'so ransacked': Petrie in Drower 1985, p.195

p.54 'the vigorous and determined': Petrie 1894, p.39

p.55 'may well have married': Petrie 1894, p.42

p.55 'truly devoted': Petrie 1894, p.41

p.55 'good living': Petrie 1894, p.39

p.55 'Akhenaten stands out': Petrie 1894, p.41

p.56 'found the remains': Sayce in Martin 1974, p.37

p.56 'the body of a man': Pendlebury in Martin 1974, p.37

p.56 'lamenting over the body': Carter in Reeves and Taylor 1992, p.42

p.57 'We found the tomb': Ward in Martin 1974, p.106

p.59 'the new excavations': Davies 1908.b, p.37

p.61 'what the German people': Reeves 2001a, p.24

p.61 'not that of an Egyptian': Hall in Kemp 2002a, p.2

p.61 'plundering, self-glorifying': Petrie 1894, p.42

p.61 'the world is still far': Petrie 1934, p.676

p.62 'a brave soul': Breasted in Aldred 1968, p.13

p.62 'Praise to thee': Breasted 1988 II, p.409

p.62 'Among the Hebrews': Breasted in Aldred 1968, p.13

p.62 'If Moses': Freud in ENO 1985, p.35

p.62 'conscientious objection': Weigall 1923, p.200

p.63 'not only a Christ': Hankey 2001, p.119

p.63 'Darling, I know I'm frightfully': Christie in ENO 1985, p.20

p.64 'was set as far': *Wigan and District Observer* 1936, p.1

p.64 'been any hot drink': Pendlebury 1951, p.114

p.65 'the quarters of the six': Pendlebury 1951, p.87

p.65 'much has been written': Woolley 1953, pp.43–4

p.65 'is scarcely consistent': Woolley 1953, pp.44–5

p.65 'This was a public affront': Woolley 1953, p.45

p.66 'the young prince whom Akhenaten': Pendlebury 1935, p.564

p.67 'almost certainly Akhenaten': Aldred 1988, plate 25

p.67 'Meritaten and the young man': Fay 1984, p.98

p.67 'if Neferneferuaten': Davies 1923b, p.43

p.67 'stories – about as wonderful': Chubb 1954, p.114

p.68 'interest in archaeological work': *Wigan and District Observer* 1936, p.1

p.68 'an attempt to keep': *Wigan and District Observer* 1936, p.1

p.69 'seems to be that': Fairman in Pendlebury 1951, p.232

p.72 'It is hard to avoid': Redford 1984, p.79

p.73 'the devaluation': Krauss in Samson 1982b, p.296

p.73 'ingenious': Aldred 1988, p.228

p.73 'iconoclasts': Martin 1974, p.77

Chapter 4

p.81 'having added to the knowledge': Murray 1963, p.94

p.94 'Nefertiti and her daughters': Luxor Museum 1978, p.67

p.95 'every vestige': Murray 1910, p.8

p.96 'Unrolling a Mummy', *Manchester Evening News*, 1908, p.5

p.98 'a copious wig': Petrie 1890, p.39

p.98 'the person was light-haired': Petrie 1890, p.41

p.98 'Egyptian priests shave': Herodotus, *Histories* 11.36 1984, p.143

p.100 'plait of hair': Petrie 1902, p.5

p.106 'took the rigid Pharaoh': Dawson ed. 1938, pp.38–9

p.107 'the sudden transition' Dawson ed. 1938, p.49–50

p.107 'in a peculiar manner': Smith 1912, p.11

p.107 'had very little hair': Smith 1912, p.13
p.108 'the least unlovely': Smith 1912, p.12
p.108 'made a hasty': Smith 1912, p.36
p.109 'a small, middle-aged': Smith 1912, p.38
p.109 'the right arm placed': Smith 1912, p.39
p.109 'shaved from the greater part': Smith 1912, p.39
p.109 'presented an extraordinary': Smith 1912, p.40
p.110 'whereas it requires': Smith 1912, p.40
p.111 'hurriedly made during': Smith 1912, p.41
p.111 'the exact age cannot': Smith 1912, p.40
p.112 'more similar to that': Harris and Wente 1980, p.379
p.114 'a near perfect superimposition': Harris et al 1978, p.1151
p.115 'head was shaved but': Loret in Romer 1981, pp.161–2
p.116 'wig of wavy hair': Daressy 1902, p.182

Chapter 5

p.118 '64 huge cases': Smith in Dawson ed. 1938, p.36
p.118 'this scientific examination': Carter in Leek 1972, p.3
p.120 'sufficient of the head': Carter in Leek 1972, p.7
p.120 'able to definitely declare': Carter in Leek 1972, p.7
p.120 'the only thing I ask': Carter in Leek 1972, p.1
p.120 'will be reverently re-wrapped': Carter in Leek 1972, p.8
p.121 'had one of those babes lived': Carter 1933, p.28
p.121 'an abnormality': Carter 1933, p.281
p.123 'is now impossible to say': Smith 1912, p.50
p.124 'it came off in a black mass': Davis 1910, p.3
p.125 'a plump little person': Winlock 1921, p.48
p.126 'flat, spiralled discs': Lansing & Hayes 1937, p.26
p.128 'damaged, particularly the skull': Harrison et al. 1979, p.14
p.131 'never was the habitation': Hoskins in Thompson 1992, p.104
p.153 'the prominence of the upper teeth': Smith 1912, p.16
p.156 'probably due to foreign influence': Petrie 1894, p.29

Chapter 6

p.157 'the son of Jack Morgan': Petrie in Reeves 2000, p.82

p.158 'de Morgan was but': Petrie in Reeves 2000, p.101

p.160 *'spectacle effroyable'*: Loret 1899, pp.100–1

p.161 'opened into blackness': Loret in Romer 1981, p.161

p.161 *'un pêle-mêle inimaginable'*, Loret 1899, p.106

p.162 'the sarcophagus, open': Loret 1899, p.102

p.163 'Three corpses': Loret 1899, p.103

p.164 'that of a child': Loret 1899, pp.103–4

p.164 'seemed to be that': Loret 1899, p.104

p.165 'I distinguished nevertheless': Loret 1899, p.105

p.165 'Such were the impressions': Loret 1899, p.105

p.166 'the mummies, rigid as wood': Loret 1899, p.108

p.166 'Was I in the midst': Loret 1899, pp.108–9

p.167 'the most quaint': Loret 1899, p.112

p.168 'requested M. Loret': *The Times* 1898, p.12

p.169 'The Valley of the Tombs': Carter MSS.VI.2.11, p.150

p.169 'the ultimate fate': Carter MSS.VI.2.11, p.158

p.169 'worthless successors': Carter MSS.VI.2.11, p.158

p.169 'two nameless women': Carter MSS.VI.2.11, p.182

p.169 'Very rightly the Egyptian Government': Carter MSS.VI.2.11, pp.183–4

p.170 'an administrative question': Carter MSS.VI.2.11, p.184

p.170 'the three naked mummies': Carter MSS.VI.2.11, p.184

p.170 'the original plan was changed': Carter MSS.VI.2.11, p.184

p.171 'accessible to the public': Carter MSS.VI.2.11, p.184

p.171 'as the reader will': Carter MSS.VI.2.11, p.185

p.171 'therefore focussed my energies': Carter MSS.VI.2.11, p.186

p.172 'for eighteen months': Carter MSS.VI.2.11, p.189

p.172 'kept house for him': Wilson 1976, p.274

p.172 'coffin and cartonnage': Andrews in Reeves and Taylor 1992, p.63

p.173 'rifled mummy': Andrews in Reeves and Taylor, 1992, p.70

p.173 'A king she would be': Carter and Mace 1923, p.82

p.174 'By Jove!': Andrews in Wilson 1976, p.275

p.174 'it is quite impossible': Davis 1910, p.1–2

p.175 'found seven & six': Currelly 1956, p.142

p.175 'I expect I shall be here': Jones in Bosse-Griffiths 2001, p.103

p.175 'I stayed till 10 o'clock': Jones in Bosse-Griffiths 2001, p.103

p.175 'Certainly, take two!': Davis in Bosse-Griffiths 2001, p.97

p.175 'so decorated that': Currelly 1956, p.143

p.176 'protruding from the remains': Weigall in Hankey 2001, p.86

p.176 'gold pendants and inlaid plaques': Ayrton in Davis 1910, pp.9–10

p.176 'evidently that of a woman': Davis 1910, p.3

p.177 'nothing but a mass': Andrews in Wilson 1976, p.278

p.177 'soaked the bones': Weigall 1923, p.xxii

p.177 'considerably damaged': Derry 1931, p.116

p.177 'Are you sure that the bones': Smith in Hankey 2001, p.89

p.177 'exhibits in an unmistakable manner': Smith in Davis 1910, p.xxiii–xxiv

p.177 'the surgeons were deceived': Davis 1910, p.3

p.177 'The mummy . . . was found': Smith 1912, p.51

p.179 'may be those of a man': Derry 1931, p.118

p.179 'the very reverse': Derry 1931, p.118

p.180 'rather fragile constitution': Hussein and Harris 1988, p.140

p.180 'Unless the anatomists': Reeves 2001a, p.84

p.180 'a man between the ages': Filer 2000, p.14

p.180 'Egyptology's most controversial': Reeves in Grimm and Schoske eds. 2001, p.121

p.180 'the ages assigned by': Smith 1912, p.52

p.181 'a comparison of our results': Wente 1995, p.3

p.181 'it is recognized': Leek 1972, p.26

p.181 'relatively easy': Waldron 2001, p.19

p.182 'whilst it is tempting': Robins 1981, p.66

p.182 'made a hasty examination': Smith 1912, p.36

p.182 'around 25': Smith 1912, p.40

p.183 'still lies in state': Smith 1934, p.558

p.183 'Since then a marked silence': Carter MSS.VI.2.11, p.193–4

p.183 'I really nearly fainted': Weigall in Hankey 2001, p.56–7

p.184 'his eyes peacefully closed': Weigall in Hankey 2001, p.57

p.185 'such treatment of the head': Thomas 1966, p.239

p.185 'Does this feature suggest': Thomas 1966, p.240

Chapter 7

p.188 'Creator of all, who makes them live': Lichtheim 1976, p.87, p.91

p.189 'Isis has your arm': Pyramid Texts, Spell 477, in Faulkner 1969, p.164

p.193 'attending market and taking': Herodotus, *Histories* II.34, 1984, p.142

p.196 'the vizier has written to me': McDowell 1999, p.45

p.198 'it can hardly be doubted': Griffith in Petrie 1900, p.35

p.201 'quite possibly the first free-standing': Lesko 1998, p.152

p.201 'an alternative translation': Gardiner 1961, p.83

p.203 'when there was a secret charge': Callender 1994, p.10

p.203 'her historical existence': Gardiner 1961, p.102

p.204 'read to me from a written record': Herodotus, *Histories* II.101, 1984, p.166

p.204 'a woman instead of a man': possibly Eratosthenes, in Gera 1997, p.101

p.204 'with fair complexion': Gardiner 1961, p.436

p.204 'strung on the necks of female slaves': Lichtheim 1975, p.152

p.205 'flew up to heaven': Lichtheim 1975, p.223

p.205 'Hear what I tell you': Lichtheim 1975, pp.136–137

p.205 'her head adorned': Lichtheim 1975, p.229

p.207 'there seems considerable likelihood': Gardiner 1961, p.141

p.210 'she looked after Egypt's soldiers': Janosi 1992, p.99

p.213 'governed the land, and the Two Lands': Gardiner 1961, p.181

p.214 'I educated the king's daughter': Dorman 1988, p.124

p.215 'seize the chiefs': Lesko 1996, p.14

p.215 'thirty-one fresh myrrh trees': Breasted 1988, p.112

p.215 'the best of myrrh': Breasted 1988, p.113

p.215 'her majesty praised me': Dorman 1988, p.38

p.216 'found the queen': Manniche 1987, pp.59–60

p.216 'when I sat in the palace': Lichtheim 1976, p.27

p.217 'The temple of [Hathor]': Lesko 1996, p.17

p.218 'supervised the excavation': Reeves and Wilkinson 1996, p.91

p.219 'be eternal like an undying star': Lichtheim 1976, p.28

p.221 'a beautiful youth who was well developed': Lichtheim 1976, p.41

p.222 'sitting drinking and making holiday': Wente 1990 pp.27–28

p.223 'as a father speaks to his son': Steindorff and Seele 1957, p.71

p.224 'spent thirty-five years lying': Breasted 1988, p.330

Chapter 8

p.226 'the Great Royal Wife is Tiy': Marriage Scarab, based on Davies 1992, p.38

p.228 'Say to the king': Amarna Letter EA.187, based on Moran 1992, p.269

p.229 'brought to his majesty': Kiluhepa Scarab, based on Davies 1992, p.37

p.229 'My father loved you': Amarna Letter EA.17, based on Moran 1992, pp.41–42

p.230 'Your messenger came to take': Amarna Letter EA.20, based on Moran 1992, pp.47–48

p.230 'May Ishtar grant you': Amarna Letter EA.21, based on Moran 1992, p.50

p.230 'Tushratta is the Mitannian king': Amarna Letter EA.24, based on Moran 1992, p.71

p.230 'If you really desire my daughter': Amarna Letter EA.32, based on Moran 1992, p.103

p.231 'Now you are asking to marry': Amarna Letter EA.1, based on Moran 1992, p.1–3

p.231 'my daughter about whom you wrote': Amarna Letter EA.3, based on Moran 1992, p.7

p.231 'You are king, you can do': Amarna Letter EA.4, based on Moran 1992, p.8

p.231 'Now as to the gold': Amarna Letter EA.4, based on Moran 1992, p.9

p.232 'It's a fine thing when': Amarna Letter EA.1, based on Moran 1992, p.2

p.232 'Tell my lord so speaks': Amarna Letter EA.12, based on Moran 1992, p.24

p.232 'I am sending you my official': Amarna Letter EA.369, based on Moran 1992, p.366

p.232 'the children of the princes': Lichtheim 1976, p.44

p.233 'Come, Golden Goddess': based on Manniche 1991, p.61

p.238 'I love to go and bathe': Manniche 1987, p.88

p.238 'I wish I were her laundryman': Manniche 1987, p.91

p.239 'the Morning Star': based on Lichtheim 1976, p.182

p.243 'I have just heard': Amarna Letter EA.5, based on Moran 1992, p.11

p.246 'the making of a lake': based on Davies 992, p.36

p.249 'Let my soul come to me': based on Faulkner 1985, p.84–85

p.252 'to the Golden One': based on Wente in Roberts 1995, p.27

p.252 'the great portals were closed': based on Lichtheim 1975, p.223–224 p.253 'When I heard that my brother': Amarna Letter EA.29, based on Moran 1992, p.94

p.254 'When they told me': Amarna Letter EA.29, based on Moran 1992, p.94

p.254 'my husband always showed love': Amarna Letter EA.26, based on Moran 1992, p.84

p.255 'Tiy your mother knows all': Amarna Letter EA.27, based on Moran 1992, p.88

p.255 'There are only five chariots': Amarna Letter EA.11, based on Moran 1992, p.21

p.256 'the evidently foreign queen': Petrie 1896, p.229

p.257 'she was descended from Queen': Aldred 1988, p.261

p.259 'the offerings for all the gods': based on Wente 1990, p.28

p.260 'shall die by the axe of the king': Amarna Letter EA.162, based on Moran 1992, p.249

p.262 'it was worse than those': based on Murnane 1995, p.78

Chapter 9

p.264 'did not belong to a god': based on Murnane 1995, p.75

p.267 'Heiress, Great One of the palace': based on Davies 1908, p.28 and Murnane 1995, p.74

p.268 'My heart is joyous': based on Davies 1908, p.32 and Murnane 1995, p.83

p.270 'Oh my ladies': based on Lichtheim 1975, p.220

p.273 'mounting his great chariot of electrum': based on Murnane 1995, p.74

p.273 'in his charior whose horses': in Steindorff and Seele 1957, p.71

p.274 'a set of bridles': Amarna Letter EA.22, based on Moran 1992, p.51

p.274 'the Great Royal Wife Neferneferuaten': based on Muranane 1995, p.135

p.275 'great offerings were made': based on Lichtheim 1980, p.77

p.276 'put on the sacred garments': based on Lichtheim 1980, p.77

p.276 'beautiful in their finely adorned appearance': based on Lichtheim 1980, p.56

p.277 'the singers and musicians shouting': based on Lichtheim 1976, p.91

p.278 'maintaining the god in a state of perpetual arousal': Aldred 1988, p.223

p.278 'took his phallus in his fist': Spell 527, based on Faulkner 1969, p.198

p.278 'the great god spent a day': Lichtheim 1976, p.216

p.278 'whenever they pass a town': Herodotus, *Histories* II.60, 1984, p.153

p.280 'my Mistress, I fall at your feet': Amarna Letter EA.48, based on Moran 1992, p.120

p.291 'luxuries, a bathroom and mirrors': based on Lichtheim 1975, p.233

p.294 'Why should my messengers': Amarna Letter EA.16, based on Moran 1992, p.39

p.301 'may partake of things which issue': based on Murnane 1995, p.131

p.302 'where you fill your mouth': based on Kemp 1991, p.310

p.307 'You stagger about, going from street': based on Lesko 1977, p.35

p.310 'My voice is not loud': Murnane 1995, p.192

Chapter 10

p.314 'a jar of sweet oil': Amarna Letter EA.34, based on Moran 1992, p.106

p.317 'the tribute of Syria and the Sudan': based on Davies 1905, p.9

p.319 'There are all kinds of bread': Watterson 1998, p.106

p.322 'Although I am only a child': based on Lichtheim 1980, pp.58–59 p.328 'May you breathe the sweet breeze': based on Murnane 1995, p.182

p.331 'my wish is to see you O Lord': based on Reeves 2001a, p.164

p.332 'the temples of the gods and goddesses': based on Gardiner 1961, pp.236–237

p.334 'My husband is dead': based on Reeves 2001a, p.175

p.338 'There is every reason to believe': Reeves 1990, p.190

Chapter 11

p.355 'The days of days': Carter and Mace 1923, p.94

Chapter 12

p.367 'gold pendants and inlaid plaques': Ayrton in Davis 1910, p.9

Picture Acknowledgements

Ägyptisches Museum, Berlin: 1 (photo Corbis), 2 bottom right (photo BPK Berlin), 4 top right and bottom left (photos BPK Berlin), 5 top (photo AKG London), 6 top (photo BPK Berlin), 8 (photo BPK Berlin), 9 bottom (photo BPK Berlin), 12 (photo BPK Berlin). Ashmolean Museum, Oxford: 11 bottom. Bolton Museum and Art Gallery: 10 bottom left and right. Brooklyn Museum of Art, New York: 7 bottom Charles Edwin Wilbour Fund (photo Bridgeman Art Library), 9 top Charles Edwin Wilbour Fund (photo Bridgeman Art Library), 11 centre Gift of Christos G. Bastis (photo Corbis). Cleveland Museum of Art, Ohio: 4 top left Leonard C. Hanna Jr. Fund 1961.417, 11 top Purchase from the J. H. Wade Fund 1959.188. Martin Collins: maps x, xi, xii, 265 and figures 2, 4, 5, 8, 9. N. de G. Davies *The Rock Tombs of El Amarna*, 6 Vols, 1903–1908: figures 1, 3, 6, 10, 11, 12, 13. N. de G. Davies *The Tomb of the Vizier Ramose*, 1941: figure 7. Egyptian Museum Cairo: 2 top (photo Joann Fletcher), 7 top left and right (photos Joann Fletcher), 13 top (photo Bridgeman Art Library), bottom (photo Corbis). Joann Fletcher: 15 top. Musée du Louvre Paris: 6 bottom (photo RMN Paris), 10 top (photo The Art Archive/Dagli Orti). G. Elliot Smith *The Royal Mummies* 1912: 2 bottom left.

Discovery Channel and Atlantic Productions: 3 bottom, 4 bottom right, 5 bottom, 14, 15 bottom, 16.

INDEX

Numbers in italics indicate captions; those in bold indicate maps. 'A.' indicates Akhenaten and 'N.' Nefertiti.